SAYYID AHMAD KHAN
Asār-us-Sanadīd

SAYYID AHMAD KHAN
Asār-us-Sanadīd

First edition 1847
Second edition 1854

Translated and edited by
Rana Safvi

 Tulika Books

First published by
Tulika Books
44 (first floor), Shahpur Jat, New Delhi 110 049, India
www.tulikabooks.in

in collaboration with

Publications Division, Sir Syed Academy
Aligarh Muslim University, Aligarh 202 002, Uttar Pradesh, India

First edition (hardback) 2018
ISBN: 978-93-82381-87-7

Designed by Alpana Khare

Printed at Chaman Offset, Delhi 110 002

I dedicate this translation to
my beloved alma mater, Aligarh Muslim University
and to its founder, Sir Sayyid Ahmad Khan
– I am what I am, because of them

Contents

Acknowledgements

RANA SAFVI

When I decided to write a book on the monuments of Delhi in a trilogy titled *Where Stones Speak*, the first reference book I located was the second edition of Sir Sayyid's monumental work, *Asar-us-Sanadid* (published in 1854; henceforth referred to as *Asar-2*). I then tried to find a translation of it and came across R. Nath's *Monuments of Delhi*, published in 1979. This book is now out of print and though it has abridged some of the descriptions, it was of great help to me. It was also this book that gave me an idea that a complete translation of *Asar-1* and *Asar-2* was needed for lovers of Delhi's heritage.

I began this endeavour and had almost completed the translation of the 1854 edition (*Asar-2*), when I came across an article by Professor C.M. Naim which mentioned that Sir Sayyid had written a previous edition as well, and which highlighted the differences between the two editions. Since I like to add interesting historical anecdotes while writing about monuments so as to make them come alive for readers, this finding was invaluable to me. Here, I have used the original text published by Sayyid-ul-Akhbar in 1847 for the translation of *Asar-1*, and am very grateful to the British Library which provided me a soft copy (PDF) of the same. I have also referred to an edition of *Asar-1* published by Munshi Nawal Kishore in Lucknow, in 1900. For the translation of *Asar-2*, I used *Asar-us-Sanadid*, edited by Khaliq Anjum, published by the National Council for Promotion of Urdu Language (Qaumi Council Baraye Farogh-e Urdu Zabaan), 2003, as well as *Aasar-us-Sanaadeed*, published by the Urdu Academy, reprint 2014. I began by comparing the two editions, initially planning to add only whatever had been left out in my translation of *Asar-2*. However, at a later meeting with Professor Narayani Gupta, she impressed upon me the importance of translating both editions in their original form. I will forever be grateful to her for her guidance in this. I am also extremely grateful to Professor C.M. Naim for his article which opened up a whole new world of Delhi to me.

I was fairly well versed with the monuments of Delhi and their history, but given my lack of knowledge of Persian and Arabic, I could not have translated a book of such monumental proportions – running into two editions, *Asar-1* and *Asar-2* – without the help of a large number of people.

I owe the biggest debt to Professor Shamsur Rahman Faruqi, who is not only someone I greatly admire but whose selfless service to Urdu inspires me greatly. Without concern for the time of night or day, I would ask for his help – and he was always there, ready to help me find the correct words and nuances in the Persian verses. I contacted him very late in the process of my translation, but he nevertheless helped me correct the innumerable mistakes I had made in the transliteration and translation of many of the verses. I can also never forget the motivation and encouragement he gave me when my energy and confidence regarding this translation were flagging. May he be blessed with good health, for the world of Urdu literature needs his guidance to flourish.

Professor Dr Syeda Bilqis Fatima Hussaini was also always ready to answer my queries, whether in person or over the telephone, despite her ill-health. I can never repay my debt to her and I pray for her good health.

Another person who unfailingly helped me was Mufti Waseem Anwar, the Imam Khateeb of Pi-1, Aicher Masjid in Greater Noida. Both he and Maulvi Muhammad Shahid Saharsavi of Aicher helped me read and look up the meanings of difficult words, many of which are no longer in use; they were of great help during the process of translation. When it was decided that we must translate the *alqaab* or honorifics as well, I could once again only think of Professor Dr Syeda Bilqis Hussaini – and though she was not keeping well, it was she who set the ball rolling by translating more than half of them. After that Mufti Waseem Anwar would read and explain them to me in simple Urdu, and I would note them down in English.

It was Azra Naqvi who discovered that they were in verse, for which I am eternally grateful as it has reduced the margin of error. I am also thankful to her for identifying and translating a few sample verses of the lesser-known poets mentioned by Sir Sayyid in his chapter on the people of Delhi.

It was by chance that I met Ajmal Siddiqi during a recording of Urdu poetry. I think the gods were smiling on me that day, because without his help I could not have polished the verses or the honorifics. I deluged him with screenshots and voice messages asking for help at odd hours, and like a true champion, he delivered. He would promptly decipher words that made no sense to me whatsoever and reply with solutions.

A huge shout out of thanks also to Professor Saiyid Zaheer Husain Jafri of the Department of History, University of Delhi and my class-fellow from the Department of Advanced Studies, Department of History, Aligarh Muslim University. He very kindly checked all my translations of Persian verses, correcting them where necessary.

Handicapped as I was by my lack of knowledge of the Persian language, I will forever be grateful to Usman Ghani, my Twitter friend from across the border in Pakistan, to whom I would send screenshots of verses and who would send me translations. Dr Syed Faizan took out time from his medical studies to do many translations of verses. I also sent screenshots and messages via Twitter to Dr Muhammad Taqi in Florida, who helped me with the Persian verses. I owe a debt of gratitude to the Rekhta Foundation, whose online resources – especially the dictionary – proved extremely useful to me while translating.

I am extremely grateful to my friend Anil Chandra for his encouragement during this long-drawn-out process. His idea of adding the lithographs in the original to the translation was a path-breaking one. I am grateful to the National Archives of India for providing me with scans of the same. I would also like to thank Dr M.A. Haq, Dr Zakir Hussain, Mr Muzaffar Islam and, in particular, Dr Faizan Ahmed who painstakingly earmarked the lithographs to be scanned. The hour I spent holding the copy of *Asar-us-Sanadid* with coloured illustrations that had come from the collection of Maulvi Basheer-ud-Din Ahmed was exhilarating. Thank you, Faizan.

It has been a mammoth exercise: over four years of hard work, research and help extended by the very special people mentioned above, but all that will be worth it if this translation can bring alive that period of history for other heritage lovers. My family has always supported me through every endeavour and I am blessed to have them in my life. I am grateful for being born into a family of Aligarians; starting with my grandfather Khan Bahadur Syed Muhammad Abbas Zaidi, my mother, aunts, uncles and sisters, we are all alumni of Aligarh Muslim University (AMU). I am especially happy that our family placed so much importance on female education.

I am very grateful to Indira Chandrasekhar and Tulika Books for publishing this important work and giving so much time to it. In fact, without the editorial team at Tulika Books, this book would not be what it is: thank you, Amaal Akhtar, Shad Naved, Sashii Ayer and Nilanjana Dey, for the insightful edits. Alpana Khare has designed it just the way I envisaged it. I am also indebted to Professor Amar Farooqui of the Department of History, University of Delhi, for painstakingly going through the manuscript and offering valuable comments, which have made the final book so much better.

Last but not the least, I am thankful to the Sir Syed Academy, its former Director, Professor Tariq Ahmed and the Assistant Director, Syed Hussain Haider, for all their help.

Translator's Note

RANA SAFVI

Sir Sayyid Ahmad Khan (CE 1817–98)[1] was a judicial officer [munsif] in the service of the East India Company, posted in Agra. In 1846, following the death of his brother Munsif Sayyid Muhammad Khan, he was transferred to Delhi from Fatehpur Sikri, Agra. Here, apart from his official duties, he took charge of continuing the newspaper *Sayyid-ul-Akhbar* that had been started by his brother, and also began working on a book on Delhi. In 1847, the first edition of *Asar-us-Sanadid* ('The Remnants of Ancient Monuments', henceforth referred to as *Asar-1*) was published at the *Sayyid-ul-Akhbar* printing press.

This, his seventh book, was very special to Sayyid Ahmad Khan – it was the fulfilment of a dream to write about 'the buildings in and around Shahjahanabad, the Red Fort, and about the people of the city and their ways'. Various constraints had prevented him from doing so until now. He hoped that this book would be a source of enlightenment and bear witness to the impermanent nature of the world, that it would caution a negligent person and make a wise man even wiser. The book was divided into four chapters that described:

- the buildings outside the walled city;
- the fort and the structures within it;
- the walled city of Shahjahanabad; and
- Delhi and the people of Delhi.

For the first time in India, a book had lithographically produced illustrations. These 130 illustrations of Delhi's monuments were drawn by Faiz Ali Khan and Mirza Shahrukh Beg. The drawings were probably based on rough sketches provided by Sayyid Ahmad Khan himself. He made many sketches – a fact he mentions in the book – and also copied the inscriptions on each of the monuments, often at great risk to life and limb, as in the case of the Qutub Minar.

Asar-1, brought out in 1847, was presented to A.A. Roberts, who took it to England and presented it to the Board of the Royal Asiatic Society. It was much appreciated by the Board and one of its members, Colonel Saxon, suggested that it be translated into English. But by this time Sayyid Ahmad Khan felt it imperative that the book be rewritten with additions and improvements. This was duly done, and the second edition (*Asar-2*) was brought out in 1854.

Asar-1 had been dedicated to Sir Thomas Theophilus Metcalfe, with a Preface that included a long Persian poem [*qasida*] of 78 verses. Metcalfe died in 1853. The second edition, *Asar-2*, expresses gratitude to Edward Thomas, A.A. Roberts and Colonel Saxon. *Asar-1* ends with a paragraph on Emperor Bahadur Shah Zafar, and his presence is strong throughout the book; however, *Asar-2* only mentions him in relation to the monuments built by him.

Asar-us-Sanadid is an invaluable work. Both editions – *Asar-1* and *Asar-2* (published in 1847 and 1854, respectively) – were written before the Revolt of 1857. As is well known, much of Shahjahanabad was changed during and in the aftermath of the events of 1857. The British broke down many structures to make governance easier and there was massive restructuring, in particular, of the Red Fort. Later, when Lutyens' Delhi was being built, many more changes were brought about, not to mention the changes that are still taking place today. Thus, in his descriptions of the buildings and monuments of Delhi prior to 1857, Sayyid Ahmad Khan gives us a glimpse of their lost glory.

The first chapter in *Asar-1* describes around 130 monuments outside the walled city of Shahjahanabad. The second chapter describes 32 buildings inside the Red Fort. The third chapter describes 70 buildings, gateways and canals, etc., inside the walled city. The fourth chapter, the longest in the book, is devoted to the people of Delhi and their environs. Sayyid Ahmad Khan opens this last chapter with a note on the climate and language of Delhi, and goes on to list the Sufi masters [*masha'ikh*]; 'men of ecstasy' [*majazib*]; noted physicians [*hakims*]; the *ulema*; reciters and memorizers of the Quran [*Qurra* and *hafiz*]; the nightingales, as he called the city's gifted poets [*bulbul-e-navayaa'n*]; and the calligraphers [*khush naviz*], artists [*musawwiran*] and musicians [*arbab-e-mausiqi*].

I have faithfully copied the titles by which he lists these people. These titles, in often abstruse Persian and Arabic prose, are an education in themselves. I was helped in translating these by Professor Dr Syeda Bilqis Fatima Hussaini and by Mufti Waseem Anwar, who is the Imam Khateeb of Pi-1, Aicher Masjid in Greater Noida and has studied Persian and Arabic. It was Mufti Waseem Anwar who discovered that the same terms were repeated – first in Persian and then in Arabic. It was quite a struggle to decipher the text since old Urdu texts have no punctuation marks and we could not always figure out where one honorific stopped and another began.

I am grateful to Azra Naqvi, an Urdu scholar and poet, from whom I sought help and who discovered that there was a rhyming pattern to the honorifics; after that the task became easier. Despite all this there may still be mistakes, and I hope I will be excused as I have tried my best.

While I have faithfully translated all the descriptions in *Asar-2* as well as the first three sections of *Asar-1*, I have taken liberties with the fourth section of *Asar-2* by abridging the description of the people of Shahjahanabad. I hope I will be forgiven for this as my translations have been undertaken from a historical perspective, and thus, while I was able to translate the most difficult words and phrases used for the monuments, I was handicapped by my lack of knowledge of literary Persian and Arabic. In both *Asar-1* and *Asar-2*, wherever I could, I have translated the Persian verses used to describe the monuments with help from various scholars, as mentioned in the Acknowledgements. Since the typesetting of *Asar-2* was archaic, we were presented with many difficulties and had to leave out a few sections of text that were unintelligible. All mistakes, if any, in the remaining transcription are mine.

It was especially difficult to translate the highly Persianized Urdu idioms from the fourth section of *Asar-1* into English, much of which was hyperbolic praise repeated in several different ways. Therefore, I have abridged these expressions in the descriptions of the *ulemas*, *mashaikhs* and poets, and paraphrased them instead, while keeping the meaning intact. I have also left out most of the Arabic, Persian and Urdu verses that Sayyid Ahmad Khan has cited in his section on the people of Delhi, as translating these was beyond my ability. The few I have translated fall within the section on poets, many of whom who are unknown to most of us today. I have translated these only to offer the reader an example of their talent. I hope that some day, a scholar of Persian and Arabic will translate all the verses in the book into English.

Asar-1 also had four *Taqriz* (Reviews), each one written by a luminary of that time – the one by Nawab Zia-ud-Din Khan Bahadur 'Nayyar Rakshan' was placed at the beginning of *Asar-1* in the original, while those by Mirza Asadullah Khan Ghalib, Maulana Imam Baksh Sehbai and Maulana Muhammad Sadr-ud-Din Khan Bahadur were placed at the end. They were all stalwarts of the age. Sayyid Ahmad Khan has described these luminaries reverentially and in great detail in his chapter on the people of Delhi (Chapter 4, *Asar-1*). These texts were written in very difficult Persian (from a present-day translator's point of view); moreover, while Ghalib wrote in prose, Maulana Imam Baksh Sehbai used a mixture of prose and poetry, and Nawab Zia-ud-Din Khan Bahadur 'Nayyar Rakshan' and Maulana Muhammad Sadr-ud-Din Khan Bahadur wrote in verse. Thus, of the four, I was only able to translate the Urdu version of Mirza Asadullah Khan Ghalib's 'Praise' (or Review), and for this I am grateful to Professor Aleem Ashraf Khan, Head of the Department of Persian, University of Delhi. He translated it into Urdu and I further translated it into English.

Compared to *Asar-2*, which was written in simple language, *Asar-1* was written in ornate language with free use of hyperbole. In his biography of Sir Sayyid Ahmad Khan, *Hayat-i-Javed*, Maulana Altaf Hussain Hali (1837–1914) attributes this difference in style to a fact revealed by Sir Sayyid himself – that Maulvi Imam Baksh Sehbai had been involved in the writing of *Asar-1* (see Appendix III, at the end of *Asar-2*).

Special mention must be made of the notes added by me (see 'Editor's Notes' at the end of the chapters) in the translation of both editions. These seek to explain a point or add information about this historical city, and its buildings and monuments, that might interest the reader. The author's notes remain at the foot of the page, within the chapters.

As I have already mentioned, the translation of the two editions has not been an easy task since Sayyid Ahmad Khan used very Persianized language; many of the architectural terms were difficult to decipher as well. For this, I would like to acknowledge the immeasurable help I received from Maulvi Zafar Hasan's *Monuments of India*. There are also many instances in the text where the author has used generic words that had to be translated with reference to context. For example, the word '*burj*' has been variously used by him to refer to tower, cupola and dome, as well as pavilion and, in some cases, bastion; it was only on the basis of my own knowledge of the building in question that I was able to find equivalent terms in English.

The two editions of *Asar* also highlight Sayyid Ahmad Khan's change in perspective and style of writing. His association with the Archaeological Society of India led him to write *Asar-2* in a more 'scientific' manner. However, it resulted in his deleting all the interesting anecdotes he had mentioned in *Asar-1*. In *Asar-2* he mentions dates using both or only the Gregorian calendar (CE) and the Al Hijri (AH) Islamic calendar. In this translation of *Asar-1*, therefore, I have added dates as per the Gregorian calendar to the Al Hijri dates, to make it easier for modern readers to place historical events. [All the dates were converted using the converter provided at http://binoria.org/islamic-applications-online-apps/gregorian-to-hijri-and-hijri-to-gregorian-date-converter/]

Sayyid Ahmad Khan was also able to provide detailed notes on the builders of various monuments in *Asar-2*, whereas in *Asar-1* he states that he was unable to locate any historical reference to them. *Asar-2* thus carries a list of the books the author consulted in the interim period between the two editions, which resulted in the discovery of these details.

Asar-2 has no Review (unlike *Asar-1*, which in the original has four Reviews), but it includes a Preface by the author in English. The biggest difference, however, between the two editions – apart from language and style – is that *Asar-2* does not include a chapter with a description of the notable persons of Delhi, but does include, at the very beginning, a chapter describing the ruling dynasties of India. The second chapter of *Asar-2* describes the origins of Delhi and the various forts that were built by rulers through the ages. Even the Red Fort [Qila-e-Mubarak or Auspicious Fort], built by Shahjahan, is described in greater detail. The third chapter has a chronological description of monuments built by the nobles and rulers of Delhi. This is followed by a section on inscriptions, with sketches of the inscriptions on various monuments, which I have left out – as I have translated them in *Asar-1* (I have made a note of these in English from the translations of inscriptions in Maulvi Zafar Hasan's book,

Monuments of India). The longer inscriptions, such as those found on Ashoka's Pillar, can be found in Appendix II, where I have added the inscriptions Zafar Hasan missed out, so that the book becomes a definitive and complete guide to modern Delhi's monuments. I have also added another appendix (Appendix I), which briefly narrates the present state of each of these monuments, including a mention of those lost to us forever.

Another difference between the two editions is that *Asar-2* does not include the inscriptions in the text but those that have been written by Sayyid Ahmad Khan in the lithographs. With regard to the lithographs, since this volume includes both *Asar-1* and *Asar-2*, it showcases the lithographs only in *Asar-1* alongside the monument that each refers to; it does not replicate the lithographs in both editions.

Translating both editions has been a monumental task, as *Asar-us-Sanadid*, written on such a scale, has formed the basis of almost every work on Delhi's monuments that has been attempted ever since. Through this translation, I am fulfilling a dream of mine to be able to make this book available in English to lovers of Delhi's history.

Any errors in translation remain mine.

Note

[1] He received his knighthood in 1888 and was made a Knight Commander of the Star of India.

ASĀR-US-SANADĪD

1

Praise [*Taqrīz*]

MIRZA ASADULLAH KHAN GHALIB

Lovers of intellect and wisdom have given the changing fortunes of time such good news that it is as though the picture galleries [*nigar-khane*] of China have revealed themselves to us; which is to say that this work – indispensable for recording the rules, customs and common practices of an era – actually heralds the advent of something new, wonderful and intoxicating, and opens up the path to wisdom and sagacity.

Sir Sayyid Ahmad Khan's *Asar-us-Sanadid* is a book that will numb the hands of other writers once they read it. In other words, no one has been able to reach the very high standard it has set; and even if people keep trying till doomsday to write such an account they will not succeed no matter how hard they try, even if they are as skilled a painter as Behzad. A picture-gallery worthy of being lauded even in paradise, this book describes fairytale-like palaces and narrates the deeds of emperors from a bygone era.

Set by the writer of time to the tune of a soundless flute, it describes the eras and tells its tale in a manner such that everyone finds an echo of their own story in it. But even though its decorated walls and gateways resemble fairyland, a man as jaded and cynical as me is left struggling to appreciate the peace, calm and reflection that it holds. It is beyond the grasp of my imagination. Therefore, conscious of my own infirmity and lost in the desert of my thoughts, I find myself disappointed with myself – much like a cheetah exhausted by the extreme heat having lost its way and unable to find its way out. My bosom is scarred, much as holes mark a beehive, and my eyes droop like a beautiful maiden's, lashes downcast and fanning one's cheeks.

This work, written in a manner that unveils the stories of people who think themselves very clever, who sleep in peace in their bedchambers, and for whom the insignia of royalty is commonplace, also helps a common man like me partake of the thoughts and events in the lives of emperors past, much as a cluster of flowers skirts the edge of a beautiful garden. Though I myself am unable to describe the armies of conquerors whose flying standards gave many a heart the notion of security, or describe their rule and dominions – others able to present their views fearlessly have innumerable admirers. No doubt that wise man is happy who knows the skill involved in his work, is aware of his accomplishments, whose character is very lofty and mind very superior, whose heart is full of love and whose temperament precludes complaints, who is an enemy of evil, a friend of the pious, is extremely intelligent, whose grandeur and literary attainment is immeasurable, and that man is Jawad-ud-Daulah Sayyid Ahmad Khan Bahadur Arif Jung.

He has brought the dead back to life with the power of his pen in such a way that they have become immortal. He has strung together all the virtues of his own temperament like pearls for others to enjoy. This lovingly strung pearl necklace, further dipped in the syrup of love and the light of enlightenment, has become manifest to all.

Thanks to his intelligent disposition, he has been able to gift the world a guide on the customs and traditions of wise and intelligent people. The beauty and attraction of this guide now resides in our hearts bestowing the gift of composure upon us, much as an old bird picking a pearl out of an oyster feels that the pearl is baring its teeth.

This work makes even the most difficult of tasks and skills seem as if an emperor has changed into new clothes. Since free men have accomplished such noble tasks without payment and their work has been much appreciated in the world, these informative works have added to the glory and respect of their ancestors and ensured that coming generations will be aware of the deeds of these eminent personalities.

This book makes it obvious that a man like Ghalib, seated on the carpet in robes of honour bestowed by the emperor, is not so very distant from his own generations-to-come, though he will soon be on the list of the departed. Every moment in this book testifies to the fact that this dear friend and guide in keeping with the commendable personality, virtues and examples of his ancestors, speaks for future generations. It can be said that my words serve as a wake-up call for people now, so that they may hear the voice of those long gone.

I am very happy that this work has reached a happy conclusion and that the pen has ceased its movement. It is also a felicitous moment and I am very pleased with it. In fact, I am so happy that it would be appropriate to say at this juncture that I was kept awake, thinking of this the whole night and by the grace of the intellect gifted to me by the Almighty was able to understand that this work was extremely difficult and challenging. I concluded however – guided by reason and my concerns – that reflecting upon it thus [through the night] had taken me out of the tavern of nothingness and placed me on the illuminated path of being. I realized that the craving and desires present in my disposition, because of my lack of wisdom, had left me forever. I was finally able to see my inferiority with my own eyes.

Thus I can conclude that the happiness that [I] Ghalib derived from reading *Asar-us-*

Sanadid is above every other thing. In reality, I have no desire for anything else, nor is any ego or sense of self-accomplishment left in me.

O Ghalib, I have cut myself off from everything else,
In fact, I have become a worshipper of the Almighty.

CHAPTER ONE

A Description of the Monuments Outside the City

See the monuments of the Beloved's city,

The tyranny of changing times has destroyed them all

In the past this city (Shahjahanabad) was oriented to the south and all its old monuments are therefore located in that direction. There are very few old buildings in any other direction in Shahjahanabad, because as the various emperors [*badshahs*] built their forts and cities, they kept shifting towards the north.

The oldest monuments in the south are those built by Tughlaq Shah and Adil Shah, who had built their forts to the south of the older habitations. So, I start my descriptions with the Fort of Tughlaqabad, not only because it is the southernmost monument, but also because its ruins serve as a warning about the intransience of the world. These ruins hold up a mirror to one's mortality for those who have the eyes to see.

TUGHLAQABAD

Upon becoming Sultan, Ghiyas-ud-Din Tughlaq began building this fort and city in AH 721 [CE 1321–22]. In CE 1323 [AH 722–23], when news of the conquest of Warrangal reached the sultan, the city of Tughlaqabad was completely ready and both Delhi and Tughlaqabad were magnificently lit up in celebration. Tughlaqabad Fort was [thus] built in a short period of time. It contained many beautiful buildings.

Sultan Ghiyas-ud-Din Tughlaq was the son of Malik Tughlaq, a slave of Sultan Ghiyas-ud-Din Balban. The fort, which must have been very beautiful and elegant at one time, is now uninhabited and in a bad state. Portions of the wall still remain, but the structures inside have crumbled, some stones and potholes being the only signs that they ever existed. There used to be a lofty building in the middle of the fort, [called the] *baithak* which the sultan used for public audiences[1] and which was named Jahannuma [world-reflecting].

Though the fort is popularly thought to be huge, on investigation I found it was not very large. It is said that this city and the fort had 56 bastions and 52 gates and it is quite possible that this is true. However this could not be verified, since much of it now lies in ruins.

The emperor located the fort in the west and on the other three sides, i.e. the east, north and the south, he established the city of Tughlaqabad – joining the walls of the city and the fort so seamlessly that they appeared as one. The fort is located 6 *kos*[2] [13.5 miles] to the south of Shahjahanabad, and is now under the control of Raja Nahar Singh of Ballamgarh, though only herdsmen called Gujars, reside here now. The Gujars have been living within the remains of the fort for the last 50 to 60 years, and they have got a wonderful place to live in just as they please. The fort is situated on a hill and is made of lime and sandstone. Though very strong yet elegant, its doors are very small and the arches are of very inferior quality as was common in those days. However, when it was built about 500 years ago, it must have been a very impressive and strongly built monument for its time. The fort and the city have been made in such a way that they all seem to be one entity.

MAQBARA TUGHLAQ SHAH

Sultan Ghiyas-ud-Din Tughlaq's mausoleum [*maqbara*] is located near Tughlaqabad Fort. When he died in CE 1324 [AH 724], his son Sultan Muhammad Tughlaq (also known as Muhammad Adil Shah)[3] built this tomb for his father. It is a very beautifully constructed tomb,

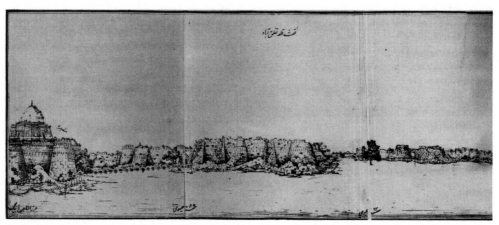

Tughlaqabad

Maqbara Ghiyas-ud-Din

and I don't think there would have been any other monument as beautiful as this in that era.

There is a popular belief among the populace that it was built by Ghiyas-ud-Din Shah[4] [Sultan Ghiyas-ud-Din Tughlaq], but this is incorrect. It was actually built by his son Malik Fakhr-ud-Din Juna – anointed as the heir apparent and bestowed the title of 'Alif Khan' by his father – who took on the title of Muhammad Tughlaq Shah when he came to the throne. Since both father and son were popularly known as Tughlaq Shah, people get confused as to which of them actually built the tomb. It was built after AH 725 [sic; CE 1324–25] and 537 years have passed since then.

The walls are built of local quartzite [*sang-e-khara*] and limestone, while the dome is made of marble with red sandstone. This combination of red and white is breathtaking. There is a red sandstone finial over the dome, damaged in places. Near the entrance is a small dome [that belongs to a pre-existing tomb] which contains a grave of an unknown person,[5] and which has been enclosed within the compound of the tomb. The tomb was called Dar-ul-Aman during the reign of Firoz Shah[i] who had a canopy of sandalwood built over the grave and had curtains from the sacred Ka'ba in Mecca installed there.

[i] *Futuhat-i-Firoz Shahi* [Sultan Firoz Shah's autobiography].

Firoz Shah received letters of forgiveness from those who had been tortured, maimed or persecuted by Sultan Muhammad Adil Tughlaq Shah [Muhammad bin Tughlaq], and [also received letters of forgiveness] from their heirs, as well as from the heirs of all those who had been killed – and he kept these letters in a box that was placed near the head of the grave.

This tomb falls under the aegis of Raja Nahar Singh of Ballamgarh, who has no appreciation for such a beautiful monument and has let it go to ruin – cattle are tied within and peasants live inside too. These peasants call themselves 'Sheikh' and claim their ancestors have been living here ever since Tughlaqabad was first inhabited. When the Gujars began living in the fort, the peasants shifted into the tomb. A bridge leads from the tomb to the fort, as water once surrounded the tomb.

Graves within the Mausoleum

This tomb's interiors are very beautiful as is made evident in the drawing. There are three graves inside the tomb, the one in the centre being that of Sultan Ghiyas-ud-Din Tughlaq himself. I have not been able to verify who is buried in the second of the three graves. People say that it belongs to Ghiyas-ud-Din Tughlaq Shah's son Muhammad Adil Shah, but Ghiyas-ud-Din did not have a son of that name. His son was called Sultan Muhammad Tughlaq and he had this tomb constructed. Sultan Muhammad Tughlaq Shah died in AH 752 [CE 1351] on the banks of the River Indus, but I wouldn't be surprised had he been brought back and buried in this tomb. The third grave here is that of his wife, who bore the title of Maqduma-e-Jahan or Queen of the World. The headstones of all three graves have vanished and no one knows where they have disappeared to. Cenotaphs of brick and limestone have been built in place of the headstones.

The Mausoleum's Dome

The dome is very beautiful and only a tall man can reach up to the dado! I am incapable of describing its beauty. There are beautifully constructed arched doors on the east, south and north and in the west, there is a wall with a niche that indicates the direction of Mecca [such a wall is called a *mihrab*]. The tomb is so sturdy and well-built that it is difficult to imagine that it will ever be destroyed. The courtyard, which is so beautiful that even walking on it with shoes was considered uncivilized, is now populated by cattle and covered in cowdung.

The Walls

The walls and entrance gateway [*darwaza*] of the tomb are very finely constructed. The gateway is made of red sandstone and there are twenty-three steps that lead into the tomb. Though this tomb is famous as 'Tikonia Kot' or the Triangular Fort, this nomenclature is wrong as there are two more sides giving the structure an irregular pentagonal shape.

It is difficult to understand why the walls were given this singularly irregular shape; maybe it was because it had to be adapted to the shape of the hill. There are five bastions projecting from the walls – one in the south and the second in the west. On the third bastion is another dome and it houses some unknown graves. The fourth and fifth bastions face the north and east. There is also a stone well on the western side, used by the peasants that now live inside the tomb complex. There are rooms in the interior that were built for the poor and the destitute [*fuqra aur masakin*] to live in. It was near this mausoleum that Sultan Firoz Shah had a dam constructed and also built a causeway to connect it with the fort, giving the structure its unique beauty.

The Causeway

Though I cannot say with certainty that the causeway was built by Sultan Firoz Shah – the son of Salar Rajab, who ascended the throne after Sultan Muhammad Tughlaq – everything points to Sultan Firoz Shah, since he had many bridges and dams built during his reign. If my guess is correct, then it was built in AH 752 [sic; CE 1351–52] and 510 years have passed since then.

Connecting the fort and the tomb has greatly added to the attraction of both. On the east is the fort, to the west are the mountains, to the south is the building called Hazar

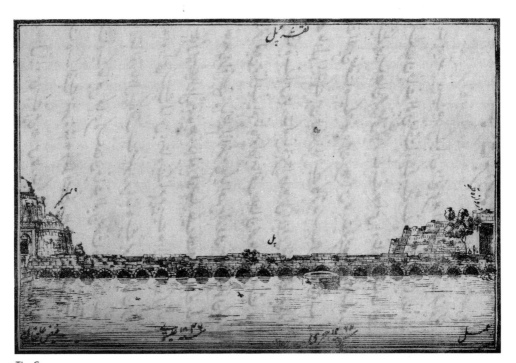

The Causeway

Sutun [Thousand Pillars], and to the north there would have been water lapping at the foot of the fort. The tomb complex, surrounded by water, must have been an amazing sight. The tomb must have appeared like a bowl [katora] in the middle of the water. The waves, the cool breeze, the greenery on the mountains must have brought paradise to mind. So much water surrounded the tomb that there was no way of reaching it. That's why a causeway had to be made from the entrance of the fort to the entrance of the tomb.

When I went to make a sketch of the tomb, I had to pass through quite a lot of water, and the waves in the water and the cool breeze made me think that had this dam been maintained, it would have made for a wonderful recreation spot [sairgah]. Unfortunately, the land it is situated on belongs to Raja Nahar Singh of Ballamgarh, who has no appreciation for this beautiful monument. The causeway is broken in places and has clogged the openings of the dam. In olden days there were many streams in this area that were diverted to this dam. Water that overflowed for twelve months, from the Hauz-e-Shamsi reservoir in Qutub Sahib's dargah area, was also diverted here.

ADILABAD/MUHAMMADABAD/IMARAT HAZAR SUTUN

Adilabad/Muhammadabad [Fort] is located near the Tughlaqabad Fort. When Sultan Muhammad Tughlaq Shah – alias Fakhr-ud-Din Juna Ghiyas-ud-Din, son of Ghiyas-ud-Din Tughlaq – became the sultan, he built a new fort near Tughlaqabad in CE 1327 [AH 727] and named it Muhammadabad or Adilabad. It was called Muhammadabad as that was his name and Adilabad because that is the title he adopted when he ascended the throne.

However, since Muhammad Tughlaq Shah killed so many thousands of innocents he came to be known as Sultan Khooni. 'Adil' was removed from his title as no one called him Adil anymore, and this is also why I had written in the description of Ghiyas-ud-Din Tughlaq Shah's tomb that he had no son by the name of Adil, because the name fell out of use.

The construction of this fort began after AH 725 [CE 1324–25], was completed in AH 728 [sic; CE 1327–28] and 534 years have passed since then. Contemporary poet Badar Saashi has recorded the date of this palace as AH 725 [CE 1324–25], in a chronogram: Fad-kuluha [to come in/to enter].

They say that this monument was once very beautiful, and because it had a thousand pillars of local quartzite it was called Imarat [building] Hazar Sutun. The fort now lies in ruins. Only some remnants of a few gateways and some walls remain, everything else has collapsed. Situated on land belonging to Raja Nahar Singh of Ballamgarh, the fort has been utterly neglected. The state of a fort built by and for a tyrant sultan, and which is now used for cattle-grazing, serves as a grave admonition:

> Take warning, then, O ye, with intelligence (Quran 59:2)

Adilabad/Muhammadabad

KALKA TEMPLE

This temple is built on the border of Bharpur village (*mauza*), which lies 6 *kos* [13.5 miles] south of Shahjahanabad. It is a major place of Hindu worship [*badi parastish-gah*]. Though it is difficult to fully comprehend the religion of the Hindus, I am writing whatever I have been able to understand.

According to Hindu mythology, millions of years ago there were two demons named Simba and Nasba, who gave a lot of trouble to the gods. The gods complained to Lord Brahma who refused to interfere and recommended that the people pray to Goddess Parvati instead. When they performed a ritual prayer ceremony, a goddess – Kaushiki Devi – was born from the mouth of Goddess Parvati. Kaushiki Devi killed the leader of the demons, Raktbhanch, but thousands of demons were born from the drops of his blood that fell to the earth.

Then the Goddess Kali was born from the eyebrows of Kaushiki Devi. Goddess Kali, 'whose lower lip rested on the hills below and the upper lip touched the sky above', drank the blood of the demons before it could fall on the ground, as Kaushiki Devi slaughtered them. Thus Kaushiki Devi emerged victorious over the demons. At the end of *Dwapar Yug*,[6] which was 4945 years ago, Kali Devi began residing on this hill. She has been worshipped since the time of the Pandavas.

Whoever comes here must first prostrate before the idol, then perform a circumambulation and make an offering, after which the priests also give the devotee some sweets [prasad]. I too got some sugar candy [batasha], raisins [kishmish] and almonds [badam], when I went there to sketch. I took the offering helplessly as I didn't want to anger the priests or they wouldn't have let me sketch. So, I tried to please the priests in every way.

> I imitated the infidel and became an infidel for a few days;
>
> I read the Zand texts and became a Brahman.

Not many people came here earlier, but now there is quite a crowd and they have great faith in the goddess. The priests here tell the devotees that if travellers offer their hands, legs, head and tongue to the goddess, she will return these on the third day. The priests are committed to keeping a lamp [diya] filled with clarified butter [ghee], lit twenty-four hours a day, till eternity. This is known as the Goddess' Flame [Devi ka jyot].

Maharaja Scindia had earlier given them the village of Bahapur, tax-free, for the maintenance of the temple. Later, the village was taken away and they received one hundred rupees annually. Now, however, they get nothing and the priests take care of expenses via tilling and offerings made to the temple. Huge crowds of people come every Tuesday and on the eighth of every month to pray to the goddess, as per their religion.

Kalka Temple: the interior

Semi-annual fairs [melas] are held here on the eighth [ashtami] of the [Hindu calender] months of Chait and Ashochki [probably corresponding to the Hindu calendar month of Ashvin], and are visited by thousands. There is a shortage of water here as there is only one well, though it is quite deep. Someone had built two tanks, but these exist in a state of disrepair and don't hold any water.

Murat Mandir

There is no idol [murat] of the goddess in this temple [mandir], just a round stone, which represents Shiva. This is actually the place dedicated to Goddess Kali [Kali ka sthan] and frequent usage of the term 'Kali ka sthan' has resulted in a shorter name, 'Kalka'. Originally there was no building on this spot, and some thousands of years later, it became a place dedicated to Goddess Kali. Some person, whose name cannot be verified, made a vaulted, twelve-arched pavilion [baradari] in this place. This was done in *Samt 1821*,[7] which was 82 years ago and it is still standing. A person named Durga Singh made a marble and red sandstone enclosure around it. To the left of the enclosure is an inscription in Farsi and Shastri *khat* (Sanskrit), which reads:

> Sri Durga Singh is mounted on a lion – 1821 *Samt Fasli.*

The Shape of the Temple

The priests wanted a pinnacle [shikhar] made on top of the temple, but could not find anyone ready to undertake this task. Finally, they decided to let the goddess give the orders herself. They wrote out the names of all the rich Hindus of the city on small bits of paper and placed these in front of the goddess.

The person whose name was selected through this process was Mirza Raja Kedarnath, the accountant [peshkar] in the administration during Akbar Shah's reign. He was a *bania* by caste and had been given the title of 'Mirza Raja'. When he heard that the chit of paper with his name had been chosen by the goddess, he had the pinnacle built over the vaulted structure. He also built twelve doors and a circumbulatory verandah with thirty-six arches around the temple.

Thirty years have passed since this temple was built and many buildings have now sprung up. These were built by the moneylenders [mahajans] to accommodate people who visit the temples during the fairs. There are two red sandstone tigers and a trident [trishul] in front of the door of this temple. As per the Hindu faith, lions pull the goddess' chariot and that is why they are stationed at the doorway.

The temple priest conducts prayers twice a day, in the morning and evening, and at 11 a.m. makes offerings of food etc. [bhog] to the idol. A huge bell hanging on a tiger's head is rung during prayer to the slogans of 'Victory to the Mother Goddess' [Devi Ma *ki Jai*]. There is a

The shape of the temple

red sandstone trident next to these tigers and a marble slab with a footprint engraved on it.

> Every people (nation) has its right path,
>
> Its faith and its focus of worship.

DARGAH HAZRAT ROSHAN CHIRAGH DEHLI

This very famous *dargah* of Hazrat Roshan Chiragh Dehli lies to the south of Shahjahanabad, at a distance of 6 *kos* [13.5 miles]. It is the resting place of Sheikh Nasir-ud-Din Mahmood, a very important Sufi saint who bore the title 'Roshan Chiragh Dehli'. He was the successor of the Sultan of the Sufi Masters, Hazrat Nizam-ud-Din Auliya.

Hazrat Abdullah Yafai asked Hazrat Makhdum Jahaniyan-e-Jahangasht who the resident saint of Delhi was. Makhdum Sahib told him that the lamp of Delhi was illuminated by Hazrat Nasir-ud-Din Mahmood, and that is how the saint got the title. Sultan Firoz Shah sincerely revered and served the saint.

The dome of his burial site was built by Firoz Shah in his lifetime itself, in AH 749 [CE 1348–49]. In AH 757 [CE 1356], on Friday, the eighteenth of [the Islamic calendar month of] Ramzan [September 14] when the saint left this world for paradise, he was buried under this dome.

The *dargah* has twelve arches with quartzite pillars. All the arches have stone-lattice

Dargah Hazrat Roshan Chiragh Dehli

screens, with the exception of the one on the south, which has a door. The dome is made of rubble and mortar and has a golden finial with a golden bowl hanging inside [the dome]. The Mughal prince, Mirza Ghulam Haider, had constructed a pavilion around the dome with columns from the shrine and the tomb of Nizam-ud-Din Auliya, but it was so badly constructed that it collapsed a decade later.

Near the *dargah* is a mosque said to have been built by Emperor Farrukhsiyyar. It has no inscription that could give details as to its construction. However, as 135 years have passed since Farrukhsiyar's reign, this mosque must have been built then.

The courtyard of the *dargah* has two pavilions. The grave of the granddaughter of Hazrat Sheikh Farid Shakar Ganj is located in the first, and the other has the grave of Makhdoom Zain-ud-Din, the former's nephew and spiritual successor [*khalifa*]. Near this lies the grave of Maqdoom Kamal-ud-Din, the Master [*Pir*] of Maulvi Fakhr-ud-Din, and the grave of Nawab Faiz Talab Khan Bangash. There are two more pavilions belonging to the Afghan period, but the names of those buried there are not known.

The dome of the *dargah* and that of the mosque have fallen into utter disrepair, especially after the circumambulatory aisles [*ghulam gardish*] built by Mirza Ghulam Haider fell into disrepair. The *dargah*'s hereditary caretakers [*khadim*] requested people for help in repairing the dome and mosque. Khwaja Muhammad Khan took on the rest of the repairs and almost built it anew. He got a stone eave [*chajja*] constructed which has given it a new life. A boundary wall and a three-arched hall were built by Maulvi Fakhr-ud-Din. The columns that marked the aisles still lie fallen in front of the *dargah*. On every seventeenth of [the Islamic calendar month of] Ramzan, a great many people gather here and sleep overnight to celebrate the saint's death anniversary [*urs*] and then leave after the *Qul* ceremony [8] that takes place on the eighteenth.

Entrance of the Dargah

The inscription on the gateway of the *dargah* reads:

> *In the name of God, we finished it with his name. The august dome was constructed during the auspicious reign of he who is expectant of the help of God, (named) Abul Muzaffar Firoz Shah the king – may God perpetuate his kingdom – in the year AH 775 from the flight of the Prophet – may the peace of God be upon him.*

Twelve years after the passing of the saint, Sultan Firoz Shah got a domed gateway constructed for the *dargah*. The dome is quite big. The sultan's name is inscribed on the gateway. The hereditary caretakers of the *dargah* got together and built a huge hall in front of the gateway for the convenience and use of the people who come here to pay homage. It has made a lot of difference, as the people who come here now have a proper place to rest.

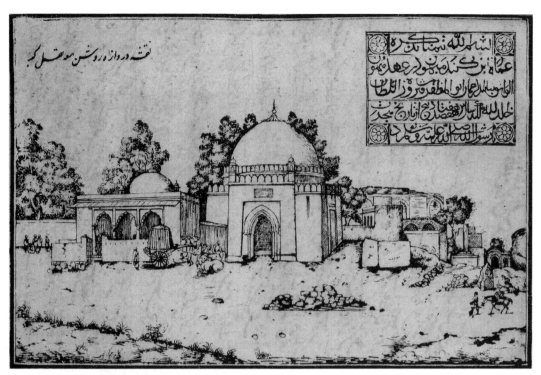

The gateway of the dargah

In front of this gateway is a bed [*takht*] made of a single piece of wood. It is 4 feet wide, 8 feet long and a foot and 4 inches high. It was sent by Dakhini Beg from Bangala and has a verse carved on it, which reads:

> *This wooden throne has been presented by Dakhini Beg in the service of his holiness*
> *Nasir-ud-Din Mahmood, May his tomb be purified/hallowed by Allah,[9] AH 1143.* [CE 1730–31]

Legend has it that it was sent by Hazrat Khwaja Banda Nawaz Gesu Daraz who was the disciple of Hazrat Roshan Chiragh. It is possible that he may have used the name Dakhini Beg because he had gone to the south and established a place [*khanqah*] there for the gathering of his Sufi brotherhood.

MAQBARA SULTAN BAHLOL LODI

This mausoleum lies behind Hazrat Roshan Chiragh Dehli's *dargah*. According to legend, this mausoleum was built before the *dargah* was built, but I find that hard to believe because Hazrat Roshan Chiragh Dehli's *dargah* was built during the reign of Sultan Firoz Shah and Bahlol Lodi came on the scene much later. This mausoleum would be about 368 years old [sic], since Sultan Bahlol Lodi died in Bhadaoli village near Saket in AH 892 [CE 1486–87],[10] and his son Sultan

Maqbara Sultan Bahlol Lodi

Sikandar sent his father's body to be buried near the *dargah* and had this mausoleum built.

It is built in a very unique style, with twelve arches and five cupolas on top, and must have been very beautiful. Alas! The tomb is today in a state of disrepair and to add to it, the *dargah*'s hereditary caretakers have built mud walls and have started living here. A graveyard has also come up, with many graves inside the red-stone screen enclosure. The walls and one of the entrances of the *dargah* Roshan Chiragh Dehli are clearly visible from here and I have drawn a sketch of this in such a way so as to include all of them.

SATPULA: THE SEVEN-ARCHED BRIDGE

This bridge-and-dam is located near the *dargah* of Hazrat Roshan Chiragh Dehli, adjoining Khirki village. The walls of this bridge form part of Sultan Firoz Shah's hunting lodge [*shikargah*]. In AH 776 [CE 1374–75], his beloved son Fatah Khan died and the sultan went into depression, losing all desire to live. Feeling it was better to be a mendicant [*faqir*] than a king, he lost all interest in the affairs of state and this impacted governance. The nobles of his court consoled him and built this dam to divert him. They chose an attractive piece of woodland, erected enclosing walls in a large area and planted various trees, thus turning it into a hunting lodge.

The seven-arched bridge makes up one of the walls of that hunting lodge. In the middle of this [bridge] wall is a huge channel [*nala*], into which all the water from the channels in Qutub Sahib's area (Mehrauli) flows. Arches have been built in the wall to ensure easy flow, which is why it is known as the '*satpula*' [seven-arched bridge].

There are a few buildings on these arches and two very famous gateways add to the beauty of the dam; 486 years have passed since it was built. The wall has crumbled in some places and a temporary dam was built here under British government-rule. The arches were also closed with mud and the flow of water stopped. It used to provide water for the fields and benefit cultivators.

On this Shab-e-barat, the strong flow of the water damaged the wall of the dam, and this has been temporarily repaired. I pray that the British government takes cognizance of the beauty and attraction of this place and restores it to its original state.

The hereditary caretakers of Hazrat Chiragh Dehli's *dargah* have woven a web here to earn money and ensnare and cheat ordinary folk who visit it. The caretakers tell them that Hazrat Chiragh Dehli had once visited the location where the arches are built. The time for afternoon prayers [*Asr*] was drawing to a close and Hazrat couldn't find water for his ritual ablutions [*wuzu*], so he dug up the ground with his bare hands and water gushed out. He completed his ablutions and blessed the water, saying that whoever bathed in it would be miraculously cured of all disease.

His disciples refer to this as a miracle. They have made small holes in front of these arches and sell the water to people. The water from these holes wouldn't even be pure for the ritual ablutions for prayers as per the Shariah. No reference to this incident has been found in any book, and even if true, it is not a miracle because there has been a small river flowing here for thousands of years. It is common in any area where water flows in this manner that if one digs one is sure to find water beneath the surface.

Satpula

Muslims now believe these holes to be as sacred as Ganga *jal* [water of the Ganges]. They have established it as a pilgrimage spot and bathe the sick here. In the [Hindu calendar] month of Kartik before Diwali, a huge crowd gathers here on Saturday, Sunday and Tuesday. Women bring children to bathe them in this water and also take it away in small packets as a token of blessings [*tabarruk*]. Many ignorant [*jahil*] men also believe this and they too come and bathe here and say that all effects of magic performed by evil persons are washed away. These days the hereditary caretakers are doing well for themselves, charging 6 *takkas* for a packet of water. When I visited it on a Sunday to sketch it, many Muslims and Hindus had come on pilgrimage and there was such a huge crowd that I found it difficult to sketch.

May Allah save the Muslims from disbelief, ingratitude, placing anything or anyone on parity with Allah [*kufr* and *shirk*], and from wrong beliefs. Amen, O Lord of the Universe. If anyone prays to another, other than Allah, then he/she has lost his/her faith.

MASJID KHIRKI

In ancient times, there used to be a village called Khirki close to the famous Satpula dam. On this location, Khan-e-Jahan Firoz Shahi built a mosque at the same time as the dam and since then this mosque has become famous by the name of the village itself, i.e. Khirki.

This mosque is uniquely built and I have not seen one such as this ever before. It is square on the exterior and is divided into four equal quadrangles inside. Between the four quadrangles is placed an open court, in the middle, like a crown. It has doors on three sides except on the side that faces the west,[11] which is closed. The mosque has numerous columns that form the aisles. There are nine domes in each square, and under every dome

Masjid Khirki

are four columns. Apart from these, there are other pillars as well. There are also four open quadrangles inside the mosque.

The mosque is now inhabited by Gujar herdsmen, who have closed all the arches and established their dwellings within. I wanted to sketch the mosque from the inside, but since the herdsmen have spread their dwellings and cattle all over it, all I could manage was a drawing of the houses inside and the walls. There is no inscription on this mosque that would indicate the year of its construction. However, since we estimate that this mosque was built at the same time as the dam, it may have been built 486 years ago. Its uniqueness can be gleaned from the sketch.

DARGAH YUSUF QATTAL

This *dargah* was built in the reign of Sultan Sikandar Shah, son of Sultan Bahlol in AH 903 [CE 1497–98]. Sheikh Ala-ud-Din, the grandson of Hazrat Sheikh Farid Shakar Ganj, built this monument, as mentioned in an inscription. This *dargah* is near Khirki Mosque.

The dome and screens of the *dargah* are made of red stone, while the dome is plastered with lime mortar and has glazed tile decoration on its edges. There is a lime-mortar mosque near it, which is now in ruins. The mosque and *dargah* must have been very fine when they were made, but now their condition is poor and there is no one to repair them. The dome is in

Dargah Yusuf Qattal

a better shape than the mosque, which is in a state of total disrepair. The peasants who live in Khirki have immense respect for this *dargah* and call it Al-Yusuf Auliya Sahib's *dargah*. One can make out the elegance of the *dargah* from the sketch. The inscription on the tomb reads as follows: [12]

> *This dome was erected in the reign of the great Sultan Abu Muzaffar Sikandar Shah*
> *Sultan, may his reign and kingdom be perpetuated.*
> *The founder of the dome was Sheikh Ala-ud-Din Nur Taj, the grandson of the Sheikh, the*
> *pole star of the world, Sheikh Farid Shakar Ganj.*
> *The [Islamic calendar] month of Moharram of the year [AH] 913 [CE 1507–08].*

DARGAH SHEIKH SALAH-UD-DIN

Hazrat Sheikh Salah-ud-Din was a very pious mendicant who lived in the reign of Sultan Muhammad Adil Shah,[ii] and was the disciple of Sheikh Sadr-ud-Din. His *dargah* is near Roshan Chiragh Dehli. No one knows when this was built and by whom, but it is very similar

---

[ii] *Akhbar-ul-Akhiyar.*

Dargah Sheikh Salah-ud-Din

in style to the monuments built in Firoz Shah's reign, from which we can conclude it was built around that time. There is a dome on the enshrined tomb and screens enclose it. There is a small mosque nearby and adjoining that is another very large domed mosque of which just a few arches remain. It lies ruined and even the niche in the wall [*pesh takh* or central *mihrab*] that indicates the direction of Mecca, is broken. To the west of Sheikh Salah-ud-Din's [tomb's] dome is another smaller domed pavilion which houses an unknown grave. A small hall is built near it and this could be called a meeting hall. No fairs or death anniversary celebrations of the saint [*urs*] are held here. The hereditary caretakers of the *dargah* of Hazrat Roshan Chiragh Dehli take whatever they can by exploiting the few people who do come here.

MAZAAR SAR NALA

Near the *dargah* of Hazrat Roshan Chiragh Dehli, at the end of the lower stream [*nala*], is a tomb. Though I tried my best, I could not find out who built it and who is buried in it. Its location at the edge of a stream is very attractive, especially when the water is flowing. The tomb itself is very well decorated and finely made, with carving and inlay work. Its floor and pillars are of red sandstone with elaborate ornamentation, and one can make out its beauty from the sketch.

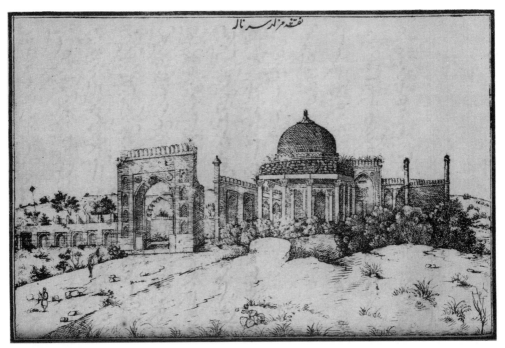

Mazaar Sar Nala

PANCH BURJA, ZAMARUDPUR

Zamarudpur village lies six miles to the south of Shahjahanabad and has been inhabited since the time of the [Lodi] Pathans. The area was earlier known as Kanchan Sarai and it seems that in the reign of Sultan Sikandar Bahlol it was included in the landholding [*jagir*] of Zamarud Khan and was thus renamed Zamarudpur. Zamarud Khan's graveyard falls in Zamarudpur village and there are five [*panch*] small domed pavilions [*burja*] supported on columns that are built on the graves [hence, the name by which it is commonly known – Panch Burja]. The pavilions are made of lime and stone, and the location contains many graves.

Nobody knows who Zamarud Khan was, but it seems quite obvious from the style of construction that these domed pavilions are from the reign of Sultan Sikandar and were built in the fifteenth century [CE 1488/AH 893–94]. The graves bear no inscription. There is a huge well near the graves, which is of the same vintage, but is almost dry now and in ruins because of its age. It is not in a position to even be repaired. Some villagers from Zamarudpur live near these tombs and some peasants have built huts there.

MAQBARA LANGAR KHAN

This tomb lies on the border of Raipur village, which is near Zamarudpur village. Raipur is totally desolate and the peasants of nearby areas and from Roshan Chiragh Dehli plough the

Maqbara Langar Khan

land and grow crops here. I have not been able to find out who Langar Khan was, except that Langar Khan was a noble from the Lodi era.

There are many graves in the tomb and one grave is so high that no one has seen the top of it. When I went to sketch the grave, I stood near it, raised my hand and tried to touch the top but couldn't reach it; it was a few inches higher. There is no inscription on this grave to indicate the exact date and so it can only be said that it was made in the reign of the Pathans. In the courtyard of this mausoleum is another small square pavilion with a grave that probably belongs to someone from the same family. The state of these graves serves as a warning that [even] such notable men today lie in the dust.

BASTI BAORI

This tomb is situated near the *dargah* of Hazrat Nizam-ud-Din, and was built by Basti Khwaja Sara for himself.[13] There is a domed pavilion, a mosque, as well as a step well [*baoli*]. Since step wells were also called *baori*, it became famous as such. It is very beautiful, with very attractive halls constructed on different levels. A mosque is located to the west of the step well, with Quranic verses engraved in cut plaster. This step well seems to be the tank [for ritual ablutions] at the mosque, but is now dry. The inscriptions on the mosque cannot be read as they have become very faint due to age and state of disrepair.

Basti Baori

To the left of the mosque is a domed gateway, which was used as a common passage. From this gateway one can view the dome of a tomb that was built on the roof of a facing building [possibly a *madarsa*]. There are stairs to reach the top where there is a grave and a dome that stands on beautiful red stone columns. The screens, which were there earlier, have been taken away and only the pavilion and columns remain.

The plinth itself has been beautifully made with four cupolas on its four corners, of which three still remain, while one has broken down. There are holes inside the pavilion from where finials were pulled out. On the four corners of the platform are four small, square-shaped domed pavilions, of which three now remain as the one on the west has collapsed. This building must have been very beautiful in its day. Even today it is well worth a visit. There is no inscription here to indicate the date, but it seems to have been built during the Pathan period, and must have been built during their reign. The sketch includes the mosque, gateway, step well and tomb.

KHIZR KI GUMBATI

Khizr Khan's mausoleum is built on the banks of the river in Okhla village, at a distance of 6 *kos* [13.5 miles] from Shahjahanabad. I consulted numerous books to find out who Khizr Khan was,

Khizr ki Gumbati

but couldn't find an answer. Though this building has become famous across countries, it is not particularly beautiful or even finely constructed. Its only special feature is that it is situated on the banks of the river. Many say that there used to be a temple here in ancient times and that this pavilion replaced it, but I haven't been able to authenticate this information.

DARGAH HAZRAT SAYYID MUHAMMAD MAHMOOD BAHAR

This *dargah* is situated on the border of Kilukhari village, near Barapula, at a distance of 4 *kos* [9 miles] from Shahjahanabad. Though the structure is ordinary, it is sanctified because of the saint buried in it, and who confers a certain beauty to it.

Hazrat Sayyid Muhammad Mahmood Bahar was a descendant of Hazrat Sayyid Nasir-ud-Din Sonepati and was a great scholar and saint. He was called *Bahar* [the ocean], because he was a great scholar, considered to be an ocean of knowledge. He performed a miracle worthy of a saint when he revived a man from the dead. As the story goes, there was an old widowed woman whose son had gone on a journey and she loved him greatly. This woman was always in service of the saint and would ask the saint to pray for her son. Allah revealed to him that the woman's son had died and only a pile of bones remained. The saint prayed to Allah and his prayer was accepted – the dead boy was revived and brought back to life and was united with his mother. The titles: 'Muhiyyul Izaam' [One who gives life to/revives bones] and 'Raja Had Goad' were bestowed on him, along with another, 'Badshah Ustakhwanha' [The emperor of bones; all the titles in one form or other meant the same].

> The saints of my nation are like the prophets of the Bani Isra'il.
> If others receive the benefit of the Ruh-ul-Qudus (Archangel Gabriel),
> They will also do the same (perform miracles) as Jesus the Saviour did.[14]

There is no need to recount his miracles, as he was very famous in his time. He left this world on 27 Safar AH 778 [16 July 1376] and was buried here. His devotees made a wall of mud around the *dargah*. Even though it is very ordinary, it is blessed because of the saint. A chronogram indicates that it has been more than 384 years since the tomb was built.

BARAPULA: THE TWELVE-ARCHED BRIDGE

This bridge is very beautifully constructed and is located four miles south of Shahjahanabad, on the way to Faridabad, near an inn [*sarai*]. Though this bridge is famous as Barapula, it has only eleven arches. It was built 241 years ago and has also been repaired by the British government.

Members of Meherban Agha Khwaja Sara's family were hereditary employees of the Timurid family [the Mughal dynasty]. When Prince Jahangir got married, Emperor Akbar

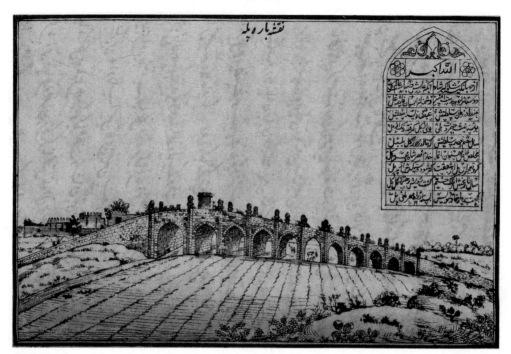

Barapula

removed him [Meherban Agha] from the service of the princess [Shahzadi Khanum], and placed him in the service of Jahangir to look after his palace. This was the reason why Jahangir respected Meherban Agha tremendously. Meherban Agha reciprocated this respect and always stayed by Jahangir's side, holding the latter's complete trust.

In Jahangir's twelfth regnal year, Meherban Agha retired due to old age and came to live in Dehli. Jahangir instructed the Governor of Delhi to accord him full respect and to make sure that he received all the comforts of life. It was during his retirement in Delhi that Meherban Agha had this bridge built. Its beauty and elegance speak volumes about his special relationship with Jahangir.

MAQBARA KHAN-E-KHANA

This mausoleum is located near Barapula bridge and Hazrat Nizam-ud-Din Auliya's _dargah_. It houses the tomb of Abdur Rahim Khan-e-Khana, son of Bairam Khan, who was an important noble during the reigns of both Akbar and Jahangir. Abdur Rahim Khan-e-Khana built this mausoleum for his wife who unfortunately could not be buried here. It was in Emperor Jahangir's twenty-first regnal year that Abdur Rahim Khan-e-Khana left this world at 72 years of age and his mortal remains were buried here.

The tomb was very beautifully constructed and decorated with floral designs, but its marble and stones have been mercilessly pulled out. The stone of this tomb was removed during Asaf-ud-Daulah's reign, taken to Lucknow and sold, thus destroying its beauty. Even the headstone of the grave was not spared. Today the mausoleum lies in ruins, with cows and buffaloes stationed on its premises. It resembles a skeleton

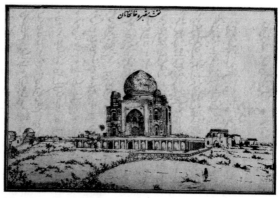

Maqbara Khan-e-Khana

of lime mortar and brick, cow dung is spread all over the place and the odour makes it very difficult for one to venture inside.

Just compare this to the grandeur and magnificence of Khan-e-Khana himself! Verily it is foolish to place importance on worldly things. He was a Turkman by descent and his grandfather Saif-ud-Din Ali Kosha Ismail had been in the service of Babur and fought at the battle of Mawarun Nahr. His father, Bairam Khan Khan-e-Khana, held a very high rank during Humayun's reign and was involved in all the important decisions in court.

Abdur Rahim Khan-e-Khana was a very important noble during Akbar's reign, but his fate was very fickle in Jahangir's reign. At times he was respected and at others, humiliated. Eventually he died and now there remains neither respect nor humiliation. He was buried under *maunds* of mud. He had built this mausoleum as a testament to his high station in life, but all that now remains is this shell. Glory be to God [*Subhan Allah*]! One whose house [*diwan khana*][15] was scented by the showering of thousands of rose petals, his mausoleum now stinks from the urine and dung of thousands of cattle.

Take warning, then, O ye, with intelligence (Quran 59:2).

Abdur Rahim Khan-e-Khana is praised for his scholarship and knowledge and is credited with translating the *Waqeat-e-Baburi* [Tales from Babur's Reign]. He was very well versed in Turki, Persian, Arabic, Hindi and Urdu.

NEELA BURJ

This tomb is called 'Neela Burj' [Blue Tomb] because of the blue (*neela*) glazed tile-work on it. It is located near Humayun's tomb; it is not known when it was made. In the years gone past, tile work on monuments was very popular and it was known as *kar-kashani*. Tiles of different colours were used and wherever they are still intact, their beauty is evident.

According to some it is the tomb of the barber [*hajjam*], but I couldn't verify whose tomb it is since even the grave has disappeared! It could be that someone broke it while trying to steal the headstone. It was once counted among the most beautiful monuments. I am unable to write more since I have not been able to find any reference to it in any history book. However, even though the tomb is not particularly well made, it has still become very famous due to its attractive tile work. One can see its present state from the sketch.

MAQBARA HUMAYUN

There is a mausoleum that lies 2.5 *kos* [5.6 miles] to the south of Shahjahanabad in the city of Kilukhari, which was built by Muiz-ud-Din Kaikobad and it contains the tomb of Humayun Badshah, apart from many other graves. It is a matchless monument and has been built using marble and red stone. The marble is of such purity that it would put a pearl to shame. The red stone is so exquisite that it resembles the leaves of a red rose. The dome is made entirely of marble and looks as if it is a pearl from the bounty of God. The design is so beautiful that the sky seems like a water bubble in comparison. It is so well proportioned that it appears delicate in spite of its size. Its width, length and height are exquisitely symmetrical, which

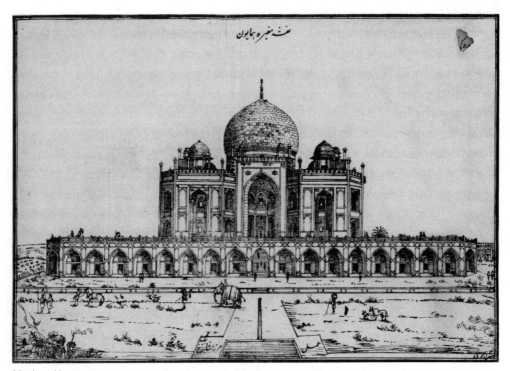

Maqbara Humayun

sets it apart from any other monument. Despite its size it appears so delicate that its beauty is beyond description.

The courtyard [*sehan*] and its buildings are extremely attractive and pleasing to the eye. The red stones with white stripes mesmerize the senses. Flowers and vines of different colours inlaid in stone also provide an amazing spectacle. At one time, there used to be a splendid garden with water channels on all four sides, tanks at frequent intervals, flowing fountains, blooming flowers, with tall cypress trees and different varieties of blooming flowers and chirping birds, all of which bring paradise to mind. A poet has described it thus:

> Anybody who wants to have a glimpse of Heaven on earth,
>
> Should be invited to see this tomb and gardens of Humayun.

Though the monument is largely in good shape, the latticed screens [*jalis*] have broken down in many places and the garden is totally desolate. The tall cypress which used to taunt a man's height, and the flowers which resembled the ruby-red lips of beauties, have completely disappeared. There are no signs of flowers and birds now, the canals have broken, the tanks are choked, the fountains are silent, the wells are blind and there are no remnants of the waterfalls either. In the north is a building from where water once cascaded and a treasure trove of fountains and streams flowed.

Burj *inside the complex*

Even today, if this mausoleum were to be repaired and the garden planted anew, it would make for an extremely pleasing and attractive place for recreational visits. Nawab Haji Begum, wife of Emperor Humayun, started the construction of this tomb in AH 973 [CE 1565–66].[iii] It took sixteen years and Rs 15 lakh for her to bring paradise down to earth and to build this little piece of heaven here. For many years members of the royal family were buried here, but now this practice has been stopped.

All the arches in the plinth of this monument house graves of people from the royal family. This complex houses the graves of Hamida Bano[16] who bore the title of Mariyam Makani. She was the mother of Akbar Jalal-ud-Din Badshah or in other words, she was Haji Begum the wife of Humayun who built this mausoleum. Alamgir II, Farrukhsiyar and Dara Shukoh are also buried here. We can see its attraction/splendour from the sketch.

[iii] *Mirat-e-Aftab-e-Numa.*

Humayun's Tomb: the western gate

The Dome within the Complex

This is a smaller tomb built inside the compound of Humayun's tomb and is made of red sandstone with marble used in a few places. There are two marble graves inside it. I made every effort to find out whose graves these were, and poured through history books but could find no reference to those buried here. Those who say it is the tomb of Humayun's brother Shah Kamran commit a grave error. Some say it is the tomb of Nizam Saqqa,[17] but even that doesn't sound credible and there is no inscription that could provide some clues as to the date of its construction. It is, however, a small and attractive monument and the proportions and beauty of the structure must still be appreciated.

The Gateways of Humayun's Tomb

This exquisite and elegant mausoleum has two magnificent gateways: one towards the south of the tomb and the other in the west. The western gateway has beautiful apartments built into it, unparalleled in their attractiveness and elegance. Every apartment has a different entrance, with beautiful stairs leading up to it. The southern gateway doesn't have apartments built in it, but the arches and platforms built around it give it a unique magnificence. These gateways seem as though they were the Gates of Heaven. Built of red sandstone and alabaster [sang-e-rukham], the alabaster has been used in such a manner that when viewed from a distance, it seems as if marble has been used in the red sandstone. The walls are made of lime and stone and they have channels for water to flow through.

ARAB SARAI

This inn [sarai] was built near Humayun's tomb with great determination and dedication by Nawab Haji Begum. It is said that the Begum brought 300 Arabs from Harmain Sharif (Mecca), of whom 100 were from very elite Sayyid families, 100 were Sheikhs or people well versed in religion, and 100 were ordinary men for day-to-day service.

Though these people have today scattered all over in search of livelihood, there are still about fifteen to twenty families, descendants of those Arabs who stayed on. From the Sayyid lineage, Sayyid Mohsin Sargiroh who is now 60 years of age, still lives in Arab Sarai. He is the head of the people who reside here and a very pleasant person. Zain-ud-Din Rais, who was an extremely nice person, hailed from the Sheikh lineage and though he passed away, his brother Sheikh Abdur Rahim still lives there.

Arab Sarai was built in the sixth year of Akbar's reign in AH 968 [CE 1560–61]. Now people from all communities live here. It has three gateways, of which two are very ordinary but the northern gateway must have been very splendid once upon a time. I have sketched it.

دروازهٔ عرب سرا

Arab Sarai

MANDI

The *mandi* or wholesale grain market, [also] a market for buying and selling food items, stood close to the eastern gateway of Arab Sarai. There was an extremely well-made mosque inside the market, which has now broken down. A large step well attached to the mosque still exists and is famous as the *bain*. Its steps are intact and there is water inside. The gateway is all that remains now and that too only in name, but it is very attractive and beautifully decorated with tiles of different colours.

Meherban Agha Khwaja Sara built this market at the same time as he constructed Barapula, in CE 1612 [AH 1020–21], during the reign of Jahangir Badshah. The phrase, 'In the name of Allah, Most Gracious, Most Merciful' is engraved on the red sandstone of the gateway, along with the *Kalima* and a few verses from the Quran. I have sketched it so that it can be clearly read. Look at the sketch of the gate and the engraving and consider it a warning (of the transitory nature of life).

MASJID ISA KHAN

To the west of Arab Sarai is a compound wall famously known as Isa Khan ka Kotla [Isa Khan's Citadel]. The mosque built inside the compound wall is made of local quartzite

Masjid Isa Khan

and lime mortar, with some red stone in the wall-niches that indicate the direction of Mecca.

Though today this mosque doesn't appear very attractive, it must have been remarkable for the period it was made in. Isa Khan built it in AH 954 [CE 1547–48] in the reign of Salim Shah. Isa Khan Hijab was a Sher Shahi noble and he helped Salim Shah ascend the throne. It was Isa Khan who [again] helped Adil Shah prevail over his elder brother, the heir apparent, and became king. Around 308 years [sic] have passed since the Isa Khan Mosque was built. There is also a well near the mosque, but I don't know why it was made in such an inappropriate place so as to spoil the look of the mosque's platform.

Maqbara Isa Khan

Isa Khan's tomb also lies inside the citadel. Though very small, it is very attractive. There is a dome in the middle and a beautiful verandah runs around the tomb. This monument has been built with local quartzite and limestone but the cupolas on top have red sandstone columns. There are many graves inside the tomb along with Isa Khan Hijab's grave. There is an inscription inside, on the western side of the tomb, with verses from the Quran as well as details of the builder and the year. This makes evident that Isa Khan himself built this tomb

Maqbara Isa Khan

during his lifetime in the reign of Salim Shah in AH 954 [CE 1547–48] and 308 years [sic] have passed since then.

Peasants now live in this tomb and the fires from their wood-burning stoves [*chulha*] are spoiling it. Unfortunately no one seems to care. One can see its beauty from the sketch. The inscription inside the tomb on a red sandstone slab fixed over a wall-niche that indicates the direction of Mecca, has a quotation from the Quran (Sura 2, verse 256), and thereafter reads:

> This tomb, which is an asylum of Paradise, was built during the reign of Islam Shah, son of Sher Shah.
>
> May God perpetuate his kingdom and sovereignty
>
> – by Masnad Ali Isa Khan, son of Niyaz Aghwan, the chief chamberlain,
>
> the year nine hundred and fifty-four from the flight (of the Prophet).
>
> The year [AH] 954 [CE 1547–48].

DARGAH HAZRAT NIZAM-UD-DIN AULIYA

What a devout and pious man! Hazrat Nizam-ud-Din Auliya is a *Waliullah*, one of the most important friends of Allah. It is our good fortune that we are blessed with such a Friend of God, who is so pious and good intentioned. Innumerable books are filled with a description of all that he evidently achieved [*zahiri* or matters obvious to the world], all his attributes and deeds that were mostly hidden from the public eye [*batini* or matters hidden from the world] and his miracles [*kamilat*], so I will content myself with describing his *dargah* here.

His father Ahmad bin Daniyal came to Hindustan from Ghazni. Hazrat Nizam-ud-Din Auliya was born in the [Islamic calendar] month of Safar in AH 634 [CE 1236–37] in the city of Badayun and came to Delhi at the age of 25. He was in search of knowledge and it is here that he met Sheikh Najib-ud-Din Mutawakkil and stayed with him. Later, he went to Ajodhan to be near Sheikh Farid-ud-Din Masood Shakar Ganj and returned to Delhi after becoming his disciple and taking an oath of allegiance to him. He took up residence in Ghiyaspur[18] and people benefited greatly from his instructions and religious discourse.

Since this world is transient and everyone has to leave, Hazrat left this world for the hereafter on a Wednesday, the eighteenth day of [the Islamic calendar month of] Rabi-us-Sani[19] in the year AH 725 [3 April 1325]. This Emperor of Faith was laid to rest on the border of Ghiyaspur village, where his *dargah* stands today. The date he left the world [*rehlat*] is inscribed on a wall in the mosque:

> The administrator (Nizam) of the two worlds, the king of water and earth, surely became a lamp for both the worlds.
>
> When I sought the date of his death from the invisible, the invisible crier said, 'the Emperor of Religion. [AH 725/CE 132–25]

Dargah Hazrat Nizam-ud-Din Auliya

The Dargah's Dome

The dome of the blessed *dargah* is unique. From the time the saint was buried here, its glory was continually enhanced and many additions, each better than the last, were made to it. At the time of the Khilji Sultans, an enclosure was built, but there are no traces left of it now.

During the reign of Akbar Badshah in AH 970 [CE 1562–63], Sayyid Faridoon Khan built columns around the shrine with twelve arches. He also built a dome over it with beautiful marble screens around it and an inscription on the latticed screen on the northern side that reads:

> There is no God but Allah and Muhammad is his Prophet.
>
> Thanks (be to God) that the Khan of the dignity of the sky resolved to build the tomb of His Holiness, The Saint [Ghaus] of the world [Sheikh Nizam-ud-Din Auliya]. He [the Khan] is the glory of the sun of [his] family and a star of the height of honour, a Sayyid of high descent and a chief of the standing of a king. Its [the tomb's] founder was a Hashmi[20] and its builder was [also] a Hashmi, in whose time flourished poetry and prose. When I sought to discover its date, the pen of wisdom wrote Qiblagah of nobles and commoners [AH 970/ CE 1562–63].

> O Faridun! Turn your face with truth towards his tomb, perchance by the favours of the
> saint your work may be accomplished. The scribe of this: Husain Ahmad Chishti.

In AH 1017 [CE 1608–09], during the reign of Jahangir, some more changes were made by Farid Khan, who bore the title of Murtaza Khan and in whose name the city of Faridabad was established. He offered an exquisite canopy of mother-of-pearl at the *dargah*, which is an example of God's majesty and bounty. It boggles the mind. There are verses inscribed on the canopy in a mother-of-pearl mosaic and some of these are as follows:

> For the Sheikh of Delhi [named] Nizam,
> Two Farids made ready all [that is required] in this world and the next.
> One Farid gave him a transitory building.
> And the other raised him to the position of everlasting life.
> Murtaza Khan erected a dome over his grave, [lofty] as the sky.
> A blue cloud rose from the world and a pearl dropped into the oyster-shell.

Aziz-ud-Din Alamgir II was a great devotee of the saint. In AH 1169 [CE 1755–56], he said some verses in Urdu in praise of the saint, and to describe the troubles of his own heart. These are inscribed in the dome towards the west:

> He who becomes the slave of Nizam-ud-Din with [all] his heart receives the royal crown of
> [marking him king of] the whole world.
> Aziz-ud-Din [known as Alamgir II] performed the services of a slave with true faith: the
> kingly crown of Hind has now been given to [Aziz-ud-Din].
> Through him is healed my wounded heart without recourse to food, prayer, medicine or
> physician.
> Much afflicted are the people now,
> O! Beloved of God.
> Confer your favours on sinners,
> You who are a friend of God
> Under the supervision of Hoshyar Ali Khan, the eunuch slave.
> The year AH 1169 [CE 1755/56]

Khalilullah Khan had a circumbulatory aisle of red sandstone built around the shrine in AH 1063 in the reign of Shahjahan. It had five arches on all the four sides, making twenty arches in all. On the arch on the south, he had the following inscribed:

> In the reign of the Exalted Majesty Sahib Qirani Sani [the Second Lord of Happy
> Conjunction], the most humble of men – Khalilullah Khan, son of Mir Miran Al Husaini
> Nimatullahi, who was the Governor of Shahjahanabad, erected this verandah round the
> blessed tomb in the year AH 1063. [CE 1652–53]

For a long time, the aisle was intact, adding to the beauty of the shrine. When it was God's will that this place be made better, it was divinely communicated to Maulvi Muhammad Fakhr-ud-Din Sahib, a prominent saint. He dreamt that this marble aisle should be replaced with marble and accordingly he decided to replace it with marble columns. His grandson Ghulam Nasir-ud-Din Sahib, known as Kale Sahib Bahadur, bought marble columns but before the work could be completed, he left this world. Nawab Ahmad Baksh Khan Bahadur of Firozpur Jhirka, with God's grace and with good intentions and steadfastness of purpose, replaced the sandstone columns with marble. Forty years must have passed by now.

The ceiling of this circumbulatory aisle was still of sandstone, and was in a state of decay as its decoration was falling off. Allah gave divine guidance to Faizullah Khan Bangash, who got a copper ceiling installed under the sandstone one, with golden and azur work on it, which is still intact. This ceiling was made twenty-five years ago in AH 1236 [CE 1820–21]. The date mentioned on the ceiling inscription has become mostly unreadable due to lime plaster falling on it.

By God's grace all these decorations were done but the dome, which was of lime mortar, was weakened by these [decorations], particularly by the circumbulatory aisle. Allah put pious intentions in the heart of Akbar Shah II,[21] who got a beautiful dome made of marble with a golden finial around it, twenty-four years ago. This building has no parallel in its beauty, grace and attraction.

Every seventeenth of [the Islamic calendar month of] Rabi-us-Sani a huge fair is held here, with thousands of people staying overnight. The emperor also graces the occasion with his presence in the mornings. An assembly of Sufi Masters [mashaikhs] is conducted by the caretakers of the dargah, though it is forbidden in Islam as being an innovation [biddat]. May Allah give divine guidance to those who have strayed and guide them to use this blessed dargah for the purpose for which it was intended.

Masjid Dargah

This mosque is constructed next to his shrine and one may get the details of its construction from the book Kutub Tawarikh. During the reign of Ala-ud-Din Khilji, there was a very prominent noble called Qurra Beg Turk Sultan, a devotee of the Sultan-ul-Mashaik [the Sultan of Sheikhs], who saw that the saint was in a divine trance [sema] and was deeply troubled by something. He wrote these points down and took them to Sultan Ala-ud-Din Khilji, narrating the entire episode. The sultan then described the obvious [zahiri], hidden [batini] facets and miracles [kamilat] of the saint.

Qurra Beg said, 'Alas! It's very sad that if you have such faith in the saint, why don't you take the opportunity of spending time in his company and being blessed by him,' to which the sultan replied, 'I am submerged in evil sins and wrongdoing and I am too ashamed to go near him. You take my sons Khizr Khan and Shadi Khan to him.' Qurra Khan took Khizr Khan into the saint's presence, who blessed Khizr Khan. Khizr Khan thus gained the company of the pious saint and became his devotee. During this period he had the middle dome and hall built.

Though the inscription carved in it cannot be read, according to the *Kutub Tawarikh* it seems that it was built before AH 712 [CE 1312–13], and more than 550 years [sic] have passed since then. This part of the mosque, which is made of red sandstone with a lofty dome, is very majestic. The middle section is 14 *gaz* long, with a golden bowl hanging from the centre. The Jats thought it was made of gold and fired shots at it, but the bowl didn't fall. It is not known what metal this bowl is made of.

Later, when Muhammad Tughlaq Shah, son of Ghiyas-ud-Din Tughlaq Shah became the sultan, he took the title of Adil Shah, but gained fame as Sultan Khooni. He added two halls on either side of the mosque, and to these halls he added two domes each. Thus, there are now five domes in the mosque.[22] Even though we don't know the dates on which these domes were built, it seems probable that this took place around AH 725 [CE 1324–25], and thus 520 years have passed [sic]. On the façade of the mosque are various inscriptions, including verses from the Quran in the Kufic script. However, none mention the year of construction.

Emperor Muhammad Shah built a marble courtyard in the *dargah*. There are three enclosures in this courtyard: one for Jahan Ara, a second for Muhammad Shah, and a third for Mirza Jahangir.

Muhajjar Jahan Ara Begum

This stone enclosure [*muhajjar*] is made entirely of marble, with marble screens on all sides. It contains four graves, three are those of adults and one is that of a child. The enclosure is a sanctuary of light [*nur*] and I would not be very far wrong if I called it the destination of the moon [*manzil-e-mah*] because a moon-faced beauty [*mahpara*] lies sleeping here. It can also be called the House of Light [*makan-e-nur*] because it is the resting place of one whose countenance was like that of the sun [*khurshid talat*].

Jahan Ara Begum, daughter of Emperor Shahjahan, had great faith in the Chishti order. It is said that she gave her entire property – valued at three crore rupees – to the *dargah*'s hereditary caretakers [*khadims*] and bought this land for her grave. After her death, however, [her brother, the emperor] Alamgir only gave [the hereditary caretakers] property worth a crore and said that only one-third of one's property could be willed away by a person as per law. Princess Jahan Ara built this enclosure in her own lifetime. The enclosure has a marble epitaph with a verse by her and a few more lines inscribed:

> *He is living and self-subsisting.*
> *Let naught cover my grave save the green grass;*
> *for grass well suffices as a covering for the grave of the lowly.*

Muhajjar Muhammad Shah

Emperor Muhammad Shah's grave lies in the same courtyard, but is far superior to Princess Jahan Ara's stone enclosure, in terms of beauty and attraction it is a crore times superior. The marble used here is so pure and white with such a beautiful sheen that a pearl would pale in comparison. Its beauty and elegance is beyond the ability of my pen. It is stunningly decorated with inlay and stone carvings. Its screens are so beautiful that when light falls on it, it seems to twinkle like stars. It seems that there is a sheet of light [chadar-e-nur] spread over the grave.

There are seven graves in this enclosure. Apart from the grave of the emperor, it also contains the graves of his wife, the queen Nawab Sahiba Mahal Begum,[23] Mirza Jigar [his grandson] and Mirza Ashoori, as well as three other graves of princes of the royal family. Emperor Muhammad Shah had bought this land from the hereditary caretakers of the dargah and had built it himself. Since he died in AH 1061 [CE 1650–51], it can be safely presumed to have been built around that time. This enclosure has two beautifully decorated marble doors and each side of these is carved out of a single piece of marble. Its beauty is enough to stun viewers.

Mirza Jahangir's Grave

This stone enclosure is very similar to the one that contains the grave of Emperor Muhammad Shah. [Though] it was meant to be a copy of it, there is a world of difference between the real and the copy. Though the work on Mirza Jahangir's enclosure is very finely made and beautiful, the marble is not of the same quality: it is not as pure and flawless. Even though there is a very stark and bleak feeling here, it is still one of a kind.

Mirza Jahangir, the son of Akbar Shah II, was exiled to Allahabad and placed under house arrest by the British for taking a potshot at the British Resident of the fort with his pistol. He died there and his mother Nawab Mumtaz Mahal who loved him greatly, sent Nawab Mukhtar-ud-Daulah Khwaja Wahid-ud-din Ahmad Khan Bahadur – son of Akbar Wazir-e-Azam Dastoor Moazzam Nawab Dabir-ud-Daulah Amin-ul-Mulk Khwaja Farid-ud-Din Ahmad Khan Bahadur – to Allahabad to bring her son's body back and had it buried here.

The stone enclosure was built twenty-four to twenty-five years ago in AH 1248 [sic; CE 1832–33]. I have made the sketch in such a way that all the buildings described above can be seen and the viewer is transported into the dargah.

DARGAH HAZRAT AMIR KHUSRAU

His real name was Abul Hasan and his father was Saif-ud-Din Mahmood and both his father and he were very senior nobles in the royal court. Hazrat Amir Khusrau served the sultan in his capacity as a noble [*Amir*] for a long time and ultimately traversed the distance from service [*amiri*] to royalty [*khusravi*].

His manifest [*zahiri*] and hidden [*batini*] miracles are well known. He was a fervent devotee of Hazrat Nizam-ud-Din Auliya, and was devastated when the saint left this world. He gave up all his worldly possessions and spent time near his Master's shrine and his grief was so great that within six months he too passed away on a Thursday night in AH 725 [CE 1324–25]. He was buried in a grave on platform called the 'Yarani Chabutra' to the left of his Master, Hazrat Nizam-ud-Din Auliya's *dargah*. For ages his grave was without a dome or enclosure which were built much later in AH 1014 [CE 1605].

In the last years of Akbar's reign and in the initial years of Jahangir's reign, Tahir, who was known as Imad-ud-Din Hasan, constructed a stone enclosure and beautiful marble dome on his grave.

> Oh matchless Khusrau
> I have faith in your shrine

The above lines by Tahir Imad-ud-Din Hasan were inscribed by Abun Nabi bin Ayyub. There are red sandstone screens around the dome and arches have been added in the south and on which a roof has been made. For some reason the dome doesn't look as beautiful.

Dargah Hazrat Amir Khusrau

During Babur's reign an inscription was placed on a marble tablet, situated outside the tomb on the north, between the tomb and the pierced stone-screens of the inner enclosure, [which reads]:

> There is no God but Allah and Muhammad is his Prophet. The earth attained honour in the reign of Babur, the emperor and champion of faith through the presence of this tablet.
> Mir Khusrau the king of the kingdom of words (poetry), the ocean of accomplishment and sea of perfection; his prose is more attractive than flowing water, his poetry is clearer than pure water. (He is a) peerless singing nightingale and an incomparable sugar-tongued parrot.
> For the date of his death, when I bowed my head above the knees of thought. A chronogram gave 'peerless', and another 'sugar-tongued parrot'. [AH 725; CE 1324–25]
> The tablet of my dust is without even a word of hope of a meeting with my beloved; my simplicity is the one (evident) sign of true love.
> Mehdi Khwaja, a Sayyid of rank and dignity, became the founder of this matchless and incomparable building. I said, 'the good efforts of Mehdi Khwaja' when asked the date of the foundation of this building. Written by Shihab, the Enigmatist of Heart.

There are many graves of notable people near the foot of his grave. On the seventeenth of [the Islamic calendar month of] Shawal, a fair is held here with great pomp and glory.

BAOLI DARGAH

This is a very beautiful step well [baoli] and is praised by people from far and wide who say they have never seen such a clean and attractive step well anywhere. The water level is very close to the surface, and ignorant people bathe in it thinking that the water has healing powers. People pray and make vows [mannat] here to get rid of djinns and evil spirits, and women also pray for a child.

This step well is famed for having being made during Hazrat Nizam-ud-Din Auliya's own lifetime and that he and his disciple [mureed] were the ones to dig it initially. As they say, 'God helps the courageous', and this step well was ready in a very short time.

The buildings and southern houses adjacent to the step well, however, seem to have been built in Firoz Shah's reign. There are some very famous buildings here. One is an ancient dome from the Pathan era, of which not much is known and there is a marble pavilion to the west with a beautiful marble tomb inside. The 99 names of Allah and Quranic verses [ayats] are inscribed on it. I have not seen such beautiful calligraphy anywhere else.[24] The year is inscribed on it, but due to some error by the inscriber it is difficult to figure out whether it is AH 1008 [CE 1599–1600], or AH 1080 [CE 1669–70]. However, the verse inscribed rhymes with AH 1080.

There used to be a passage from the mosque to the step well and devotees would come here to perform ritual ablutions before prayers. Muhammad Shah has built a vaulted roof

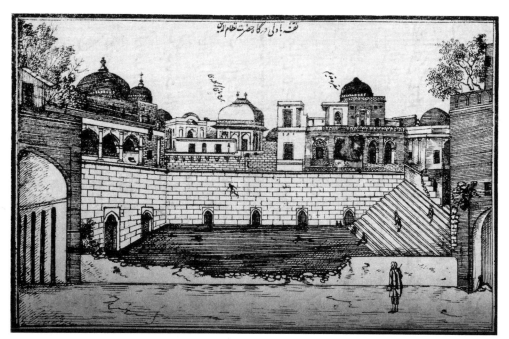

Baoli Dargah

over it. On the southern side are some arches from the reign of Firoz Shah and there is a passage to enter the step well from that side. There is a stone with an Arabic inscription at that location, but it is so badly inscribed that it can't be read. However, the year of construction and the builder's name are legible, and are given as AH 781 [CE 1379–80] and Firoz Shah respectively.

On the occasion of the death anniversary of the saint, there is a grand spectacle here. A great crowd collects and sits in the apartments around the step well, and watches young boys jumping into it from the rooftops of houses built on its sides. These boys dive from there and show-off their swimming skills. They ask spectators to throw coins into the step well and dive to retrieve them from the water.

The *dargah*'s boundary wall was in a ruined state, but when Nawab Ahmad Baksh Khan, the Bahadur of Firozpur Jhirka, built the circumambulatory aisle, he got this repaired too. His noble deeds are still remembered here. This verse is inscribed and painted golden on the gate to the step-well complex:

> *The Lord has unique ways,*
> *To honour supplicants.*

Near it is a building, which is called 'the citadel', but I didn't find it attractive enough to make a sketch.

MAQBARA TAGHA KHAN

This is the tomb of Shams-ud-Din Muhammad Khan Ghaznavi whose title was Azam Khan.[25] He was the husband of Emperor Akbar's wet nurse, Maham Anga. Akbar Badshah called her Jiji Anaga. That is why he [Azam Khan] was also called 'Takka', 'Tagha' or 'Atagha' Khan.[26]

[Azam] Tagha Khan occupied a very honoured position in Akbar's court and was the Chancellor. This made Maham Anga's son Adham Khan very jealous, and on the twelfth of [the Islamic calendar month of] Ramzan in AH 969 [16 May 1562] Adham Khan killed him [Azam Khan]. The emperor in turn killed Adham Khan, by throwing him down from the fort twice [in case he had somehow survived the first fall]. Two murders were committed [*do khun shud*]. The chronogram for the date [of the murder of Azam 'Tagha' Khan by Adham Khan] reads: 'The cruelty against Azam Khan has been avenged'. Some say that the following lines are also another chronogram for his death:

> *The great commander and soldier Khan Azam Khan,*
> *No one has seen such a brave man in this era.*
> *The month of Ramzan bore witness that,*
> *A fasting man tasted the syrup of death.*
> *Alas! Had he been martyred some other year,*
> The year of his death lies [hidden in the phrase] the 'Martyred Khan'.[27]

Maqbara Tagha Khan

[Azam] Tagha Khan's murdered body was brought to Delhi and buried near Hazrat Nizam-ud-Din's shrine and tomb. His son, [Mirza Aziz] Kokaltash Khan, built this tomb in AH 975 [CE 1567–68]. It is a very beautiful structure of red stone and white marble, decorated with Quranic verses and floral designs. The date of construction is inscribed on top of the door; 288 years have passed [sic] since this tomb was constructed. The inscription on the southern doorway reads:

> This noble edifice was finished in the year AH 974 [CE 1566–57] under the superintendence of Ustad Khuda Quli.

[Around the arches on all the four sides run Quranic inscriptions, which conclude with a reference to Baqi Muhammad, the scribe].

CHAUSATH KHAMBA

This matchless monument is made entirely of marble. I don't think there is any other monument with such a unique design. It gets its name from the 64 [chausath] marble columns built inside it. Wall-niches are carved to indicate the direction of Mecca and the arrangement of the arches is very beautiful. The monument is the tomb of Mirza Aziz Kokaltash Khan, the son of Khan-e-Azam Tagha Khan.[28] After his father's murder at the hands of Adham Khan,

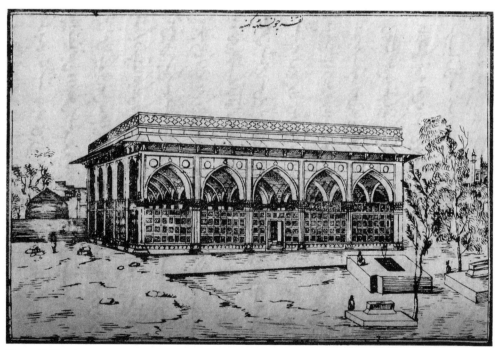

Chausath Khamba

Kokaltash Khan was bestowed the title of Khan-e-Azam, and he held this position until the nineteenth year of Jahangir's reign, sometimes with respect, sometimes in humiliation. When Mirza Aziz Kokaltash died in Ahmedabad in CE 1624 [AH 1032–33] still under Jahangir's reign, his body was brought and buried here and this tomb was built on his grave.

This building is exquisite and it is said that Mirza Aziz Kokaltash was an extremely talented man, an expert in Nastaliq calligraphy having learnt it from Mirza Baqar, son of Mullah Mir Ali. He was also an occasional poet. This verse is attributed to him:

> Love calls me with every breath I take,
> It keeps me away from the company of the wise ones.
> I am freed from the captivity of religion as well as reason,
> Now I am a captive of someone's dark tresses.
> It has been 228 years since this building was constructed.

LAL MAHAL

Lal Mahal [the Red Palace], also referred to as 'Kushk-e-Lal' by historians, is a building from the Khilji period. In the days when Ala-ud-Din Khilji had laid siege to the Fort of Ranthambhor, Haji Maula Ghulamzada Mulk-ul-Umara Fakhr-ud-Din Kotwal, rebelled and sat on the throne

Lal Mahal

of Delhi, in this Kushk-e-Lal. Today there are no remnants, only ruins that people have made famous as 'Lal Mahal'.

It is possible that there was a palace nearby and when that building was wiped out, the name Lal Mahal was transferred to this one. This building too is very ancient and has graves inside it. It is surprising that this building contains graves. I can't say whose graves these are, or who built it; I just present a sketch for the reader's perusal. There is a building known as Barakhamba near it, but it is not worthy of attention. Faizullah Khan Bangash recently built his mausoleum near it. It's an unremarkable monument.

MAQBARA SAYYID ABID

Between Hazrat Nizam-ud-Din Auliya's *dargah* and the Purana Qila [Old Fort], is a domed tomb made of limestone with some tile work on it. Some people also call it Shahid Sahib's *dargah*. Sayyid Abid Khan was the friend and associate of Nawab Khan Dauran-e-Khan who was martyred in battle [hence, *shahid*]. I could not find any details of this tomb, or who built it and when. It is an attractive building with a grand gateway and a pretty three-door pavilion [*sehdari*]. The structure is also very elegant. It had an attractive tank and water channels in the courtyard, but these now lie desolate.

Maqbara Sayyid Abid

All of it is in a ruined state and the tile work has disappeared. No longer in pristine condition, it is nevertheless a reminder of the grand old days. I have sketched it in such a way that the dome and gateway are included.

LAL BANGLA

Near this tomb lies another monument [a small domed building] famed as 'Lal Bangla' [the Red Bungalow]. I have found no reference to it in history books, but have heard from Emperor Bahadur Shah Zafar that before Nasir-ud-Din Muhammad Humayun Badshah[29] left for Iran, someone from his harem was buried here and some structure was built.

When Lal Kunwar, the mother of Firdaus Manzil or Shah Alam Badshah, died later, she too was buried here in a small domed building. It became famous as Lal Bangla. Later his beloved daughter Begum Jaan, who was affianced to Mirza Makhoo, was also buried in another domed building, which he built. This building would be about 70 years old now.

This also houses the graves of princes of the Timurid family. Mirza Sultan Parvez, Mirza Dara Bakht, the brother of the heir apparent, Mirza Dawood, Nawab Fatehabadi and Mirza Bulaqi are buried here. The emperor's wives are also buried here. These buildings are very beautifully built of red sandstone. There are two graves with stone enclosures in the

Lal Bangla

courtyard, which have been built in the emperor's reign. These are of Nawab Fatehabadi and Mirza Bulaqi. I have sketched them as they are.

PURANA QILA

It is very well known amongst the people that this fort is very old. In fact, it is said that the date of its original construction is unknown. However this does not appear to be accurate, as history books suggest that Raja Anekpal first built a fort here in 440 Bikramjiti [Hindu calendar era]. No signs of this fort now remain and one does not know when it was destroyed. Perhaps it was present during Emperor Humayun's reign. Emperor Humayun built it anew 324 years ago [sic] in AH 938 [CE 1531–32]. The building now called Purana Qila was constructed by Nasir-ud-Din Muhammad Humayun, and though people call it the Purana Qila, its actual name is Dinpanah.

Three of its huge gateways and one wicket gate [khirki] are very famous. There are many other wicket gates but none so famous. One gateway in the north-east has been shut for a long time and people call it the 'Talaqi Darwaza' [Divorce Gateway]. It is said that once, years ago, some army had left for a campaign from this gateway and it was closed after their departure. It was said that if the army returned defeated, the wives would divorce the men. But I couldn't ascertain under which king this incident took place.

The walls of this fort are made of local quartzite and limestone, and have been very solidly built. The fort must have been very strong and attractive when it was inhabited. Today

Purana Qila

it lies desolate and in ruins, and the peasants of Indarpat village live here. But for a lofty and beautiful mosque and one building called Sher Mandal,[30] both of which still stand, not a single other building remains – they have all been destroyed. The fort is situated at a distance of 2 *kos* [4.5 miles] to the south of Shahjahanabad. To its west [once] lay old Delhi [*purani* Delhi], now destroyed. Except for a few doors and walls, there are no other remnants.

KHAIR-UL-MANAZIL MOSQUE–MADARSA COMPLEX

This complex [famous as 'Masjid o *Madarsa*' in Sir Sayyid's time] was built by Maham Begum, Badshah Akbar's wet nurse, in CE 1561 [AH 968–69] in front of Purana Qila. Built of lime mortar and stone, the complex is now in ruins. However, an inscription still remains on the façade of the mosque:

> In the time of Jalal-ud-Din Muhammad who is the greatest (Akbar) of just kings,
> When Maham Begh the protection of chastity, erected this building for the virtuous.
> Shihab-ud-Din Ahmad Khan, the generous, assisted (in the erection of) this good house.
> How blessed is this good building that its chrongram is 'best of houses'.
> Composed by Niyaz Baksh under the supervision of Darwesh Hussain.

GULAL BARI

Near the Khair-ul-Manazil complex, and directly opposite the entrance of Purana Qila, is a building called Gulal Bari, which is now just a heap of lime mortar, and there is no inscription to reveal any details of it either.

KHAS MAHAL

Near Gulal Bari lies Khas Mahal [Palace of Note], built in the reign of Shahjahan, but which is also in ruins. However, an inscription [part of which is a chronogram] remains on its gateway:

> During the reign of Shahjahan, the second Lord of the Happy Constellation [Sahib-e-
> Qiran] who is the cherisher of the Universe in this world and has a heaven-like court.
> Know that the daughter of Zain Khan built Khas Mahal, the noblest structure of the
> period, on this piece of ground, through her generosity. May her enlightened mind be ever
> inclined to virtue and integrity under a changing sky.
> If you would [wish to] know the date of its erection, add the numerical value of 'Jawab'
> [answer] to that of 'Sarai Mahal-e-Khas', AH 1052. [CE 1642–43]

NEELI CHHATRI

Near Khas Mahal lies the mausoleum of Nawab Naubat Khan. The mausoleum is now almost in ruins. Once upon a time it had [blue] tile work on it and that is why it was called *Neeli Chhatri* or the Blue Canopy. Only a ruined gateway still stands. I drew the sketch of the Old Fort [Purana Qila] from the top of the gateway of this building. There is an inscription on it:

> The eyes of Time have not seen in this world,
>
> Such a beautiful and lofty building.
>
> Of Knowledge, the date of its completion.
>
> I asked; [it] replied, [it has] attained completion.

SHER MANDAL

Purana Qila has a lofty minaret-like building near the mosque called Sher Mandal, built by Sher Shah; 313 years have passed since then. The entire fort was [once] called Sher Mandal because of this beautiful building, which is constructed completely of red sandstone. The design includes a narrow circumambulatory aisle constructed around a central room. On top on the roof is a small cupola. This was built as a place for recreation. When Emperor Nasir-ud-Din Muhammad Humayun regained the throne of Hindustan, he established a library in this building. He would also climb to the top to study the sun, moon and stars [astronomy was a passion].

Sher Mandal

Death needs but an excuse! Once, while going down the stairs he heard the call for evening prayers and sat down until the call was completed. Then, as he pulled himself up, holding on to the chain that acted as a banister [*jarib*], it slipped from his hands and he fell down the length of the staircase, dying a few days later from the severity of the injuries he sustained. Look at its sketch and let it serve as a warning of man's mortality. Today people live in and around this Sher Mandal. One can see the habitation in the sketch.

MASJID QILA

This mosque[31] was built by Nasir-ud-Din Humayun Badshah at the same time that he was building the fort [hence the name, fort-mosque]. I cannot describe its beauty and attractive aspects. It is so beautifully and elegantly made that it has no parallel in any other monuments of the period. There are five arches of very unique design. Though the mosque is built of local quartzite its façade has been made of red sandstone with beautiful inlay of marble. On every arch and niche is beautiful calligraphy done in the Naskh style and Kufic script.

The courtyard has is a beautiful octagonal tank [*hauz*], now in a state of disrepair, but still a reminder of the hard work of people from a past era. The way to the top of this mosque is unique [as there are] attractive niches on the walls of the staircase. Only one central dome

Masjid Qila

remains on the roof. There used to be two canopies on either side of the dome, but these have since broken down. The dome is so attractive that you don't want to remove your eyes from it. In fact you want to keep gazing at it. There is no inscription giving a date but a few verses are inscribed on the side-niches. On a marble slab in the second niche towards the north, and marking the direction of Mecca is inscribed:

> As long as the world is populated, may this edifice be frequented and may the people of the world be cheerful and happy with it.

On a marble slab in the second niche towards the south, and marking the direction of Mecca is inscribed:

> O God show mercy for we are polluted and our liver is washed with the blood of our heart. Instruct us as is best in thy sight for we have been wanting in our duties.

KABULI DARWAZA

A little way from Shahjahanabad's Delhi Darwaza [today called Delhi Gate], is a gateway leading from Purani [old] Delhi, called Kabuli Darwaza [today Kabuli Gate], which is one of the remnants of old Delhi. It has been beautifully made of local quartzite and has a red sandstone façade. There are beautiful halls, small rooms and alcoves on top of it. Today the sentries of the jailhouse live in the rooms of this gateway as the jailhouse is near it.

I could find no historical reference as to who built Kabuli Darwaza, but it seems probable that Humayun built it at the same time as he built Purana Qila. I have also heard the same from people. Nothing is left of the buildings of old Delhi except for this Kabuli Darwaza. The jailhouse is nearby.

JAILKHANA

This jailhouse [jailkhana] was actually an inn. When old Delhi was desolated, this inn too became desolate, to the extent that during the reigns of Alamgir II and Shah Alam, it was totally

Kabuli Darwaza, Jailkhana, Me'nhdiya'n

deserted. The British Government considered it to be most suited to serve as a jailhouse, and so had it repaired and converted into one. This jailhouse has a grand gateway with apartments on its upper storey which are suitable as living quarters for the superintendant [darogha] of the jailhouse. Two or three years ago the British built a new jailhouse near the old one, and on the other side, they constructed a hospital. Thus this erswhile inn, which used to provide a place of rest to travellers, is now filled with the anguish of prisoners. Nowadays, any prisoner who is on death row is hanged here. May Allah protect us from the perils of the world and the afterlife.

ME'NHDIYA'N

This was a very unique round building with rooms on the ground floor and pavilions on the two upper floors. The truth is that no one knows why it was built, or when, or by whom. According to legend it was built by a Nawab to commemorate Saint Hazrat Ghaus-ul-Azam (Sayyid Abdul Qadir Jilani). In Hindustan there is a tradition to hold annual ceremonies to honour the deceased, when small paper-encased bamboo lanterns called me'nhdiya'n [the singular for lantern, being me'nhdi] are used to illuminate the area.[32]

One such ceremony is held here in honour of the Bara Pir or Great Saint (Sayyid Abdul Qadir Jilani-Ghaus-ul-Azam). This building looks as if it was built for illumination and has become well-known as Kushk-e-Me'nhdiya'n. It is a wondrous monument and has been constructed in a unique style. It has an arched plinth with five cupolas on top of it, four on the corners and one in the centre. When the Nawab succeeded to the title and became very prosperous he built a monument where these lanterns could be illuminated each year. He would illuminate these pavilions and distribute food to the poor. Since then, this building has become famous as Me'nhdiya'n, but no one knows who the Nawab credited with constructing it, was.

Near Me'nhdiya'n is open ground where lie the graves of family members and friends of the family of Maulana Shah Abdul Aziz Sahib. Therefore, the shrines of Janab Maulana Shah Waliullah Sahib, Maulana Shah Abdul Aziz Sahib, Maulvi Rafi-ud-Din Sahib and Maulvi Abdul Quddus Sahib Qudd-us-Allah are situated here.

This building [Me'nhdiya'n] is in very bad shape and can be seen in the sketch. Between the Purana Qila and here, there is now no place from where I could sketch properly. In the middle [of this space between the Purana Qila and here] are two famous buildings – one [that contains] Sheikh Muhammad's step well, now in the possession of Shah Sabir Baksh Sahib's successors, and [the second called] Mahabat Khan ki Reti[33] as that is where Mahabat Khan's mansion [haveli] used to stand. The river used to flow below it, which was why it was called Mahabat Khan ki Reti.

KOTLA FIROZ SHAH

The citadel was built during the period of Firoz Shah's reign and is situated at a little distance, outside Shahjahanabad's Delhi Darwaza [Delhi Gate], on the banks of the river. There is a very famous and tall pillar, called Firoz Shah's pillar [*lath*], installed here.[34] I have not been able to find any credible source mentioning an exact date regarding the building of this citadel, but I think it was built in the same period as the city of Firozabad, which was built by Firoz Shah in AH 755 [CE 1354–55], i.e. around 508 years ago [sic]. This monument is now in a very bad state and is deteriorating day by day. One can see this in the sketch. However, the pillar is very famous.

I tried to find out why this pillar was built or when, but could not find any details. There are inscriptions on the pillar in an ancient language that no one has been able to decipher. There are some inscriptions in the Shastri script (Sanskrit), but even these cannot be deciphered. Whatever words I could decipher from the Shastri script, I am noting down:

> In the year 1220 on the fifteenth day of the bright half of the [Hindu calendar] month of Vaisakh, Vishnu Das Narayan Shah Bahadur.

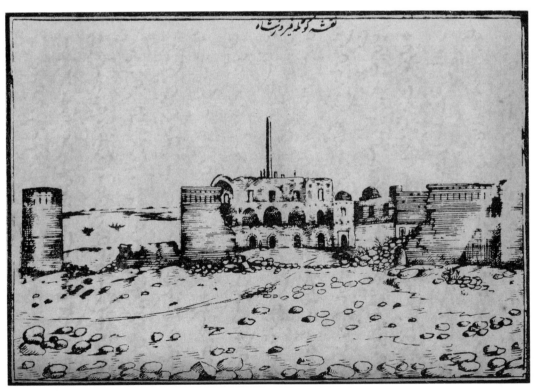

Kotla Firoz Shah

May Muiz-ud-din [one who strengthens religion] have a long life for he is the scale on
which honour can be measured.

It seems that at the time that Sultan Muiz-ud-Din bin Sam Ghori[35] ruled over the mountains of Sivalik in the north of Hindustan, this was written on this pillar, which was already standing at this present location and Hindus used to worship it. The history of the pillar, from what I could gather, is that there were two pillars in the mountains of Kumaon in the north of Hindustan. The Hindus believed that these were sticks used by the gods when taking their cattle to graze. They used to worship the pillars and believed that doomsday would come only if these pillars broke or were removed from this place. Sultan Firoz Shah wanted to prove this wrong and so he broke one and brought the other and installed it here, and since then it is famous as Firoz Shah's pillar.

This pillar is from a wondrous and miraculous age [*ajaib rozgar*] in itself and is made of a single stone which people say is a kind of stone [*korund*]. It is said that the pillar is twice as much under the surface as it is on top, and many say that it has been installed over priceless treasures. According to history texts, the length of the pillar is 60 *gaz*, but I measured it with my astrolabe and found that the portion above ground is 48 feet and 5 inches, and its circumference is 10 feet. The top of this pillar has been damaged, which some say was due to a lightning strike, while others say a cannon ball was shot at it. Now that the monuments on this side have been described, I will now describe the monuments near the Qutub.

MASJID QUWWAT-UL-ISLAM

This is the mosque[36] that has the minaret [*minar*] which is famous as Qutub Sahib *ki Lath* or Qutub Sahib's Pillar [today popular as the Qutub Minar]. The mosque is unique. I am sure that there is no other mosque as big as this on the face of earth, and nor can the vault of the sky have seen [*chashm-e-falak*] such a mosque. In reality this mosque can have no parallel on earth, it is so delicate and attractive despite its huge size. One has to see the beautiful carving and decoration on each stone to believe it!

May the curly locks of a thousand beloveds be sacrificed upon each of its intertwining tendrils, and may hundreds of rosy cheeks and life-giving lips be sacrificed upon each of its tiny flowers and petals. Calligraphy, done in the Naskh style, adorns the whole mosque with such exquisite beauty that is incomparable. It is very unfortunate that the tides of time did not even have the ability to countenance this lofty building on earth.

I was scorned, when towards love I started turning,

No one cared that a young sapling was burning.

First, when somehow work was started on the building, the builder's life was cut short and the building remained incomplete. Whatever was built was not allowed to stay, and is now broken in many places. Today, we have reached the stage where every stone of this beautiful building is like an old woman's teeth – the stones keep falling, and those that haven't fallen are shaking and ready to fall.

The truth behind the construction of this mosque is that a temple built by Rai Pithaura [Prithviraj Chauhan] used to be located here. It was very famous, and at par with the temple of Somnath. This mosque was made on the location of this temple. When Sultan Muiz-ud-Din Muhammad bin Sam who was famous as Sultan Shahab-ud-Din,[37] defeated Rai Pithaura in AH 577 [CE 1181; sic],[38] he captured this temple, smashed all the idols in it and laid the foundation of this lofty mosque.

> See the miracle of the house of my idols, O Sheikh,
>
> Even when destroyed it becomes the House of God.

Once the foundation of this mosque had been laid, its construction continued under different rulers, however it could still not be completed. It is now difficult for spectators to understand its various edifices or why they were built, as it is in ruins and also left incomplete. That is why I thought it appropriate to include a description and explanation of its design and how it was supposed to be and why it was started, so that those who read this or go to see the mosque can understand its beauty and the reason behind its present state.

When Rai Pithaura's temple was captured and it was decided that a mosque would be built on that location, the people realized that the temples were very exquisitely built. It was decided that a mosque would be built, but that the temple building was to be kept intact. There were two advantages here, one that such a beautiful temple would not be broken and second that the authority and the power of Islam would be stamped on it. Thus, the builders of the mosque divided the temple into five parts, with different buildings on each of the five parts. The temple was so cleverly converted that it seemed to have been made for the mosque itself.

Those parts of the temple that could not be fitted in the mosque, were removed and used elsewhere. There were thousands of columns in this temple but no proper building. The columns were beautifully carved with idols, but the Muslim builders defaced the idols, and these are still present. But since the defaced idols are still present on these columns and are remnants of a very ancient monument, I will sketch them too and describe them in a separate place.

Now I will describe the different parts of the mosque starting with its minaret which is called Qutub Sahib *ki Lath* [Qutub Minar today].

Qutub Sahib ki Lath

In reality this pillar [*lath*] is the minaret of Quwwat-ul-Islam Mosque. Its loftiness,[39] beauty and magnificence cannot be put into words. It is so lofty that travellers from all over the world

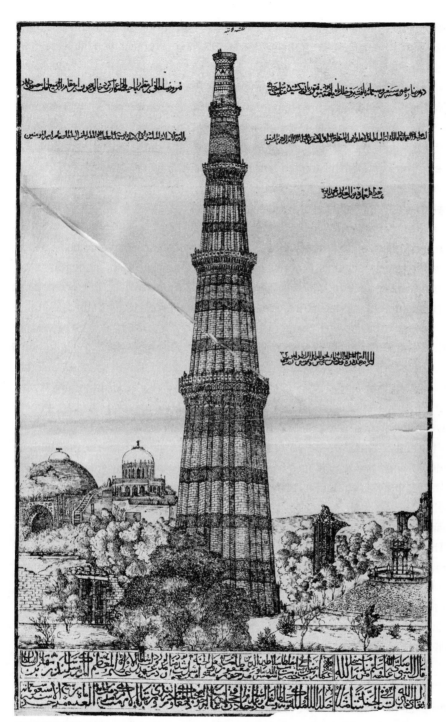

Qutub Sahib ki Lath

have not seen anything like it, except at one or two places. It is famously said that whoever is looking up at it has to hold on to their caps and turbans! It is so lofty that men think they can catch hold of the sky from its top and climb onto it. In the monsoon, during the procession called Phool Walo'n ki Sair,[40] on descending from the top of this minaret, twelve people found that it had been raining. God is the greatest! Even the clouds are lower than this minaret!

When viewed from the top of the minaret, those below seem very tiny like toys. It seems to those who are watching from below that there are angels on top. In short, this is a unique minaret. One wants to keep looking at it, as it is so exquisitely made, despite its size. The first three parts are made of red sandstone and the fourth is of marble with calligraphic verses and intricate carving on all the levels. The flutings on the pillar-minaret and its corbels are so beautiful that they can't be described in words. I will therefore describe its construction since words fail me regarding its beauty.

Sultan Shams-ud-Din Altamash built this minaret during his reign.[41] Since he ascended the throne in AH 607 [CE 1210–11], it can be said that this minaret was built 656 years ago [sic]. In my view, after reading historical texts, I feel that it was completed after AH 626 [CE 1228–29]. Anyway, this pillar was built by Sultan Shams-ud-Din Altamash and is a sign of his grand intentions. Many sultans after him, awed by its designs and grandeur, kept repairing it.

During the reign of Firoz Shah, it was struck by lightning and damaged. In AH 770 [CE 1368–69] Sultan Firoz Shah got it repaired. It was damaged once again in the reign of Sultan Sikandar bin Bahlol Lodi and he got it repaired in AH 909 [CE 1503–04]. It was again damaged by an earthquake and lightning and some stones fell down near its base.

The British government took up the task of repairing it with great fortitude. Captain Smith was put in charge of the repairs and twenty years have passed since then. The British government spent around a lakh of rupees in repairing the minaret, other buildings near it and in making a road. In reality this minaret is still standing because of these repairs; otherwise it would have fallen down long ago.

Earlier this minaret looked very different from what it does today. On talking to old people I found that there were no railings on each storey, but beautiful merlons instead. Smith Sahib added the railings as the merlons had been destroyed. If one reflects on the minaret, one realizes that the merlons were actually suited to this monument and would have added to its beauty.

It is also famous that it used to be seven-storeyed [haft manzari] and old people confirm this fact by saying that earlier this minaret was much taller. They say that there used to be a small section [khand] on top of the fifth storey which had four doors on the four sides and people would go up there, sit and enjoy themselves, and on one side of this there were small steps to go on top, and perhaps there was some room/building on top of that too, but no one remembers it now. From books and what is popular amongst the general population here, it seems that this minaret indeed had seven sections.

Two portions on the top had already broken before the British government came into power and the third – which is the top-most part of the structure today – had also suffered some damage. The British government got it repaired and in place of the sixth storey constructed a stone pavilion, and on top of that a wooden pavilion, and thus the British once again took the minaret back to its original height. But due to light and strong winds, neither the stone not the wooden pavilion remained standing and were damaged. While the stone pavilion stands near the minaret as a reminder, there are no traces of the wooden one. It is present in the sketch.

I measured the height of this minaret with an astrolabe, and then confirmed it by measuring each part with a rope. The first part of this minaret is 96 feet and a few inches, which is 32 *gaz* and some inches. The second part is 50 feet and some inches, which is approximately 17 *gaz*. The third part is 40 feet and some inches, which is about 13 *gaz*. The fourth part is 25 feet which is about 8.25 *gaz*. The fifth, along with the protruding part inside the wooden pavilion, is around 25 feet or 8.25 *gaz*. The wooden pavilion is 3 feet high, thus the total height comes to 80 *gaz*. The stone pavilion (made by Smith), which has now been taken down, stood 17 feet high/6 *gaz*.

It is said that there was a 5-*gaz*-high wooden pavilion on which the flag used to fly. At its base the circumference is 150 feet/50 *gaz* and 30 feet/10 *gaz* on the fifth storey where the pavilion was installed. It seems that the wooden and stone pavilion along with the flag would have been tapering in alignment with the rest of the shape. It would have culminated in the flag and thus given it a conical shape.

The minaret is hollow from within and has a circular staircase built inside it. I don't know how many steps there were earlier but now the first storey has 156 steps, the second storey has 78, the third 62 steps, and the fourth and fifth have 41 steps each. All together that makes 378 steps.

On the fourth and fifth levels, there are some steps to climb towards the stone and wooden pavilion. There are five steps on the fourth level and the three steps on the fifth level seem separately built. The entire minaret is inscribed with Quranic verses, the beauty of which is beyond words!

Six inscriptions are worth describing and therefore I am noting them down. They are very important as they give details of the builders and repairers of this minaret, while one of them also mentions the architect. I have copied them in the same script and style. The one on the fourth storey is written on the wall, while all the other inscriptions are inscribed on top of the door. It was difficult to read the words as they are written in a different style, so please excuse the mistakes of the copier. They are written on the sketch.

Masjid Quwwat-ul-Islam: The First Section

The three sections in front of the minaret on the northern side are the first sections of the mosque. Though built later, the first section has been labelled such because it is at the entrance of the mosque. It has three red sandstone arches towards the west [qibla].[42] The central arch is bigger while the ones on the sides are smaller with Quranic calligraphy in the Naskh style in the Kufic script, along with floral carving around it. All three arches have been damaged, while half of the smaller arch on the south has broken down. The arch in the centre and on the north has almost broken down, with only its arm standing.[43] A building from the Rai Pithaura temple stands on the southern end. A roof has been made on those columns.

There used to be a door for common use on the southern side, but it has now broken. There was an identical building with a doorway towards the north, which has completely broken down as well. There used to be a similar door here too for going into the second section but that too is broken and not even a single wall-niche showing the direction of Mecca remains. Only a few remnants of the arms of the arches of these wall-niches remain.

To the south of this part, on the arm of the smaller arch, the date AH 627 [CE 1229–30] is inscribed. This proves that this part was built in the reign of Sultan Shams-ud-Din Altamash,

Masjid Quwwat-ul-Islam: the first section

636 years ago [sic]. These arches are so lofty that I do not think I have seen any to equal them anywhere. Even though the central arch has broken down the others are intact. I measured these arches with my astrolabe. The central arch must have been 48 feet and the smaller ones are 28 feet in height. The width of all three is 112 feet. These arches in themselves are enough to understand the magnificence of this mosque. I am making a sketch of all that I have described. The inscriptions of this mosque are also given.[44] Read them and heed the warning of the transient nature of life.

Masjid Quwwat-ul-Islam: The Second Section

The second section of the mosque is the biggest. The reason for that is that out of the three parts designed for it, only two could be completed and thus this became the central one. There are five arches towards the west [qibla], with one larger arch flanked by two smaller arches on each side with exquisite calligraphy and floral designs. These arches are of the same height as the other arches. The carving and calligraphy on these arches is the most beautiful of all the designs and its beauty is beyond description. It is difficult to read the Quranic verses as many of the letters have broken.

On the south pier at the foot of the inscribed band framing the central arch of the great screen is the inscription:

> … date, the twentieth of [the Islamic calendar month of] Zil Qada of the year five hundred and ninety-four.

This was built in the reign of Sultan Muiz-ud-Din Muhammad bin Sam and from the date inscribed [23 September CE 1198] it seems that it was built 669 years ago [sic]. This is the earliest construction in this complex and was built on the actual spot of Rai Pithaura's temple and is the foundation of the Quwwat-ul-Islam Mosque.

Later rulers added to it. To its south are the columns of the temple. There was a door for common use in this area but it has fallen down, though its remains still stand. There is a door for use on the northern side, which also still stands. There are columns on the eastern side with one door for use that is still intact. In this area, the columns on the west are very beautiful and the beautifully carved idols are visible. I will separately make a sketch of this part of the Rai Pithaura temple.

This second part is 138 feet from the west to the north and consists of the iron pillar in its courtyard.

The Iron Pillar

I have not been able to ascertain the facts about this pillar called the Iron Pillar [Lohe ki Lath], including who got it made and when. However, there is no doubt that it is very old as inscriptions that cannot be read exist on its surface from a bygone era. Some people say that Sultan Muiz-ud-Din Muhammad bin Sam[45] got this pillar installed here as the needle of a sundial [miqyas], but this seems incorrect. However, it is possible that this pillar was already present in Rai Pithaura's temple and Sultan Muiz-ud-Din Muhammad bin Sam let it remain as the needle of a sundial, thinking that it would be useful as a tool to measure the hours of the day and add to the glory of Islam.

Some people say that the soothsayers of Rai Pithaura told him that they would install a nail and as long as that nail held firm, his kingdom would too. They quoted the movement of stars as an argument in its favour. Rai Pithaura could not grasp the purpose and as a great amount of money was being spent on it, he did not make haste to get it finished. Finally, an old and learned priest decided on a course of action that would make the Raja understand its importance. Sometimes a common man's language can be understood by all. He once again raised the topic of the nail.

Rai Pithaura, as usual, asked why it was important. With folded hands, the priest said, 'Maharaj Prithviraj, this is not something which can be told in public. However, if you insist on knowing then let us go to a place where we are alone and I will tell you, but don't let anyone else know what I tell you.' Rajaji immediately took the priest aside, who said, 'Listen Maharaj Prithviraj, the Master of this whole world is the God, Raja Basik, the Emperor of snakes and he traverses the whole earth. He is about to come to this area in a few days. If we install this nail firmly on his head, then he will remain permanently in this area and your kingdom will remain forever too.'

Rai Pithaura could now understand the importance of this task and immediately gave orders for the nail to be installed. All the priests gathered together, ascertained an auspicious time and installed the nail. The Raja asked, 'O Panditji, tell me has this nail been firmly struck on Raja Basik's head?' The priest replied, 'Yes Prithviraj, it is firmly set on his head.'

After a few days Raja Prithviraj started having doubts whether the nail had actually been set on Raja Basik's head or not, and he gave orders to the priests to uproot the nail and see if it was indeed wet with Raja Basik's blood. The priests tried to explain the folly of this action to him but he refused to listen and got it uprooted.

There was no blood on the nail but the priests, to prove their point, smeared its base with blood and showed it to him as proof that the nail had indeed pierced Raja Basik's head. Prithviraj, very dismayed that he had doubted them, immediately had it reinstalled. This time, however, it was not set properly, and a little while later he tasted defeat at the hands of the Muslim invaders. Some say that he was killed, while others say that he was sent to Ghazni. Thus Muslim rule came to be established here.

Readers may think that this is just a tale, but those who have some knowledge of astrology and history will know that such things were made by ancient soothsayers and astrologers. They won't find it strange that the priests got such a nail made and installed. This pillar is very unique and is a single piece cast in iron. People are awestruck at how it was made or put up. When I sketched this pillar I measured it with a tape and astrolabe and found that it was 22.6 feet high and 5.3 feet in circumference at the base. Whoever wanted has got their name inscribed on this pillar, while some have done so with some floral decorations and animals inscribed around the inscription.

But its actual inscription cannot be read or understood, as it is in an ancient language. I have heard that someone could read just the words 'Sri Rai Prithviraj' on it. When the general public came to see it, there would be a strange spectacle. It is said that whoever can encircle the pillar with their arms backward are legitimate, and those who cannot are illegitimate. It is easy for tall people to grasp it, while shorter ones have a hard time doing so and their friends tease them with the words 'you are illegitimate' ['haram ka hai'].

One day, I was sitting and writing about this pillar when a group of young and beautiful girls came to see it. Perchance, all could encircle it except the prettiest girl. Her friends started teasing her and she became tearful. I was quietly sketching and writing in a corner. For some reason these girls thought that either I was a religious teacher [mullah], or a hereditary caretaker [of a mosque or dargah], or someone knowledgeable and came to me and asked, 'Miyanji, [Sir] is the person who can't encircle this pillar of illegitimate birth?' I was very amused and thought to myself that I had landed myself a task fit for a judge.

Then I said to the girls, 'What you say is true for those who are above the age of twenty. Tell me if you're that old, for only then can I say anything further.' Since none of them was that old, they all burst into laughter and went away, and I returned to my own work.

> When everyone sets out at dawn to do the mundane chores,
>
> Those who are burdened with love trek to the beloved's door.

Look at the sketch and think of the power of the Almighty.

Masjid Quwwat-ul-Islam: Eastern Part of the Second Section/ Rai Pithaura's Temple

The columns, which I am sketching, are in the eastern part of the second section, just as they were in the northern and southern sections. I have sketched them only so that people can get an idea of what the temple looked like, though I can't be sure whether it is still in the shape it was under Rai Pithaura or whether the Muslims have changed it. However, it is believed that these columns were arranged in the same fashion from the time of Rai Pithaura and under the Muslims; the idols were defaced but their positions left undisturbed. In case there were any changes, then Sultan Qutub-ud-Din Aibak built a door here that I will describe later and make a sketch of.

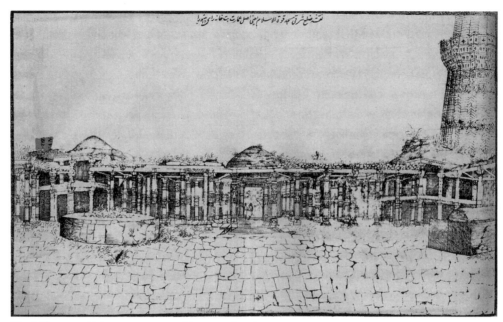

Masjid Quwwat-ul-Islam: eastern part of the second section

It is said that the wall of the complex – opposite to the columns and the doorway set in it – is completely different. It becomes evident by just looking at these columns that they were placed here before that wall and door were built. Therefore I feel that these columns are from the time of Rai Pithaura and I am describing it considering it as Rai Pithaura's memorial. These columns are far superior to all the other columns and have very fine carvings on them. Many idols carved on them were defaced under Muslim rule and are still present in the same condition. Looking at this building I am reminded of the verse:[46]

> The marks and engravings on the ruined walls and gates,
>
> [They are] the remnant signs of Persia's ancient monuments.

It is the power of God that such mighty people have lived in this world and the incidents that have passed in their lives! It's a warning for all men to come that one must never place trust in this intransient world or in the worldly pleasures of life as everything passes.

> Nobody can complete the tasks of the world,
>
> Whoever attempts can only complete a part of it.
>
> I have sketched it in such a way that you can see the idols. Look at it and remember God.

Masjid Quwwat-ul-Islam: Eastern Gate of the Second Section

This gate is behind Rai Pithaura's temple that I have sketched above. The gate seems incomplete. The square door on the inner side seems to have been built in the reign of Sultan

Muiz-ud-Din.[47] The year of the conquest and the word 'temple' are inscribed on it. I couldn't read the inscription clearly, as it was very fine and in a new script, but whatever I could read I will note down. On the lintel is inscribed:

> In the Name of Allah, Most Gracious, Most Merciful.

This is followed by a verse from the Quran:

> And whoever enters it shall be safe. And [due] to Allah from the people is a pilgrimage to the House – for whoever is able to find thereto a way. But whoever disbelieves – then indeed, Allah is free from need of the worlds. (Aali-' Imran, 3:97)

[Next], the inscription is as follows:

> This fort was conquered and this Jami Masjid was built in the year AH 587 [CE 1191–92] by the Amir, the great and glorious commander of the army [named] Qutb-ud-Daulat-Waddin Aibak Sultani, may God strengthen his helpers. The material of 27 temples on [the erection of] each of which 2,000,000 deliwals had been spent, were used in [the construction of] this mosque. May God the great and glorious have mercy on him who should pray for the faith of the founder of the good [building].

On the arch tympanium of the eastern gate is inscribed:

> This mosque was built by Qutb-ud-Din Aibak.
>
> May God have mercy on him who should pray for the faith of the founder of the good [building].

Masjid Quwwat-ul-Islam: the eastern gate of the second section

Sultan Qutb-ud-Din Aibak has built the large wall-niche that indicates the direction of Mecca, in front of this door and his name is inscribed on it. But I have doubts that it was made in his reign. It is possible that since Sultan Muiz-ud-Din Muhammad bin Sam had left Qutb-ud-Din Aibak in charge here, after the conquest of Delhi he got his name inscribed on it. But I can't find the verification of it in any book. This gate is very beautiful and that can be ascertained by looking at the sketch.

Masjid Quwwat-ul-Islam: The Northern Gate of the Second Section

This gate was made before all the other buildings in this mosque, in the reign of Sultan Muiz-ud-Din Muhammad bin Sam,[48] the conqueror of this temple, in AH 592 [CE 1195–96]. Thus his name and the year of the foundation of the mosque are inscribed on it. From this inscription we can also understand that this mosque was made on the orders of this emperor. On the arch tympanium of the north gate is the inscription:

> In the months of the year five hundred and ninety-two this building was erected by the high order of the exalted Sultan Muiz-ud-duniya-waddin Muhammad bin Sam, the helper of the prince of the faithful.

This gate is very attractive and its beauty can be seen in the sketch. The third part of the mosque is near this gate which I will now describe.

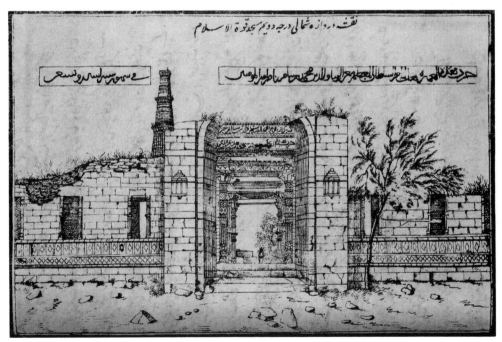

Masjid Quwwat-ul-Islam: the northern gate of the second section

Masjid Quwwat-ul-Islam: The Third Section

The third section of the mosque is very similar to the first. Even though the stone on which the year of construction was inscribed has broken, its similarity to the first section in terms of ornamentation and the size of its arches leads to the conclusion that it too was built in the reign of Sultan Shams-ud-Din Altamash, i.e. at the same time as the first part, in AH 627 [CE 1229–30] and 636 years have passed since then [sic]. There are three arches here with a larger central one flanked by two smaller ones. The first arch is almost intact barring a few stones that have fallen down. The central arch has also crumbled, and only its arms are standing. Only one arm of the third arch remains, with no remains of the rest. Perhaps they have been absorbed in the road.

The road from Lado Sarai, which goes towards Qutub Sahib [Mehrauli] via Bhul Bhulaiyya, passes through this third arch. This part is 108 feet wide from the western direction [towards Mecca: *qibla*]. It seems that Sultan Shams-ud-Din Altamash wanted to expand the mosque and build a second pillar here, but it was not to be. When Sultan Ala-ud-Din Khilji became the emperor, he decided to expand the mosque and build a minaret loftier than the one standing there. He laid the foundations and started construction, but his life was soon cut short. I will describe that further [below].

Masjid Quwwat-ul-Islam: the third section

Masjid Quwwat-ul-Islam: The Fourth Section

There is nothing in this section; if something was built here, it no longer exists. One can just make out the base of the arches, and it seems that the foundation for it was laid and construction started. Even now there exists some masonry work measuring 2 to 2.5 *gaz* in height. People have taken the stones away for use in their houses and only the lime mortar remains.

This section is similar in style to the other sections. Five arches were being built here, with one taller central arch and two smaller ones flanking it on each side. According to history books, Sultan Ala-ud-Din Khilji started construction of this part in AH 711 [CE 1311–12]. As he died around the same time [CE 1316], it was left incomplete. Since there is nothing here except mud and stones, I am not sketching it, and will describe its dimensions along with the fifth section.

Masjid Quwwat-ul-Islam: The Fifth Section

This part was started by Sultan Ala-ud-Din Khilji in AH 711 [CE 1311–12] along with the fourth section, and this too was left incomplete. This was to be very similar in style to the first section, with three arches, but was not completed. Both these parts are 258 feet from the western side [*qibla*]. Thus the total size of the width of all parts of the mosque, along with 30 feet for its walls, would be 646 feet. Only mud and stones are to be found in this area too and so I am not sketching it.

The Incomplete Pillar

Sultan Ala-ud-Din Khilji started construction of this minaret along with the arches in AH 711 [CE 1311–12]. He wanted to make it double the size of the first minaret. But now all its stones have fallen down. I am describing whatever remains as it is a very famous monument. Amir Khusrau, in *Khazain-ul-Futuh*, writes in praise of this minaret:

> This Minar is like a stone pillar,
>
> The roof of the sky is lustrous as glass.
>
> Alas! The roof of Heaven has become old and worn out,
>
> It was for this purpose that the minaret was made.

MAQBARA SULTAN SHAMS-UD-DIN ALTAMASH

This is the tomb of Sultan Shams-ud-Din Altamash who built a lofty minaret, but even he could not escape the hands of time and was interred in the dust. It is indeed a warning that time does not leave anyone unscathed, such famous names lie beneath the earth, turned to dust.

The incomplete pillar

> All those famous and noteworthy shall be buried underground,
>
> Not a sign of them shall remain above ground.

He was an excellent emperor, blessed with an exemplary character and intentions. People lived in peace and prosperity under him. In all probability, his tomb was built during the reign of Sultan Rukn-ud-Din Firoz Shah or Raziya Begum. Though there is no date in any book for the construction of this tomb, Sultan Shams-ud-Din Altamash died in AH 633 [CE 1236], so we can guess its date from this date and 630 years have passed since then [sic].

The inside of this tomb is made of local quartzite and of red sandstone. In some places we find marble. The walls are covered with Quranic calligraphy and exquisite carving. It seems that there was a dome on this tomb, which has now fallen and only the walls remain and they too are broken in many places. There used to be a road going from Lado Sarai towards Qutub Sahib [Mehrauli] from the side of this tomb. I am sketching it in its present condition. Look at it and take heed at the changing fortunes of time.

MAQBARA SULTAN ALA-UD-DIN KHILJI

Such is the majesty of God, that a sultan such as Ala-ud-Din Khilji – in front of whom djinns, men, animals and birds stood with folded hands – was interred into the dust in a moment. Now

نقشه مقبره سلطان شمس الدین التمش

Maqbara Sultan Shams-ud-Din Altamash

no one knows about his grave as he lies abandoned; helpless that people stole his tombstone, stones from his grave and he could do nothing!

Some more arches and ruins can be seen towards the south behind the arches of the first part of Quwwat-ul-Islam Mosque. Sultan Ala-ud-Din Khilji's grave lies nestled in these ruins. Though this grave is not worthy of a sketch, I am making it so that people may take it as a warning of the transitory nature of this world. Anyway, he was a famous ruler. This tomb was constructed in the reign of Sultan Shahab-ud-Din and Sultan Qutb-ud-Din Mubarak Shah who were the sons of Ala-ud-Din Khilji. Though we don't know the exact date of this construction we can guess its date from the fact that Sultan Ala-ud-Din Khilji died in AH 715 [CE 1316].

BADA DARWAZA

This is a large [bada] gateway [today better known as the Alai Darwaza] near the large minaret [Qutub Minar] made completely of red sandstone. It has four arched doors on all four corners with very intricate work. Its dome is so lofty that it seems to be touching the sky. The arches of the doors have beautiful Quranic calligraphy on them. The history of the gate is also written on the four doors. The following is inscribed:

Constructed on fifteenth of Shawal, the year [AH] 716 . [31 December 1316]

Maqbara Sultan Ala-ud-Din Khilji

From the dates it seems that this gateway was built in the reign of Sultan Ala-ud-Din Khilji who constructed it as an entrance gate to the mosque. He had decided to expand the mosque and build more such gates but this intention remained incomplete. This is a unique gate and I have not seen such a lofty domed gateway [anywhere else]. Near this lies Imam Zamin's *dargah*.

DARGAH IMAM ZAMIN

Imam Muhammad Ali Mashhadi was also known as Sayyid Hussain. His *dargah* is, therefore, also known as 'Sayyid Hussain *pa-e-minar*'[iv] [near the minaret], as it is located near Alai Darwaza, next to Qutub Minar. This tomb was built in his lifetime and he had willed that he should be buried in it and so it was. The tomb was constructed in AH 944 [CE 1537–38]. Since the inscription is very large, it cannot fit inside the sketch I made, so I have written it separately. [See Appendix II at the end of *Asar-2*].

---

iv *Mirat-e-Aftab-e-Numa.*

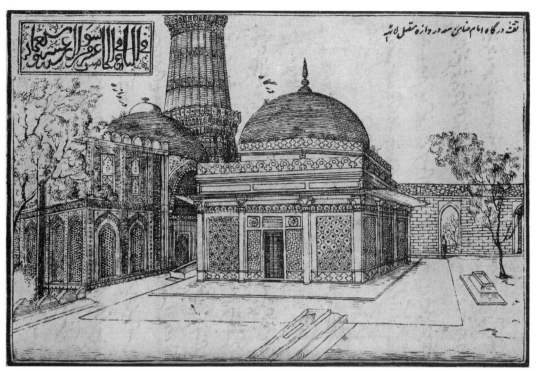

Dargah Imam Zamin and Bada Darwaza

KOTHI JANAB FAIZ MUAB MUALLIUL ALQAB
SAHIB-E-KALAN BAHADUR DAAM IQBALAHU

[The above title may be loosely translated as: The mansion of he who is blessed, honoured and holds the highest office. May his glory increase.] This building [Thomas Metcalfe's mansion] near Qutub Sahib *ki Lath* [Qutub Minar] had fallen into disrepair and was in a bad shape. It was known as the mausoleum of Emperor Akbar's foster brother Muhammad Quli Khan. This monument would have been made either in Akbar's reign, or during that of his son, Jahangir. But the fortunes of this building only changed for the better when Sir Thomas Metcalfe – thanks to whose justice lions and goats drank water on one shore, and who has annihilated oppression and tyranny from this world, and the praises of whose noble intentions and virtues reach the skies – decided to build a mansion on this spot![49]

Just ruler, the exalted son and most beloved of the emperor, the most honourable person of the government, custodian of the country, and distinguished friend, Sir Thomas Theophilus Metcalfe Sahib Baronet Bahadur Firoz Jung Sahib Senior of Shahjahanabad, may your glory increase. [You] bought this desolate building and turned it into the envy of paradise. This beautiful and elegant mansion is ready. Each building [that Sir Thomas ADDED to the original]

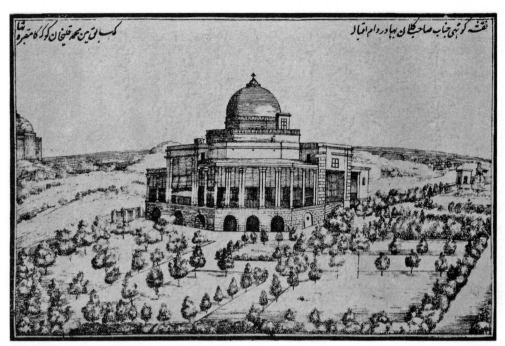

Kothi Janab Sahib-e-Kalan Bahadur Daam Iqbalahu

of this monument seems to taunt the palaces of Heaven and even the sky is envious of it. The gardens are beautifully laid out with waterways on all sides and various kinds of trees and flowerbeds that remind one of paradise, and the waterfalls and cool breezes make one long for Heaven. Without doubt, this mansion is proof of this verse [by Amir Khusrau]:

> If there is a paradise on earth,
> It is here, it is here, it is here.

RAJO'N KI BAIN

Near the building called Dilkusha,[50] is a building called Rajo'n ki Bain which hails from the period of the Pathans. Daulat Khan built it in the reign of Sikandar Shah, son of Sultan Bahlol Lodi in AH 912 [CE 1506–07]. Words cannot describe this delicate and exquisite work. Even though this building is made of lime mortar, it is a thousand times better than those made of stone.

There is a step well [*baoli*] here which is extremely beautiful and well made. It is so well maintained, attractive and pleasing to the heart that it feels as though the architects have just got up and left. There is a mosque on an elevated plinth by the step well, which is very beautiful and pleasing to the heart, and the soul is uplifted on seeing it. There are two

Rajo'n ki Bain

graves in a very sturdy and attractive pavilion located in the mosque's courtyard. There is an inscription on the pavilion, which describes its construction. I have written it on the sketch.

Once upon a time, masons [raj] used to live in the buildings around the step well and since then it has been famous as Rajo'n ki Bain ['bain' derives from baoli]. The masons have long gone and now some villagers have settled here. When the Emperor [Huzur-e-Wala] goes to Qutub Sahib [Mehrauli], his special bodyguards stop at this mosque. The beauty of this step well can be seen in the sketch.

DARGAH MAULANA JAMALI

Maulana Jamali was a great poet and a godly person. I don't have the capability to describe his many miracles. His dargah is near Rajo'n ki Bain [see above] and is built of stone and mortar. It is beautifully decorated with glazed tiles and ornamentation. This interior of the dargah is beautifully ornamented with designs on the plaster, and these designs have to be seen to be believed. Verses written by the Maulana are incised in plaster. These are translated below:[51]

> *Even if our wickedness may approach blasphemy, we still cherish hope of your pardon,*
> *At your threshold we are ashamed because your dogs cannot rest at night on account of our wailing.*

If I should have the honour to approach the curtain [that guards] your secret, an angel will be proud to act as porter.

Covered with dust of your street we look contemptible to [common] people, but this meanness is an honour in the estimation of persons of wisdom.

By the cloud of your kindness the dust of sin has been washed away, but the blot of our shame could not be cleansed.

On the day of separation from you in helplessness and loneliness, nothing consoles us but the sorrow we feel for you.

O! Jamali, resort for protection the door of the friend, for our refuge is the door of the beloved.

————

Our restlessness in your love has passed beyond bounds, our hope is that you will pity our weeping.

How could your pardon be known, had we not shown ourselves guilty!

Although we are deserving of wrath for our guilt, yet we hope from your kindness.

We may attain the honour, glory and dignity of angels if you observe our humility.

If we become those who may hold your secrets [even] an angel would not be worthy of acting as our porter.

With one shower from the cloud of beneficence you wash away the dust of crime from our shamed faces.

Cast your eyes upon Jamali and do not look at his idleness and shortcomings.

————

O thou, whose mercy won the game from wrath, and whose kindness ordered rage to depart! Wherever there is talk of thy immense forgiveness, people's sin is not weighed there against [them]; [or] barely [such that it is it is of little consequence].

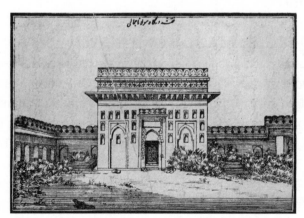

Dargah Maulana Jamali

The saint died in AH 942 [CE 1535–36] in the reign of Humayun and the chronogram for his death is *Khusrau-e-Hind*; 321 years have passed since this *dargah* was constructed.

Masjid Maulana Jamali

Near his *dargah* stands a grand stone and lime mortar mosque which looks like it must have been attractive and appealing once upon a time. There is no date or inscription on it, nor could I find any reference to the year it was built, so I cannot give an authentic date for its construction or name its builder. However, I can conclude that it was built at the same time as the shrine and tomb, as it is attached to it. It bears many similarities to mosques built during Humayun's reign, so we can say it was built during that period. [Hence] 321 years have passed since it was constructed.

Though this mosque lies desolate today, it was once situated in the midst of habitation. Qutub Sahib used to live here, and there are still ruins of houses at this location. The state of this mosque can be seen from the sketch. Look at it and heed the revolution of time.

MAQBARA SULTAN GHIYAS-UD-DIN BALBAN

Near the mosque of Maulana Jamali, next to the ruins of the old mansions of the old abode of Qutub Sahib, is the near ruined, broken down and damaged tomb of Ghiyas-ud-Din Balban.

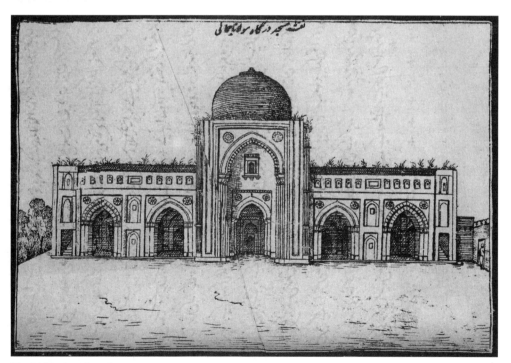

Masjid Maulana Jamali

Maqbara Sultan Ghiyas-ud-Din Balban

Stones from this tomb have been taken away, some were taken to Lucknow and some were used for the mansions and monuments built during the reigns of the Delhi emperors.

As in the case of the tomb of Sultan Ala-ud-Din Khilji, there are just ruins here, but because it is the tomb of a very famous sultan, I am describing it, even though its condition doesn't merit a description. There are no records of the date of its construction. However, since Sultan Ghiyas-ud-Din Balban died in AH 686 [CE 1287], we can say that it was made by Sultan Muiz-ud-Din Kaikobad, Sultan Ghiyas-ud-Din Balban's grandson who succeeded him, Balban's son Nasir-ud-Din [and Muiz-ud-Din's father] having died during Balban's lifetime. If we go by that date, it was made 577 years ago [sic].

Adjacent to this tomb, in fact so close that it appears to be a part of the same tomb, is a smaller tomb in the same broken-down state. This is the tomb of Khan Shahid, who died fighting infidels near Lahore, in AH 683 [CE 1284–85]. On his death, Mir Hasan Dehalvi wrote an elegy [*marsiya*]. One can see the state of these two tombs in the sketch.

BAGH-E-NAZIR

This is a beautiful, attractive, verdant and luxuriant garden near the waterfall of Qutub Sahib [in the Mehrauli area]. It is still very well maintained, with blooming flowers and green trees.

Bagh-e-Nazir

The buildings around it are still intact and thousands of people come here during the Phool Walo'n ki Sair procession, to enjoy its beauty. The spectacle is as entertaining as though one were at a fair. This garden was built by Nazir Roz Afzun during the reign of Muhammad Shah Badshah. I will write down the verses inscribed on the entrance as they give the date of the construction and name of the builder:

> By the orders of Muhammad Shah Adil,
> Whose head bears the sacred crown.
> He founded this garden near [the shrine and tomb of] Qutub Sahib,
> And has adorned it with the flowers of paradise.
> It should remain green till the Day of Judgment,
> By the Grace of the Holy Quran.
> The year of its construction,
> Was found to be the blessed date,
> AH 1116 [CE 1704–05] in the thirty-first regnal year of Muhammad Shah.

A wall surrounds the garden and there are red sandstone buildings of great attraction built all around, within the wall. There is one building in the middle of the garden that is the biggest and best of all the buildings there. Thus I am attaching its sketch here.

JHARNA

This is a place for recreation and pleasure; it is exotic and unearthly, elegant and refined, interesting and delightful, happiness bestowing and heart pleasing. Qutub Sahib's waterfall [jharna][52] is famous for its verdant green trees and reminds one of heaven. Initially, Sultan Firoz Shah had constructed a dam here and the wall of the waterfall is that dam. It is still intact.

He had diverted the excess water of Hauz-e-Shamsi reservoir into Naulakh canal [nala] towards the moats of Tughlaqabad Fort. After some years however, the fort was abandoned and water stopped going to that area. The excess water from the Hauz-e-Shamsi then started flowing into the jungles from this dam and was wasted. Nawab Ghazi-ud-Din Khan Firoz Jung built a tank, water channels, and chutes for the water to flow through. The waterfall is an awesome spectacle and pleases the heart, causing the spectator to involuntarily exclaim in delight. There are various buildings around this waterfall which I will describe here.

Pavilion on the Western Side

On the western side, adjoining the wall of the dam stands a pavilion at an elevation of 11 feet and 5 inches. It has three arches, and the waterfall cascades down on it. There is an attractive

Jharna

tank in front of it, into which people jump from the roof of this building. During the Phool Walo'n ki Sair festivities people diving into this tank and swimming in it, make for a huge spectacle. They use various diving styles including somersaulting into the water, they also make a pyramid by climbing onto the shoulders of men standing below until the man at the top of the pyramid reaches tree-branch height. Then those at the bottom dive into the tank and all those on their shoulders plunge into the tank. This is called a 'tree dive' [darakht ka kudna] or a 'wild growth dive' [jhad-jhankar ka kudna].

There are thirteen small water pipes under the roof of this building and water from the waterfall flows down through these, via the pavilion, and into the tank. There is a 3.2-feet-wide water chute inside the pavilion which falls from a height of 4.3 feet into the tank. There are niches built under the chute in the pavilion wall, and water flows over lighted lamps that are placed within the niches.

This 25-feet square tank has an opening of 1.7 feet for water to flow into it and is 7.6 feet deep. There is a 22 feet long, 6 feet wide and 3.6 feet deep water-channel, which flows out of this tank in a 5.6 feet cascade and is joined by two smaller cascades from the north and south. There are beautifully carved stone chutes [salami pathar] measuring 3 feet 7 inches, to receive the cascade. The water winds its way down the carvings on the chute creating a mesmerizing effect.

The water channel in front of this pavilion is 26 feet long, 6 feet wide and 2 feet deep, while the water channel in front of the smaller cascades is 15.3 feet wide, 2.9 feet wide and 8 feet deep. All the water collects at this point and flows into the jungle. The waterfall passes over all these pavilions and the water channel, and in reality it is a truly spellbinding sight. The sound of the flowing water mingles with the singing of the nightingale, the chirping of doves, peacocks dancing and the sounds of merriment of finely attired men and women. It is a mesmerizing scene, which could put Raja Indra's[53] assembly in the shade.

Pavilion on the Northern Side

There is a very attractive double pavilion on this side. Muin-ud-Din Muhammad Akbar Shah Badshah built the double pavilion in his reign, around three years ago. These are the most attractive buildings in the place.

Pavilion on the Southern Side

There is a three-arched pavilion in this area, with two smaller pavilions on its sides which gives it the impression of being five arched. In addition to this there are two doors next to it, thus making it seven arched. This pavilion was built around 50 years ago in the reign of Shah Alam by Shahji's brother, whose name was Sayyid Muhammad.

Pavilion on the Eastern Side

There are only mountains on this side and no buildings, but Muhammad Shah Badshah built a stone slide [phisalna pathar] 18 feet 3 inches long and 7 feet 7 inches wide.

The Mango Orchard

There are many mango trees in this area. People tie swings to the branches and have fun swinging on them. Numerous dancing and singing girls gather here to enjoy themselves. In short, this place is magical and the mind boggles at its attractions. There is also a grave here with the following verse inscribed on it:

> Abid who was wise, learned, pious and man of intellect,
>
> Was martyred by a dishonest robber.
>
> The invisible crier told me the chronogram of his death,
>
> The soul of Abid, the martyr entered paradise [in] AH 1209. [CE 1794–95]

HAUZ-E-SHAMSI

This reservoir [hauz] was one of a kind. Sultan Shams-ud-Din Altamash built it during his reign and that is why it is famous as Hauz-e-Shamsi. Once upon a time this reservoir was made of red sandstone but now all the stone has been torn off and it is just a simple reservoir and that's why people call it Qutub Sahib's reservoir, while some still call it Hauz-e-Shamsi. The water from here feeds the waterfall and also fed the moats of Tughlaqabad in olden days.

It is difficult to imagine there is a reservoir of this size on the face of earth. It is spread across 276 bighas [a land measurement] and its water reaches eight provinces [subahs]! The pavilion has been built around the mark of a hoof which people call the hoofprint of the Prophet's celestial steed Buraq, but to me it seems a made-up story. God alone knows the truth.

Auliya Masjid

On the eastern side of the Hauz-e-Shamsi is a platform and on it another smaller platform about a gaz or so with a small wall. According to legend, Hazrat Khwaja Qutb-ud-Din Bakhtiyar Kaki and other Sufi saints undertook their spiritual retreat/penance [chillah] on it. They built the mosque with their own hands, bringing baskets [of mud from the reservoir] and that's why it is called Auliya [The Saint's] Mosque. Now people have plastered it with mortar and lime.

JAHAZ

On the same side as the Auliya Mosque is a unique building known as Jahaz and also as Lal Mahal. They say that a merchant got it made as a spiritual retreat for mendicants. Many other rooms etc., have been built on the banks of the reservoir. I will list them, starting from the western side.

1. Balkhi Shahzade *ka bagh* [Prince Balkhi's garden]
2. Zain-ud-Din Zamar-ud-Din's mausoleum
3. Sheikh Wajih-ud-Din Khalifa Hazrat Sultan-ul-Mashaikh Sultan-ul-Sheikh's [Hazrat Nizam-ud-Din Auliya's] mausoleum
4. Shadi *ka bagh* [Shadi's garden][54]
5. Chandni Chabutra [Moonlit Platform] built by Muhammad Shah, which now lies broken. Only five or ten trees are left in Andheria Bagh [the Dark Garden], so called because of the density of trees.
6. *Pipulwala kuan* [the well beside the banyan tree]
7. The mausoleum of Khwaja Sama-ud-Din [Maulana Jamali's *Pir* or Master]
8. Sohan Burj, a bastion on the original wall of Lal Kot fort built by the Tomar and Chauhan rulers.
9. Chihaltan-Chihaltain, a *dargah* that has the graves of forty Sufi saints.
10. Auliya Masjid [the Saints' Mosque]
11. Yaarani Chabutra [the Platform of Friends] of Lal Mahal/Jahaz, the place where saints gathered and conversed with their disciples.
12. Deen Ali Shah's *takia* [seat]
13. Inayatullah Khan's *khanqah* [the saint's spiritual retreat where he also dispensed healing and undertook charitable work, including providing food and healing.]
14. Nawab Hafiz-ud-Din's *khanqah*
15. Wali Mosque
16. The mausoleum of Sheikh Abdul Haq

MAQBARA SHEIKH ABDUL HAQ MUHADDIS DEHLVI, MAY THE MERCY OF ALLAH BE ON HIM

He was a very famous saint [*auliya*] and a person who interpreted the sayings [*muhaddis*] of the Prophet, peace be upon him. His qualities are brighter than the sky and beyond the capacity of a lowly man like me to describe. His mausoleum is situated on the bank of the Hauz-e-Shamsi reservoir and is very attractively built and was built after his passing away. There are some inscriptions in plaster on a wall inside the small single-domed pavilion from which we get details. I have copied them down here:

> An extract from the blessed account of the glorious and eminent leader of the age [named] Abdul Haq, may God show immense mercy on him.
> As he entered with heart and soul into the worship of God and acquiring knowledge from

early childhood, he had learnt many sciences by the time he reached the age of 22 years, having finished all of them, learned the Quran by heart and applied himself to teaching. While he was young he felt a longing for God and having renounced his friends and country proceeded to the sacred sites of Mecca and Medina. He stayed for a long time in these holy places and having been in the company of most saintly people of the age had the honour of receiving the sacred charge of instructing seekers [after God].

Besides this he completed the study of the hadith and returned home with abundant blessings, where he remained with peace of mind for a period of 52 years and engaged himself in educating his sons and other students, as well as in propogating various sciences specially the hadith in which he surpassed all the ancient and modern savants of Ajam[55] and received much prominence and distinction through it.

He wrote many authentic books on various subjects especially on the hadith, such that learned men of the age study and have recourse to, and people high and low purchase even at a very high price.

The works of this eminently generous man – including all the big and small – are some hundred volumes while the number of verses amounts to 5000.

Maqbara Sheikh Abdul Haq Muhaddis Dehlvi

This most perfect light [Sheikh Abdul Haq] illuminated this material world, [he was born]
in the [Islamic calendar] month of Moharram, the year AH 958 [CE 1551] and departed to
paradise well-informed and happily in the year AH 1052 [CE 1642–43].

The chronogram for his birth is 'Shaikh-e-Auliya' and that of his death is 'Fakhr-e-Alam'.

DARGAH HAZRAT QUTUB-AL-AQTAB
KHWAJA QUTUB-UD-DIN BAKHTIYAR KAKI

I cannot even dare to write about the various obvious and hidden miracles of Qutub Sahib, may the mercy of Allah be on him. His miracles are so extraordinary they seem contrary to nature. Every person is well acquainted with his abstinence, noble deeds and miracles. It is unnecessary to write about the attributes of such a saint who is known to all and [whose qualities and achievements one] cannot even fit into words. Thus, I will just write about his *dargah* and adjoining buildings.

Please note that his *dargah* is not a permanent structure and his grave is just a pile of mud. There is no dome or structure over it. He sleeps under the open sky. Yet the splendour of this illuminated shrine has to be seen to be believed! A divine light shines there which gives a sense of peace and fulfilment to visitors. Glory be to God, this humility is the pride of emperors.

The beauty of the beloved is in no need of our incomplete love,

Your lovely face has no need of lustre, colour or beautification.

He left this world on the night of Monday on fourteenth [of the Islamic calendar month of] Rabi Awwal AH 633 [27 November 1235] and this blessed shrine and tomb would have been built then.

Once Badshah Sher Shah came to this area for a hunt and was blessed to pay homage to this pious *dargah*. He saw that the holy *dargah* was very simple and decided to get a compound wall built around it, and a place set aside for people to leave their shoes and proceed barefoot.

With this thought in mind, he shot three arrows into the air and built a gate and a compound wall on the spot where the arrows landed. That compound was very extensive and no longer exists. One can only find the ruins of the gates and the wall. After this, subsequent kings built a compound wall and doorways.

The Ajmeri Darwaza or the western gate [gives access from Zafar Mahal side and is] also known as the New Gateway [Naya Darwaza]:

People acquired the treasure of felicity here; at last Shakir Khan threaded the pearls of supplication.

I enquired of myself 'What shall I write for its date?' Rizwan [the gardener of Paradise] said to my heart 'The secrets of the gate of Paradise', AH 1119. [CE 1707–08]

Inscriptions on the gate next to the meeting hall [*majlis khana*] of the *dargah* are as follows:

> *During the reign of the sun of the sky of empire, Sher Shah the king, with the moon for his standard, the stars for his army, and heaven for his slave.*
>
> *The majestic tomb, in respect of which the saying, 'This is the door of the house of peace', is verified.*
>
> *Was completed in the year AH 948 [CE 1541], under the superintendence of the Sheikh, the cherisher of religion, Khalil-ul Haq.*

In AH 1252 [CE 1836–37], the Empress and wife of the Emperor of the World, Abul Zafar Siraj-ud-Din Muhammad Bahadur Shah, Ghazi Khulullah had got a sandalwood railing put around his blessed shrine and gained felicity in this world and thereafter.

Dargah Qazi Hamid-ud-Din Nagauri, May the Mercy of Allah be upon Him

Qazi Hamid-ud-Din Nagauri's *dargah* is near the base of Qutub Sahib's *dargah*. There are many other graves near his *dargah*. I will now describe the main shrine.

Dargah Hazrat Qutub-al-Aqtab

A Reference to Miya'n Ghulam Noor Sahib Khadim

Even though there are many hereditary caretakers of the blessed shrine of Qutub Sahib, each more superior than the rest, Miya'n Ghulam Noor Sahib's qualities and virtues are particularly noteworthy. His conduct is exemplary and his virtues are innumerable. He is fond of history and he is very knowledgeable about the buildings in this area. He was with me when I was researching this area, and he described each of the buildings to me very beautifully.

Gateway to Dargah Qutub-al-Aqtab[56]

To the east of the *dargah* are marble screens and gateways, built in the reign of Mughal Emperor Farrukhsiyar. These have verses inscribed on them, which give us the date of construction and name of the builder. Built by Emperor Farrukhsiyar during his reign, the inner gateway leads to the shrine of Qutub Sahib. On this gateway we find inscribed, on a marble slab over the doorway:

> By the efforts of the meanest of the emperor's slaves who is faithful, confident and of a perfect standard.
>
> The angel went into the land of the paradise of Eden and they found its date 'The fort of the paradise of Eden.'

Gateway to Dargah Qutub-al-Aqtab

Finished under the supervision of the meanest of slaves Farukh Shah. The seventh year of accession. The year AH 1130 [CE 1717–18].

Written by Ubaidullah Shirin Raqim.

The verse on the outer gate reads:

By the order of the emperor of the world, the king of the world, Farrukhsiyar, who is the emperor with the nine firmaments for his slaves.

Round the grave of the chief of faith and the pole star of the nine heavens, about whose mausoleum mankind and angels walk.

A beautiful well arranged enclosure was built, which is as exalted as qibla [the direction of Mecca] and as sacred as Ka'aba.

Dargah Maulana Fakhr-ud-Din, May God's Mercy be upon Him

Near this gateway and behind the mosque, is the *dargah* of Maulana Fakhr-ud-Din Sahib. He is blessed to have got such a pious and elevated place for his grave. The *dargah* is made of marble and has the following verses inscribed on it:

When Fakhr-ud-Din left the transitory world, that Qutb [pole star] of the eternal world offered him a place at his threshold,

When I enquired of the invisible one the year of the death of that moon, the unseen crier said 'The sun of both worlds'. AH 1199 [CE 1784–85]

Composed by Poet Laureate [Sayyid-us-Shu'ara] Fakhr-ud-Din, the accepted of God, 1222.

All these screens and the gate are very elegantly built of marble, the beauty of which cannot be put into words.

Mosque and Dargah

Adjacent to the *dargah* and near the screens is a mosque. Its status is equivalent to that of Bait-ul-Muqaddis [now known as the Al Aqsa Mosque in Jerusalem] and is definitely as blessed as the House of God in Mecca. There are three parts to it. The first two parts have two wall niches that indicate the direction of Mecca, but are made of mud and were built by Qutub-ul-Aqtab along with his companions, each of whom was a saint in his own right. When Islam Shah built a compound wall around the *dargah* he built a permanent structure in front of this mud wall.

During the reign of Muhammad Farrukhsiyar, when a marble enclosure and gateway were built, he built another section in front of this mosque, which is the third section and has the following inscription:

His exalted majesty the Emperor Farrukhsiyar, the emperor who is a master of the neck ['neck' refers to the people] and is favoured [by God].

Built a beautiful mosque with good intention and firm faith as a place of worship for the old and young.

The invisible crier whispered into the ears of Wisdom the chronogram for when it was erected: 'The accepted abode of God.'

Under the supervision of the despicable . . .' [the rest is illegible]

Baoli Dargah

Though the above mentioned *dargah* and mosque had reached a status of elevation and blessings, there was no water available for the worshippers to perform ritual ablutions before prayers and this led to much inconvenience. Thus, as a means of gaining divine blessings Nadeem-ud-Daulah Khalifat-ul-Mulk, Hafez Muhammad Daud Khan Mustaqeem Jung built an elegant and attractive step well out of the generosity of his heart. Now, members of the public that come here to pray find it convenient as this step well serves as the mosque's tank. Very few people are so blessed as to be able to perform such a wonderful task for such a blessed place.

The construction of this step well commenced in AH 1260 [CE 1844–45] and was completed in AH 1263 [CE 1847]. Hafez Daud Sahib is a very generous and largehearted man and belongs

Mosque and dargah, *including the step well (*baoli)

to a very illustrious family. He is descended from Imam Abu Hanifa Kufi Rahmatullah Alihe and his ancestors held high offices in the royal court.

Hazrat Zill-e-Subhanahu Abu Zafar Siraj-ud-Din Muhammad Bahadur Shah Badshah Ghazi [the emperor] had received guidance in reading the Quran from Hafez Daud Sahib's father Hafez Muhammad Khalil. He has a degree of intimacy with the emperor which no other courtier has achieved. He has been appointed Superintendant [Darogha Nazar Nisar] and also been given charge of the Department of Household Expenses [Khan Samani].

It is difficult to describe all his noble traits and attributes, which are without count. He is always on the lookout for undertaking works of public welfare and this step well is a result of that policy. He has donated hundred copies of the Quran Sharif to a mosque and may God keep him safe as he serves mankind.

MOTI MASJID

This mosque is famous for having been built by Shah Alam Bahadur Shah. It is built completely of marble, even the flooring has areas demarcated with black stone edging that make them look like prayer mats. There is only one wall between this mosque and the *dargah* of Qutub Sahib. The *dargah* is to the east of this mosque and the enclosure with the grave of Shah Alam

Moti Masjid

Bahadur Shah is to its south. There is a door near this enclosure, which is used by the emperor when he visits the Dargah Sharif [Qutub Sahib's *dargah*]. This mosque has three arches and three domes with two marble minarets on the two corners of the mosque's courtyard. The middle dome fell down during an earthquake and was repaired in the reign of Shah Alam.

There were two very attractive cupolas on its minarets, but in AH 1262 [CE 1846] Emperor Abu Zafar Siraj-ud-Din Muhammad Bahadur Shah removed them as they had become old and unsteady and it was feared they would fall down. Alas! No one has had the guidance to repair them.

Muhajjar Shah Alam Bahadur Shah

An elegant and beautiful enclosure[57] built of marble may be seen adjacent to the mosque, Moti Masjid. This enclosure is very attractive; the pristine beauty of its marble has more lustre than a pearl. Its splendour can compete with any palace in heaven. Shah Alam Bahadur Shah's son built this enclosure in AH 1124 [CE 1712–13]. This emperor is buried here and on the screens near the headstone is this inscription:

> According to the sayings of Mustafa [a name of the Prophet] may Shah Alam be rewarded
> by heaven for his good intentions.
> [Written by] Ghulam Hayat Khan AH 1124. [CE 1712–13]

Sultan-e-Aali Gauhar Shah Alam's grave is next to it and has the following verse inscribed on it:

> Alas the sun of the Zenith of Royal Dignity has been concealed below the earth,
> By the gloom of the eclipse of death.
> He is the forgiver and the partner.
> … and may God make paradise his residence.
> [That is to say that Shah Alam, Protector of the World]
> Departed from this world to the pleasure ground of paradise.
> O Sayyid, my miracle-working pen has written a verse,
> Each line of which is a chronogram thereof.
> He was the sun on the face of the earth before this [his death],
> Alas that the sun is buried under the earth.
> The scribe Mir Kallan, the year AH 1221. [CE 1806–07]

Near this grave is the tomb of Moin-ud-Din Muhammad Akbar [Akbar II] Badshah who now resides in heaven.[58] The date of his death is inscribed on the headstone in a chronogram which may be translated as:

> He is God. He is great and powerful,
> Shah Akbar, the giver of light to the world.
> [He] was eclipsed, like the full moon, by death.

Of the date [of his death] Zafar [Victory] said,

The empyrean of heaven is the resting place of the exalted in dignity AH 1253. [CE 1837]

HAKIM AHSANULLAH KHAN BAHADUR'S HAVELI AND MASJID

Though this mansion [*haveli*] and the mosque are new constructions, they have been so beautifully made that I want to describe them. A man, whose munificence and virtuous traits make the ocean appear as a drop, built this mosque and mansion. His wealth can put the treasures of Qaroon[59] to shame. Hakeem Muhammad Ahsanullah Khan was a very honourable and virtuous man and there is hardly anyone high or low who has not benefited from his generosity. He was given the title, Ehtram-ud-Daulah Umdat-ul-Hukma Muttahid–ul-Mulk Haziq-us-Zaman Hakeem Muhammad Ahsanullah Khan Bahadur Sabit-e-Jung.

In reality, the entire administration and magnificence of the Mughal court rests on his shoulders and thus, I wanted to describe this blessed place. This mosque was built in AH 1261 [CE 1845] and the mansion in AH 1263 [CE 1846–47].

Tarikh-e-Masjid: The Year the Mosque Was Built

The construction of this mosque is beauty in action by Ahsanullah Khan, the pious, in the reign of Zafar. 'The house of God is full of light' [is the chronogram for the date of construction].

Tarikh-e-Makaan: The Year the Mansion Was Built

The year of the construction of [this mansion] *near the dargah,*

My spiritual leader sent me a sign.

He looked towards Delhi [Mehrauli].[60]

[It was] constructed by this humble man, Ahsanullah Khan.

MAQBARA ADHAM KHAN/BHOOL BHULAIYYA'N

This is the tomb of Adham Khan, foster brother of Emperor Akbar, who murdered Shams-ud-Din Muhammad Khan Atgha. As punishment, the emperor threw Adham Khan from the ramparts of Agra Fort and killed him. This incident took place on the twelfth [of the Islamic calendar month of] Ramzan AH 969 [16 May 1562], and its chronogram was, 'two murders committed' [*do khun shud*]. The tomb was built after that and we can therefore surmise the date of its construction.

The tomb is made of mortar and stone and has a staircase that leads into a skillfully made labyrinth. The labyrinth runs all round the dome and at one place there is such a trap that a person feels that whichever route he takes will lead him below to the entrance, but

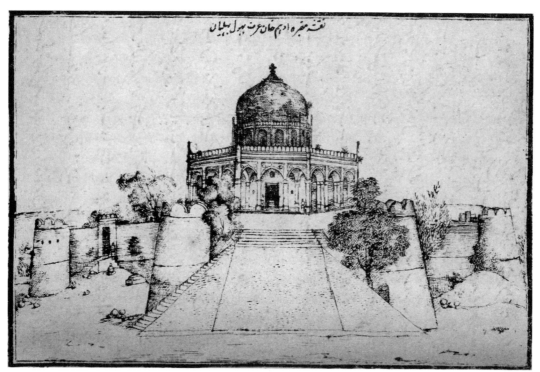

نقشہ مقبرہ ادہم خان حضرت بہول بھلیاں

Maqbara Adham Khan/Bhool Bhulaiyya'n

he keeps ascending further into it. The passage that leads down has been skillfully hidden in one corner, thus escaping notice. It is easy to get lost in it and so it has become famous as the maze [*bhool bhulaiyya'n*] or as 'the place where one gets lost' [*maqam-e-gum gushtagi*].

It is a famous monument among the monuments of Qutub Sahib. Senior British officers came and stayed because of which the cenotaphs have been removed. Though built in Akbar's reign, it is made in the style of the Pathans. One can understand its shape from the sketch.

JOGMAYA TEMPLE

This is a very famous temple near the Qutub Minar on the boundary of Yusuf Sarai. This temple is dedicated to a Hindu Goddess [Jogmaya]. There is a stone in this temple around which a marble screen has been built and people worship it since the days of Rai Pithaura [Prithviraj Chauhan] since approximately 800 to 825 years ago.

I have not been able to get an accurate description of this goddess from any Hindu, but they say Jogmaya was the sister of Krishna avatar and flew here like lightning during an internal feud. Since then, it has become the abode of Jogmaya ji. Some people say that when Rai Pithaura's daughter, Maya, went to Haji Rozbih, many friends accompanied her. When

Jogmaya Temple

Rai Pithaura's daughter converted to Islam her friends, fearing his punishment, were apprehensive of facing Rai Pithaura, and so they all jumped into a well which was near this temple. People say that it is the same well which is still near the temple.

When Raja Pithaura learnt of the incident, he got all their bodies out and cremated them on the site of this temple and said that they had earned *jog* [a union of the individual soul with the divine] and since then this temple has been called Jogmaya and people started offering flowers, sweets and betel leaves [*pan*] here. Slowly it reached the stage where people started calling her a goddess and started praying for their needs here.

These are all stories put out by the hereditary caretakers and priests of every religion to earn money. There is no credible reference for any of these stories.

This temple has three steeples of varying sizes. The steeple with the bell in front of it has the stone, which is worshipped. All the buildings of this temple are of new construction and were built some twenty years ago. Raja Sidhmal, who was a courtier in the reign of Emperor Akbar Shah II, built the present structure. There is a golden pinnacle on the steeple of the temple, which contains a mirror. This mirror casts its reflection for quite a distance. The temple is 41 feet high as measured by the astrolabe.

The buildings of this temple are not very beautiful and seem built more for practical use than beauty. Nevertheless it is a very famous Hindu temple. Every week there is a fair here on a fixed date. The priests here say Jogmaya is more powerful than Kalka Devi, as animals are sacrificed to the latter while flowers are offered to Jogmaya.

The compound of this temple was built in the reign of Akbar Shah II. The sketch has been made in the way it is. When looking at the sketch of this temple, I ponder on the customs of various religions and reflect on the Oneness of God. Every people (nation) has its right path, its faith and its focus of worship.

QILA RAI PITHAURA

This is an ancient fort [*qila*] which is 7 *kos* [15.75 miles] to the south of Shahjahanabad, near Qutub Minar. Even though this fort now lies in ruins, in some places we still find a few remnants of broken walls. One can only imagine its grandeur from these ruins. The ruins of this fort can be seen from a distance of 3 *kos* [6.75 miles]. It encompassed the entire area, including the Rai Pithaura temple and Qutub Minar.

It was built on a small hill and encircled by a moat. This moat was filled with water from nearby jungle streams. A dam was also built here so that this moat would be filled with water all year round. It is learnt from historical texts that Rai Prithviraj – whom the populace calls Pithaura – built this fort in 1198 Bikramajit [Hindu calendar era], 705 solar [*shamsi*] years have passed since. This fort lies in ruins on every side, though remains of some walls can be seen. On the western side stood the Ghazni Darwaza [gateway]; its ruins and the moat can also be seen. I have measured the walls with the help of an astrolabe from this direction.

When I went to sketch this fort, I measured the walls with an astrolabe and found that the fort is at a height of 65 feet from the moat even today, so it must have been much taller before it broke down. The walls are very broad. The wall and bastions have been built from the direction of the moat. Once the wall became equal to the height of the fort, a gap of 17 feet was left and a second 21-feet-wide wall has been built. Then, after leaving a gap of 11 feet towards the fort, another 8-feet-wide wall has been built. It seems certain that merlons were also built on this wall. One can see the present state of this fort from the sketch and is a reminder of the previous era.

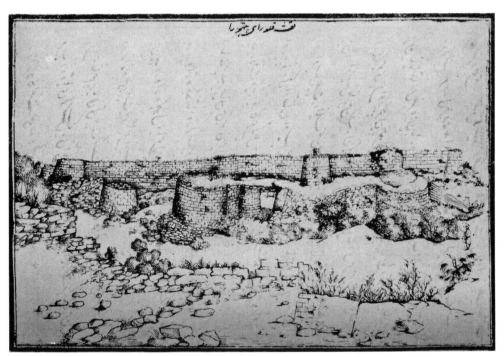

Qila Rai Pithaura

Dargah Baba Haji Rozbih

In the middle of the dried-up moat of this fort, under a neem tree, is the *dargah* of Baba Haji Rozbih. He was a much-respected saint who came to this area in the reign of Rai Pithaura and settled in the moat outside the fort. The astrologers of Rai Pithaura's kingdom prophesied that the coming of Haji Rozbih predicted the advent of Muslim rule and that is indeed what happened. They say that Rai Pithaura's daughter became his disciple and converted to Islam; it is said that the woman's grave near Baba Haji Rozbih's grave is that of Rai Pithaura's daughter. During his lifetime, Baba Haji Rozbih had many Hindu disciples who converted to Islam. When he passed away, he was buried in the same place where he used to live.

> Brother! The world remains with none,
>
> Bind the heart to the Creator, it is enough.

MAQBARA SULTAN GHAZI

Hazrat Sultan Ghazi's mausoleum is very beautiful, elegant and pleasing to the heart. It is situated 2 *kos* [5 miles] from the *dargah* of Qutub Sahib, towards the west. Sultan Shams-ud-Din Altamash built it in AH 720 [CE 1320–21]. It has buildings all around it with a small mosque built completely of marble in the west.

Maqbara Sultan Ghazi

In the centre is a cave which one enters by going down fifteen steps. Columns built inside it have covered the cave and the saintly prince is buried inside it. On the roof outside is an octagonal platform with a marble plinth and a base of lime and mortar. The height of this platform [*chabutra*] is 4.7 ½ feet. Every part of the platform is 15 feet and 1.5 inches and its total measurement is 121 feet. On the eastern side of the platform are seven steps and the entrance to the cave is on the south.

It is said that this entrance was earlier locked and people would pay homage to the platform itself. It was opened in the reign of Tughlaq Shah after which people started going inside to pay obeisance. This entrance is very small and measures 1.11 feet in width and 3.9 feet in height. There is a shortage of water here and people who visit face problems. The nearest water source is 2 to 2.5 *kos* [5 to 6.25 miles] away. At this point, I will the sketch the tomb. The sketch of the gateway will be given separately.

The Gateway to Sultan Ghazi's Dargah

The gateway to this *dargah* is very beautifully made, with a threshold [*chaukhat*] of marble. The wall around it is made of strong quartzite stone set upon a high plinth. There are four

The gateway to Dargah Sultan Ghazi

bastions on the four corners. The entrance to the tomb is to the east, and up to the level of the plinth it is made of quartzite; beyond that the threshold and the gate are made of marble. The gateway to this tomb is made of marble with Quranic calligraphy in Naskh and Kufic script along with inscriptions. Whatever I could read, I have written down and placed flowers in the portions, which I could not:

> This blessed building was commanded to be created by the great Sultan, the exalted Emperor, the lord of the necks of the people,[61] the shadow of God in the world, the bestower of safety on the (believers, the heir of the Kingdom of Sulaiman, the Master of the Seal in the Kingdom of the World) the Sultan of Sultans, Shams-ud-dunya-wa-Din who is especially favoured by the Lord of the Worlds, Abu Muzaffar Altamush [Altamash] the Sultan, the Helper of the Chief of the Faithful, may God perpetuate his rule, as a mausoleum for the King of Kings of the East Abul Fath Mahmood, may God forgive him with his indulgence and make him dwell in the centre of the paradise in [the months of] the year 629. [CE 1231–32]

This dargah is very beautifully built and is on such a high plinth that one has to climb twenty-two steps to enter inside. I am placing its sketch here and one can see its beauty in that.

HAUZ-E-KHAS AND MAQBARA FIROZ SHAH

This is a very beautiful reservoir [hauz] built by Firoz Shah and must have been very pleasing to the eye. Once upon a time it must have been so beautiful that people must have been uncontrollably drawn to it. It must have been a lovely place of rest and recreation [sairgah] but now exists in a bad state to the extent that it can't even retain water and stays dry. The peasants have started growing crops in it.

There are buildings towards the south of this reservoir, where Firoz Shah's tomb is also located. There is a limestone inscription on the façade of the gate, which is now broken in many places. Whatever is left of the inscription reads:

> Sultan Firoz Shah, may his dust be sanctified and paradise be his resting place....

Therefore, it seems probable that this reservoir was also made in the same era. This tomb was built by Sultan Muhammad Shah bin Sultan Firoz Shah who became the emperor in AH 793 [CE 1390–91] after the death of his nephew Abu Bakr Shah bin Zafar Khan bin Firoz Shah. This reservoir is situated on a large expanse of land measuring over 100 bighas with many small pavilions built on it. One of the pavilions contains the following inscription:

> This monument was built in the reign of Sultan-ul-Azam Sikandar Shah Sultan. May he get a place in heaven for Sheikh Shahab-ud-Din Taq Jaan and Sultan Abu Saeed.

Near it at a distance of a kos [2.25 miles] is the mausoleum of Mir Khan Wazir Khan who was a noble in the reign of Firoz Shah. The administrative divisions of Mirpur and

Maqbara Firoz Shah, Hauz-e-Khas

Wazirpur have been named after him. Muhammadpur has an unknown mausoleum. However, these mausoleums do not merit a sketch and only Firoz Shah's mausoleum has been sketched.

BADIH MANZIL, [FAMOUS AS] BIJAI MANDAL

This is a building in front of Hauz Khas along the road which goes towards Qutub Sahib. Built by Firoz Shah, it is very lofty and majestic, and is also called 'Jahannuma' [World-reflecting] or 'Badih' [Extraodinary] Manzil [Building]. Somewhere along the line, people have begun calling it Bijai Mandal [possibly a corruption of Badih Manzil]. From a perusal of historical texts, it is found that this building was constructed in the same period when Firoz Shah built Firozabad which was constructed in [AH] 755 [CE 1354]. This may have been built a few years later.

The shape of this building is very unique. A four-door room has been built on the top of a lofty building with a staircase running up the wall for access. On top of this room, there used to be a beautiful 12-arched pavilion [*baradari*] which is in ruins now. Such buildings were built for the king to inspect his troops and that must be the purpose for constructing this one too. They say that Firoz Shah had built a 3 *kos*-long tunnel [6.75 miles] from Firozabad through which horsemen could go all the way to Hauz Khas via Badih Manzil

نقشہ بیرنی منزل جو فیخے منڈل

Badih Manzil/Bijai Mandal

[Bijai Mandal]. Now, the whole monument is in ruins but its size and shape can be seen in the sketch I have made.

MASJID BEGUMPUR

Near Bijai Mandal lies Begumpur where Khan-e-Jahan Khan-e-Firoz Shahi [Sultan Firoz Shah's prime minister] has constructed a mosque. It is very similar to the Khirki mosque. I didn't find the building attractive enough to sketch, so have left it out.

MOTH KI MASJID

This is a very famous and eminent mosque. People say that this mosque dates back to the Shahjahan era but I don't agree, as the building seems to be from the [Lodi] Pathan era. There is no inscription on it to indicate its year of construction. The mosque has five arches with two additional but smaller ones on each side, which have steps. Its gateway, now broken, used to be very beautiful with Quranic calligraphy inscribed on marble.

They say that the emperor once picked up a grain of *moth* [a type of legume] from the

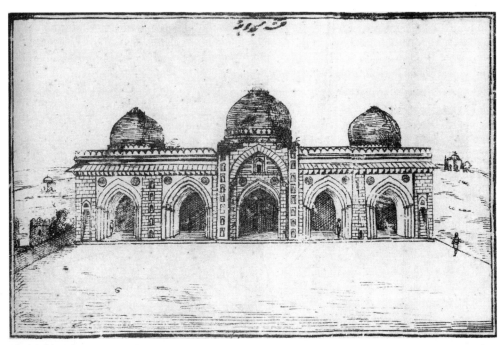

Moth ki Masjid

ground, sowed it and repeated the process over the years till a lot of money was collected from the sale of the harvests. The proceeds were used to build this mosque, which is why it is called 'the mosque built from one *moth*' [*ek moth ki masjid*]. There is no doubt that this mosque is very grand but now peasants have built their huts within and have begun living inside it. The sketch of the mosque is given here.

TI-BURJA

Near Masjid Moth are three domed tombs [*ti-burja*]. They also lie close to Mubarakpur Kotla [see below] and have been there since the reign of the Pathans but no one knows whose tombs these are. It is not known under which Pathan king they were built, but according to legend, one domed tomb is that of Bade Khan, one of Chhote Khan and the third of Kale Khan.

The construction of two of the domed tombs isn't very good and is in fact of such inferior quality that I doubt if it belongs to the Pathan era either. The biggest domed tomb is better constructed and is definitely from the Pathan period. It is built of lime and quartzite and red sandstone has been used in places. It seems that it was probably built towards the end of the [Lodi] Pathan rule. Even though not much is known about these monuments whatever we know is enough. Therefore I provide the sketch here which includes all three domed tombs.

Ti-burja

MUBARAKPUR KOTLA

Mubarakpur Kotla [the Citadel of Mubarakpur] is actually a village at a distance of 3 to 4 *kos* [6.75 to 9 miles] from Shahjahanabad and it has a mausoleum. From its construction, it seems to be from the period of Sher Shah and Islam Shah. Isa Khan's mausoleum near Humayun's tomb is built in the same style. However, this mausoleum is famously known as Mubarak Shah's mausoleum, and this village is thus known as Mubarakpur Kotla.

The mausoleum is very beautifully made of local quartzite and is worth seeing. The building is very attractive, with a beautiful octagonal circumambulatory aisle all around it. If one takes this to be the tomb of Muiz-ud-Din Abul Fath Mubarak Shah, then it was built some 425 years ago [sic] as Mubarak Shah died on the fifth day [of the Islamic calendar month of] Ramzan in AH 837 [15 April 1434]. However, I don't think that this building is that old. I am placing its sketch here.

DARGAH SHAH-E-MARDAN

This *dargah* is located in front of Mansoor's tomb. There is an imprint of a foot on a slab of marble which is said to be that of Hazrat Amir-ul-Momineen Ali Karamallah Wajhu. That is why this place is also known as Aliji or Shah-e-Mardan. Many other buildings have sprung up around

نقشه مقبره مبارک پور کوتلا

Maqbara Mubarakpur Kotla

it. This footprint has been placed in a marble tank on which the following verse is inscribed:

> *On the piece of ground where there is a mark of your foot.*
>
> *For years there will be prostrations by men of insight.*
>
> The year AH 1173 [CE 1759–60]

Under the tank is laid out marble flooring and a marble enclosure has been built around it. It is a very venerated building and is always crowded with people. The twentieth of every lunar month[62] is celebrated with great pomp and splendour, and huge crowds gather in the [Islamic calendar] month of Moharram.

Burj Kasa Hazrat Fatima

Near this enclosure is a pavilion into which men are not allowed, as it is said to contain an imprint of the *kasa* or cup of Bibi Fatima, the Prophet's (peace be upon him) daughter.

Jahaz

There is a huge courtyard near this pavilion. It is said that a rich merchant whose prayers had been answered here, built it as fulfillment of his vow and called it 'Jahaz'.

Dargah Shah-e-Mardan

Majlis Khana

Near the pavilion is an arcaded hallway built by Ishrat Ali Khan, used for purposes of congregation and the singing of elegies during the [Islamic calendar] month of Moharram [*marsiya khwani*];[63] that is why it is called a congregation hall [*majlis khana*]. The following was inscribed on a piece of marble built into the wall on the left side of the arch on the south-east corner:

> *At the court of the Emperor of both the worlds, Ali, the king of heroes and the friend of God.*
> *By order of the renowned king Akbar, when Ishrat Ali Khan adorned the place,*
> *I enquired of the Sayyid the year of its foundation and he wrote, 'Nazir built it.'* AH 1223. [CE 1808–09]

Naqqar Khana[64]

Sadiq Ali Khan got a beautiful gateway built, housing the drum-house [*naqqar khana*] near this monument on which a date is inscribed:

> *When Sadiq Ali built a high edifice at the threshold of Haidar[65]*
> *For the date of the foundation [chronogram] of that edifice Sadiq said, 'the drum house'*
> *The year* AH 1230. [CE 1814–15]

The Boundary Wall

These buildings are enclosed within a permanent boundary wall [ahatah] with a date inscribed on its north gateway:

> Muhammad the friend of God said,
> I am the city of learning and Ali its gateway.

In AH 1162 [CE 1748–49] in the auspicious reign of Ahmad Shah Bahadur Badshah Ghazi, the building of the fort, congregation hall, mosque and tank was completed in one year, according to the orders of Nawab Qudsia Hazrat Sahiba Zamania under the supervision of Nawab Bahadur Javed Khan Sahib and under the control of the humble Lutf Ali Khan. AH 1164 [CE 1750–51]. I will place the sketch of the *dargah* here.

KARBALA

Mirza Ashraf Beg Khan got a permanent boundary wall made around a piece of land near this compound where the *taziyas*[66] of the entire city are buried during [the Islamic calendar month of] Moharram. This area is known as Karbala.

MAQBARA NAJAF KHAN

Near this *dargah* is the tomb of Najaf Khan who was the prime minister[67] of the Mughal Emperor. The date [of his death] is inscribed on his tomb.

MANSOOR KA MAQBARA

This is the famous mausoleum that holds the tomb of Mansoor Ali Khan Safdarjung [famous today as Safdarjung's Tomb] who was the Prime Minister of Emperor Ahmad Shah. The beauty of this monument is beyond words. It is made completely of red sandstone interspersed with stripes of marble. Its dome is made of marble and marble has been used up to the dados inside the tomb. The headstone of the tomb is also of marble.

The actual grave is in the basement below it. The monument is so delicate and finely made that there is nothing comparable to it. The planning of the structure and gardens has been very well done. The enclosing wall, made of lime and stone, has beautifully designed gardens inside it. There are canals and tanks on all sides which are still flourishing.

There are attractive buildings built on three sides of the garden. The one on the south is called Moti Mahal. English sahibs stay in Moti Mahal for enjoyment and recreation. The one on the west is called Jungli Mahal and is very attractive. The elegant and beautiful building on the north is known as the Emperor's Favourite [*Badshah Pasand*]. To the east is a lofty gateway with numerous rooms and apartments built in it. There is a very attractive twelve-arched pavilion built on the gate and a suitable place for rest and recreation.

There is a beautiful mosque near the gateway towards the north, which is built of red sandstone. It is very unfortunate that prayers are not held here.[68] There are cupolas on the four corners of the compound wall with very fine-latticed screens of red stone which give it a very attractive look. The lattice screens of the cupolas give the effect of clouds swirling. This tomb was built under the supervision of Shaidi Bilal Muhammad Khan at a cost of Rs 3 lakh. The date is inscribed on a marble slab over the gateway:

> *Ya Allah!*
> *When the brave hero departed from the transitory world,*
> *The following date of* [his departure] *was written 'may he be a resident of the highest paradise'* AH 1167. [CE 1753–54]

Khairpur

In front of Mansoor Ali Khan Safdarjung's tomb is a very attractive domed pavilion, which bears great similarity to the tomb in Mubarakpur Kotla and Isa Khan's tomb. I haven't been able to ascertain the exact date, but it is undoubtedly from the Pathan period. There must have been a nobleman after whom this village was named, and these tombs are his and those

Mansoor ka Maqbara/Safdarjung's Tomb

Khairpur

of his family members. The building is extremely attractive, as can be seen from the sketch.

Masjid-o-Maqbara

Near this domed pavilion is a mosque and mausoleum from the Pathan era but I couldn't find any details regarding them. The mosque near the tomb is very elegantly built. Though built of lime and mortar, its ornamentation is exquisite. Quranic verses are inscribed on the façade in plaster. Peasants are living inside this *dargah* and have spoilt the entire monument. Whatever condition it is in can be seen clearly in the sketch.

Maqbara Sultan Sikandar Bahlol

In front of these domed pavilions is another very attractive pavilion which bears great similarity to the tomb in Mubarkpur Kotla and the tomb of Isa Khan. This is the tomb of Nizam Khan, whose title was Sultan Sikandar Shah bin Bahlol Lodi. This tomb must have been built soon after Sikandar Shah died, on the thirteenth [of the Islamic calendar month] of Zil Qada, AH 915 [22 February 1510]. Around 348 years have passed since then [sic]. This monument is also very beautiful and this can be seen clearly from the sketch that I will place here.

Masjid-o-Maqbara

Maqbara Sultan Sikandar Bahlol Lodi

JANTAR MANTAR

Jantar in Hindi means an instrument used for observing the stars, but in common parlance people refer to these instruments as *jantar mantar*. These instruments are used for observing stars and were built in the reign of Muhammad Shah Badshah under the supervision of famous Hindu and Muslim mathematicians. It is worth a close look to observe the attention to detail paid while making these complicated instruments that make even the celestial arrangement seem comprehensible thanks to their vast reach.

Alas! These instruments are now in a state of disrepair and have broken in many places. Instead of an observatory, this place is now a lavatory! There are such heaps of excrement and dung that I found it difficult to stand there and make a sketch because of the stench coming from it. All that is on earth will perish [*kullo man Alaihe fa'an*].

This building is an observatory and is a sign of the passage of time and a testimony to the changing fortunes of men. I will need a separate book to describe the workmanship, use and effectiveness of these instruments. If life supports me and God is willing, I will write an article on them. Here, I make a sketch of these instruments. Please note that many have broken down and only four instruments are left standing which I will describe along with their sketches.

Miqiyas

This [the *miqiyas*] is an excellent instrument with many uses. Its structure is such that it is built like an equatorial sundial [*madalun nahar*]. Each part is 10 inches and 4 *ashr* (1/10th) and has an upper and lower level. Each part was divided into 10 parts which were then further sub-divided into 6 parts each. Thus, every part had 60 minutes [*daqiqa*] because of this division.

There is a sidewall/ramp [*pakha*] and there are 66 stairs to climb to the top. However, the last 5 steps are broken. The rest are intact. This ramp is 116 feet from top to bottom. There was a perpendicular pole (for a tent) made on the top where the telescope would be kept for observation. Similarly there are stairs on both sides of the sundial arcs to facilitate the observation of shadows.

There was a basement below it which is now filled with mud and thus closed. The basement had a small hole and astronomers would sit in there and observe the stars through it. This arc is 106 feet and the walls of the staircases are 2 feet wide, every step is 1 foot and 5½ inches each. This can be seen in the sketch.

Karah-i-Maqar

[A spherical instrument.] Two concave hemispheres are placed below this observatory in such a way that the axis of the zodiac is incomplete without each in place. The sphere or

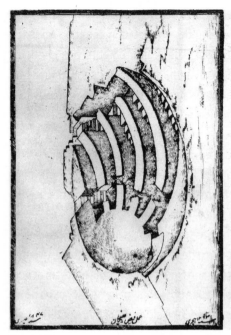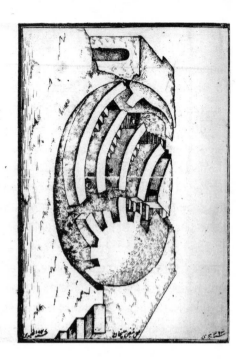

Karah-i-Maqar

karah is completed only when one half is placed on the other. There are twelve arcs in these spheres. The signs of the zodiac have been divided such that six are filled in and six are empty.

Towards the south, there is a small iron nail which has been uprooted now. Both the southern and northern parts are now in ruins. A mark has been made to denote mid-day. Four platforms have been built around these arcs from where the shadows inside were observed. In every empty arc, there are stairs that allow one to climb to the top.

The diameter of these spheres is 26.7 feet. It is difficult to make an exact sketch but I have tried to do the best I could. Look at this and think of its shape.

Davair-uz-Zil

Between these two instruments, towards the south, are four levels of concentric circles [*davair-uz-zil*] to measure shadows. The four levels have been built like a well with one level sunk into the ground and three above the ground. This has then been further divided into sixty sections, in which niches have been created, and which are left alternatively open or filled up.

In the middle is a perpendicular pole [*umud*] which is a measuring instrument [*miqyas*]. Its width is 17.1 feet and half the diameter [*nisf qatar*] is 24 feet, excluding the perpendicular

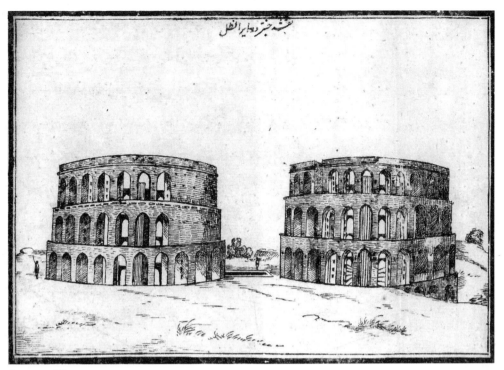

Davair-uz-Zil

pole. The pole's circumference is 5.8 feet. Thus, the total horizontal circumference of the circle would be 53 feet and 8 inches. There are steps inside which are filled and empty to denote numbers. I will give the sketches of these circles here.

Qasih Dair-ul-Uzam

This is another measuring instrument located to the north of the first instrument. This instrument is a raised platform with has four arcs, two towards the west and two towards the east. The inner arc has a circumference of 20.9 feet. There is one more arc with a circumference of 32 feet and a few inches. There are stairs on both sides of the arc so that the effect of the shadows can be studied. Each arc [originally] had measurement units to record the time and zodiac. However the signs on this raised platform have now all been erased, and the arcs are also broken in many places. I am making a sketch which will describe it better.

DARGAH QADAM SHARIF

This is a very famous *dargah* and houses the grave of Prince Fatah Khan, son of Firoz Shah and the imprint of the [foot of the] the Prophet, peace be upon him. A miracle of the Prophet

Qasih Dair-ul-Uzam

Muhammad resulted in his footprint being imprinted on stone.[v] It is said that one of those stones with the footprint came to Firoz Shah and when his beloved son died, he installed it on his son's chest in order to sanctify [the body]. He made various buildings, a school and a mosque around it. There is a big tank near this *dargah*.

Firoz Shah built all the old monuments in this *dargah*. There is a marble enclosure on top of the grave and this is filled with water and devotees wash the blessed footprint [*qadam mubarak*] of the Prophet in it and take the water away as a token of blessing [*tabarruk*]. They take it far and wide and recite this verse:

O Khizr, the heart finds solace when one drinks it,

The water of Qadam Sharif is the elixir of life.

On the twelfth of [the Islamic calendar month of] Rabi Awwal, an annual fair is held to celebrate the birthday of the Prophet, peace be upon him. It attracts huge crowds that include thousands of mendicants [*malangs* and *faqirs*] who gather near the entrance and

[v] *Quasida-e-Hamzia.*

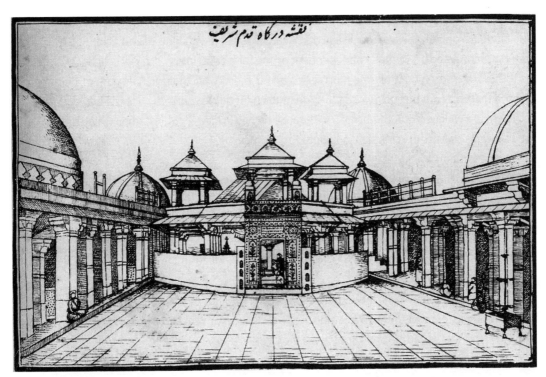

Dargah Qadam Sharif

enjoy themselves to the tune of their own music and songs. This *dargah* has many gateways and this verse is inscribed on the eastern one:

> There is no God but Allah and Muhammad is His prophet.
> Muhammad Mir, custodian of the chinaware of Emperor Alamgir.

On a marble slab over the eastern entrance to the inner enclosure of the shrine is inscribed:

> The guide of those who have lost their way [is] Muhammad; the director of directors is Muhammad.
> Glorious is the school, the pulpit and the court where is read the praise of Muhammad.
> For the broken-hearted he is balm, for the hearts of the afflicted he is medicine.
> The sky becomes secure under the feet of him who has become the dust of the foot of Muhammad.
> I am one of the dogs of his lane, and Shirwan has become a beggar of Muhammad.
> Shirwan Khan, son of Raihan Khan the Abyssinian, wrote these lines on the twenty-third of [the Islamic calendar month of] *Rabia II of the year* AH 1082. [29 August 1671].

DARGAH KHWAJA BAQI BILLAH

This is the *dargah* of Khwaja Baqi Billah and Allah is pleased with him. Hazrat Baqi Billah is very well known and his fame is not dependent on me for a description, so I will only describe his tomb. The *dargah* built of lime mortar lies under the sky and has such an aura of being blessed that it cannot be put in words. In spite of the heat of the sun, this place is always cool.

There is a wall near the tombstone with many niches in it for lighting lamps which bears the following long poem in Persian [*qasida*]:

> *He* [God] *is immortal.*
>
> *The qibla of spiritual persons[69] and the Ka'ba of religious people, the object of Divine Grace and the master of true knowledge.*
>
> *The defender of the religion of the Prophet, the most perfect leader of the pious, the recipient of the revered grace, and the descendant of the last of the prophets [Muhammad].*
>
> *The revealer of the supreme secrets, having knowledge of the truth ascertained by evidence, absorbed in the sacred person and faithfully firm with God.*
>
> *Ghaus-e-Azam,[70] having the faith in the Lord of the Universe, a Qutub (pole star) showing the right way to the world and the significance of the true faith in God.*

Dargah Hazrat Khwaja Baqi Billah

Perfect, of excellent manner, the guide to the firm path [religion] a sea of knowledge of God and the chief of the wise.

The will and pleasure of God is manifested through his person and disposition; this dignity is from the beloved of the Lord of the universe [the Prophet].

The Light of God shone on his forehead through true faith and the hearts of the true believers were brightened by the felicity of his attention.

How can I praise him, the best of saints? The person of Khwaja Baqi is a blessing for the worlds, Baqi was a gift of God and verily he continued to be a refuge to men and angels by the grace of God.

Khwajgi Amkana was the spiritual guide of that king of religion, but he belonged to the sect of Owais and knew the secrets of religion.

As his perfection was ever to have communion with [God] and its meaning was stamped on his heart, he was absorbed at last into the invisible[71] at the age of forty. Know, the year of the death of the polestar of the age and the support of Muslims was 1012 after the flight. Whoever comes to his shrine with sincerity and belief, his desires will be fulfilled, as well as his secular and religious objects.

The helpless and sinning rubs his forehead at his threshold, so that there may descend the regard of compassion, as well as salvation on the day of Judgement.

May the blessing of the Lord of the Universe descend upon Muhammad Khwaja Baqi, who is one of the favoured saints.

Copy of the original verses, executed by the pen of the sinner Abul Muazzam Siraj-ud-Din Ahmad during the time of Mir Amir Ali Sahib's taking over as spiritual successor in 1319.

DARGAH SAYYID HASAN RASUL NUMA

Dargah Sayyid Hasan Rasul Numa

Hazrat Sayyid Hasan Rasul Numa[72] was a descendant of Sayyid Usman of Narnaul. He is so famous and well-known that he needs no description. Through his piety, he had reached such a degree of closeness to the Prophet, peace be upon him, that he could enable others to see the Prophet [*Rasul*] too [probably in their dreams or subconscious]. That is why he was given the title of '*Rasul Numa*' [Revealer of the Prophet]. On a piece of marble over the central arch of the southern verandah is inscribed the chronogram:

Rasul Numa remained firm with the Prophet.

Written by the sinning slave Yaqut Raqam Khan alias Ibadull AH *1103* (CE 1691–92)

On a piece of marble that is set in the west hall of the inner enclosure, the following line is inscribed:

Hasan Rasul Numa the most glorious of the descendants of Hussain, the second Owais Qarni and the third Hasnain[73] 1103.

[CE 1691–92]

BHOOLI BHATIYARI KA MAHAL

This monument is on a small hill beyond Hazrat Rasul Numa's tomb and shrine. It was built by Bu Ali Khan Pathan[74] and people have started calling it Bhooli Bhatiyari Mahal. Since it sits on an elevation, one gets a beautiful view of the scenic beauty all around the hill. The scene is beautiful especially during monsoon when the water is running down the slopes and the entire area is green and verdant.

Every year, all the Brahmans of the city with an interest in astronomy put their flagstaff in the ground and predict the weather thereafter. There is a fair called 'Parcha ka Mela' and Hindus and Muslims participate in it in great numbers.

Masjid Sirhindi

MASJID SIRHINDI

This mosque is situated outside Lahori Darwaza. It was built completely of red sandstone by Sirhindi Begum, wife of Emperor Shahjahan. The mosque has three beautiful domes and a large, attractive courtyard. Marvah Ikram's inn stood outside Lahori Darwaza and saw a great movement of people. The congregation at prayer times used to be quite large but once the inn was demolished on the orders of the Company [East India Company] very few people come here to pray except during the evening prayers. The boundary wall has also been destroyed. Though this is a very old mosque, it has been so strongly built that it can last till Doomsday!

It is said that the inn was a very busy one and it was so crowded at all times that it was difficult to walk. There would be such huge crowds of vendors outside its gates that it seemed like a proper market. It not only served travellers staying at the inn, but also residents of the city. Many would come there just to enjoy the sights and sounds. There is a very beautiful inscription on its gate giving its date of construction.[75]

KOTHI JANAB SAHIB BAHADUR DAAM IQBALAHU

This mansion [kothi] is situated outside Kashmiri Darwaza [gateway]. It was built by the just ruler, dispenser of justice, the ruler of the time, the Nausherwan of the age, founder of justice,

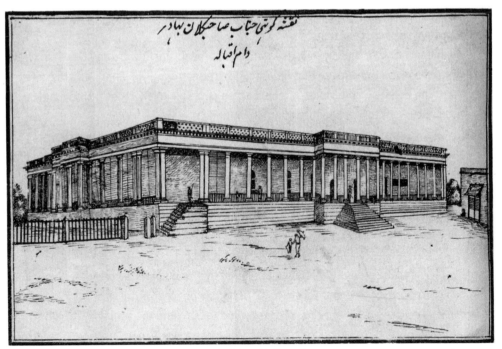

Kothi Janab Sahib-e-Kalan Bahadur Daam Iqbalahu [Metcalfe House]

of just disposition, the most honourable person of the government, custodian of the country, the exalted son and most beloved of the emperor, Sir Thomas Theophilus Metcalfe Baronet Bahadur Firoz Jung Sahib Senior, resident of Dar-ul-Khilafat Shahjahanabad.

It is so immense that if another universe was to be created it could fit in here. It would be suitable to say without any exaggeration that it is the envy of the garden in paradise [Iram] and even paradise itself would be jealous of it. Every possible decoration and all types of ornamentation are present here. The walls are so beautifully polished that they reflect like a mirror and create a mirage when there is a breeze. This is an extremely beautiful mansion. It is very worthy of this verse:

> What a beautiful monument, that the spectator
>
> Cannot tear away his gaze from it.

A whole book can be written in its praise. Each part of the mansion is more beautiful than the last and one doesn't want to leave any part of it to go to the other.

QUDSIA BAGH

Qudsia Bagh is a garden [bagh] located very close to the mansion of Kalan Bahadur Daam Iqbalah [Sir Thomas Metcalfe] outside Kashmiri Darwaza. It was built by Nawab Qudsia Begum and seems to have been built many years ago. Within it is a very beautiful and lofty mosque in red sandstone. A big twelve-arched pavilion has also been built in the garden with very attractive alcoves for sitting.

Behind the twelve-arched pavilion is a garden with beautiful flowers and trees which are the envy of the world. The breeze that flows from here seems as rejuvenating as the breezes of heaven. The beauty of the violets in this garden puts the lovely faces of the maidens to shame and they want to hide their faces as a result.

The water from its stream seems as life-giving as a stream from heaven. Every tree is the envy of a tall man and every blossom the envy of a beautiful maiden. Its stream is prettier than the Milky Way and its greenery more attractive than any other garden. The garden provides a view of the Yamuna River and one can see people enjoying themselves on the river from here. It is a wondrous spectacle – the beautiful river on one side and the verdant garden on the other.

NIGAMBODH GHAT

This is an area for the cremation of dead bodies of the Hindus and is considered very holy. They believe that anybody cremated here will definitely be forgiven all sins. The Hindus also believe that a corpse burnt here requires less wood to burn and the soul gains a high status in the afterlife. Here, I am reminded of an anecdote when a Hindu man described the virtues of this land as a cremation place that it requires less wood to cremate a dead body here. The

لعثه باغ قدسیه

Qudsia Bagh

Muslim replied that it went to prove that the stratum of the earth, which contains fire, is very close to this place.

Another reason for the piety attached to this place is that priests keep themselves busy in prayers near *Neeli Chhatri*, a temple across the river near Salimgarh Fort. A unique crowd of men and women come to bathe here and the beauty of the scene even affects the sun which comes out orange. It is beyond my ability to describe the beauty of the ladies who come here to bathe every morning; all I can say is that if the sun's path were not fixed it would feel shy to come out.

> Patience and tolerance are both ended in heresy,
>
> The power of control and restraint was lost,
>
> and fell into the hands of the infidels.
>
> Beware and avoid the beautiful waists decorated with the sacred thread,
>
> They waylay travelers on the highway,
>
> Who have wealth and property of [Islamic] faith.
>
> And in the morning they loot and take away,
>
> The wealth of the heart and soul.

Nigambodh Ghat

NEELI CHHATRI[76]

This is a small domed-pavilion built like a building with a curved roof and is famous as *Neeli Chhatri* [the Blue Canopy]. Humayun Badshah built it in AH 939 [CE 1532–33] near Salimgarh on the banks of the river towards Nigambodh Ghat. Humayun Badshah would often sit here and enjoy the beauty of the river. Some even call it the pavilion of Emperor Jahangir. The Hindus say that it is an ancient ruined edifice and that Humayun built a new structure on the same location. There must have been an ancient canopy here from the time of the Pandavas which was demolished by Emperor Humayun and replaced by this new building. Emperor Jahangir repaired this and got an inscription put in it. The first inscription reads:

> *O Revealer, God is Great.*
>
> *At the time when the King of the seven climes, Nur-ud-Din Jahangir, the King champion of the faith, started from his capital Agra for paradise-like Kashmir, this verse came to his inspired tongue.*

[An impromptu verse by Jahangir Shah Akbar]:

> *What a graceful and happy place,*
> *The seat of a dweller in Paradise.*
> *The fourteenth year of the reign of Jahangir corresponding to AH 1028. [CE 1618–19]*

The inscription put up on his return:

> O Protector. God is Great.
>
> When the Emperor, the protector of the World, returned from the delightful country of
> Kashmir and honoured this place of Grace with his presence, he ordered that this verse
> also be engraved: Humayun Shah, son of Shah Babur, whose pure blood is [drawn] from
> Sahib Qiran [Taimur].
>
> The sixteenth year of the propitious reign of Jahangir, corresponding to AH 1030. [CE
> 1620–21].

Emperor Humayun was given the title of Jannat Ashiyani after his death.

THE GARDENS

There were many beautiful gardens outside Lahori Darwaza and Kashmiri Darwaza. Sirhindi
Bagh, Roshan Ara Bagh, Mahaldar Khan Bagh and Shalimar Bagh are all from the reign of
Shahjahan. Hamid Ali Khan Bahadur's Bagh and Bagh Janab Maulana Sadr-ud-Din Khan
Bahadur were built recently. However, I have not described them as it is such a waste of time
now. [All the gardens lay in ruins at the time Sir Sayyid was writing this book.]

Editor's Notes

1. Not to be confused with the Diwan-e-Aam, the Hall of Public Audience.
2. One *kos* is equivalent to 2.25 miles.
3. History books today refer to him as Sultan Muhammad bin Tughlaq.
4. 'Shah' in a name, here Giyas-ud-Din Shah, indicates rulership and the fact that he was the sultan.
5. An inscription placed on the southern side by the Indian Archaeological Society states that this tomb houses the remains of Zafar Khan who was a general under the Khilji rulers. Thus, this grave was probably already present and was incorporated into Sultan Ghiyas-ud-Din Tughlaq's tomb.
6. The third of the four ages described in the Hindu scriptures.
7. *Samt* probably corresponds to the word *Samvat*, the Hindu calendar era.
8. Verses from the Quran starting with the word '*Qul*' (four in all, in the Holy Book) are recited and consecrated to the memory of the saint.
9. *Quddisa sirru-hu-ul-Aziz* is the honorific used.
10. Today it is commonly believed that Sultan Bahlol Lodi died in CE 1489.
11. In India, the west is the direction of *qibla* (the direction of the Ka'ba) and the Islamic faithful face westwards when offering prayers.
12. Maulvi Zafar Hasan writes that Sir Sayyid erroneously assigns to this tomb an inscription found on the doorway of the tomb of Sheikh Ala-ud-Din. I have therefore quoted the correct inscription taken from Maulvi Zafar Hasan's book.
13. The term '*khwaja sara*' refers to eunuchs who held many important posts during this period. Depending on their talents they were chosen to serve in the army, in the administration, to protect the royal harem etc., and many rose to very high positions. Therefore, Basti Khwaja Sara must have held a fairly important position and been a person of means to be able to build such a tomb for himself.
14. Sir Sayyid has quoted a saying [*hadith*] of the Prophet, substituting the word *auliya* [saint] for the word *ulema*.
15. More specifically: a hall near the entrance where the male head of the household meets formal guests. Women would rarely enter the *diwan khana* which was always located in the section apportioned to the males of the household [*mardana*].
16. Nawab Haji Begum and Hamida Bano Begum are two different people. Gul Badan Begum, the writer of *Humayun Nama*, identifies Bega Begum as Haji Begum, Humayun's first cousin and first wife.
17. He is said to have saved Humayun from drowning when the latter was fleeing after the battle of Chausa. '*Saqqa*' means water-carrier, so Nizam Saqqa must have been a water-carrier by profession.
18. Today, this area is known as the Hazrat Nizam-ud-Din Basti.
19. In *Asar-2*, Sir Sayyid has corrected this to 17 which is the accurate date [2 April 1325].
20. A descendent of Hashim, the ancestor of Prophet Muhammad.
21. Penultimate Mughal ruler (ruled from 1806–1837) succeeded by the dynasty's last ruler Bahadur Shah Zafar II.
22. As seen from the sketch and otherwise, the *Dargah* Mosque actually has only three domes. However, since both *Asar-1* and *Asar-2* state it has five domes, one can only assume there may have been a typesetting error during the printing of both the original works.
23. The queens were all addressed as *Nawab Sahiba*. In addition, some were also given titles, such as Malika-e-Jahan [Queen of the World].
24. The tomb has been encroached upon but the Aga Khan Trust for Culture is at present in the process of restoring it. The calligraphy is indeed stunning and surprisingly intact.
25. Azam Khan was killed by Adham Khan in CE 1561.
26. The words 'Takka', 'Tagha' and 'Atagha' were used to indicate that Emperor Akbar considered Azam Khan a foster brother. During this period, Azam Khan was commonly known as Tagha Khan or Atagha Khan.
27. The term 'Martyred Khan' is indicated by the chronogram *Khan-e-Shahid*.
28. Refers to Azam Khan who was murdered by Adham Khan.
29. The word 'badshah' refers to 'emperor'.
30. Named after the ruler, Sher Shah (CE 1486–1545); the building is described later.
31. Today it is known as the Masjid-e-Qila-e-Kuhna or 'Mosque of the Old Fort'.
32. The lighting of these *me'nhdiya'n* or lanterns is possibly what gave it the name Me'nhdiya'n.

33 The word *reti* refers to the sands of a riverbank and the mansion was built near the riverbank in what is now the area around ITO.

34 Today, this is famous as Ashoka's Pillar at Kotla Firoz Shah which in turn is today called Firoz Shah Kotla.

35 Known as Muhammad Ghori [today] and also as Sultan Shahab-ud-Din [in the period that Sir Sayyid wrote this seminal work].

36 According to Professor Irfan Habib, the name of the mosque translates to 'Dome of Islam', i.e., The Sanctuary of Peace as per the reference found in the fourteenth-century work of Zia-ud-Din Barani – the *Tarikh-e-Firoz Shahi* – and should therefore be spelt as Qubbat-ul-Islam. Sir Sayyid, by referring to it as the Quwwat-ul-Islam, names it the 'Might of Islam', altering completely the meaning of the name.

37 Also known as Muhammad Ghori.

38 The two battles fought by him against Prithviraj Chauhan (Rai Pithaura) are known to have taken place in CE 1191 and CE 1192, which would be AH 586–87 and AH 588.

39 The Qutub Minar was popularly called the staff of Saint Qutub-ud-Din Bakkhtiyar Kaki as it was believed that a Sufi saint connects to heaven with the staff that he always carries with him.

40 A festival started in the reign of Akbar II as the result of a vow made by his wife, Mumtaz Mahal, whose son Jahangir had been exiled from Delhi by the British. Upon his return, she duly offered a floral *chadar* [a sheet of flowers] to lay on the grave of Saint Qutub-ud-Din Bakkhtiyar Kaki. To this the emperor added a floral offering to the temple of Yogmaya in the vicinity of the *dargah*. This practice still continues and is called 'Phool Walo'n ki Sair' which can be loosely translated as 'The Journey of People with Flowers'.

41 Sir Sayyid does not give credit in *Asar-1* to Rai Pithaura for the first level of the minaret.

42 'Qibla' signifies the direction of Ka'ba from anywhere in the world; in India *qibla* is toward the west.

43 These are the arches added by Sultan Shams-ud-Din Altamush who died in CE 1236.

44 See Appendix II in *Asar-2*.

45 Sultan Muhammad Ghori.

46 This verse by Urfi gave the book its title, '*Asar-us-Sanadid*'.

47 Sultan Muhammad Ghori.

48 Ibid.

49 Sir Sayyid reserved the highest honorifics for Sir Thomas, the British Resident of Delhi at the time of writing. Sir Thomas not only converted the mausoleum into a residence but also rented it out to honeymooners. The tomb's cenotaph was put to use as a dining table. Sir Thomas also added more structures to the original building. As concrete graves are not allowed in Islam – a body must only be buried in earth and thus under the monument in this case – the cenotaph is an empty tomb that marks the place of the actual grave.

50 Having added a lot to the tomb – including a billiards room, a library, a guesthouse with a small swimming pool, a boathouse and a dovecote – Sir Thomas named this residence of his 'Dilkusha', i.e. 'That which pleases the heart'.

51 The translations from the original Persian are taken from Maulvi Zafar Hasan, *Monuments of Delhi* (Delhi: Aryan Books International, 2008).

52 The excess water of the Hauz-e-Shamsi used to fall here, so, the place came to be called '*jharna*' [waterfall]. Later, other pavilions were built here too.

53 The king of heaven in Hindu mythology.

54 Shadi, in this case, would have been someone's name. It does not refer to a venue for weddings [*shadi*].

55 Ajam is a word used to refer to non-Arab countries, specifically Persia.

56 The title given to Hazrat Qutub-ud-din Bakhtiyar Kaki.

57 This is inside Zafar Mahal, a summer palace built by Shah Alam II. Later, his son and successor, Bahadur Shah Zafar, added a large gateway to it, because of which the palace came to be called Zafar Mahal.

58 The actual term used was '*Arsh aramgah*', which may also be translated as 'rests in heaven'.

59 An immensely rich man of the time of Moses who was said to be possessed of a legendary treasure.

60 Mehrauli was known as Delhi and what is now called Old Delhi was Shahjahanabad.

61 A metaphor for 'having power over', or 'being head of'.

62 Hazrat Ali was stabbed on the nineteenth of the Islamic calendar month of Ramzan and attained martyrdom on the twenty-first. Sir Sayyid probably means the *night of* the twentieth as, according to lunar calendars, the day starts at sunset.

63 Various assemblies commemorating the memory of Imam Hussain where speeches are made and elegies recited, describing his martyrdom.

64 A large apartment, or set of apartments, where drums and other musical instruments were kept. The drum-players would ceremonially perform on a daily basis as would the other musicians playing on various instruments, such as the shehnai etc.

65 Metaphorically refers to Hazrat Ali called the King of Men [Shah-e-Mardan].

66 Replicas of the tomb of Imam Hussain carried in procession during the month of Moharram.

67 Normally referred to the bailiff, but in this case Sir Sayyid used it to refer to the Prime Minister.

68 Congregational Friday prayers are now held in the mosque under the aegis of the Delhi Waqf Board.

69 The phrase refers to the fact that he was a magnet to whom spiritual persons were drawn.

70 Abdul Qadir Gilani, a very revered twelfth-century Sufi saint, whose shrine is in Baghdad.

71 The Persian word for invisible is 'ghaib', which has the numerical value 1012, which is the year that Khwaja Baqi Billah died.

72 Though he lived in the lifetime of the Prophet, he never met the Prophet but accepted him as his spiritual guardian. Such was his spiritual bond with the Prophet that he felt the Prophet guided him at all times.

73 Hasnain is the collective name given to Hasan and Hussain, the grandsons of the Prophet.

74 During the reign of Sultan Firoz Shah in CE 1354.

75 Neither the Sirhindi Mosque, nor the inn exist any longer, so, it is impossible to accurately pinpoint their location.

76 This building is different from the mausoleum of Nawab Naubat Khan described earlier and from the temple referred to above though they all have the same name.

CHAPTER TWO

A Description of the Buildings Inside the Qila-e-Mu'alla

QILA-E-MU'ALLA OR QILA SHAHJAHAN

What can one say of a fort where the gardens bloom,

There's perpetual spring, with no sign of gloom.

What an exalted edifice.[1] If the sky were to create something as exquisite as even one of its cupolas, *then* it could add a feather to its cap! Even the celestial sphere cannot compete with its grandeur. This fort [the Red Fort] is such that one's imagination boggles when trying to imagine the height of its walls, or its width. Its walls soar up to the sky and its moats are uncommonly wide.

This fort was built in the twelfth regnal year of Shahb-ud-Din Muhammad Shahjahan Badshah. As per his imperial command [*farman*], construction on the fort started on a Thursday, the twelfth [of the Islamic calendar month of] Zil Hijj, AH 1048 [16 April 1639] when after finding an auspicious time, Ustad Hamid and Ustad Ahmad laid the foundation. Both these architects had no parallel in their field and were experts in mathematics [*hindasa* and *hisab*][2] and their intellect was the envy of all. This date is inscribed in a room in the female section of the royal residential area within the fort.

However, I have found some old papers which contain an astronomical chart [*zaicha*] that gives the time and date the foundation was laid – on Thursday at 5.12 p.m., on the ninth [of the Islamic calendar month of] Moharram, AH 1049 [12 May 1639].

The respected emperor gave strict orders to complete it as soon as possible and to take this magic, which would be the envy of the heavens, to its conclusion. Therefore, from every

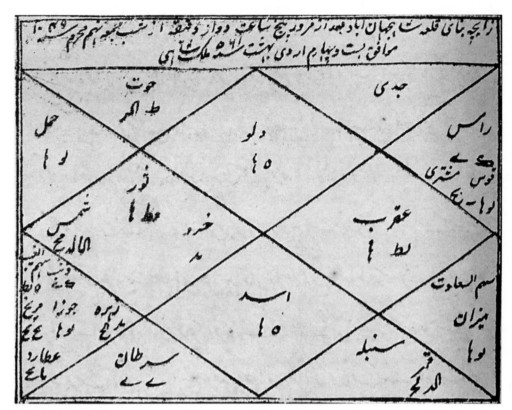

Chart for Qila Shahjahan

corner of the empire, talented and famous architects [*miamar*], sculptors [*sang-tarash*], artisans, embossers and carvers [*munabatkar*], and those who do inlay work on stone [*parchin saz*], were called. In the beginning, Izzat Khan was given the charge of supervision of the fort and for five months two days till the fifteenth of [the Islamic calendar month of] Jamad-ul-Awwal 1049, [13 September 1639] the entire foundation of the fort was dug and materials were accrued.

In some places, the foundation was raised too. Then Izzat Khan was appointed to the governorship of Thatta and charge was handed over to Ali Vardi Khan. Under his supervision, 12-*gaz*-high walls were built all around the fort in two years, one month and eleven days. Supervision then passed on to Makarmat Khan and the fort was completed in the eighth year under him. It took nine years to complete the fort which was the twentieth year of Shahjahan's reign.

Emperor Shahjahan was in Kabul when the fort was completed and Makramat Khan sent him the message that the royal residence, that is the palace and the Halls of the Shadow of

God, that is the emperor's residence had been completed, and that the Diwan-e-Aam and Diwan-e-Khas [halls of Public Audience and Special Audience, respectively], the baths and streams were waiting to be blessed by the fall of his footsteps. And his noble self should sanctify this piece of heaven which is the envy of heaven itself.

The emperor, very impatient to see the fort gave orders to march from Kabul to Agra and reached as soon as he could. On the twenty-fourth [of the Islamic calendar month of] Rabi Awwal AH 1058 [18 April 1648], he entered the fort. Everyone was awestruck by the level of work, the fountains and streams transported one to another world. It did not seem strange to think that this was indeed heaven. The fort, twice the size of Akbarabad Fort [Agra Fort], was built in eight years at the cost of Rs 50 lakh for the superstructure, and Rs 50 lakh for the buildings within it.

The fort has two large gateways, two wicket gates [*khirkis*] and twenty-one bastions. Of these, seven are round and fourteen are octagonal. The architecture of the fort is in the form of a chamfered square or irregular octagon [*musamman-e-baghdadi*], 1000 *gaz* long and 600 *gaz* wide, with an area of 6 lakh *gaz*. The walls of this fort are 25 *gaz* high and its foundations are 11 *gaz* deep. The width is 15 *gaz* at the bottom and tapers to 10 *gaz* on the top. The eastern side, towards the Yamuna, is set on an elevation of 12 *gaz*. The river flows to the east of this

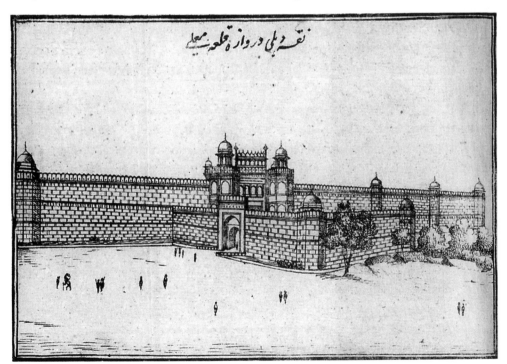

Qila-e-Mu'alla: Delhi Darwaza

fort and on the other three sides is a deep moat that is 3,600 *gaz* long, 25 *gaz* wide and 10 *gaz* deep. It is kept filled by water from the river.

All the towers have been built of red sandstone from top to bottom. All the buildings in the north – Hayat Baksh Bagh, Hammam, Shah Mahal better known as the Diwan-e-Khas, the emperor's retiring rooms [*aramgah muqaddas*],[3] Burj Tila or Musamman Burj [also known as the Golden Tower], the emperor's sleeping quarters [*khwabgah*], Rang Mahal,[4] the apartments assigned to the royal ladies, the palaces belonging to the royal consorts – all have been made in such a way that there is river water on the eastern side and gardens on the west.

The 4- *gaz*-wide Nahr-e-Bahisht stream flows from the north winding its way through the buildings towards the south. I want to describe the incomparable buildings in this fort that have so fascinated me in a way that the reader can enjoy them too and come to know about them.

The Southern Gateway

The southern gateway is so lofty that even the sky seems inferior in front of it. Made completely of red sandstone with a few instances of marble inlay work [*pichikari*] on its dome, it soars higher than the sky and the decoration is prettier than the constellations [*kahkashan*].

It is also called Delhi Darwaza [and Delhi Gate today] as it faces old Delhi, and some even call it Akbari Gate as it leads to Akbarabad [Agra]. It is even called 'Hathiya Pol' or Elephant Gate in Hindi, which means Darwaza-e-Filan, as there used to be two life-sized statues of elephants in front of this gate. However these elephants were broken and removed under [the orders of] Emperor Muhammad Aurangzeb Alamgir as he felt they were un-Islamic. He forbade statues and paintings of living beings on buildings.

Earlier, one could see all the way to the jungle from here but Hazrat Alamgir [Emperor Aurangzeb] thought this inappropriate, and leaving a space in front of it had a barbican built in front with its opening to the west. When Shahjahan [placed under house arrest in Agra Fort by Aurangzeb who deposed him] heard about the barbican in front of the two gates, the deposed emperor wrote to his son: 'My illustrious son you have made the fort into a bride and veiled her!'

There is a moat around the gate with a wooden drawbridge which was raised when not in use. Once the drawbridge was raised, there was no access to the fort due to the deep water-filled moat. However, during the reign of Hazrat Arsh Aramgah[5] Muhammad Akbar Shah II, the Sarkar Daulat Madar Angrezi[6] got a concrete bridge built in front of it which had a marble inscription:

> God is munificent! In AH 1226/CE 1811 in the fifth year of the reign of Shah Jamjah
> Muhammad Akbar Badshah Ghazi Sahib Qiran Sani[7] this bridge, Faiz Manzil was built by
> Dilawar-ud-Daulah Robert Macpherson Bahadur Diler-Jung.

Entering from the Lahori Darwaza, we come into the square called the Jilau Khana Chowk which is 200 x 140 *gaz* with doors on three sides, and the drum-house [*naqqar khana*] on the western side. From the southern gate, one goes to Nurgarh [Salimgarh Fort] via the royal stables. There is also a tank in the middle of this courtyard and a 4-*gaz*-wide stream that flows into the south moat.

Qila-e-Mu'alla: Lahori Darwaza

Qila-e-Mu'alla's [Red Fort's] Lahori Darwaza has no equal with regard to its lofty height, rising upwards to the sky, resembling a mountain. Its carving and ornamentation have no parallel. This is similar in construction to Delhi Darwaza. Hazrat Alamgir [Emperor Aurangzeb] has built a barbican in front of it as one could see all the way to Fatehpuri Mosque via Chandni Chowk from here.

Earlier, the nobles had to dismount at Fatehpuri Mosque and then walk to the Diwan-e-Khas. There was a moat in front of it too with a wooden drawbridge. A masonry bridge was built here in the reign of Hazrat Akbar Badshah II with an identical inscription to the one in front of Delhi Darwaza. This gate is in the possession and use of the Commander of the Palace Guard [*Sahib-e-Qiladar*; a position at this time held by a British Officer] who lives [in an apartment built] on top of it. Since both the gateways are similar, I will only sketch Delhi Darwaza.

Chhatta Lahori Darwaza

To the west of this square can be seen the vaulted arcade [*chatta*] of the Lahori Darwaza. This arcade is one of a kind; its builders have created different types of magic here. The height of its arched ceiling is such that it appears to be the roof of the sky with waves and designs which are very attractive. Made very well, the ceiling of this arcade is very high and extends a great distance. It has been beautifully ornamented with paintings on the plaster. There are very pleasing and attractive two-storeyed rooms on both sides with a courtyard in the middle which has an open roof for light. This arcade was called the covered market [bazaar *musaqqaf*] in the reign of Shahjahan.

Naqqar Khana

To the west of Jilau Khana Chowk [no longer there; this was the forecourt] stands a very lofty gateway that soars to the sky and leads to the Diwan-e-Aam. The gateway has attractive hallways and buildings built in its vicinity. The royal drum-house [*badshahi naqqar khana*] is situated here in a set of apartments. The sound of the kettledrums [*naubat*] that play day and night remove all sorrows and instil a sense of happiness. It intoxicates not just people but also djinns, animals, birds and inanimate objects. The art of playing the drums [*naqqar-shahi*] is such that it inspires the loyal and the brave and terrifies enemies, who turn pale with fear.

This building is made of red sandstone with a huge doorway in the middle. It has two

Naqqar Khana

apartments and two floors on either side. In front of the apartments are wall-niches indicating the direction of Mecca and steps leading up to the drum-house. There is an arched hallway on either side within which is located the section that mends and repairs all the musical instruments [*naubat karkhana*], and from where music for the royal family is played, and that is why it is called the drum-house [*naqqar khana*] too. There are very attractive cupolas on its four corners which add to its beauty. I will draw its sketch here.

Diwan-e-Aam: The Hall of Public Audience

This unique building is situated in a large courtyard in front of the drum-house. The emperor held court here on the days he granted the public an audience. There is a nine-arched hallway divided into three aisles. The length of this majestic hall is 67 *gaz* and it is 24 *gaz* wide. Each section has pillars which support extremely beautiful arches. Though the hall is made of red sandstone, it has been plastered white to resemble marble, and has stucco and gilded ornamentation.

The outer hallway (after the middle doorway) has an enclosure with a marble railing in it. It is beautifully decorated with golden finial [*kalsi*] on its kiosks. Nothing remains of these finials, but the marble railing still exists, albeit in a ruined state. The outer hallway is built

Diwan-e-Aam

on a platform and its measurements are 160 x 104 *gaz*. There is a red sandstone enclosure around it which was the height of a man. It was decorated with golden finials which have now disappeared. This enclosure had also been destroyed but was rebuilt in the tenth regnal year of Siraj-ud-Din Muhammad Bahadur Shah Badshah Ghazi Khuldallah.[8]

There is a huge courtyard in front of it, measuring 204 x 60 *gaz*, which can rival the world. There are beautiful hallways and corridors built next to this courtyard. To its south, there is a passage which leads to the royal apartments and palaces. There is a door on the north which leads to the Office of Household Expenses [*Khan Samani*] and the gardens and the drum-house is on its west.

Nasheman-e-Zill-e-Ilahi[9]

In the middle of the innermost hallway is the throne called the Takht-e-Shahi or Aurang Zill-e-Ilahi. Even the inhabitants of the sky would not have seen anything comparable to this throne. The canopy is made of pure marble and is 4 *gaz* square in width, with four columns that support a curved dome. On the wall behind the throne, is a special marble recess measuring 7 x 2.5 *gaz* with various exquisite types of birds and beasts of pietra dura on it. The artistry of these pietra dura plaques would confound the inhabitants of the sky.

On the wall behind the throne is a door through which the emperor would enter the Diwan-e-Aam on the days he held a public audience. He would grace the throne room with his presence and illuminate the world by sitting on this throne with all the nobles, emissaries and officers of the army standing according to their status near the marble and red sandstone railings with folded hands. The plinth of the throne is higher than a man's head and there is a beautiful marble dais kept in front of it, which is decorated with inlay work.

When any noble had to present a petition, he would take permission from the emperor and stand on this dais. He would only speak after kissing the legs of the throne and offering salutations to the emperor. It has been an age since the emperor held court here, and this building, where once emissaries of the important emperors of the world aspired to enter, now lies desolate and the royal guards idle away their time. I will describe this building [Diwan-e-Aam] in a sketch at this point.

Imtiaz Mahal/Rang Mahal

This royal palace lies behind the Diwan-e-Aam and is the biggest palace in the fort. It used to have a huge courtyard with canals, fountains and gardens inside it but all of this is now ruined and ugly houses have been built in the once charming courtyard. The courtyard earlier had a tank 48 to 50 *gaz* in size that had five fountains; the Nahr-e-Bahisht stream, with its twenty-five fountains also flowed through this courtyard. There was also a garden, 107 x 115 *gaz* in size, surrounded by a red sandstone screen that had 2000 golden finials. Three sides had charming mansions and arcades and each side measured 70 *gaz*.

Towards the west of the buildings, overhanging the stream and the Pai'n Bagh [a miniature garden], is Imtiaz Mahal the praise of which is beyond the capacity of a mere mortal. A terrace on a plinth is visible from the outside[10] and below it are two attractive basements. On this terrace is an intricate three-aisle hall with a five-arched façade which is 57 x 26 *gaz* in size. In front of the middle arch and towards the courtyard is a huge marble basin made from a single piece of marble which is raised above the ground on legs. Into it flows a 3-*gaz* wide cascade of water from a height of 1.5 *gaz*, down to the sunken lower pond, from where it overflows into streams that in turn flow into every parterre and channel of the gardens. It [the basin] has been made entirely of marble.

Engrailed arches were situated in strategic places in the garden with such exquisite embossing and carving that it amazes the mind. On four corners of the roof are four dome-shaped pavilions which magnify the beauty and majesty of the building. There were four stone kiosks on all four corners of this courtyard, so that in the summer screens made of *khus* [vetiver grass] would [be drenched and the breezes blowing through them would] keep the interiors cool.

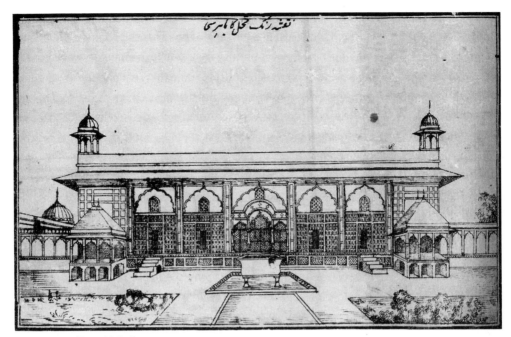

نقشه رنگ محل جا باہرسی

Imtiaz Mahal / Rang Mahal: exterior

It is beyond the capacity of a mere mortal to praise the buildings in the Imtiaz Mahal. Just imagine the scene: streams flowing through the palace, water gushing from the fountains, a cool breeze wafting through the vetiver-grass screens that were constantly drenched with water, and each eye damp with that water as though glistening with pearl drops. In reality, it is a piece of heaven and cannot be described in words. This is just a description of its courtyard. Its interior, which is even more magical, confounds the mind. Here, I will describe its façade via a sketch.

Imtiaz Mahal/Rang Mahal: Interior

How can I describe this majestic palace, my words do not have the strength to capture its beauty. However, I will do my best as its builders have done wonders with their skill. It is magical and has to be seen to be believed. The façade consists of five arched doors with arched square bays and vaults within. May the eyebrows of a thousand beloveds be sacrificed to each arch!

In the middle is a square with a pool, the beauty of which baffles the mind – it is made of marble and built to resemble a flower in full bloom. Its petals are so beautiful that every jasmine from all the gardens can be sacrificed at the altar of its beauty. The inlay work of flowers and foliage in various coloured stones inside it has been executed so exquisitely that it is beyond description. It is like a picture gallery opened to an ardent audience. Although the pool is 7.5 *gaz* square, it is very shallow, just like the palm of one's hand. Its beauty is such that when it is full of rippling water, all the flowers and foliage inside it seem to be swaying in the morning breeze, giving the impression of a garden in full bloom that reminds one of paradise.

Inside the pool is a marble cup shaped like a beautiful flower, and on whose beauty many thousands of flowers could be sacrificed. On every curve and arched cusp, flowers and leaves of coloured stones spring from creeping plants, and the creeping plants in turn emerge from flowers and leaves. A hidden underground stream bubbles out of a bowl and as the water overflows, the swaying of the flowers and plants make it a magical moment. The Nahr-e-Bahisht stream flows out of Moti Mahal and the Diwan-e-Khas through the middle of this palace before flowing out towards the south. There is another stream which flows from this tank from east to west, and cascades into the tank located towards the east in the courtyard, in front of the façade.

Every stream has been decorated with the same carving; pietra dura and mosaic are used for ornamenting the tank. The columns supporting the arches in Imtiaz Mahal are made of marble up to the dado and decorated with inlay work. The marble of this palace is fairer than the complexion of a thousand beloveds, and the redness of the stones used is more attractive than the ruby-red lips of innumerable beauties.

Imtiaz Mahal/Rang Mahal: interior

Almost the entire palace has been gilded with dazzling gold floral designs. They say that this palace had a pure silver ceiling, but the silver was for some reason and requirement replaced with copper in the reign of Farrukhsiyyar. About thirty-five years ago, during the reign of Emperor Moin-ud-Din Muhammad Akbar Shah II, the copper ceiling was also removed and replaced by wood but even that is now in ruins. Everyone upon the earth will perish. Next to the Imtiaz Mahal are small apartments and the building called the Chhoti Baithak. I am describing it [Imtiaz Mahal] with a sketch.

Chhoti Baithak

This building [in the female-only section of the royal residences] lies to the south of Imtiaz Mahal and is an annexe to the emperor's personal apartments. It is very beautiful and pleasing to the eye. The late Mirza Jahangir Bahadur had made new additions to it, but it lost its beauty, not remaining the way it was initially built by Shahjahan. Therefore I am not making a sketch of it.

Jharoka

'Jharoka' refers to windows facing [in this case] the sands of a riverbank. If the emperor wanted to watch a spectacle, he would watch it from these windows [and the building came to be called by this name: Jharoka]. However, Jharoka was built with the intention of allowing the public to see the emperor when he appeared before his people at fixed times during the day. This was a custom started during the reign of Akbar the Great.

The Hindu subjects of Emperor Akbar [Bandagan-e-Khas Akbari], the people of his realm would not talk to anyone until they had seen the emperor's face. Thus, the emperor would appear before his people. Once this became an established custom, this building came to be called 'Jharoka'. This custom continued till the reign of Shahjahan and was stopped during Aurangzeb's rule.

Asad Burj

This is the southern tower of the fort and is built in the same manner as the one to the north which is famous as Shah Burj. This tower was destroyed in the chaos that followed the bombardment between Ochterlony and Harnath Chela but was restored to its original state in the reign of Moin-ud-Din Muhammad Akbar Shah II who now resides in paradise.

Khwabgah/Badi Baithak

These are the emperor's personal apartments, and lie to the north of Imtiaz Mahal. They are very elegant and beautiful and do not have a parallel on the face of this earth. The entire area is built completely of marble with beautiful floral designs and gilded decoration of flowers and foliage. In the middle stands a raised platform on which the emperor's throne is placed. To the north and south of it are two marble-arched doorways decorated with glazed-tile ornamentation.

The raised platform, on which is placed the emperor's throne, is 15 x 6 *gaz* in size. An inscription written by Sadullah Khan is present on two of its arches in addition to verses written in gold water. The inscription on the central arch reads as follows:

> God is pure! How beautiful are these painted mansions and charming residences. They are a part of high heaven. I may say the high soul'd-holy angels are desirous of looking at them. If residents of different parts and directions of the world would come to walk round them, as [they walk] round the old house [Ka'ba] it would be allowable; or if the beholders of the two worlds should run to kiss their highly glorious threshold as [they do] the black stone [of the Ka'ba it would be proper and fitting].
>
> The commencement of the great fort which is higher than the Palace of the Heavens is the envy of the wall of Alexander; and of his pleasant edifice; and of the Hayat Baksh [life-bestowing] garden, which is to these buildings as the soul is to the body, and the lamp to an assembly; and of the pure canal, the limpid water of which is to the person possessing sight as a mirror showing the world, and to the wise, the unveiler of the secret world; and

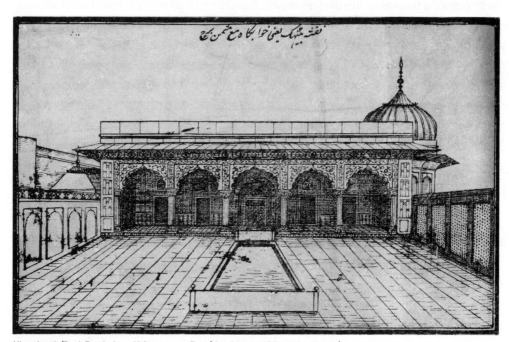

Khwabgah/Badi Baithak and Musamman Burj (the dome visible in the sketch)

of the water-cascades, each of which you may say is the whiteness of the dawn, or a tablet containing secrets of the Table and Pen [of Fate].

Inscription on the northern arch [a continuation of the above]:

And of the fountains, each of which is a hand of light inclined to shake hands with the inhabitants of heavens, or is a string of bright pearls made to descend to reward the inhabitants of the earth; and of the tank, full to the brim of the water of life and in its purity the envy of light and the spring of the sun announced on the twelfth of [the Islamic calendar month of] Zil Hajjah in the twelfth year of the holy ascension, corresponding to AH 1048 [16 April 1639], the tidings of happiness to men. The completion of it, at the expense of Rs 50 lakh, by the power of the auspicious feet of the sovereign of the earth, the lord of the world, the originator of these heavenly buildings, Shihab-ud-Din Muhammad, the Second Lord of Felicity, Shahjahan the King, the champion of the faith, opened on the twenty-fourth [of the Islamic calendar month of] Rabi Awwal in the twenty-first blessed year of the ascension, corresponding AH 1058 [18 April 1648], the door of grace to the world.

Beyond this is a five-arched hall which is a very elegant and made completely of marble. It is exquisitely decorated with pietra dura work and is 20 x 6 *gaz* with arches and chambers on either side. From the western chambers is a passageway called the '*khasi deorhi*' that leads to the Diwan-e-Khas. There is also a unique marble basin placed in the middle of Badi Baithak. I don't know how the artists of those days could conjure up such wondrous designs. It is actually an exquisite oblong basin but instead of fountains, it has thousands of beautiful floral decorations in stones of various colours on its surface. The petal of every flower has a hole from which water spouts out as from a fountain into the stream. Since there are thousands of petals in the inlay of the basin, a thousand streams of water spout out of the flowers and enchant the viewer. The work on this marble basin is exquisite and its beauty cannot be envisaged without laying eyes on it. Beyond this hall is a courtyard which is very big and has a fascinating marble-paved floor. The Nahr-e-Bahisht flows through here and then goes into the Rang Mahal [Imitiaz Mahal].

Burj Tila/Musamman Burj

To the east of the wall of the emperor's private apartments is the Burj-e-Tila, also called Sunehri Burj [or the Golden Tower] as its dome is golden in colour. It overlooks the riverside and is also known as the Octagonal Tower [Burj-e-Musamman] since it is octagonal [*musamman*] in shape. Made entirely of marble, it has floral decorations and displays work in gold and pietra dura just like the other buildings. Three sides of this tower face towards the emperor's private apartments and five jut out towards the river. There are marble screens on these five sides and on one of the sides is a balcony towards the river. I am drawing a sketch here which includes the emperor's private apartments and the tower.

Shah Mahal/Diwan-e-Khas

This is a very famous building, and has no parallel on the face of this earth. It is so attractive that I have never seen another like it. To the north of the emperor's private apartments is a huge square, to the east of which is a platform that is 1½ *gaz* high, 80 *gaz* long and 26 *gaz* wide. In the middle of it stands the Diwan-e-Khas, 34 x 26 *gaz* in size and made of marble from top to bottom. The marble is so pure that the whiteness of dawn would seem darker than the darkest night.

The Nahr-e-Bahisht, 4 *gaz* wide here, flows through the centre of the hall. In the middle of this edifice is another room measuring 18 x 10 *gaz*, that has been built by erecting square columns around a platform in the centre. It is on this platform that the Takht-e-Taoos [the Peacock Throne] is placed and when the emperor graces the court with his presence, this is where he sits.

Around this is a row of elevated columns that constitute the hall. The columns, arches and floor are made of marble inlaid with cornelian, corals and other precious stones reaching

Shah Mahal/Diwan-e-Khas

up to the dado where flowers and foliage have been carved. Their beauty forces one to remember God's bounty. From the dado to ceiling, it is decorated with golden work. The following famous verse is inscribed on one of the inner arches of the Diwan-e-Khas in gold:

> If there is Heaven on earth,
>
> It is here, it is here, it is here.

The eastern side of this building overlooks the river, and the doors on that side have finely carved marble screens with glass inlay work in the perforations. Towards the west lies a courtyard measuring 70 x 60 *gaz* and around it are mansions and arcades of red sandstone. Towards the west is the entrance connected to the Diwan-e-Aam by a passage. A red curtain screens the entrance door. When the emperor holds court, it is from here that the nobles present their respects and salutations.

Towards the north is the way to Hayat Baksh garden and towards the south is the passageway leading to the royal harem. In front of this entrance, towards the courtyard, is a marble enclosure called the Chaukhundi Diwan-e-Khas or the Square Hall of Special Audience. This building is also a unique wonder. Its ceiling was also made completely of silver but was torn-off during the Maratha and the Jat rebellions.

Tasbih Khana/Prayer Hall

Towards the south of the terrace on which this beautiful Diwan-e-Khas is built is a hall which is famous as the Tasbih Khana or Prayer Hall. It lies to the rear of the emperor's private apartments. Whenever the emperor wants solitude, or calls a meeting with special nobles, he comes and sits here.[11]

In the middle of this hall is a weighing scale engraved in marble with 'scales of justice' [*Mizan-e-Adl*] carved on it. It has a lot of golden work on it. The man who engraved these scales must have been virtuous as at the time of prayer and meditation, the emperor glances at it and remembers that on the Day of Judgment, the Divine Scales of Justice [*Mizan-e-Adl-e-Ilahi*] will be taken out and the rich and the poor treated alike, their deeds being judged on merit. Thus it is an imperative reminding the emperor to be just and to issue orders only after weighing them on the scales of justice.

The way to the emperor's private apartments is called the 'special private passageway' [*khasi deorhi*] and is located inside this Prayer Hall.

Hammam

To the south of the Diwan-e-Khas is an incomparable bathhouse [*hammam*] and the building is referred to as lying 'behind the royal baths' [*aqab-e-hammam*]. I will provide a sketch of the Diwan-e-Khas. The Prayer Hall can be seen in it, as can the buildings behind the royal bath. These baths are incomparable and unique. I am convinced they have no parallel anywhere in the country. There are three parts to them, therefore, I though it prudent to describe each separately.

Jam-e-Kun

This was the changing room, the place to disrobe and to wear robes, relax and partake of refreshments after a bath and it is therefore referred to as a *jam-e-kun*. Built to resemble a large room, it is made of marble till the dado, with pietra dura decorations. To the east are screens decorated with mirror-work in which the flowers, greenery and the river are reflected very clearly. I did not sketch this area. It is this room that many people call the *aqab-e-hammam* [behind the baths].

Sard Khana

This room is so unparalleled that even inhabitants of the skies (*chashm-e-falak*) would not have seen anything like it. Though called the 'cold room' [*sard khana*], its special feature is that its temperature, and that of the water in the stream and the fountains, can be kept cool.

Sard Khana

If one wishes then the room can be heated from the floor to the ceiling. Cold or hot water would flow from this rivulet as per need.

A throne for the emperor, made of marble and decorated with mosaic and pietra dura is placed to the north. Beyond it is a quadrangle made completely of marble with a mosaic of various coloured stones from the floor to the ceiling and all kinds of floral designs. The mosaic on the floor is so beautiful that a thousand Persian carpets would look dull in front of its design.

In the middle of this room is a square pool with pietra dura work which has golden fountains on the four corners. They have been designed in such a way that the jets from all four fountains combine to fall together in the centre of the pool. Near it, adjacent to the wall, flows a shallow rivulet, about a *gaz* wide. No other room is as beautiful as this. I will make a sketch of this section here.

Garam Khana

This is the third room of the royal bath and to its west are the tanks that provide heated water [hence the name, 'hot room' or *garam khana*]. The tanks are made completely of marble. It is said that even 125 *maunds* of wood were but a morsel for heating water here. As you enter

Garam Khana

you see a square with a marble platform in the centre which was used for sitting upon while bathing. Towards the north is another throne for the emperor with a rectangular pool in front of it that can be filled with hot or cold water.

The floor, platform, pools and the walls are all beautifully carved and decorated with mosaic and inlay work up to the dado. The floral inlays are studded with precious and semi-precious stones and with such skill that they give the effect of a garden. The skill and artistry [that has gone into the building] of the royal baths cannot be put in words and the following verse seems to be apt here:

> The beauty of the building is such,
>
> That one can't stop gazing at it.

Here, I will sketch this building so that you can get some idea of its beauty.

Hira Mahal

To the north of the royal baths is Moti Mahal and between it and the royal baths lies a small courtyard through which flows a 4-*gaz*-long marble stream taking a winding course (*marpech*). This is a continuation of the Nahr-e-Bahisht that flows down here from the Diwan-e-Khas and Imtiaz Mahal/Rang Mahal. In the middle of the courtyard and to the side of the stream is a twelve-arched marble pavilion with four small cupolas with golden domes on the

Hira Mahal

four corners of the roof. This marble pavilion is very delicately and aesthetically made. This is not an old building but was built four to five years ago on the orders of Hazrat Abu Zafar Siraj-ud-Din Muhammad Bahadur Shah Badshah Ghazi,[12] may God preserve his reign. It has been very finely made and its attractions cannot be written down.

The course taken by the stream in this courtyard also defies description. It is so attractive and twists and turns so beautifully that the beauty of this sight cannot be captured in words. In yesteryears there were twenty-four golden and silver fountains installed in this stream which used to flow constantly. Now, it is in ruins and there is no trace of those fountains. The fountains drink their own tears and are silent. Look at the sketch and reflect on the power of the Almighty.

Moti Mahal

This palace is made of red sandstone plastered white and generously decorated with floral designs and gilding. The first part is 15 x 8 *gaz* wide and includes two seats built for the emperor. In the middle is a 4 x 3 *gaz* wide pond. Behind each seat is an 8 x 5 *gaz* section. There are lofty rectangular halls with five arches overlooking the river on the east. Towards the west, they overlook the Hayat Baksh garden. Each rectangular hall is 30 x 60 *gaz* in size. The inner building is made of marble up to the dado, and the rest is made of red sandstone plastered white. The palace also has a canal from which a 2-*gaz*-wide cascade of water falls

Moti Mahal

into a pool towards Hayat Baksh garden via a chute. This wondrous pool is incomparable and here I will describe it separately.

Description of the Pool

The reality is that this large, flawless stone was mined from the Makrana mines and was incomparable in whiteness and quality. A large basin, 4 *gaz* square and 1.5 *gaz* deep, was carved out of it on the orders of the emperor. The whole basin, along with its legs, was carved out of one monolithic stone. After it was completed, the basin was brought carefully from Makrana, which is 200 *kos* [450 miles] from the capital city [or the *dar-ul-khilafat*], and was safely installed here. There were mansions to the north and south of Moti Mahal which still exist, although they now show some signs of damage. The emperor has now had a small basement built under this palace where he rests. It is a very finely built palace and I will make a sketch so that everyone can see and appreciate its beauty.

Moti Masjid

This mosque lies behind the bathhouse near Hayat Baksh garden. Built completely of marble, its flooring, walls, engrailed arches, wall-niches marking the direction of Mecca, parapets, and ceiling are all of marble with beautiful ornamentation. The floral designs are exquisite. In reality no other building in the entire fort can match the workmanship and ornamentation of this mosque. In fact, it would be difficult to find such work anywhere in the world.

This mosque has three attractive arches, two small minarets and three gilded domes, because of which many refer to it as Sunehri Masjid [Golden Mosque]. There is a small water tank in the courtyard. As it was difficult to keep the water in the tank pure for purposes of ablution, it was cleverly arranged so that water from Bhado'n [described below] flowed here and overflowed.[13] There is a small room on the northern side of the mosque for the purposes of prayer and meditation. This room also contains a small, shallow but very beautiful tank. It is decorated with glass mosaic. Hazrat Aurangzeb Alamgir built this mosque in his second regnal year at a cost of Rs 1,60,000. There is a chronogram of its date written by Aqil Khan: *Doubtless all mosques are the House of God, so do not call anyone except Allah here.*

This yields AH 1036 [CE 1626–27] as the year of its construction. This mosque is unique and I am placing its sketch here.

Bagh-e-Hayat Baksh

The 250 x 125 *gaz* Hayat Baksh [life-bestowing] garden is a sign of God's divine grace and rejuvenates the heart of the onlooker and makes him ecstatic and cheerful. The gardens of heaven are seen by one's own eyes. The height of the trees can make men envious of their stature. Every flower can make a fair maiden blush and its tendrils put to shame the beloved's curls. Even the finest poet would find it difficult to describe its beauty. In the middle of this garden is a large tank and all around it flow streams through red sandstone channels that are 6 *gaz* wide. Each stream has thirty silver fountains where water used to once flow continuously. This garden with its fragrant flowers and trees is the reason for the ever-present freshness here. There are two pavilions on either side of this, which are called Sawan and Bhado'n,[14] which I will describe in detail later. The ambience produced by the greenery of the plants and trees and the fragrance of the flowers, the soft flowing breeze cannot be adequately captured in words.

> A hundred-thousand flowers bloom in this garden,
>
> The greenery is fresh and sweet sound of the water is soothing.

Hauz Bagh-e-Hayat Baksh

In the centre of Hayat Baksh Garden is a large pool [*hauz*] and even the fountain of life and immortality [*chashm-e-khizr*] is thirsty for its pure water. The pool measures 60 x 60 *gaz*. There were once 49 silver fountains in the middle of it from which water used to flow constantly. On its corners were 112 silver fountain jets which also spouted water day and night. Now there are only holes to remind us that once there were fountains on this spot.

> Rivals always trouble a lover's heart,
>
> Only a scar remains, where once there was an ache.

Bhado'n Pavilion

To the south of Hayat Baksh garden is an elegant and beautiful marble pavilion called Bhado'n, built within the garden premises. It is very unique and the flowing water inside it gives the impression of rain in the [Hindu calendar] month of Bhado'n [around August], thus its name. The pavilion itself is an attractive and elegant hall built on a platform with a plinth supported by sixteen columns. On the four corners of the roof are four golden cupolas. The sixteen columns divide the pavilion into two sections on the east and west creating square bays in between. Below this, on ground-level, is a square marble tank which measures 4 *gaz* x 15 *tasu* [the twenty-fourth part of a *gaz*] in width and is 1½ *gaz* deep.

A channel from the Nahr-e-Bahisht stream cascades into the tank. From here, water flows through another chute and falls into the canal. Small arched niches were made in the tank and in the chutes. During the day, flower bouquets were placed in these niches, and at night camphor candles would be lit in them. When water cascaded over these candles and flowers, it created a wondrous impression. There is now no way for water to flow into it. I will make its sketch here so that you can see its uniqueness.

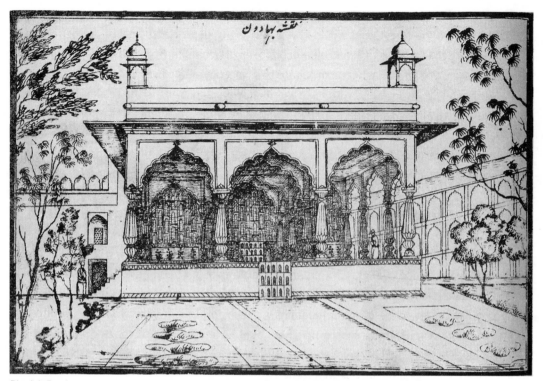

Bhado'n Pavilion

Zafar Mahal

Four or five years ago, Hazrat Abu Zafar Siraj-ud-Din Muhammad Bahadur Shah Badshah Ghazi got this palace built in the tank in Hayat Baksh garden. It is made completely of red sandstone. There is an empty and open space in the middle and around it are built alcoves and enclosures for sitting. On one side is a bridge for entry and exit. This is a new building and it has been elegantly built. I am making a sketch which will show both these buildings.

Sawan Pavilion

On the northern side of this garden is the other exquisite pavilion called Sawan, also made entirely of marble. There is not even a hair's breadth of difference between the two pavilions. Sawan is identical to Bhado'n with the same arched niches for flowers and lamps, arches, tank, chutes and flow of water. As both are identical, I sketched Bhado'n from the outside and Sawan from the inside. The streams, their flow and the noise are all similar to the sound of the rain during the monsoons and the pavilion was thus named Sawan.

Zafar Mahal, including the hauz of Mehtab Bagh

Burj Shumali/Shah Burj

This bastion with a triple-storeyed domed pavilion is also incredible. It has a diameter of 100 *gaz*. The first storey stands on a 12-*gaz* plinth. The central hall with a vaulted soffit is round from the inside and level from the outside. It is built of stone with marble up to the dados, and is beautifully decorated with mosaic and inlay work. The remainder has been plastered white, over which floral designs have been painted in gold. This second storey is octagonal and on the top of that is the domed pavilion. The second storey has an 8-*gaz* diameter with four alcoves and two canopied seats that are semi-octagonal and the whole projects over the river.

The façade is marble and the alcoves on both the northern and eastern side measure 4 x 4 *gaz*. The ones on the western and southern sides are 4 x 3 *gaz*. In the centre is an extremely attractive tank with a diameter of 3 *gaz*. The ornamentation on the tank leaves one breathless and reminds one of divine grace. From the western alcove, with its small arched niches for flowers in the daytime and lamps at night, flows a waterfall. In front of the waterfall is a marble basin measuring 3.5 x 2.5 *gaz* and from this basin towards the east extends a 1.5-*gaz*-long marble channel through which flows a stream. The basin and marble

Sawan Pavilion

channel are beautifully decorated with pietra dura and floral embossing. Both are inlaid with cornelian [*aqiq*], coral [*marjan*] and other priceless precious stones.

Another stream flows from this which falls into the tank on the western alcove and joins the stream of the Shah Burj, subsequently reaching the eastern alcove via the octagonal [*musamman*] tank. Underneath it, towards the river, is a waterfall. From this point onwards, a stream runs through the entire fort, and in fact the water system for the entire fort is controlled from here. Each pipe bears a label of the tank or stream it flows into.

The second storey is also octagonal [as mentioned above], made very neatly with an 8 *gaz* diameter and a gallery supported on twenty-four pillars. The third storey is an alcove with a domed pavilion that has eight pillars. The dome is made of marble and has a golden finial. It is a very astonishing building and I am making its sketch here.

Mehtab Bagh

This garden is situated to the west of Hayat Baksh garden. Once upon a time it must have been marvellous, but it now lies in ruins. Through the centre of this garden flows an attractive and large stream. Now Emperor Siraj-ud-Din Muhammad Bahadur Shah has replicated the waterfall of Qutub Sahib[15] to the west of this garden, and has added to its beauty. It is made of red

Burj Shumali/Shah Burj

sandstone. This garden contains the shrine of Qadam Sharif [the imprint of the footprint of the Prophet, peace be upon him] which is built in a very ordinary way so I am not including its sketch.

Chobi Masjid

If one goes a little beyond Mehtab Bagh, there are two buildings used as kitchens and are famous as the Little Kitchen [*Chota Khasa*] and Large Kitchen [*Bada Khasa*][16] respectively. Near these once stood a mosque which had been built in the reign of Emperor Ahmad Shah. Now, it is in ruins and just a pile of stones. There is only an inscription left on its door:[17]

>*This mosque was built by the Emperor, Protector of the Faith,*
>*Who received help from Divine power.*
>*Whoever performs prostrations of supplication here,*
>*Is sure to be guided by the light of worship.*
>*The foot of wisdom slipped in astonishment,*
>*When he began to deliberate upon the date.*
>*The angel, though very proud, was thus inspired,*
>*The mosque of Ahmad Shah has attained the rank of the Zodiac sign.*
>AH 1104. [CE 1692–93; the date revealed by the chronogram]

Description of the Qila-e-Mu'alla from the Riverbank

Viewing the Qila-e-Mu'alla [Red Fort] from the riverbank is a unique experience. On one side are the waves of the River Yamuna, boats plying and waving greenery seen from a distance. When the walls, merlons and especially the Golden Tower are reflected on the surface of the Yamuna, it is an incredible experience. When the rays of the sun reflect on the Golden Tower, it shines so brightly that those gazing at it from the river have to avert their gaze. In the evening, the murmur of the water, the chirping of the birds which come to rest in the trees below the fort and the breeze, all force the mystic and the enlightened [the *arif*] to come and witness such a scene for themselves.

Nurgarh

Towards the north of the Qila-e-Mu'alla lies Salimgarh Fort built by Islam Shah in AH 953 [CE 1546–47]. The Timurid family[18] calls it Nurgarh. This has now integrated so well that it has become a part of the fort. This fort was built in the middle of the river and during the reign of Islam Shah, one had to alight on it from the river.

The original entrance of the fort is on the south towards Nigambodh Ghat. In the reign of Emperor Jahangir, a bridge was made towards the north and a gateway built there. When Shahjahan built this fort, the bridge got integrated so well in it that it seemed as if the bridge was made specifically for the Qila-e-Mu'alla. On either side of the bridge is an inscription.[19] On the eastern side is inscribed:

> God is Great.

On the western side is a longer inscription:

> By the order of the ruler of Seven Climes, the emperor [who rules]with equity, justice and good government,
> Jahangir, the son of Emperor Akbar, whose sword has subdued the world.
> When this bridge was built in Delhi, the praises of which cannot be expressed
> For the date of its completion wisdom spoke thus: 'the bridge of the Emperor of Delhi [named] Jahangir.'

The value of the letters of the chronogram, '*pul-e-Shahenshah-e-Delhi Jahangir*', come to AH 1031 [CE 1621–22]. The year and auspicious date [it was erected in] – AH 1031/CE 1621–22 – [is also found in the following chronogram]: 'That is the right path'. It was built on the orders of Emperor Nur-ud-Din Jahangir the Great. I will make a sketch of the riverside which will include Salimgarh and all the buildings of Salimgarh towards the riverbank. Please note that wherever I have given measurements of the fort, it is by the Shahjahani *gaz*.

ABU ZAFAR SIRAJ-UD-DIN MUHAMMAD
BAHADUR SHAH BADSHAH GHAZI

May Allah keep his country and his empire safe and may the people of his realm benefit from his just and benevolent rule. Praise be to God! This Exalted Palace [Qila-e-Mu'alla or the Red Fort] and Supreme Fort whose humblest mansion is superior to heaven is illuminated by the prestige and status of an emperor in whose court of law Nausherwan[20] would be a humble servant and Sikandar [Alexander] would hold the lowest rank.

Even autumn [khizan], a term used to express desolation, was a season as bountiful as spring here. Thorns were the pride of flowers [ghairat-e-gulzar]. It is obvious that anything I write is lowly and inferior compared to the glory of my subject. That's why at the outset I am acknowledging my inability to do justice. His Exalted Honour was born on the twenty-eighth of [the Islamic calendar month of] Shabaan, AH 1189 on a Tuesday at sunset [24 October 1775] so that the world would know that when this blessed child was born even the sun [feeling small] hid behind a veil.

'Abu Zafar' is a chronogram for his date of birth and his name is a proof that he will be victorious over his enemies. [Zafar means victorious]. His blessed reign started on the twenty-eighth of [the Islamic calendar month of] Jamadi-us-Saani in AH 1253 [29 September 1837] on a Friday. There is a chronogram at the end of the following verse for the date of his reign.

> Due to the intoxication produced by Bahadur Shah's reign,
> Delhi's cup runs over with the wine of happiness,
> He sat on the throne and the power of his empire grew every day,
> Because of him fragrance spread and increased in the garden of Delhi.
> The date of the ascension of the ruler of great value came on the lips of wisdom as
> 'Chiragh-e-Dehli'.[21]

Editor's Notes

1. The structure today known as the Red Fort was originally just called 'Qila' [fort] according to Prof. Shamsur Rehman Faruqi and later came to be known as the Qila-e-Mubarak or the Auspicious Fort. Under the Later Mughals it was called the Qila-e-Mu'alla or the Exalted Fort. In the nineteenth century the residents of Shahjahanabad called it the Lal Haveli [Red Palace], or just 'Haveli'. Since by the time the British came, the white plaster had peeled off revealing the red sandstone beneath, the British called it the Red Fort and the locals, Lal Qila.

2. 'Hindasa' or mathematics was so named after a delegation from India visited Baghdad in CE 771. They carried the works of Aryabhatt and Brahmagupt, which were subsequently translated into Arabic, and became popular all over the Muslim world. The Arabs called this new system 'Hindasa', or 'from Hind'.

3. The aramgah muqaddas was where the emperor retired to rest and only those ladies he invited could enter, the remainder would retire to the ladies' section of the palace. These areas were in the female [zenana] quarters of the palace that were guarded by eunuchs and female warriors.

4. Rang Mahal [Palace of Colour] was called Imtiaz Mahal [Palace of Distinction] in Shahjahan's time.

5. Hazrat who now resides in paradise.

6. Honorifics used to refer to the British government.

7. Honorifics used to refer to Emperor Akbar II.

8. This title refers to Emperor Bahadur Shah Zafar and indicates that 'May Allah grant him heaven'.

9. Refers to the throne or seat [nasheman] of the Shadow of God on earth [Zil-e-Ilaahi] – a title that the Mughal emperors had bestowed upon themselves.

10. This terrace on a plinth is no longer accessible.

11. The durbar [quote] was held here daily sometimes twice a day. The durbar was held on the terrace. A famous painting by Ghulam Ali Khan (1838) shows Bahadur Shah Zafar seated on his throne under the scales of justice with three of his sons flanking him.

12. Hazrat Abu Zafar Siraj-ud-Din Muhammad Bahadur Shah Badshah Ghazi refers to Bahadur Shah Zafar and this was the name that had been used during his coronation excluding the words 'hazrat' and 'badshah'. 'Zafar' was the pen-name he used when writing poetry.

13. Still water is not considered pure.

14. Both names refer to the monsoon season and are months of the Hindu calendar.

15. Khwaja Qutub-ud-Din Bakhtiyar Kaki, a Sufi saint whose dargah is in Mehrauli. It is possible that the term 'jharna of Qutub Sahib' was used to describe the entire complex rather than just the waterfall. However the garden is now in ruins so there is no way to confirm this.

16. Khasa actually refers to royal food, the terms Chota and Bada Khasa thus refer to the royal kitchens where food was prepared for the royal family.

17. Gordon Sanderson, Delhi Fort: A Guide to the Buildings and Gardens, Delhi: Asian Educational Services, 2000; reprint of the facsimile edition of 1914.

18. The phrase 'Timurid family' refers to the Mughals.

19. Gordon Sanderson, Delhi Fort: A Guide to the Buildings and Gardens, Delhi: Asian Educational Services, 2000; reprint of the facsimile edition of 1914.

20. Nausherwan, the Sassanid king of Persia, famed for his justice.

21. 'Chiragh-e-Dehli' or the 'lamp of Delhi' is the chronogram.

CHAPTER THREE

Khas Shahr Shahjahanabad: A Description of the City of Shahjahanabad

Everyone would be happy in life,

[If] they lived in Shahjahanabad.

An ordinary mortal does not have the ability to describe the miracles of this city, so, I will only describe the city itself. People started living in this city in the twelfth regnal year of Shahjahan, which corresponds to AH 1048 [CE 1638–39].[1] The city and the moat were made after the fort was completed. The city was made as per a very elegant design with gateways and squares built at planned intervals. Every alley and street could make the residents of heaven jealous.

The city did not have a parallel on the face of earth as far as delicacy and elegance of design is concerned and was completed in AH 1058 [CE 1648]. Mir Yahya Kashi composed the following chronogram for the city: *Shud Shahjahan abad az Shahjahan abad* [Shahjahan built Shahjahanabad]. A canal called Faiz Nahr runs through the centre of the city, giving its beauty a heavenly touch, flowing into every street and alley. It provides [the city with] water, taunting the life-giving waters of the river [Ab-e-Hayat] that flows in heaven. I therefore thought it appropriate to describe the canal first, so that those who are weary from the pursuit of vanity in Delhi are refreshed.

FAIZ NAHR

I will start the description of the city with the canal [*nahr*] as it is its lifeblood. Faiz Nahr flows into the centre of the city and its water reaches every nook and cranny. It appears to be taunting the Ab-e-Hayat as it nourishes the soul of Delhi.[2] It was constructed by Sultan Firoz Shah bin Salar Rajab who had also built Firozabad, Kotla [the Citadel] Firoz Shah and Badih Manzil or Bijai Mandal.[3] He was a very pious and well-intentioned ruler who constructed many dams and bridges. Thus, during his reign, he carved out a canal from the river Yamuna and started its construction from Pargana Navahi[4] in Khizrabad.

They say that he built a very strong square and beautiful building with entrances and casements at the point where the canal began. Only as much water as needed is released from here. He took it to a distance of 30 kos [67.5 miles] to Pargana Safidon where he had a hunting lodge. After Firoz Shah's death, Faiz Nahr was extremely neglected and was left to choke and dry.

In the reign of Emperor Jalal-ud-Din Muhammad Akbar, the Governor [Subedar] of Delhi, Shahab-ud-Din Ahmad Khan had Faiz Nahr cleaned as it was part of his fief [jagir], and restored its flow from Safidon to Khizrabad, naming it 'Nahr Shahab'. After him however, no one bothered to keep it clean and eventually this canal dried up again. When Emperor Shahb-ud-Din Muhammad Shahjahan built the fort and populated Shahjahanabad, he gave orders for it to be cleaned and got it started from Khizrabad to Safidon once again. He ordered that a new 30 kos [67.5 mile]-long canal was to be dug from Safidon which would reach Qila-e-Shahjahani [as Red Fort was known then] and the people of Shahjahanabad.

In the twelfth regnal year, on the fifteenth day of [the Islamic calendar month of] Jamadi-ul-Awwal, after four months and two days, Izzat Khan, the nephew of Abdullah Khan Bahadur Firoz Jung, decided to undertake the task of rebuilding this canal. And after Izzat Khan was appointed Governor of Thatta, this task was given to Ali Vardi Khan. For two years, one month and fifteen days, he worked on this task and in the fifteenth regnal year, on the first day [of the Islamic calendar month of] Jamadi-us-Saani, the work was handed over to Mukarammat Khan Mir Samaan wa Khan Samaan. Under him, it was completed in the twentieth regnal year and completed at the same time as the fort.

There was no building in the fort that the canal did not reach and there was no alley or street in the city it did not flow into. It even went into the royal kitchens, making the task of cooking easier. But by the reign of Alamgir II, this canal had broken and become choked with mud, thus preventing the flow of water. The city lost its freshness and attraction. When the British Government gained control of the city, [it was as though] spring had come to the city once again. They had it repaired and even improved it. Now it once again flows into every building and alley of the fort and city. Inspired by the success of this canal, the British Government has even made provisions for water to rural areas, and it now flows into most provinces and districts.

There are two branches of this canal. One flows to the west towards Sirsa and Hissar, where it ends since there is a desert beyond it. The other branch flows via the city of Shahjahanabad into its markets and the fort, towards the southern direction of Karnal, Ambala and Panipat. Once again the buildings of the fort have been refreshed and rendered attractive. The canal then flows into the River Yamuna.

As a result of the efforts of the British Government, the country now has five canals. The first one on the west is called Faiz Nahr that I have described above. Its branches extend all the way to Hissar and Rohtak. The second, the eastern canal stretches from the River Yamuna till Saharanpur, the third runs from Dehradun to Bijapur, the fourth from Rajpur, near Dehradun, and the fifth canal was taken from Nagina in district Bijnor, Rohilkhand.

I will now describe the best of cities, namely Shahjahanabad.

HAL SHAHR PANAH:[5]
A DESCRIPTION OF THE CITY OF REFUGE

When the Qila-e-Mu'alla [Red Fort] was ready and the city's population started increasing, the emperor ordered that a city wall be built around it, strengthened by a moat and bastions. Thus, in the emperor's twenty-fourth regnal year, this task was given to Mukarammat Khan.

As per the emperor's orders, a stone and mud wall enclosing the city was built within four months at a cost of Rs 1.5 lakh. However, in the monsoons of the next two years it crumbled in many places. Therefore, on the twenty-second day of [the Islamic calendar month of] Rabi Awwal, Shahjahan – then in his twenty-sixth regnal year – ordered it to be rebuilt with lime mortar and stone. This was completed within seven years, at a cost of Rs 3.5 lakh. A total of Rs 5 lakh was thus spent on this city wall. It was completed on the eleventh day of [the Islamic calendar month of] Jamadi-us-Saani, AH 1069 [6 March 1659].

The length of this boundary of the sky [hisar-e-falak] is 6364 gaz long, 4 gaz wide and 9 gaz high up to the merlons. It has 27 towers with a diameter of 10 gaz. There were originally six gateways and five wicket gates, but now a few more have been added. All the gateways are similar in size and shape. Thus, I will only sketch one of them though I will name them all.

When the British gained power, this wall had broken down in many places. The British Government gave orders for its repair, and the wall and moats were skilfully repaired. Outside Ajmeri Gate was the madarsa of Ghazi-ud-Din Khan. It was deemed unwise that such a magnificent building should be outside the city gates or that it should be broken down. Thus a new city wall was built, and this madarsa was taken inside the city. It will be described later.

As it was constructed in the reign of Emperor Moin-ud-Din Muhammad Akbar Shah, a marble tablet was installed on a new tower in this wall with the words 'The Tower of Emperor Akbar' [Burj Akbar Shah].

I will write down the names of all the gateways and give the sketch of one.

1. Delhi Darwaza
2. Rajghat Darwaza
3. Khizri Darwaza
4. Nigambodh Darwaza
5. *Kele ke Ghat ka* Darwaza
6. Lal Darwaza
7. Kashmiri Darwaza
8. Badar-ru Darwaza
9. Kabuli Darwaza
10. Paththar Ghati Darwaza
11. Lahori Darwaza (closed)
12. Ajmeri Darwaza
13. Turkman Darwaza

Khirki (wicket gates)

1. Zinat-ul-Masajid *ki khirki*/Nawab Ahmad Baksh Khan *ki khirki*
2. Nawab Ghazi-ud-Din Khan *ki khirki*
3. Musamman Burj *ki khirki*
4. Salimgarh *ki khirki*
5. Nasirganj *ki khirki*
6. Nai Khirki
7. Shahganj *ki khirki*
8. Ajmeri Darwaze *ki khirki*
9. Sayyad Bholi (Bu Ali) *ki khirki* (closed)
10. Buland Bagh *ki khirki* (closed)
11. Farrash Khane *ki khirki* (closed)
12. Amir Khan *ki khirki*
13. Khalil Khan *ki khirki*
14. Bahadur Ali Khan *ki khirki*
15. Nigambodh *ki khirki*

A DESCRIPTION OF THE CITY'S POPULATION

I don't have words to describe the beauty of this wondrous city. It is a piece of heaven inhabited by angels. All the luxuries of the world are available here. The beauty of the citizens makes even the virgins of paradise [*houris*] and the boys who attend the virtuous in heaven [*gilman*] envious.

The streets and alleys of the city are very wide and clean. Each street is like the street of the beloved and every bazaar is like a garden of flowers.

> Every dwelling I see on earth is a paradise,
>
> And every place is a garden.
>
> These meadows give pleasure
>
> As though they were a pathway to heaven,
>
> The wind is enchanting, delightful....
>
> This place is an abode of serenity on earth.

The description of this city is beyond me. How can I enclose a flowing river in a small cup? I will just describe the buildings, as the city has many elegant mansions and lofty mosques. The most beautiful of the mosques is the Jami-ul-Masajid also called Jama Masjid or Masjid Jahannuma. That is why I will describe it first.

MASJID JAHANNUMA/JAMA MASJID

This majestic place of worship is situated at a distance of 1000 *gaz* on a small hillock to the west of Shahjahanabad. The mosque completely hides the hill. Emperor Shahab-ud-Din Muhammad Shahjahan built this mosque. It is impossible to describe its exquisite design, delicate work and beauty. There is no other mosque of similar beauty on the face of earth.

It is built of the same red stone from top to bottom with marble used up to the dados. The red stone is interspersed at intervals with stripes of marble and black stone inlay. The domes are made completely of marble with black stripes of black stone. The architect has made this mosque with such artistry that not a single wall, arch, niche or wall-niches marking the direction of Mecca are free of design.

The foundation of this mosque was ceremoniously laid on tenth of [the Islamic calendar month of] Shawal AH 1060 [6 October 1659] in the twenty-fourth year of Shahjahan's reign under the supervision of Prime Minister Sadullah Khan and the Bailiff, Fazil Khan. A force of 5000 masons, stonecutters and labourers worked on it. This mosque was completed in six years at the cost of Rs 10 lakh. It has three beautiful domes, measuring 90 x 20 *gaz*. All the arches have inscriptions in Tughra script on marble tablets written in black slate. On the central arch is inscribed, 'O Guide!' [*Yaa Hadi*; one of the 99 names of Allah]. The inscriptions on the other arches praise the emperor and give details of the construction.

Arch I

> *By the order of the emperor of the world; king of the earth and age; lord of the world; conqueror of kingdoms; master of the world; powerful as the sky; founder of the laws of justice and administration; the one who strengthens the pillars of state and wealth; well-*

Masjid Jahannuma/Jama Masjid

knowing; of exalted nature; whose commands are like the decree of fate, and position like that of providence; of happy intellect, and auspicious appearance; fortunate and lucky; having grandeur like the firmament, soldiers [as numerous] as stars; glory like the sun and the court [as spacious] as the sky.

Arch II

The manifestation of the Almighty's power; the recipient of unlimited blessings; the proclaimer of the great word of God; the promulgator of the bright faith of Hanifa;[6] the asylum of princes and kings; the deputy of God on earth; the just and great king; the great and glorious lord [named] Abul Muzaffar Shihab-ud-Din Muhammad Sahib-e-Sani Shahjahan Badshah Ghazai, may the flags of his kingdom ever remain victorious and the enemies of his majesty subdued, whose eye of God-seeing perception is lit by the radiance of lights, of guidance of 'Verily, he populates mosques of God'.

Arch III

Who believes in God and the last day, and the mirror of whose truth-adopting conscience has received light from the flame of the lamp of the tradition 'The places most loved by God are mosques'; this mosque with its foundation [as firm] as a mountain and as lofty as the firmament which has for the description of its strong foundation the noble [verse], 'Verily the mosque founded on piety' and the clear [verse], 'The mountains were cast into the earth in order to make it firm' for the inscription of its strong hall; whose sky-like pinnacle and dome have gone beyond the folds of the firmament and the cornice of whose sky-like vaults have reached the height of Saturn.

Arch IV

If you want to know what the vault and cupola of its prayer chamber are like, nothing can be said except [that they resemble] the Milky Way and sky. The dome would have been matchless had the firmament not been its equal, the vault would have been unique had the Milky Way not been its pair. The brilliance of the Shamsa[7] of whose world-showing arch gives light to the lamps of heavens [stars]; the reflection of the pinnacle of whose world-adorning dome increases the light of the chandelier of paradise; whose marble pulpit like the rock of Solomon's temple is a ladder to.

Arch V

The point Qaba Qausain au adna;[8] whose grace-spreading mihrab like the true dawn with its broad and noble brow gives the good news: verily there has come to them from their God the right path; whose doors, which are the resort of mercy, have brought to the hearing of great and small the announcement, 'And God invites to the abode of peace'; whose minarets, which are the orbits of heavens, have sent the call, '[God] will compensate those who do good, with goodness' beyond the nine folds of the blue-coloured dome; whose lofty and polished roof is the pleasure ground of the spirits of the celestial sphere.

Arch VI

Whose spacious and pleasant courtyard is the place of worship of the pure, born of this terrestrial and populated world, and the favourable refreshing good and soul-strengthening air thereof resembles [the breeze of] the garden of paradise; the sweetness of the pure water of whose pleasing and purifying tank represents the spring of Sabasil, on Friday the tenth of the month of Shawal of the year 1060 Hijra, [6 October 1650] corresponding to the fourth year of the third cycle of the auspicious reign, at the propitious moment.

Arch VII

And the fortunate time obtained the wealth of foundation and ornament of stability; and during the period of six years, with the efficient exertions of expert and skilful workmen, with the great application and devotion of respectable superintendents, with the heavy effort of sagacious and wise masters; and with the great exertions of apt-handed and skilled artificers at a cost of Rs 10 lakh, obtained the form of completion and the feature of a structure finished, soon after its completion, on the day of Eid-ul-Fitr.

Arch VIII

It was adorned and embellished by the magnificence of the holiest steps of the king, the shadow of God, pure-intentioned, and God knowing; and on the day of Eid-uz-Zuha it became the resort of the crowds of people, by his [the emperor's] saying the Eid prayers and discharging the exercises of Islam as [is done] in Masjid-ul-Haram [Ka'ba] and blessed the formulation of Islam and faith with firmness and strength. To those who have made the tour of the inhabited fourth portion [of the globe] and travellers of such loftiness and strength have never been reflected in the mirror of their sight.

Arch IX

And the looking glass of their imagination, nor to the relaters of the events of the age and the careful students of prose and poetry who are the biographers of the important personages of the country and the kingdom, and are the connoisseurs of the persons of might and power, has a lofty edifice of such grandeur and magnificence been brought on the tongue of their pen and the pen of their tongue. May the builder of this mansion of life and the designer of high and low places keeping this exalted building firm, which is like the pupil of the eye of sight and the embellisher of the workhouse of creation.

Arch X

Continue the sound of the repeaters of the praises of God on a rosary, in it, giving grace to the noise of the assembly of God praising angels, and the melodious voice of the readers of the Muhammadan creed and the name of God, in it, increasing joy of the congregations of recluse angels of the highest order; and decorate the heads of the pulpits of the inhabited world world with the sermon [khutba][9] of the eternity adorning reign of this emperor who is an administrator of justice and cherisher of faith, and by the blessings of whose august and holy person the doors of peace and security have been opened for the world, for the sake of God and His people. Written by Nurullah Ahmad.

Dargah-e-Asar Sharif

To the north of this mosque, in the western hallway are kept the relics of the Prophet, peace be upon him. Almas Ali Khan Khwaja Sara got a red sandstone latticed stone-enclosure made around it during the reign of Emperor Aurangzeb Alamgir. The following date is inscribed in a chronogram on it:

> In front of this auspicious memorial of the last Prophet,
>
> In the reign of Shah Alamgir, King of the whole world,
>
> With pious intentions this screen of red stone was built,
>
> By the slave, the faithful, the clean-hearted Almas Khan.
>
> When the year and date of this building the Mir enquired, of Thought and Intelligence,
>
> Hathif replied: He has opened for himself the gates of Paradise.

Five years ago this enclosure was destroyed in a storm and was rebuilt from scratch by Hazrat Abu Zafar Siraj-ud-Din Muhammad Bahadur Shah Badshah Ghazi Khudullah. That enclosure is still present.

The Hauz

The courtyard is very attractive and pleasing to the soul. It measures 136 *gaz* square and in the middle of it stands a tank [*hauz*]. The tank is made completely of marble, and is refreshing, attractive, bewitching and exhilarating. It measures 15 by 12 *gaz* and has a fountain at its centre which flows on Fridays and on the festivals of Eid and Alvida Juma during [the Islamic calendar month of] Ramzan. This is a fountain of light which reaches the heavens, and even the sky and moon bend down to shake hands with it. To the west of this tank is a small stone enclosure built because of a dream seen by Muhammad Tahsin Khan Mahali Khwaja Sara. As per legend, he saw the Prophet, peace be upon him, sitting there. The following verses are inscribed on it:

> The Kausar [tank] of Muhammad, the Messenger of God, in the year AH 1180 [CE 1766–67],
>
> The Prophet was seen here by the saints and the people of God!
>
> This stone should be a place of worship.
>
> The year of its building, Hatif declared with joy and congratulations.
>
> The enclosure of the seat of the Messenger of God. The builder of this place of prayer, the writer of these blessed [words].
>
> Muhammad Tahsin Khan Mahali Badshahi, the year 1180. [CE 1766–67]

All around the mosque are beautiful aisles, hallways and rooms. On the four corners of the mosque stand four pavilions which add to its attraction. In front of the south-east hall is a sundial to indicate the time of prayers. This mosque has three lofty gateways. One is to the south towards the Chitli Qabr bazaar. The second is to the east towards Khas Bazaar and the third is on the north towards Paiwalo'n bazaar. All three gateways have doors installed in them with brass ornamentation. On either side of the mosque stand the beautiful buildings of Dar-ul-Baqa and Dar-ul-Shifa. I will draw a sketch of the mosque from inside as well as a separate sketch of the gateways. I will now describe each gateway and all the buildings near each.

JAMA MASJID: THE SOUTHERN GATEWAY

The southern gateway is made near the Chitli Qabr bazaar area, and its steps are generally crowded in the afternoon with peddlers who put up their shops and sell their wares. The *falooda*-seller decorates his shop and sells sweet sherbet and colourful *falooda* and cools the hearts of the lovers burning with desire of their beloved. Makers of *kababs* make every type of *kabab*, and the aromas coming from their stalls cause the parched lover to crave it.

Various types of pedigreed birds and animals, including gaming cocks, are also sold here on the steps. Young men with faces of angels indulge in cockfights, such that even the sky wonders at their cruelty. Friends roam around arm-in-arm enjoying themselves. Those who pray [the *namazi*] rush here to pray when they hear the call to prayer, and like angels make the intent to fly. The attractive redness of the thirty-three steps remind one of the betel-stained lips of the beloved. The marble is more attractive than the neck of a fair maiden. One can understand its beauty by looking at the sketch.

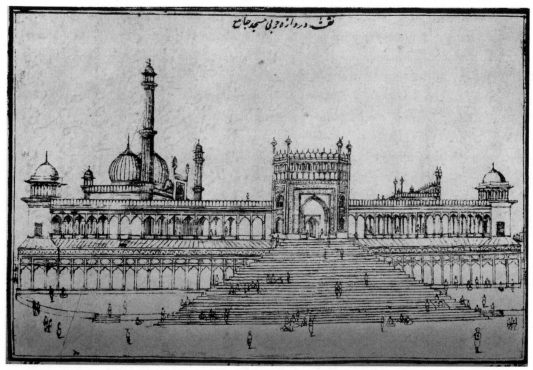

Jama Masjid: the southern gateway

Dar-ul-Baqa

The Dar-ul-Baqa *madarsa* is situated near this gateway. In the past, students used to stay here and study reason [*maqul*] and the fundamentals of religion [*manqul*]. This *madarsa* lay in ruins, but every age has its own philanthropists with generous and courageous temperaments. Janab Maulana Maulvi Muhammad Sadr-ud-Din Khan, the Chief Judge of Shahjahanabad, was guided by the Almighty to take up this task in this age. Perhaps, no one even in the past was so generous with his time and money. With great resolution of mind, he renovated this *madarsa* by spending his own money on it. Broken-down rooms were remade, teachers were employed and students have once again returned. Their board and lodging is paid for from the royal coffers.

God be Praised! His personality is blessed and generous. Only one's good deeds remain after death, and nothing accompanied us in the afterlife except our good deeds. It seems as if Allah has created these conditions specifically for him. There is a quite a big bazaar near this southern gateway which goes all the way up to the Turkman Darwaza and Delhi Darwaza. I now describe the famous locations below.

AREA AROUND THE SOUTHERN GATEWAY OF JAMA MASJID[10]

When we start from here there are some famous localities on the way.

Imam ki Gali

This street [*kucha* or *gali*] is on the right and situated here are the mansions of nobles and wealthy people. The house of the Imam of the Jama Masjid has also been here for ages, and that's why it popular as Imam ki Gali.

Ghazi Bharbhunja ki Dukan

Just at the beginning of this alley on the left is the shop [*dukan*] of Ghazi Bharbhunja [a seller of parched grain]. He is very famous, and his shop attracts many buyers at every fair, as he sets it up there and puts a fountain outside it. He illuminates his shop so well that night seems day. Thousands of people come here to enjoy the fair. During the [Islamic calendar] month of Moharram he puts up a wooden barge outside his shop and decorates and illuminates it. For ten days of Moharram, people come to see it. There is such a crowd in front of his shop that there is no standing space. On the ninth night of Moharram, a *tazia* comes here and stops in front of his shop. Fireworks are set off and people flock to see it. This bazaar looks like the Day of Reckoning [has arrived], because of the crowds present.

Matia Mahal

This is an old building on the left. Though there may have been a palace or houses of nobles here, now there are commoners' houses. I have not been able to ascertain how it got this name.

Haveli Janab Maulvi Muhammad Sadr-ud-Din Khan Bahadur Sadr-us-Sudur

To the right is the mansion of Janab Maulvi Muhammad Sadr-ud-DinKhan Bahadur Sadr-us-Sudur. It used to be the mansion of Lal Hazar Beg which was bought by Maulvi Sahib and rebuilt from scratch. It is a very attractive mansion with canals and fountains flowing in it. The gardens, canal and fountains make it look like a piece of heaven.

Shaidi Faulad Khan ka Bangla

Shaidi Faulad Khan's bungalow was also on the right. He was the chief of police [Kotwal][11] of Delhi in the reign of Muhammad Shah. But, now no traces remain of that bungalow, and just his name remains. A branch of the road which is called Churi walo'n ka mohalla [the neighbourhood of bangle-sellers], goes towards the west.

Azizabad ki Haveli

On the left of this road is the mansion of the Nawab of Azizabad. It was in the possession of Nawab Mufil Beg Khan but is now part of the crown lands. There was an old ruined mosque inside this mansion which has been repaired at great cost by Maulvi Muhammad Sadr-ud-Din Khan Bahadur. He also got a new well dug here.

Sayyid Muhammad Amir Khushnavez ki Haveli

Near the Shaidi Faulad Khan's mansion, towards the right is the mansion of Sayyid Muhammad Amir Khushnavez. In beautiful calligraphy are written the words 'May your afterlife be good' [Aqibat Ba Khair baad]. Near it is the Bhojala Pahari police station [thana].

Nawab Muhammad Mustafa Khan Bahadur ki Haveli

Beyond the mansion of Sayyid Muhammad Amir Khushnavez lies the mansion of Nawab Muhammad Mustafa Khan Bahadur towards the left. It is beautifully constructed and raises the status of its inhabitants to the sky.

Sayyid Rafa-e-Sahib ki Masjid[12]

This mosque is on the right and is very old. However, because Sayyid Sahib used to live in it and repaired it, the mosque has become known by his name. Sayyid Sahib was a very pious and devout man. He used to hold a special assembly where his devotees would gather in great numbers. Women were not allowed in this gathering. His special disciples would have knives in their hands and when they went into a state of ecstasy and forgetfulness of the world they would start reciting the *Kalima* and stab each other with these knives. However, no one was hurt. In case anyone did get hurt, Sayyid Sahib would put his spit on the wound and it would be immediately healed. It's been thirty years since Sayyid Sahib died.

Azam Khan ki Haveli

This mansion is on the left of Sayyid Rafa-e-Sahib ki Masjid. Azam Khan had built it but now it has become the residence of many people.

Chitli Qabr[13]

Near this mansion [Azam Khan ki Haveli] towards the right is a grave which is famous far and wide. They say it is the grave of Sayyid Roshan Sahib Shahid who was buried here 500 years ago. The market divides into two branches here, with one going towards Delhi Darwaza and the other towards Turkman Darwaza. The open space between Azam Khan's mansion and Chitli Qabr has become a three-way road.

Mir Muhammadi Sahib's Grave

Near this bazaar towards the left was the mansion of this saintly man. He was buried in it after his death and a commemoratory celebration [urs] is held here annually with the grave being illuminated. Mirza Salim Bahadur, son of Emperor Moin-ud-Din Muhammad Akbar, is also buried here.

Shah Ghulam Ali Sahib ka Khanqah

A little ahead and towards the left is the spiritual retreat of the revered Auliya Shah Ghulam Ali Sahib. The grave of Mirza Jan-e-Jana Mazhar, Shah Sahib himself and Shah Abu Saeed (may the mercy of Allah be on him) are all located here.

Momgaro'n ka Chhatta

Near this retreat towards the right was the area or 'hive' [chhatta] of the *momgar* or candle-makers, but now it consists of houses of the nobility and wealthy people.

Shah Kallan ki Dugduggi

Adjacent to the retreat towards the left in the bazaar is a small hallway with a short wall for lighting candles and incense sticks. Shah Kallan, a conjuror/juggler [dervish madari], used to live here. The small drum [dugduggi] he used to beat became very famous and thus this place became known as Shah Kallan ki Dugduggi. A road goes from here to Bulbuli Khana [see below] and Turkman Darwaza.

Mazaar Raziya Sultan Begum

In this area there lies the Bulbuli Khana locality. The houses of Munshi Sher Ali Khan and Maulvi Rasheed-ud-Din Khan are in this area. Between these houses is a stone compound with two graves. One is the grave of Raziya Sultan Begum and the other of Shazia Begum. The locals call this Rajji Shajji *ki dargah*. In some bygone era, this must have been a properly-built monument but now it lies ruined. The headstones of the two tombs have also disappeared. It is not even good enough for me to draw a sketch of it. However, Raziya Sultan Begum was the Badshah[14] of Hindustan in her time and increased the grandeur of the Delhi Sultanate, so I deemed it proper to mention her name.

We should know that Raziya Sultan Begum was the daughter of Sultan Shams-ud-Din Altamash who built the Qutub Minar, Quwwat-ul-Islam Mosque and the Hauz-e-Shamsi reservoir. When Sultan Shams-ud-Din Altamash died, Sultan Raziya came to the throne in AH 634 [CE 1236–37]. In AH 637 [CE 1239–40] Sultan Muiz-ud-Din imprisoned her in Bhatind Fort. She died a few days later and was buried here.

Kali Masjid

This mosque lies between Bulbuli Khana and Turkman Gate. It is popularly called Kali Masjid but it must be big as it is on a high plinth, and one has to climb thirty-two steps to reach it. The mosque was built by Junan Khan, the son of Khan-e-Jahan, Firoz Shah Tughlaq's Wazir [prime minister] in AH 789 [CE 1387]. There is an inscription on its façade:

> In the name of God, the most merciful, the most compassionate. By the grace and kindness of the Creator, in the reign and sovereignity of the religious king, strong by the help of the merciful [named] Abul Muzaffar Firoz Shah Sultan may his kingdom be perpetuated, this mosque was built by the son of the threshold, Junan Shah Maqbool titled Khan Jahan, son of Khan-e-Jahan, may God be merciful to that slave. Anyone coming to the mosque should pray for the benefit of the king of the Musalmans and recite the fatiha and the ikhlas for this slave, and may God forgive the slave. In honour of the Prophet and his posterity this mosque was finished on the tenth of [the Islamic calendar month of] Jumada II of the year AH 789. [CE 1387–88]

The mosque is very lofty and has five arches in every aisle. There are many graves in the courtyard. One of the graves is that of Junan Khan, the builder of the mosque, and the second is that of his father, Khan-e-Jahan. Look at its sketch and think of God's divine power.

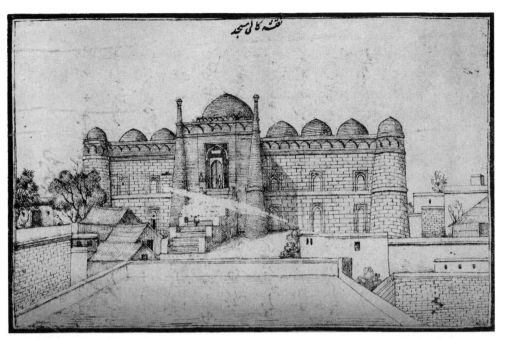

Kali Masjid

Dargah Hazrat Shah Turkman[15]

This is the *dargah* of Hazrat Shams-ul-Arifeen Shah Turkman Bayabani near Turkman Darwaza and that is why this gateway has become famous as Turkman Gate. Hazrat Shams-ul-Arifeen Shah Turkman Bayabani is a very revered saint whose miracles and qualities are beyond description, and nor does he depend on it. His grave is under the open sky with a small compound in which his shrine is located. Around his shrine is a marble enclosure with marble flooring laid around it. The rest of the flooring is of red sandstone. Near the grave is a Khirni tree[16] which was planted by Hazrat Maqdoom Jahaniyan-e-Jahan Gasht according to the hereditary caretakers here. He passed away on the twenty-fourth of [the Islamic Calendar month of] Rajab in AH 638 [8 February 1241] and a commemoratory celebration [*urs*] is held here on that date.

The festival of Basant Panchami [onset of spring in the Hindu calendar] is celebrated here with great gusto in the [Hindu calendar] month of Bahar; people from all over the city gather here to celebrate it. There are four more graves in this compound, where his disciples are buried. One grave is that of his nephew.

Amir Khan ka Bazaar

From Chitli Qabr, the bazaar branches in two directions. I have described above the branch of this market which went to Turkman Darwaza, and will now describe the one that goes to Delhi

Dargah Hazrat Shah Turkman

Darwaza. The market which goes towards Delhi Darwaza is called the Amir Khan Bazaar and has grocery and leather shops.

Bangash ka Kamra

Towards the right of this bazaar is the lofty room called 'Bangash Khan ka Kamra' which seems to be talking to the sky. It is very solidly built and seems to taunt the mountains with its stability. This room was built by Faizullah Khan Bangash at a great expense. In front of this bazaar is a three-way road and the mansion of Mirza Khajista Bakht. A road goes to Amir Khan's *Ganj* from its right side. The road on the left goes towards Chelo'n ka Kucha and Kale Mahal.

Mirza Khajista Bakht Bahadur ki Haveli

This is the mansion of Mirza Khajista Bakht Bahadur, brother of the late Muhammad Akbar Shah Badshah. It has an inscription with a chronogram for its date: '*The foundation of Khajista's home*' is what it says.

Tiraha Bairam Khan

There is a small square beyond this into which three roads converge. One is the road from the Amir Khan Bazaar, the second goes to Delhi Darwaza, and the third is on the left and goes towards Faiz Bazaar. There is a very famous mosque at this place.

Dai ki Masjid

This is a beautiful single-domed mosque. It is very famous, and many people come here to pray. This is inscribed on its façade:

> Thanks be to God that this mosque, through its glory, became a place of adoration to saintly persons. Wisdom said [of] the year of its foundation, 'Another Ka'ba has been populated'. The year AH 1064. [CE 1653–54]

Late Nawab Dabir-ud-Daulah's Haveli

Towards Faiz Bazaar [see below] is the mansion of Nawab Dabir-ud-Daulah Amin-ul-Mulk Khwaja Farid-ud-Din Ahmad Khan Bahadur Masleh Jung. It used to belong to Nawab Mehdi Quli Khan, and was bought by Nawab Dabir-ud-Daulah after Nawab Mehdi Quli Khan died.

Auliya Masjid

Beyond this is the Auliya Mosque. The chronogram for its date is: *The house of God* [*Khana-e-Khuda*]. Beyond it lies Faiz Bazaar, and a road goes to Tarachand ka Kucha.

Faiz Bazaar

This is really a bazaar of bounty, beneficence and abundance like its name. Attractive and extensive, it stretches from Delhi Darwaza till the Red Fort. It measures 1050 x 30 *gaz*. There are buildings on either side of it with a stream in the centre. It also has an exquisite tank lined with pretty trees and flowers which refreshes the soul. Vegetable and fruit shops add to the beauty and freshness.

The bubbling energy of this stream and tank as the water flowed was not found in any other stream in the city. Alas! The stream is now choked and the water has dried up and this enjoyment is lost. In a few days, no one will remember that there used to be a stream here. When water flowed through it here, this bazaar was really a piece of heaven. This verse fitted it beautifully:

> There are streams everywhere in this garden,
> Full of water, their flow is like a mad elephant.

Hakim Bu Ali Khan ka Kamra

Physician Bu Ali Khan's room is in this bazaar, which has been bought by Khwaja Zain-ul-Abidin Ahmad Khan Bahadur Masleh Jung. Once upon a time, this room was very beautiful.

Phool ki Mandi

The wholesale flower market [*phool ki mandi*] is in this bazaar and the shops of the flower-sellers would scent the entire atmosphere. However, the shops have long since been removed but the name continues. The Faiz Bazaar police station [*thana*] is located nearby too.

Masjid Roshan-ud-Daulah

There is a very beautiful and elegant mosque built by Nawab Roshan-ud-Daulah near Qazi Wada. In bygone days, this mosque had gilded decorations covering its walls. It had three beautiful golden domes and so it was called Sunehri Masjid. But now the gilding has peeled off and it looks very dull. The domes are broken and some of the minarets are damaged. There are just a few signs to testify to its name. They say that gold-plating from the domes was used to repair Sunehri Masjid near the Kotwali. Janab Maulvi Makhsusullah Sahib often comes to this mosque.

There is a very pretty tank in the courtyard. This too is now in ruins. This mosque was on the main road and so was very well-frequented by people. It was built in the reign of Muhammad Shah, and these verses are written on its façade:

> *Thanks be to God, that by the blessing of the grace of the Sayyid, a protection of the knowledge [of God], Shah Bhik who is a perfect and holy teacher, in the reign of a king glorified like Alexander and dignified like Jamshed, the spreader of justice, [named]*

Masjid Roshan-ud-Daulah

Muhammad Shah, the champion of the faith and the King Roshan-ud-Daulah Zafar Khan, the Lord of Beneficence and Bounty, built this golden mosque resembling heaven. Such a mosque that its dignified open courtyard the sky sweeps every morning with the pencil of the sun's rays. It's clear tank represents the stream of paradise, whoever performed ablution with its water became pure of his sins. Rasai obtained the date of its foundation from the invisible inspiration: [It is a] mosque like the mosque of Jerusalem where the light of God descends.' The year AH 1157. [CE 1744–45]

This mosque is very beautiful and famous and so I will make its sketch.

Masjid Akbarabadi

In this same Faiz Bazaar is a beautiful mosque that pleases the heart, refreshes the eyes and rejuvenates the spirit. It is built completely of red sandstone. There are rooms around it for students to live in. It has been built on a plinth which goes all the way to its western side. In magnificence and exaltation it even supersedes the sky. Aizaz-un-Nisa Begum, wife of Shihab-ud-Din Muhammad Shahjahan, in AH 1060 [CE 1650], built this blessed mosque in his twenty-fourth regnal year. She was given the title of Akbarabadi Mahal and the mosque also became famous by that name. It had three *burj* and seven arches and measured 63 *gaz* in length and 17 *gaz* in width.

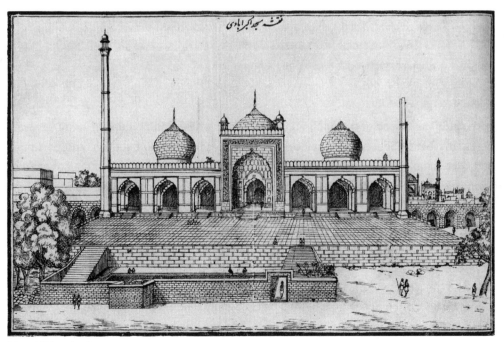

Masjid Akbarabadi

The hall is made of marble with inlay work. In front of it there is a platform which measures 63 *gaz* in length and 57 *gaz* in width and is 3½ *gaz* high. There is a marble enclosure around it in front. In front of that is a square 12 x 12 *gaz* tank which could once make the springs of the sun and moon blush. It is now dry. There are rooms around the tank measuring 154 *gaz* in length and 104 *gaz* wide. In front of each room is a gallery with a platform in front of it. This mosque also had two very lofty minarets which were destroyed by lightning, and no one has repaired it. There is an inscription on it in Naskh calligraphy.

> *This mosque is intended for the use of men only and it is such a place where the heart is at peace. The Hammam-e-Nizamat and Chowk-e-Dilkusha are located here. These are buildings where all seekers of truth observe prayers; and for the non-believers this place refreshes the soul. For the departed, it is a place of recreation, and for those of the mortal world, it is a place of gain. This mosque was built in Shihab-ud-Din Muhammad Shahjahan's reign, in the name of his Begum Aza-un-Nisa, who was also called Akbarabadi Begum. It was meant with the intent and hope for reward and salvation. All the expenses related to the mosque (both internal and external spending) were met through the waqf [trust]; so much so that when needed, its repairs could also be paid for through this trust. The rest of the money was put aside for the mosque, the hammam [tank], the students of the madarsa, and those who were in need, the poor (who have not been mentioned by name). These structures were built in two years, after an expense of Rs 1.5 lakh, and they were completed at the end of the month of Ramzan, from the twenty-fifth regnal year of the King, i.e., AH 1006. May God reward the King for this task. Amen.*

This mosque was destroyed following the 1857 mutiny.

Sunehri Masjid

Just a little way ahead of the Akbarabadi Mosque there is another mosque in the low-lying part of the fort. Its beauty and elegance are beyond description. It is beautifully proportioned and built completely of fawn-coloured stone. Both its beautiful minars are also made of fawn-coloured stone. It had three golden domes which had been built by plating the stone domes with thick copper plates and then another layer of thin golden plating. Even the *burjis* and finials of the mosque were golden. The walls inside were covered with gilded decoration. Some time ago the gold-plating came off and the domes were damaged. So, on the orders of the emperor the golden plates were completely removed. But I made the sketch before that was done.

To the left of the Sunehri Masjid is a hall with holy relics kept in it, which are taken out every year so that the faithful may see them and benefit from them. On the right of the mosque is a beautiful tank with a fountain supplied by water from a nearby well. Now the well

Sunehri Masjid

has fallen into disrepair and the fountain no longer works. The following verses are inscribed on the central arch:

> *Thanks be to God! In the reign of Ahmad Shah who is a champion of the faith, a king,*
> *a cherisher of the people, a door of justice, and a protection to the kings of the world,*
> *Nawab Qudsi [of divine] dignity built this mosque.*
> *May the common favour of that place of adoration of angels be everlasting.*
> *The exertions of the courteous and benevolent Nawab Bahadur [called] awed, of exalted*
> *power, constructed such an edifice.*
> *The clean well and the tank of its court are an honour to Zamzam;[17] whoever washed*
> *himself with its water became clean of his sins.*
> *How beautifully Khurram obtained the year of its foundation, from the invisible*
> *inspiration; [It is] the mosque of Jerusalem that rising place of the divine light.*
> *I will now make the sketch here.*

Bagwa Bari

Near the Golden Mosque is Bagwa Bari, a small garden, so named because Bagwa Begum's grave is located here. Khana garden is also in this area. Nowadays, some princes of the royal family live in it. Rajghat police *thana* is located next to it.

Zeenat-ul-Masajid

Zeenat-ul-Masajid

This famous and lofty mosque is located in Daryaganj next to the River Yamuna. It has two lofty minarets and can be seen from afar. The ornamentation and carving on the mosque, the greenery all around, the waves of the river all contribute to a beautiful mood. Very few mosques have such a beautiful atmosphere and surroundings.

The mosque is made completely of red sandstone and has three marble domes with black stone stripes in it. The black stripes in the dome are meant to ward off the evil eye. The shining golden finials on the domes seem to compete with the brightness of the sun. The minarets soar so high, as if they're in conversation with the sky. This mosque has seven arches with one large one in the centre and the rest of a smaller size. There is a tank in the courtyard, which used to be fed by a well, which is no longer functional. The tank appears to be like a spring emerging from the sun, but is as illuminated as the moon. There was a well near this which fed the tank, but the well is in disuse and is completely dry.

Zeenat-un-Nisa, the daughter of Emperor Alamgir, constructed this mosque. She is buried to the north of the mosque and near her grave is a small pavilion for placing offerings, and below it there are two stone emclosures. Inside an enclosure of fawn-coloured stone is another enclosure of marble. The flooring and headstone are also of marble. The marble headstone bears a Quranic verse and the epitaph:

For a friend in my grave, God's forgiveness is alone sufficient.

The canopy of my grave, is the shadow of the cloud of God's mercy.

In the hope of a righteous end Fathmah Zeenat-ul-Nisa Begum, daughter of Badshah

Mohi-ud-Din Muhammad Alamgir Ghazi.

May God illuminate his works: AH 1122. [CE 1710–11]

This mosque was constructed in the reign of Alamgir [Aurangzeb] and this enclosure after his death. I will give the sketch which will include the mosque and stone-enclosure.

JAMA MASJID: THE EASTERN GATEWAY AND ITS ENVIRONS

This gateway of the great mosque opens towards Khas Bazaar and there is a daily fair on its steps where clothes-sellers showcase their wares on clotheslines and decorate their shops in various striking ways to attract customers. Their innovative styles in trying to beautify this area remind one of the gardens of paradise.

The romantic youth of the city swagger about holding cages of exotic birds and animals in their hands. They stop and show-off their pets and their voices at various points. On one side stand the pigeon sellers and on the other, the horse traders with their horses. Buyers crowd the area to check out the birds and animals. All sales are made in hard cash. The scene reminds one of the saying, 'One item, a hundred buyers; one pomegranate, a hundred dying [for it]'. There are thirty-five steps in front of this gateway. The *dargah* of Shah Hare Bhare Sahib and Miyan Sarmad are located near this gateway too.

Khas Bazaar

This extensive and attractive bazaar is located near this gateway on a straight road. All kinds of vendors have their shops here but vendors selling different types of vegetables are most in number. A road from here goes to Khanum ka Bazaar and the mansion of Khan Dauran Khan.

Sadullah Khan ka Chowk

Once upon a time this chowk used to be very attractive and elegant, and a popular place for taking the air and recreation, but now it's just a memory.

Lal Diggi

Underneath the fort and facing the Khas Bazaar, at the spot where Gulabi Garden used to be located in an earlier time, the felicitous British Government has constructed a font of benefit that puts to shame even the sun and the moon. This water tank is constructed entirely of red sandstone with four small pavilions on the four corners and four extended terraces with guard-screens. There are steps going down to the water on two sides. This font of benefit was built in compliance wth the immutable command of Nawab Aali Janab *Falak Rakab* [whose feet use the heavens as their stirrups] Lord Ellenbrough Bahadur, and cost close to Rs 50,000. It measures 500 x 150 feet. The elegance and refinement of such a structure cannot be put in words.

Lal Diggi

JAMA MASJID: THE NORTHERN GATEWAY AND ITS ENVIRONS

This gateway is located near the Paiwalo'n ka Bazaar and there are thirty-nine steps leading up to it. *Kabab*-sellers sit on these steps while vendors put up their shops. However, the most entertaining are the jugglers and storytellers who show-off their skills on these steps. In the evening while one storyteller [*qissakhwan*] recites the *Dastan-e-Amir Hamza*, others narrate *Qissa Hatim Tai* or *Dastan Bostan*. Thousands of people gather here to hear these stories.

Jugglers also entertain people in such a way that even the elderly and old feel rejuvenated. There is a magical feel to the evenings on the steps of these gateways that only someone who has experienced it can understand. Something you have only heard about is like you have not seen it at all. God be praised, what a mosque, what a city, what inhabitants, what bazaars, what spectacles and what magic! Only someone who has seen it can believe it. I will make its sketch here so that you can see its beauty.

Dar-us Shifa

Near this gateway is the Shahjahani Darwaza or gateway [*dar*] of healing [*shifa*] where physicians used to sit in earlier days. There was a dispensary over here. But now it has been replaced by houses and people live in them.

R'hat's Well

This is a very famous well from Shahjahan's era. It has been dug in the hillock and a Persian Wheel [*r'hat*] fixed on it, which gives it its name. The water in the Jama Masjid mosque's tank and fountains is supplied by this well.

Jama Masjid: the northern gateway

Large Jain Temple

This temple is located in Dharmpura and is very big. It is built of brick and lime mortar with generous use of marble inside. Its construction was started in CE 1800 and it took seven years to complete. The first prayers were held here on the fifth of [the Jain calendar month of] Vaisakh Sudi in CE 1807. The cost of building this temple was Rs 5 lakh and it is said that there is one pedestal which was built for Rs 1.25 lakh. Lala Harsukh Rai and Lala Mohan Lal have built this temple.

Small Jain Temple

This temple is in a lane called Seth Gali [in Kucha Seth, Dariba Kalan] in the city of Shahjahanabad. It has been constructed by the Jains of the city and is famous as the Panchayati Temple. The construction of this temple was started in 1858 Simt[18] and took seven years to build. The deity was established in 1890 Simt. This temple is made of lime mortar and brick with marble used in many places inside. Both these temples have golden finials and many lakhs of rupees were spent on its construction. The priests don't allow people of other faiths to enter this temple and that is why I couldn't sketch both the temples.

Paiwalo'n ka Bazaar

This is an attractive and extensive bazaar in front of the North Darwaza of the Jama Masjid. There is a fork in the road from which two more roads emerge. One goes to Khanum ka Bazaar and the other to Dariba.

Dariba[19]

Even though it is much smaller in area than the other bazaars, it is much more famous and very well known. One can't describe the splendour and charm of this bazaar. There are many shops here of moneylenders and traders.

Masjid Sharf-ud-Daulah

This mosque is in Dariba Bazaar of the city of Shahjahanabad. It is built of lime mortar and bricks and has three marble domes. However, this marble is so yellow that it appears to be of brass. Nawab Sharf-ud-Daulah Bahadur built the mosque and the *madarsa* near it, in the reign of Emperor Muhammad Shah in AH 1135 [CE 1722–23]. There is an inscription on its façade.

Khooni Darwaza

At the edge of Dariba is an attractive arched gateway, which has been named Khooni

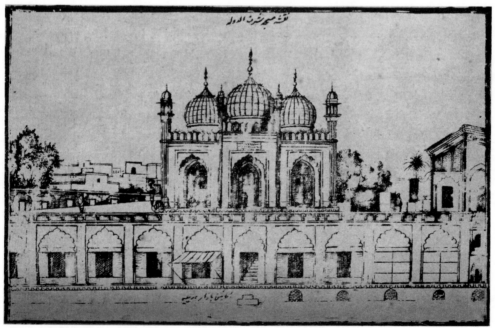

Masjid Sharf-ud-Daulah

Darwaza.[20] The main markets, including Chandni Chowk, lie beyond it. In earlier days this area used to be called Lahori or Urdu Bazaar. Since it is now known by a different name [Khooni Bazaar], I am also using the same.

Bazaar Janib Dar-ul-Sultanat Lahore

This is such an extensive bazaar that even the universe seems small in comparison. It is even more beautiful than paradise, as all kinds of vendors and shopkeepers sell their wares here. One can't describe its attraction as it is indescribable. This bazaar extends from Lahori Darwaza to the Fatehpuri Mosque. It measures 40 *gaz* in width, with 20 *gaz* on each side divided by a stream in the middle with trees planted on either side of it. The buildings on either side are uniquely beautiful.

The first part of this bazaar is called Urdu Bazaar. Beyond that is the Tripolia Darwaza and police station [*kotwali*] and so this part is known by that name. The area beyond that is called Chandni Chowk and beyond that is the Fatehpuri Bazaar. As soon as one comes out of Khooni Darwaza one sees Begum Samru's Kothi [mansion].

Samru ki Begum ki Kothi

This is a very beautiful and attractive mansion, the likes of which have probably never been seen before. This mansion is built on a plinth with a godown and rooms for the servants and employees, built at the plinth level. The mansion is like a terrestrial paradise. Apart from the beauty of the mansion itself the garden surrounding it is exquisite. The fragrance of the flowers and trees and the flow of the canal take it to a heavenly plane. This mansion was built during the initial years of the British government by Begum Samru, the estate-owner [*jagirdar*] of Sardhana. Since the mansion does not look as beautiful from the outside, I have not drawn a sketch of it. [21]

Kotwali Chabutra

This official building is located in an 80-*gaz* square with a tank, in the bazaar described above. The police station [*kotwali*], built on a platform [*chabutra*] is towards the south of it.[22] The Tripolia Darwaza was towards the north and though the gateway has now broken down, the road is still in use. They say that this place has always been a scene of calamities and trouble. Once upon a time, a river used to flow here and this was the spot where there was a whirlpool responsible for the drowning of innumerable boats. There was a jungle here with wild animals; a tiger roamed here that didn't let any living person escape. Now it houses the Kotwali Chabutra, where criminals are brought and punished. Sunehri Masjid is next to it, but do we need a tavern near the mosque, or persons looking for salvation?

Sunehri Masjid at Kotwali

This mosque is extremely beautiful and at such a wonderful location in the middle of a lively bazaar. Even though it is made of lime mortar and bricks, it is very attractive. The dome and finials are gilded which is why it is known as the Sunehri Masjid. The dome had been damaged and was replaced by the dome from Roshan-ud-Daulah's other mosque. Nawab Roshan-ud-Daulah Zafar Khan built it in AH 1134 [CE 1721–22] during the reign of Muhammad Shah. There are a few verses inscribed on the façade of the mosque:

> In the reign of the ruler of seven climes, Muhammad Shah, the sovereign who has Solomon-like splendour.
>
> This mosque was made unrivalled in the world for its magnificence, for Shah Bhik, the Polar Star of the age.
>
> O God! It is not but for the sake of laying him under an obligation that it (the mosque) is named after Raushan-ud-Daulah Zafar Khan.
>
> Its date, calculated from the flight [of the Prophet] is one thousand one hundred and thirty-four.

Chandni Chowk

Chandni Chowk [or the Moonlit Square, so called because of its beauty when seen on moonlit nights] lies beyond the platform that houses the police station [Kotwali Chabutra]. It is a 480-*gaz* bazaar, with a 100-*gaz* square [*chowk*] that has a square tank [*hauz*] in the centre. It is the 100-*gaz* square that is called Chandni Chowk. It is beyond my ability to describe its beauty and attraction. The evenings are magical here with the youth, princes and nobles coming for an evening stroll and entertainment. Very attractively built shops line both sides of the square, selling all kinds of wares. There is nothing in the world that is not sold here.

Begum ka Bagh

To the north of this square once existed a very eye-catching and appealing 970 x 240 *gaz* garden [*bagh*]. It had many striking and elegant twelve-arched pavilions and buildings inside it, and a stream flowed through it. There were tanks with fountains in it at intervals. Unfortunately, it is no longer as attractive as many people have built houses inside it and a settlement has come up here. However, the garden is still present with the stream flowing through it and serves as a reminder of yesteryears.[23]

To the south of this square was another appealing building made in response to Begum ka Bagh. It was known as Sahibabad. All these buildings were built on the orders of Jahan Ara Begum, daughter of Emperor Shahjahan's daughter, and are reminders of the past.

The ornamentations still left on the ruined walls and gates,
Are the remnant signs of Persia's ancient monuments.[24]

Masjid Fatehpuri

This mosque is at the end of Chandni Chowk. It was built with such noble intention that many good actions are still performed here. Innumerable people joined the ranks of those who had memorized the Quran [*hafiz-e-Quran*] here. Praise be to Allah. The mosque measures 45 x 22 *gaz* and is built of red sandstone. There are three arches, three aisles deep on each side of the dome. The marble flooring is ornamented up to the dado and there are two minarets on either side, 35 *gaz* in height but their cupolas have now broken and only the minarets are standing.

There is a red sandstone platform [*chabutra*] in front of it, which is 45 x 35 *gaz* in front of which is a red sandstone tank, which is 16 x 14 *gaz*. The stream that runs through Chandni Chowk flows into the tank of this mosque. The courtyard of this mosque is beyond that and measures 100 x 100 *gaz* and around the courtyard there are 69 rooms for students to reside in. Behind it is Lahori Darwaza. Nawab Fatehpuri Mahal Begum, wife of Shahjahan, constructed it. Its sketch is placed here.

Masjid Fatehpuri

Masjid Punjabi Katra

Masjid Punjabi Katra

Punjabi Katra was a residential area, where traders from Punjab would alight when they came to Shahjahanabad. That's why it became famous as Punjabi Katra. This attractive and appealing mosque is built of red sandstone and its beauty is beyond my ability to describe. It was built by such a noble woman that it is still functioning. Maulvi Abdul Khaliq Sahib and Maulvi Muhammad Nazir Hussain Sahib teach and give sermons here. The mosque is blessed as the name of Allah and the Prophet are remembered here day and night. There is a very pristine tank and beautiful buildings in the mosque complex. However, many people now have encroached and taken parts of the courtyard into their houses. Even then it's a very impressive mosque. Nawab Aurangabadi Begum, wife of Emperor Aurangzeb Alamgir, built this mosque during his reign and left it as a memorial to her piety.

Fakhr-ul-Masajid

This mosque is located inside the city of Shajahanabad, near Kashmiri Darwaza. Though not a very big mosque, it is very exquisitely designed with beautiful domes and its appearance is very elegant. The domes of this mosque are incomparable and there is no other such dome on the face of earth. Even the domes of the sky are envious of it and bow before it. This mosque has been made in the bazaar on a plinth, with many shops at the level of the plinth. Its façade is made of marble with stripes of red sandstone at intervals. Marble has been very tastefully placed inside the mosque till the dado. The domes are of marble with lines of black stone. The finial is golden in colour. The mosque has marble flooring and its outside is made of red sandstone.

There is a very well-made concrete courtyard on its southern side that has been replicated on the northern side. Both sides of the northern courtyard used to open on to a very beautifully made tank, but the tank and its fountain are now broken. There was also another tank nearby fed by the water of the stream, and it in turn fed this [now broken] tank and its fountain. Fatima Fakhr-un-Nissa Begum, wife of Nawab Shujat Khan built this masjid in AH 1141 [CE 1728–29]. When Nawab Shujat Khan left this world, his wife had this mosque built in his memory so that his afterlife would be blessed and good deeds could be registered on his deed of registers [on the day of Resurrection]. On the gate of the mosque is an inscription on a marble plaque with 'Fakhr-ul-Masajid' [Fakhr-ul Mosque] inscribed on it. An inscription on the central arch reads:

> The Khan, cherisher of religion, Shujat Khan got a place in paradise, by the will of the Exalted God and for the sake of Murtaza [Ali].
>
> The chief of ladies, Kaniz Fatima, the pride of the world, built this mosque in his memory by the Grace of Mustafa [the Prophet], AH 1141. [CE 1728–29]

Girja Ghar

This church is near the Fakhr-ul-Masajid. It is difficult to describe the beauty and majesty of this church. In reality there must be very few churches which are as beautiful as this. Its dome has been made in the shape of a cross. It is very beautiful and golden in colour. The rooms inside are very beautifully made with elegant marble flooring. Colonel James Skinner Sahib Bahadur, a very famous and resolute man, built this church at his own expense. Its construction began in CE 1826 and was completed in ten years at a cost of Rs 90,000. The marble flooring is not included in this figure asColonel Sahib already had the marble in his possession.

William Fraser, whose grave lies to the east of this church, was the Commissioner of Delhi and he was shot and murdered by some improvident men. Fraser Sahib gave a lot of respect to Indian noblemen and that's why Indians were very sorrowful at his death. His marble grave with carvings on it is very well made and is surrounded by an iron railing. I will make its sketch here so that its beauty can be seen.

Girja Ghar

Nawab Abdul Ahad Khan's Haveli

This mansion was near [Skinner's] Church. It was very beautiful with a garden, fountains and a stream flowing in it. Now, there is a government *madarsa* inside one portion of it and civil courts in the other rooms.

Mansoor Ali Khan's Haveli

Mansoor Ali Khan's beautiful mansion is near this. It is very big and well decorated with a stream flowing through it with fountains in the garden. There is a beautiful bathouse near this mansion which is still heated in winters.

Magazine Sarkari

Near these mansions is a government [*sarkari*] magazine[25] which houses an arsenal. Every day there is an increase in it.

Panchakki/Water Mill

Near the magazine is the stream that goes into the fort and flows into all the buildings there.

The water mills [*panchakkis*] are located on this water-channel. They grind innumerable *maunds* of flour every day. The area behind Jama Masjid is also very beautiful with its minarets, domes and cupolas.

THE AREA BEHIND JAMA MASJID

The minarets and domes of Jama Masjid look very beautiful even when viewed from the back of this mosque. Thus I will write about that side here.

Chawri Bazaar

The bazaar behind Jama Masjid is famous as Chawri Bazaar. It's very extensive, attractive and worth strolling in. There are many types of vendors here, but the maximum number of shops here sell pulses, oil and saffron. There are also paper-makers here.[26]

Shah Bola's Banyan Tree

Just beyond Chawri Bazaar is this very famous banyan tree. A mendicant named Shah Bola used to live here and his grave is situated under it. Though other trees have replaced this tree, it is still known by the previous name.[27]

Qazi ka Hauz

Just a little ahead of the banyan tree was a brackish well which is now in disuse. Beyond that is the very famous Qazi ka Hauz [the Qazi's tank],[28] even though it is not as attractive now, some signs of it can be found here. There is a crossroad at this point with one road going to Ajmeri Gate, one into Sita-Ram's Bazaar [Sita-Ram ka Bazaar] and a third towards Lal Kuan.

Lal Kuan Bazaar

This is a very spread-out bazaar. The mansions of Badal Beg Khan and Hafiz Abdur Rahman are located here, along with a few small mosques. There is a functional well here built of red sandstone, which has given the locality the name of Lal Kuan.

Khari Baoli

This step well [*baoli*][29] is just a little ahead of Lal Kuan. Even though the shops have encroached upon the step well, one can still make out that there is a step well here. It predates the city of Shahjahanabad and was built in Sher Shah's reign. In other words it was started in AH 952 [CE 1545] and was completed in AH 958 [CE 1551]. Some words are inscribed on this step well but I couldn't read them all. I am writing down what I could and copying the rest as I found them. The inscription on the gate reads as:

O Allah! There is no God but Allah and Muhammad is his Prophet. O Allah!

The inscription on the façade inside reads:

In the name of Allah, the most gracious, the most merciful. And with the healing by my Lord, the disease dies.

This step well was built in the [Islamic calendar] month of Ramzan in AH 958 [CE 1551] with the blessings of Muhammad Mustafa, Rasul-e-Khuda during the reign of Adil Islam ibn Sher Shah by Khwaja Imad-ul-Mulk alias Abdullah Lazar Qureishi who is hopeful of mercy and blessings. The inscription on the north wall reads:

In the name of Allah, the most gracious, the most merciful.

In the reign of Shah Sultan-us-Salateen wa Muzazafar-ul-Islam Shah bin Sher Shah Sultan, Allah gave the opportunity with the blessing from his Prophet to Mulk Imad-ul-Mulk alias Khwaja Abdullah Lazar Qureishi Badar-ul-Mulk Hazrat Dehli, AH 952. [CE1545]

Bazaar Ajmeri Darwaza

The bazaar at Ajmeri Darwaza [gateway; also, known as Ajmeri Gate, today] is very extensive with attractive buildings and small mosques on either sides. Ghazi-ud-Din Khan's *madarsa* stands outside this gateway.

Madarsa Ghazi-ud-Din Khan

Ghazi-ud-Din Khan's *madarsa* is situated outside Ajmeri Darwaza. It has three very attractive gates and when someone steps into the *madarsa* through them, one's spirit is immediately uplifted. There is a large courtyard inside. To its north and south are very spacious and elegant rooms for students to rest in. On the roof are some more rooms. There are rooms on either side of the three gates on the east as well.

Towards the west and on the opposite side is a grand red sandstone mosque with flooring of red sandstone. On both sides of the mosque, some place has been set aside for a courtyard and two halls. The southern hall has an enclosure of fawn-coloured stone which has another marble enclosure inside it with very delicately made screens surrounding it. These screens are so beautiful and delicately carved that they cannot be described in words. There are three graves inside this enclosure with marble headstones. A large and deep tank once stood in the courtyard of the *madarsa*.

This *madarsa* was constructed in the reign of emperors Ahmad Shah and Alamgir II. Ghazi-ud-Din Khan, a notable noble in the reign of these emperors, built it. The British wanted to demolish it and had already started to do so. However, as it was very solidly built, the cost of demolition was very high and since it was a beautiful building they decided to reuse it. They dug a moat around it and took it inside the city of Shahjahanabad and decided to use it for

Madarsa Ghazi-ud-Din Khan

teaching students. Teachers were appointed to teach Arabic, Persian and Shastri [Sanskrit] here.

Nawab Fazl-e-Ali Khan Itmad-ud-Daulah, Wazir Shah Awadh, donated Rs 170,000 for the maintenance of this *madarsa*. The government had this fact inscribed on the wall. The inscription on the west arch of the central eastern gateway giving access into the courtyard reads:

> *There remains no mark on the tablet, but the reward of an act and a good name.*
> *In the blessed memory of Nawab Itmad-ud-Daulah Zai-ul-Mulk Sayyid Fazl-e-Ali Khan Bahadur Sohrab Jung, who entrusted the Honourable English East India Company with one lakh and seventy thousand rupees for the advancement of learning at this school, situated in Delhi proper, his native place [this tablet] was inscribed in CE 1829.*
> *Written by Sayyid Amir Rizvi. In the name of Allah, Most Gracious, Most Merciful.*

Editor's Notes

1. CE 1638–39 was the year that the emperor gave orders to begin the building of this city. Once work began princes, nobles, courtiers and ordinary people began moving in and building their own homes.

2. Today, in place of Faiz Nahr [canal] stands Chnadni Chowk, one of the busiest and most chaotic streets of Delhi.

3. Bijai Mandal was not constructed by Firoz Shah Tughlaq, but was part of Jahapanah, the city built by Muhammad bin Tughlaq.

4. The area that was Pargana Navahi in Khizrabad is today Delhi's New Friends Colony.

5. Another name for the city of Shahjahanabad as the walls surrounding it kept it safe from invaders.

6. One of the four great expounders of Muslim Law.

7. 'Resembling the sun and offering light and radiance; here a figure resembling the sun put up as a decoration on a keystone arch'. [Taken from Zafar Hasan, *Monuments of Delhi* (Delhi: Aryan Books International, 2008).]

8. Literally a place located two bow-lengths away, or even closer than that. This is a reference to the Prophet's proximity to God during his ascent to heaven.

9. The *khutba* sermon is delivered by the Imam on the occasion of Eid and Friday prayers and used to contain the name of the reigning monarch.

10. Most of the names mentioned in this section on the southern gateway of Jama Masjid are no longer visible. Matia Mahal is now an area full of restaurants and other shops and the mansions [*havelis*] have all vanished.

11. The chief of police of a town or city was called the Kotwal.

12. The mosque still exists but in a modern form. It has been completely renovated.

13. The Chitli Qabr grave still exists and so does the market.

14. Raziya ascended the throne as Sultan Jalalat-ud-din Raziya. She titled herself Sultan Raziya. According to her, 'Sultan of Delhi' was her proper title. Sultana was a title for a consort or a princess, not for the ruler [Sultan].

15. The actual *dargah* of Shah Turkman as described and sketched by Sir Sayyid is in Mohalla Qabristan of Turkman Gate area and is famous as the *dargah* of Dada Pir. The *dargah* near the gate itself is of an unknown person, now called Shah Turkman.

16. *Manilkara hexandra* of the family Sapotaceae.

17. Zamzam is the name of a well in Mecca's Al-Haram mosque. On the orders of God, prophet Abraham had left his child and wife Hajira in the desert of Mecca. The baby was crying of thirst and Hajira was running between two hills to find water for him. A spring gushed out miraculously on the spot where the infant child Ismail was crying. The water of the well is called Aab-e-Hayat [life-giving water] as it is said to be blessed.

18. It is unclear whether the term, used by Sir Sayyid, 'Simt' refers to the Hindu calendar era Samvat. Therefore the term has simply been reproduced as it was in the original.

19. It derives its name from the Persian *Dur-e-be-baha* which translates as 'unparalleled pearl'.

20. This Khooni Darwaza is no longer extant. Now this name has been given to another gate which stands near Firoz Shah Kotla and is referred to in this book [*Asar-1*] by Sir Sayyid as 'Kabuli Darwaza'.

21. Samru Begum ki Kothi is now an urban mess with hawkers and shops crowding on to the building and its famous staircase from all sides. It houses the Central Bank of India and is in a very sad state of repair.

22. Today the Kotwali Chabutra area houses Gurudwara Shishganj.

23. When the British gained power in India after 1857 they re-named Begum ka Bagh as Queen's Park and installed a statue of Queen Victoria. Now, a statue of Mahatma Gandhi stands there and it is called Mahatma Gandhi Park. It is attached to the Town Hall which was built on the location where Begum [Jahan Ara] ki Sarai [The Begum's Inn] once stood.

24. This verse by Urfi gives the book its title [*Asar-us-Sanadid*].

25. The magazine was blown up by the British so that it would not fall into rebel hands.

26. Even today, Chawri Bazaar is famous for its books and paper business.

27. Shah Bola's banyan tree: there is still a banyan tree in the place, which is probably an offshoot of the original.

28. The name probably came because the tank might have been built by a judge [*qazi*] of the Shariah [Islamic] law.

29. The Khari Baoli area now houses Asia's largest spice market.

CHAPTER FOUR

Delhi aur Delhi ke Logo'n ke Bayaan Mei'n: About Delhi and Its People

Hazrat Dehli's attribute is that it's a huge congregation,

May those whose presence is spread all over be in Allah's protection.

If I decide to write about the beginning of Delhi and describe it according to Hindu history, then I would need a complete book as there isn't enough space to fit in everything into this brief account. That's why I will just describe it in bits and pieces.

DESCRIPTION OF DELHI AND ITS CLIMATE

A lot of praise is heaped on the way Delhi's climate once was, but today my special city does not have a good climate. Most of the wells are brackish, except for those which are on the banks or near the river where the water is sweet. The water of the river can't be described; it is just like the water of any other river. Due to the fact that the water levels of the river have gone down and been diverted into canals, even the river water isn't of a good quality any more. The water of the wells is cool in the summers and beats iced water as it is lighter, but it isn't as easily digested as one would desire. I don't say that the water is harmful, but that there's no doubt it isn't worthy of praise.

The breeze here is humid and moist and most of the people here normally suffer from many diseases particularly liver ailments, indigestion, colds and coughs. The reason for these problems seems to be the size of the city's population – people of every profession and trade live here, also – and as compared to the past – the roads and markets have become very narrow and congested. The city is not as clean as it should be, and this is why the climate has also changed. In the summers even if it is not too hot, there are outbreaks of infectious diseases.

The climate outside the city is very pleasant: the water is easily digested, the breeze is very enjoyable and there are very few instances of disease. The climate of Qutub Sahib [Mehrauli] is very famous, however since the emperor now stays there very often it has become crowded because of the people who follow him there. There is an increase in the waste thrown and though it is no longer as beautiful as it used to be, it is still better than Delhi. However, in spite of all these factors, the climate of Delhi is still a thousand times better than that of other cities. There is no specific ailment which is found here. By God's grace, the people here are attractive, fair and good looking, and the young delight in showing off their youth.

A DESCRIPTION OF THE PEOPLE OF SHAHJAHANABAD

Though people might feel that I am writing about the people of this place in a biased manner because of my love for the place, but those who are just will see that my writing is free from all bias and prejudice. In reality, the people of this place are such as cannot be found in any other place. Every individual is a collection of thousands of good traits and a bouquet of lakhs of skills and talents. Every individual wants to gain knowledge, skills and learning all the time. Virtues are so imbibed in every person's disposition that were we to write about it, thousands of books could be written. On top of that, their clemency, humanity, loyalty to friends is beyond description, and they are never envious or jealous.

> It is blasphemy to keep envy and jealousy in our *tariqa*,
>
> It is our constitution to keep our hearts as clear as a mirror.

There must be thousands of people who have forsaken the pleasures of the body and all things abominable and have adopted the teachings of the Prophet, peace be upon him. The same virtues that are found in the teachings of the Prophet are found in the people here. Even though there are some youth who are misguided and wild in their ways and according to Saadi, 'The young do whatever they want to in the days of youth.'

They are busy wandering, playing games and have no other interest except for absurd pastimes and the pursuit of love, but even then these are conducted within boundaries of modesty [they hunt behind a veil of modesty]. This modesty is a redeeming factor. There are thousands of youngsters who are so virtuous and upright, who in spite of their youth and tender years, are not tempted towards the irrational or wrongdoing and have adopted a path of piety and virtue which is very praiseworthy. I will now describe those respected men whom I have been fortunate enough to serve or those virtuous men whose existence lit the world.

Zikr-e-Kibaar-e-Mashaiqin Razi Allah hu Anhum Ajmain: Description of the Sufi Masters[1]

Janab Hazrat Master of Masters Maulana Shah Ghulam Ali, May His Tomb Be Purified and Hallowed[2]

I am not worthy of being able to write about his evident virtues, piety and status in the eyes of God as these are beyond the capacity of the writer and are not obvious to the onlooker. Glory be to God, his knowledge, accomplishments, virtue, piety, qualities, generosity, humility and clemency were ultimate. He gave away everything that he had, or had acquired, in the name of Allah and never worried about the future. He spent his entire day in remembrance of Allah and his Prophet, peace be upon him, without caring about the world.

Which of his qualities can I describe? His knowledge was incomparable, his devotion and striving in the path of God are beyond description and his piety and virtue had reached the stage beyond which it had nowhere further to go. On top of that, his humility and his level of religious attainments, achievements and virtues were at a level where one didn't want to leave his company if one were fortunate enough to be with him.

He was originally from Dotala[3] village which is in the state of Punjab near Ambarsar [Amritsar] and belonged to the descendant of the Prophet from Hazrat Ali [Sadat Alavi]. His father was also a great religious leader who used to go to the jungles and spend time in remembrance of God and would live on herbs and leaves that were found there. Before his birth, the saint's father saw Amir-ul-Mominin[4] Ali ibn Abi Talib (may Allah brighten his face) in a dream. Hazrat Ali predicted that soon a boy would be born to the family and must be named after him [Hazrat Ali]. And his mother saw a saint in her dream naming her son Abdul Qadir. And his uncle kept his name Abdullah after a revelation to him by the Prophet, peace be upon him, that is why his actual name was Abdullah alias Ghulam Ali.

He was born in AH 1156 [CE 1743–44] and illuminated the world with the beauty of his existence. A few poets have even celebrated his birth in verse. He lived till the age of 16 in this region. In AH 1174 [CE 1760–61], he was called to Delhi by his father to become a disciple of his father's Master, Shah Nasir-ud-Din Qadri, whose mausoleum lies behind the new Idgah. But Shah Nasir-ud-Din passed away before he [Abdullah alias Ghulam Ali] could reach. God had some other purpose in mind and his father allowed him to become the disciple of anyone of his own choice.[5] In AH 1178 [CE 1164–65] at the age of 22, he became the disciple of Mirza Jan-e-Jana Mazhar, may the blessings of Allah be upon him,[6] and read this verse:

> I found a door in front of which to do the prostration of love,
>
> I found my head on the ground and my eyes on the sky.

After becoming a disciple, he spent many years in the service of his Master and his devotion and hard work in striving in the way of God can't be described. He spent his life learning and in piety. He had entered the Qadriya order but took permission from his master and saints of the other Sufi orders to be associated with them too. After the demise of his master he became the administrator of the *dargah*. He had no worldly attachment and lived his life as per *sunnat*[7] and his faith in God was so strong that he never wavered. Kings and nobles wanted to fix a stipend for the mendicants who lived at the spiritual retreat [*khanqah*] but he refused to accept this. Once, Nawab Amir-ud-Daulah Amir Muhammad Khan, the ruler of Tonk requested him profusely for permission to bestow a stipend. Shah Ghulam Ali sent a verse in reply:

> I don't want to insult fasting and patience,
> Tell Amir Khan that my livelihood is ordained [by God].

His fame spread far and wide and he had disciples from many countries. I have personally witnessed people from as far Rum [Turkey], Baghdad, Egypt, China and Habsh [Africa] come to the spiritual retreat and become his disciples. Of course, people from India and neighbouring countries like Afghanistan came in large numbers.

> Just as people of distant lands head towards Ka'ba to pray[8]
> People come from thousands of miles for a glimpse of his face.

There were at least 500 mendicant disciples living in Hazrat's spiritual retreat. He was responsible for their food and upkeep, for which he didn't take any help from anyone. Allah would provide unseen [*ghaib-ul-ghaib*] help and he never needed any help from anyone for their food or upkeep. He would sell all the presents that disciples offered him and use them for the maintenance of the spiritual retreat. He would wear the same coarse cloth as his disciples and eat the same food and refused to differentiate. When pressed to wear expensive clothes or use anything for his personal pleasure, he would say:

> My sitting on the dusty earth is as if I was [equal to] King Solomon,
> It's the same for me to wear the crown of a king.
> It has been many years since I've been wearing this,
> My cloak of nakedness never becomes old.

And if ever there were a discussion of luxuries, then he would quote the famous Persian poet Bedil:

> O Bedil, greed is not content with the goods and merchandise of the world,
> Whatever I have in use also, most of it is not really needed.

And if ever there were a discussion of luxuries, then he would say that patience is not greed and that and that he did not even need the worldly goods he already possessed.

His followed a very disciplined daily routine. He knew the Quran by heart and thus was a *hafiz*. He would say his morning prayers at the correct time, would read ten chapters of the

Quran daily and be busy in remembrance of God till dawn. After the dawn prayers he would teach the sayings of the Prophet [*hadith*] and a commentary of the Quran to his disciples. He had complete knowledge of all things. He would eat a light meal after teaching and then take a short nap and then recite the afternoon prayers. From the noon prayer [*Zohar*] till the afternoon [*Asr*] prayers he would again teach. He would then sit with his disciples till sunset [*maghrib*] and share precious knowledge with them. He would not sleep at night and spend it in prayers and devotion. He would snooze in between prayers but he never slept on a bed. There was an extraordinary atmosphere at this spiritual retreat where the ground was covered by sackcloth. His character was unique.

My [Sir Sayyid's] family, especially my father, had great faith in the saint who, in turn, loved my father as a son and his blessings were on our family. This had a great influence on our family's character. I would present myself in his presence every day. Hazrat would make me sit next to him on his prayer mat. Due to my tender age, I would sometimes behave improperly, but even then Hazrat would tolerate it and bless me. Apart from this, we can't describe his miracles. On a Saturday, on the twenty-second [of the Islamic calendar month] of Safar AH 1240 [16 October 1824], he left this world and he was buried at the spiritual retreat next to his Master. He had willed that some verses in Arabic and Persian be recited during his funeral, as was done at Khwaja Baha-ud-Din Naqshbandiya's funeral.[9] Thousands mourned him and there was a huge outpouring of grief when the verses specified by him were read.

Janab Hazrat Maulana Shah Abu Saeed,[10] May Allah Illuminate His Grave

He [Hazrat Abu Saeed] is from the family of Mujaddid,[11] the Master of Masters of Janab Hazrat Shah Ghulam Ali Sahib. [Hazrat Abu Saeed was Janab Hazrat Shah Ghulam Ali Sahib's diciple.] Hazrat Shah Ghulam Ali gave him [Hazrat Abu Saeed] the same respect [that he would give his Master]. Hazrat Abu Saeed is the successor-in-chief of Janab Hazrat Shah Ghulam Ali Sahib and also the administrator. His genealogy could be traced thus: Shah Abu Saeed bin [the son of] Safiullah [the son of] Azeezul Qadr [the son of] Muhammad Isa [the son of] Saif-ud-Din [the son of] Khwaja Muhammad Masoom [the son of] Mujaddid Al Fisani – Allah is pleased with him. Mujaddid Al Fisani was descended from the second Caliph, Hazrat Umar Faruukh.

Maulana Shah Abu Saeed was a very pious man who was endowed with obvious and hidden qualities. He had memorized the Quran and was an expert in matters related to religion. He would spend his days and nights increasing his religious knowledge. His voice was so sweet and well modulated that people would come from far and wide to hear him recite the Quran. He was initially in the Qadri order, with Maulana Shah *Dargahi*[12] – Allah is pleased with him – as his master, but he took permission from him to enter the Naqshbandiya Mujaddiya order, to which Shah Ghulam Ali belonged.

His face was illumined and as long as one sat with him, there would be no evil thought in anyone's mind. He followed the same principles as laid by his master, Shah Ghulam Ali. He would write the Quran in his own hand and gift it to people. He had learnt the art of calligraphy [khat-e-naskh] from Kallu Khan [a famous calligrapher, mentioned later in this book].

Shah Ghulam Ali Sahib would often remark on how proud he was of Shah Abu Saeed who would spend his time in devotion and remembrance of God with no thought of the world. He was an able disciple and in fact went even went further than his master. Thousands benefited from his teachings and company. During this period, love for the Prophet, peace be upon him, swelled in his heart and he decided to visit Mecca and Medina [the Haramain Sharif]. He was able to perform the Hajj and the pilgrimage to Medina-e-Munavara ['the illuminated city'; Medina is referred to in this fashion even today].

On his return from the pilgrimage, Shah Abu Saeed passed away at Tonk. His body was brought to Delhi and he was buried next to Hazrat Shah Ghulam Ali at his spiritual retreat. He was born in AH 1196 [CE 1781–82] and passed away in AH 1250 [CE 1834–35] on the day of Eid.

Janab Hazrat Maulana Shah Ahmad Saeed, May the Most High God Save and Protect Him

He is the eldest son and successor of Shah Abu Saeed. His praiseworthy qualities are beyond description. He has memorized the Quran following in the footsteps of his Masters and it is from him that this spiritual retreat is illuminated and flourishing. Thousands are blessed to have his guidance and may Allah keep this man, who is responsible for continuing the Mujaddid lineage. He was born in AH 1217 [CE 1802–03] and *Mazhar Yazdaan* is the chronogram for his birth.

Even though he is just 46 years old at the time of my writing [sic], he has reached the height of excellence. He has become the disciple of Hazrat Ghulam Ali Shah and has been appointed his successor. He gained a lot of knowledge from his respected father and attained success as well as successorship from him. After his father's demise, he is now the administrator and is busy in his task of guiding and providing leadership to his people at his spiritual retreat. Oh Allah, please benefit Muslims with his long life and elevate their status.[13]

Janab Hazrat Maulana Shah Abdul Ghani Sahib, May the Most High God Save and Protect Him

Another son of Shah Abu Saeed, he too has memorized the Quran and is a renowned scholar on the sayings of the Prophet [hadith] and jurisprudence [fiqh]. He was born on Saturday, the twenty-fifth [of the Islamic calendar month] of Shaban, AH 1234 [19 June 1819]. Hazrat Ghulam Ali Sahib gave him a lot of attention in his childhood. When he grew up, he took an oath of allegiance to his father and after his father's demise took an oath to Shah Ghafoor Beg Sahib who was an important successor of Shah Ghulam Ali Sahib. He was very particular about fulfilling all his religious duties and was quite unaware of worldly matters. It is not in my capacity to praise his qualities. Truth be told, his status is an example of a Quranic verse [ayat]. May Allah keep him safe and give him fame and status.

Shah Muhammad Afaq, May Allah Keep His Grave Illuminated

His miracles are famous. He knew about obvious and hidden matters and was one of the famous saints [waliullah] of his era. He was a descendant of Hazrat Mujaddid Al Fisani Ahmad Shaheed. He was a mendicant [faqir] who followed Khwaja Zia-ud-Din Sahib of the Mujajadidiya order to whom he had taken an oath of allegiance. After the demise of his Master [Pir], he became his hereditary successor. He had permission from all the Sufi orders to become a Master or a Murshid of anyone connected to them. On the seventh [of the Islamic calendar month] of Moharram in AH 1251 [5 May 1835], a Tuesday, he left this temporary world for the eternal life after the evening prayer [namaz-e-maghrib]. He was buried in Mughalpura on Thursday.

Haji Ala-ud-Din Ahmad, May the Most High God Save and Protect Him

He is the successor and the administrator of Shah Afaq's dargah. In reality he is a remembrance of his master. His pristine character was sealed when he was in his mother's womb. From a very young age he was inclined towards spirituality. At the age of sixteen, he took the oath of allegiance and underwent various hardships to perfect his faith. Wherever he was, he was always in the service of his master. His genealogical chart meets up with Khwaja Yusuf Hamadani.[14] His behaviour always reflected his faith in God and his love for the Prophet, peace be upon him.

He performed the Hajj at a young age. Now in his nineties, he finds it difficult to see clearly and is not able to walk properly, but his devotion, prayer and piety [saum-o-salat] are at the same level as when he was young. God is great! What people these are who are never unaware of the presence of their Creator. Just reflect on the status of the man who has spent his entire life in devotion and piety. May Allah keep him safe.

Fakhr-ul-Millat-o-Deen Maulana Muhammad Fakhr-ud-Din, May God Have Mercy on Him and Forgive His Sins

Of pure descent, a chosen person, leader of the chosen persons in the court of God, frontrunner in the path of unity of God, [and] a model for the followers of Islamic tenements [such is] Maulana Muhammad Fakhr-ul-Millat-o-din.[15]

I cannot describe his status, his attributes, his miracles, the good fortune he brought to everything he was concerned with as they are innumerable and beyond my humble capacity.

His father was Maulana Nizam-ul-Haq Sahib who lived in Makravan in Lucknow District. His genealogical chart goes up to Sheikh Shah-ud-Din Suhrwardi. His mother was from the family of Hazrat Gesu Daraz.

He was born in Aurangabad but he spent his life in Shahjahanabad. His father came here from Aurangabad. Though he was not formally inducted into education, yet his destiny was to become a famous scholar. He took an oath of allegiance to Fani Fillah Baqi Billah Hazrat Sheikh Kalimullah Jahanabadi. He learnt the obvious and the hidden from him and became his successor. With the permission of his Master [Pir], he left for Aurangabad.

He spent time in the service of his father and became his successor too. After his father's demise, he spent a few years in service of Nawab Nizam-ud-Daulah Nasir Jang and Himmat Yar Khan. Later, he went to Ajmer Sharif and with the blessings of Khwaja Moin-ud-Din Chisti, Allah is pleased with him, and who is a model amongst the instruments [who can get prayers accepted] in the court of God, the polestar of polestars [saints of a very high order], he started residing there.

In the reign of Ahmad Shah he returned to Shahjahanabad. His guidance benefited the people there. His word was considered no less than a revelation. He had many disciples who greatly revered him. He had many attributes including hidden and obvious miracles. He lived like an ascetic in poverty. One of his successors is Hazrat Shah Sulaiman Sahib of District [navah] Pakpattan and his blessings guided thousands. He left this world in AH 1199 [CE 1784–85].

Janab Maulana Qutb-ud-Din, May God Have Mercy on Him and Forgive His Sins

He was the son of Fakhr-ul-Millat-o-Din Maulana Muhammad Fakhr-ud-Din and became his father's successor. There is no need to write his praises, as it is enough to say that he was the flower of such a garden and the offspring of such an illustrious father. He passed away on the seventeenth [of the Islamic calendar month] of Moharram in AH 1200 [20 November 1785].[16] His mausoleum is in the *dargah* complex of the tomb of Hazrat Qutb-ud-Din Bakhtiyar Kaki.

Janab Haji Hazrat Ghulam Nasir-ud-Din alias Kale Sahib, May the Most High God Save and Protect Him

He is the son of Maulana Qutb-ud-Din. According to *Tazkirat-ul-Fuqura* and *Tazkirat-ul-Ansab*, he was born in AH 1262 [CE 1845–46]. It is beyond me to praise him. His nature and disposition are incomparable, and his humility is at a level which is difficult to express. He is always busy remembering God. There is no other Sheikh as famous as him in these days. Emperor Bahadur Shah II and many nobles are his followers and are impressed by his conduct. Whichever gathering he graces with his presence finds people rushing towards him and falling at his feet, and they think it is their good fortune to be able to do so.

A few years ago, he became desirous of visiting Mecca and performing a pilgrimage there. On his return, he went to Pakpattan and presented himself in front of Shah Sulaiman.[17] He stayed there for a while and was very warmly welcomed. He gained spiritual blessings and knowledge of his grandfather from Shah Sulaiman, after which he returned to Shahjahanabad. At present, he is over 50 years of age, and may Allah keep such blessed personalities safe.

Khwaja Muhammad Nasir, May the Mercy of Allah Be on Him

The excellence of his nature, disposition, qualities were beyond words. He was the grandson of Khwaja Mir Dard, Allah is pleased with him, who was a famous saint and poet of Urdu/Persian. He was born in AH 1189 [CE 1775–76]. Spiritually inclined since his childhood, he took an oath of allegiance at age 10 to Khwaja Mir Dard and was inconsolable when the latter left this world. May not even an enemy's life be scarred by such a wound.

He was very interested in acquiring knowledge especially in mathematics, was very well-versed in music, and was so conversant with rhythm that masters of music were compelled to acknowledge him. He was an expert in arithmetic and could easily solve the most difficult sums. He wrote many articles on music and arithmetic. These were his obvious external qualities. His hidden qualities were far superior. He has acquired many spiritual qualities from Khwaja Mir Asar, the younger brother of Khwaja Mir Dard. Following the demise of Khwaja Mir Asar, the late Khwaja Mir Dard's son, Khwaja Mir, became the administrator of the *dargah*. Khwaja Nasir succeeded Khwaja Mir. On the second and twenty-fourth of every month, a gathering was held in his presence. His patience, tolerance and detachment from the world were legendary.

Khwaja Nasir hailed from an illustrious family, with his genealogical chart going back to Nawab Zafar Khan Jahangiri. Khwaja Mir Dard's father was a Persian poet whose pen name was 'Andalib' [nightingale]. His poems have been compiled and published as 'The Cry of the Nightingale' [*Nala-e-Andalib*]. Khwaja Nasir himself was a member of the imperial Mughal bureaucracy [*mansabdar*]; suddenly he had a spiritual experience and left everything, and presented himself in front of Sheikh Sadullah, famous as Shah Gulshan. On the latter's guidance, he took an oath of allegiance to Khwaja Muhammad Zubair and thereafter devoted himself to a life of devotion and piety and become the guiding saint of the age [*qutub-e-waqt*].

Maulvi Yusuf Ali Sahib, May the Most High God Save and Protect Him

He is the *dargah* administrator who succeeded Khwaja Muhammad Nasir. His virtues are innumerable and the writer does not have the strength to describe them. Hazrat is from an illustrious Sayyid family and his family has been made even more illustrious by his becoming the administrator of the *dargah*. He has a very cordial disposition and is approximately 40 years of age now. The writer has personally been blessed by witnessing Hazrat's virtues and the beauty of his character. I have been fortunate to see him go about his daily life.

Shah Ghiyas-ud-Din, May His Tomb Be Purified and Hallowed

The descendant of Khwaja Mawdud Chisti,[18] may the blessings of Allah be upon him, Shah Ghiyas-ud-Din Quddisa is popularly known as Khwaja Kumhariwala. He was extremely pious and spent most of his waking hours in devotion, following the path shown by the Prophet, peace be upon him. He led an ascetic life and only slept and ate enough to stay alive.

Janab Shah Sabir Baksh Sahib, May God Have Mercy on Him and Forgive His Sins

Sayyid Sabir Ali, known as Sayyid Sabir Baksh Chisti, was from the Chisti family. His father was Sayyid Shah Nasir-ud-Din, son of Shah Ghulam Sadaat Chisti, son of Sheikh Abdul Wahid. Initially he gained knowledge from the Sheikhs of his own age, and then later he became the disciple of his grandfather Shah Ghulam Sadaat Chisti. Eventually he succeeded him as the administrator of the *dargah*.

Shah Ghulam Sadaat was the successor of Hazrat Shah Muhammad Nasir who was the successor of Hazrat Sheikh Muhammad Chisti. Shah Sabir Baksh Sahib succeeded his grandfather as in his father's lifetime and with his approval. He also died in his father's lifetime. He became the successor, as against his father, because his knowledge was far more than his father's. The expenses of running a free kitchen, undertaking ceremonies marking the death anniversary [urs], looking after the travellers and pilgrims who came to his *dargah*, were all his responsibility. His generosity put even Hatim Tai to shame.

His devotion and piety is beyond the capacity of the scribe to pen. He passed away at the age of 63 on the night of the fourteenth day [of the Islamic calendar month] of Rabi Awwal in AH 1237 [9 December 1821]. His spiritual retreat, which he constructed for the poor and needy, is located in the Daryaganj area of Shahjahanabad. This is where he was buried. His son, Sayyid Abdullah – may Allah keep him safe – succeeded him and kept up his father's generous traditions.

Janab Mir Muhammadi Sahib, May God Forgive Him His Sins

His name was Sayyid Muhammad Imad-ud-Din and Mir Muhammadi was his alias.[i] He was descended from Janab Ghufran Ma'ab Maulana Maulvi Faqr-ul-Millat. He was so popular amongst the nobles and common people that everyone considered a glimpse of him as good as a big blessing and to be able to be in his presence was considered a gift from God. His qualities were so great that all the residents of the city and especially the residents of the Qila-e-Mubarak [Red Fort] and the royal princes would visit him to benefit from his spiritual experiences. The populace had great faith in him and his curative powers which were

---

[i] *Tazkirat-ul-Fuqura.*

comparable to those of Jesus. Even if he read a prayer and handed over dust to his followers, it acted as an elixir. He died some time ago, in AH 1242 [CE 1826–27] and was buried in his own premises, situated next to Chitli Qabr.[ii]

Janab Miran Shah Nanu, May God Have Mercy on Him and Forgive His Sins

Janab Miran Shah is from the same period as Sheikh Kalimullah Jahanabadi in AH 1141 [CE 1728–29]. He belonged to Thanesar[iii] and his lineage may be traced back to Janab Barkat Intesab Sargiroh Ahlul-Ullah Sheikh Jalal-ud-Din Thaneswari, who was a Faruqi Sheikh and was born a saint [wali]. In the Chisti order he was the disciple and successor of Sheikh Abdur Quddus Gangohi Rahmatullah.

He died in AH 979 [CE 1571–72]. Janab Miran Shah Nanu came to Shahjahanabad and started living in a room in Fatehpuri Mosque, and very soon his miracles became widely famous. People from all walks of life came to him and benefited from his spiritual powers. He lived up to the age of 80 and was buried in the same mosque. His death anniversary is still commemorated each year with an urs.

Janab Shah Jalal, May God Have Mercy on Him and Forgive His Sins

He was the successor of Hazrat Miran Shah Nanu. He spent his life in his master's apartment [hujra] shouldering the responsibilities of his successorship. Till his last breath, he did not glance even once at any worldly matters. Despite the fact that he had no visible source of income and only relied on Allah for sustenance, he established a free kitchen and fed the poor and indigenous every evening.[19]

Hazrat Maulana Muhammad Hayat, May the Most High God Save and Protect Him

He is originally from Punjab and after gaining initial knowledge in his own area, he lived as a student in various places in and around India for some time. Later when he came to Shahjahanabad, he started living in Shah Sayyid Sabir Ali's spiritual retreat and began teaching. He is an extremely learned man. His knowledge is the envy of the scholars of his age with students arriving from far and wide to benefit from it. Even the humblest of his students is considered better than the most accomplished student of another place. Some of his students have gone on to become famous scholars, especially Hafiz Abdur Rahman, whose praise is beyond my pen.

[ii] Ibid.

[iii] Ibid.

Even though Hazrat Maulana Sahib is handicapped because of his failing eyesight, there is no branch of religious or secular learning that he is not master of. He teaches even those lessons which require writing, in such a way that even people with a hundred eyes would not be able to match even a fraction of his teaching skills. Even though he has an ascetic nature and wanted to forsake the world, he has concentrated on his spiritual side. He has now returned to asceticism, spending time with and gaining spiritual knowledge from other saints of his age, but only after his students were ready to take over from him. He went to Pakpattan and benefitted from the company and knowledge of Hazrat Shah Suleiman, returning to Shahjahanabad only after he was spiritually and mentally satisfied with himself. In the meantime, however, Janab Sabir Baksh Sahib had departed from this world. Hazrat Maulana Muhammad Hayat then left the spiritual retreat and started living in another mosque near the Qila-e-Mubarak [Red Fort] where he still resides. He is around 70 years of age and may Allah give him a long life.

Hazrat Sayyid Ahmad [Barelvi] Sahib, May His Tomb Be Purified and Hallowed

Sayyid Ahmad Sahib was a Sayyid and one of the most respected Sheikhs of his era. He belonged to Bareilly and came to Shahjahanabad for purposes of education. After completing his education, he presented himself in the service of Maulana Abdul Qadir and began living in Akbarabadi Mosque and there mastered the grammar of Arabic.

He was inclined towards the life of a spiritual mendicant [derveshi] and spent his time serving in the mosque. He made it his personal mission to look after whoever came in the presence of Maulana Abdul Qadir. Despite undertaking these responsibilities, he would spend so much time in devotion and prayers that it was equal, if not more, to those who spent their entire lives only in prayer. Maulana Abdul Qadir would often say that Sayyid Ahmad's actions revealed his greatness and status.

In this period, he decided to take an oath of allegiance to Maulana Shah Abdul Aziz Dehlvi the 'Leader of all Ulemas', the 'Representative of Representative of Respected Orators', the 'Repository of All Evident Miracles', and the 'Preacher of the Prophet's hadith'. When Sayyid Ahmad Sahib went into the presence of Maulana Shah Abdul Aziz Dehlvi the latter said, 'you do not need to take an oath of allegiance to anyone as your position is exalted and you are not dependent on other people. However, since a Master is needed for the world, I will accept you as my disciple.'

A few days after taking the oath of allegiance, he set off on his travels visiting nearby areas and serving people. He soon became well-known and people began flocking to him. When the crowds eventually became unmanageable, he decided to adopt anonymity so that his devotion and piety could continue undisturbed, and so he left for Tonk. In Tonk, he spent his time in the friendship of Nawab Amir Khan. Despite anonymity, his bravery, courage and lineage became apparent to people, and they benefited from his guidance. Once again, he returned to Akbarabadi Mosque.

Maulana Abdul Qadir had passed away in the meantime and Maulvi Muhammad Ismail – may the mercy of Allah be upon him – had taken over his responsibilities.[20]

When Sayyid Ahmad came back to the Akbarabadi Mosque, huge crowds started coming to him for spiritual guidance. By chance, Shah Ismail and Maulvi Abdul Hai[21] happened to meet once and decided to test Hazrat Sayyid Ahmad's knowledge. They requested the latter which they could observe a special prayer undertaken by people of elevated status [the *Huzoor-e-qalb* prayer] under his guidance, since they had never observed it before. Hazrat knew from his meditation that this was his test and smiled and said, 'Maulana come to this room at night and maybe this will become evident.'

Both of them were very surprised, and they visited him at night. Maulana Sayyid Ahmad made them stand with him in prayer, and when he had finished leading the prayer he told them to set an intention [*niyat*] for two units of prayer [two *rakat namaz*][22] and to pray separately. When the two finished and finally stood up, they realized the whole night had passed and it was then morning. Realizing he was no ordinary man, they swore an oath of allegiance to him and thereafter spent their entire time with him.

After a few days, Hazrat Sayyid Ahmad told them that it was God's will that they would gain complete knowledge of what they were seeking spiritually. He sought the cleansing of their heart in travel and accompanied them to Mecca. On the way, they were joined by at least 1000 people. Everyone's expenses were borne by Hazrat. They all performed Hajj and returned to India.

Hazrat Sayyid Ahmad thereafter started preaching the values of goodness, and this resulted in a reduction of evil-doing in nearby areas. As long as he stayed in Calcutta, wine was not sold and shops selling alcohol were shut. The swelling number of his disciples there soon crossed lakhs, and those whom he acknowledged as successors reached high status. He knew from his meditation that he would be martyred along with some other believers [*momins*].

Maulana Ismail and Maulana Abdul Hai were allowed by Hazrat Sayyid Ahmad to preach in and around India and to explain the benefits of jihad and martyrdom. The former two, however, did not know the intention behind this preaching. Lakhs of people came into their fold because of their preaching and the desire for jihad and martyrdom made its way into all their hearts. After this, Hazrat Sayyid Ahmad recalled them to where he was and along with them he left for Kohistan [present-day Khyber Pakhtunkhwa area of Pakistan]. When they reached Panjtar, many Afghanis became his disciples and accepted him as their religious leader [Imam]. He declared jihad against the Sikhs. Apart from Afghanis, many people from

India gathered and read the *khutba* in his name.[23] Tributes, as per Islam started, coming to him from nearby areas.

His presence struck such a chord in people's hearts that despite the fact that it was an area populated by Sikhs, some states agreed to give him tribute and even a part of their kingdoms. This is the fear of God and not of his creation. However, since Hazrat wanted to revive Islam, he refused to accept any part of their kingdoms. This state of affairs continued for many years. Meanwhile Maulana Abdul Hai passed away from an illness [on the eighth of the Islamic calendar month of Shaban in AH 1243, or 24 February 1828, from piles].

After that the Afghanis, who are considered a very avaricious community, decided to accept the land being offered by the Sikhs and left him. They betrayed him in the midst of battle and Hazrat Sayyid Ahmad and Shah Ismail were martyred along with other believers in AH 1246 [CE 1830–31] in Balakot, Punjab.

Description of the Rasul Shahi Order [Silsila]

No detailed description of this order[24] is available in any book so I thought it appropriate to give a brief account of Rasul Shah Sahib [the saint] to whom this order traces its lineage. He lived much before my time and I did not meet anyone except Shah Fida Hussain Sahib. However, this narrative will provide the details of this order and will serve as a reference in the years to come.

Rasul Shah Sahib

The order [*silsila*] originates from the Suharwardi order and goes back all the way up to Hazrat Sheikh Shahab-ud-Din Suharwardi. Rasul Shah Sahib was completely absorbed in Allah and would roam the hills of Alwar. If he got some food every couple of days, he would eat; otherwise he wouldn't bother. He would be totally engrossed and absorbed in the worship of his God and oblivious to the world. He had reached such a stage of worship that none of the rules of the Shariah were applicable to him. He had no restrictions of clothing and would wear whatever he could lay his hands on, or just be as he was. He would stay in this state of absorption and work his myriad miracles.

Hailing from the Sayyid family of Bahadurpur in Alwar, his real name was Sayyid Abdul Rasul. The people of Bahadurpur are people of strong faith and considered a blow of his breath to be blessed as it helped them attain their wishes. The Raja of Alwar attributes his kingdom to the saint's blessings.

The order [to which Rasul Shah Sahib belonged] goes back to Sheikh Shab-ud-Din Suharwardi [as follows]: Rasul Shah was a follower of Nematullah Shah, a disciple of Shah Dawood Misri [who was] a follower of Saqi Habib who in turn was a disciple of Shah Ismail.

Shah Ismail was a follower of Shah Murtaza Anand who was a disciple of Shah Razzaq Pak a follower of Shah Allah-Dad. [Shah Allah-Dad was] a disciple of Shah Piran Bandagi. Shah Piran Bandagi was a follower of Shah Sajjan Gosha-Nasheen who in turn was a follower of Shah Muhammad, a disciple of Shah Ishaq. Shah Ishaq was a disciple of Shah Dawood who was a follower of Shah Raju Qital who was a follower of Makhdoom Jahan Gasht. Makhdoom Jahan Gasht was a disciple of Sayyid Jalal Bukhari who was a follower of Sayyid Ahmad Kabir. Sayyid Ahmad Kabir was a disciple of Sayyid Shah Buzurg who was a follower of Sayyid Makhdoom Shah Baha-ud-Din who ultimately was a disciple of Sheikh Shahb-ud-Din Suharwardi.

Rasul Shah's state of absorption in God leading to obliviousness to the world [jazb] was evident from the beginning. He had presented himself in Shah Nematullah's presence at the age of 12 and with the blow of one breath by the latter he attained a state of total absorption in Allah and left for the forest and mountains where he spent his life in that exalted state.

He left this world on the twenty-second [of the Islamic calendar month] of Jumadi-us-Saani in AH 1211 [23 December 1796] and was buried in the dwelling [takiya] of the Rasul Shahis. His body was removed from there for certain reasons that cannot be described in such a brief narrative, and he was buried in Firozpur Jhirka.

Maulvi Shah Hanif Sahib

His real name was Maulvi Muzaffar Hussain and he belonged to a rich family from Meerut. He was an exceptional scholar and his lineage goes up to Nawab Khair-ud-Din Khan and Farhat Andesh Khan. He spent his time in the mosque, always busy with his studies. One day a mendicant [faqir] of the Rasul Shahi order suddenly came to Maulvi Muzaffar Hussain and said, 'Come, Rasul Shah is calling you.' He left with him at once.

As soon as he presented himself in front of the Master, he too went into the same state of complete absorption in God and spent his whole life in that state. He would sometimes recite verses and he wrote a commentary called *Sharh-e-Gulistan* on *Gulistan* and a book on the history of Sufism called *Ek Gyan Chausar*. Two of his verses are [mentioned here]:

My heart is a manifestation of God,
A mirror which is an ocean without waves to reflect Him.
Instead of searching for God, look for yourself,
When you find yourself, you will find Him.

Shah Fida Hussain Sahib

Shah Fida Hussain Sahib's real name is Khwaja Najib-ud-Din Ahmad[25] and he is the descendant of Khwaja Yusuf Hamdani. At the age of 18, he became an ascetic and gained knowledge from his Master [*Pir*]. He had complete mastery over mysticism [*tasawwuf*] and would teach the most difficult of religious subjects very easily. As he had no interest in worldly matters, he avoided company and lived alone. All his life, he rubbed mud on his body and lay on the ground, using a brick or stone as a pillow. More inclined towards mysticism, he would enter a state of total absorption in God only once in a while. He stayed in Alwar for twenty years with his Master [*Pir*] Maulvi Muhammad Hanif, succeeding him after his death as the administrator. He also came to Delhi for some work and spent forty years in one room.

Raja Bani Singh of Alwar was very keen that Shah Fida Hussain Sahib return to Alwar to his dwelling [*takiya*], but he was very weakened due to illness and was not himself. However, his disciples took him back to Alwar where he eventually died on the eighteenth [of the Islamic calendar month] of Moharram AH 1259 [18 February 1843].

Many miracles have been attributed to him. His disciples went far and wide, to places such as Tibet and Mashhad [in Iran]. Mendicants, who are his disciples, are present in these places. He would also recite verses while in a state of complete absorption in God like his Master [*Pir*] and a long poem [*masnavi*] written by him was published. One of his verses is as follows:

> I don't have anything else to do in the world except look at Ali,[26]
> I have no other friend except Rasul Allah for deliverance on Doomsday.

Shah Tawakkul Hussain Sahib

His successors are still around, but I could not find out [much] about his lineage after his death. I only know that he was one of those who had submitted himself totally to his Master and was intoxicated by his spiritual master [*fana fi Sheikh*]. He benefitted a lot from his Master and died in AH 1262 [CE 1845–46]. He was buried in Alwar and has since been succeeded by Rang Ali Shah.

Majzubo'n ka Bayaan:
Description of Men in Divine Ecstasy

Sayyid Askari

He is one of the grandsons of Hazrat Janab Sayyid Hasan 'Rasulnuma', may God have mercy on him and forgive his sins.[27] Sayyid Askari was a soldier by profession and was serving in the army when he passed by Alwar, went into the presence of Maulvi Muhammad Hanif and recited:

> I am so intoxicated that I have lost my senses,
> I am unconscious of who comes or who goes in the world.

As soon as he heard this verse, the saint ordered him to 'Go and sit in your grandfather's

(Hazrat Rasul Numa) shrine'. He has remained in a state of ecstasy ever since and has become an ascetic. I have seen him myself and he would be found sitting, shackled in chains, near Hazrat Hasan Rasul Numa's shrine and no one had dared look at him. He left this world a few days after that.

Janab Mir Qutbi Sahib
He was from a family of Sayyids [direct descendants of the Prophet, peace be upon him] and was always engrossed in devotion and often seen to be in a state of ecstasy. Gradually, he reached such state of ecstasy that he even stopped wearing clothes. He performed many miracles and passed away a few years ago.

Shah Abdun Nabi
He was one of the most notable persons of his age and possessed miraculous powers. He had no fixed abode and would live in any corner, or in the shade of any wall that he found. As long as Maulana Abdul Qadir was alive and resided at Akbarabadi Mosque, Shah Abdun Nabi would spend the night anywhere he could, but spent the whole day in front of the mosque, near a small spring. He spent many years like this. This is where those who believed in his miracles would visit him and would ask him to pray for them so that they could attain their desires.

Maulvi Abdul Qadir would often sing Shah Abdun Nabi's praises to his students. When Maulvi Abdul Qadir fell sick and his end was near, Shah Abdun Nabi picked up his bedding and left. When people asked him in surprise about this, he replied, 'My patron is no more, why should I live here?' No one knew where he went [at that time]. Maulvi Abdul Qadir also left this world after Shah Abdun Nabi went away.

Though Shah Abdun Nabi never entered the mosque and only sat outside, yet he knew that the Maulana's end was near because of his own intuition and exalted state of mind. After a few days, Shah Abdun Nabi reappeared and started living in one of the rooms of the Jama Masjid. Many miracles are attributed to him. Though he was often in a state of ecstasy, he would spend his time in prayers though he wasn't particular about the timings. He would write the Quran in *naskh* calligraphy [khat-e-naskh] and would not talk to anyone. He remained this way till his last breath. Rich and powerful nobles would often come to serve him and to look after his needs, particularly Bakshi Bhawani Shankar, a highly-placed officer, who would look after his needs and serve him. Shah Abdun Nabi ate only yogurt [dahi] and a milk-based sweet [peda] at both meals but it never harmed him and he never fell sick. Even though he was 70 years of age, his complexion was that of a young man. He fell sick only once which was the cause of his death. He died many years ago.

Mir Ahmad Diwana

I don't know much about his early years. He always lived in a state of ecstasy, but even in such a state, people would come to him for help and their problems would disappear with his prayers. He spent his entire time in the area of Chitli Qabr. He would sleep in whichever shop he saw empty. Despite this state of heedlessness, no one ever saw him without clothes. It has been an age since he left this world.

Deen Ali Shah

He used to be in a constant state of ecstasy and would earlier roam around the area of Motiya Khan and sleep in some corner there. Since the last few years, he has been living in a domed pavilion in the Qadam Sharif area. He would stay nude because of his state of frenzy. When crowds assembled, he would talk senselessly. Though his words sounded meaningless, they had a higher spiritual meaning and were actually the answers to people's prayers. Everyone could get the answer to their questions and needs in these. He also performed miracles quite often.

Khanum Sahib

A God-fearing woman, spiritually better than a thousand men, lived in the Ballimaran area in Sher Afghan Khan's twelve-arched pavilion. She was always in a state of ecstasy, but not to the level where she would be in a state of total frenzy. People from all walks of life – rich, noble, commoner – all would come to her and ask her to pray for them, and it was found that whatever she foretold, happened. She passed away a few months ago.

Bai Ji

Bai Ji was a woman with miraculous powers who lived in a hut outside Shahjahanabad near the Eidgah. I don't know her real name, but she was popularly known as 'Bai Ji'. She would recite extensively from the Quran during her conversations, especially verse [ayat] 108 from the chapter 'Sura-e-Kausar'. When a needy person approached her, she would place seventeen cowrie shells [brought by the needy person] on the ground and pick them up one by one. Each time she picked one up she would recite the above-mentioned verse. Such is the power of God that whatever she said at that time proved to be true. She left this world one year ago.

Haji Ghulam Ali, Chief among Saints

He held a very high and influential post in the pre-British era, during the Mughal sultanate. He was in charge of giving stipends to mendicants and saints who lived in seclusion. Though now those days are behind him, his reputation still holds good. Khwaja Ghulam Ali was indeed worthy of being called 'Chief among Saints' and had miraculous powers. He was an ardent lover of the Prophet, peace be upon him, and was very particular about regular and supererogatory prayers. Dervishes – whom he spent his time with – had a huge influence on him and he left for Mecca and Medina [wrapt] in this ardour. He was a descendant of Khwaja Nasir-ud-Din Obaidullah Ahrar of whom Maulana Jami has said:

> The royal dress was glorified and elevated,
> Because of the strategy of the servants of God.

His ancestors came to India during the reign of Muhammad Shah. A very high and influential post was first given to [Haji Ghulam Ali's ancestor] Khwaja Rafi-ud-Din which, after his demise, passed on to his nephew Khwaja Muhammad Murad, and after him to Haji Ghulam Ali. His birth name was Ghulam Ali and he died on the fifteenth of [the Islamic calendar month] of Zilhajja in AH 1261 [15 December 1845]. He is buried in Chausath Khamba [described earlier in the book], outside [Delhi's] Turkman Darwaza [gateway].

Khwaja Ahmad Ali, Chief among Saints

After his demise, his eldest son Khwaja Ahmad Ali became Chief among Saints [*Naqib-ul-Auliya*].

Zikr Hukma-e-Karam, Zul Majd wa Ehteram: Description of Respected Physicians

Hakim Ahsanullah Khan

Repository of knowledge, achiever of perfection, embodiment of knowledge, founder of the edifice of knowledge, a sage in the centre of wisdom and knowledge, endowed with messiah-like powers of healing, Hakim Muhammad Ehsanullah Khan, [with the titles of] honour of the state, one upon whom the empire can rely, best of physicians, sharp intellect of his age, [such is] Hakim Muhammad Ahsanullah Khan Bahadur Sabit Jung.

He is the descendant of Sheikh Siddiqi and is originally from Herat. His lineage goes up to Khwaja Zain-ud-Din Herati, may the mercy of Allah be on him. His was a mystically inclined family and there was a tradition of [family members becoming] Sufi masters and disciples/followers. Those who were benefited by his knowledge would reach the level of Ghauz-e-Azam and Qutub Shahi.[28] Khwaja Zain-ul-Din came from Herat to Kashmir disheartened by the behaviour of the Governor of Herat. He lived in Kashmir finding it paradisical and breathed his last there.

His mausoleum and shrine, famous as Zamindar Shah, is located by the side of Dal Lake in Srinagar. The residents of the area look after his shrine and have great faith in his powers.

Hakim Ahsanullah Khan's ancestors always held influential posts in government service. His father, the late Hakim Muhammad Azizullah Khan, whose qualities and miracles are beyond description, was inclined towards the Unani system of medicine and took training under the late Hakim Muhammad Zakaullah Khan. He soon gained superiority over all the Hakims of Shahjahanabad. The family shifted to Delhi later.

Ahsanullah Khan learnt medicine [hikmat] from his father. He had a strong constitution and achieved every possible milestone in his life. His reputation as a doctor [tabib] was such that a person who could not get cured by any other doctor would come to him and be cured. The residents of Shahjahanabad would flock to him for treatment. When his reputation touched the skies, he was appointed as a physician [hakim] in the employment of Fakhr-ud-Daulah Nawab Ahmad Baksh Khan of Firozpur Jhirka. And after the death of Nawab Ahmad Baksh, Asad-ud-daulah Nawab Faiz Muhammad Khan of Jhujjhar appointed him to the same position.

Hakim Ahsanullah Khan respected Nawab Faiz Muhammad Khan and often took his guidance. After his patron's death, Hakim Ahsanullah Khan left employment and stayed at home. However, his reputation led to Mughal Emperor Moin-ud-Din Muhammad Akbar Shah summoning him and appointing him as his personal doctor. After his father's death, Abu Zafar Siraj-ud-Din Bahadur Shah Ghazi – may Allah protect his kingdom and his name spread all over the world – sent for him and appointed him as his doctor. He also bestowed upon him the title of 'Honour of the State and Constant in War'. Hakim Ahsanullah Khan gained prominence and promotions and the emperor was very pleased with him, till the stage was reached that the emperor would consult him on everything, whether it was to do with his health or the empire. The stage was reached when he was in charge of all the affairs of the fort.

Hakim Ghulam Najaf Khan

Eminent progeny, the pious dignitary, best among the best, Hakim Ghulam Najaf Khan, the son of Hafiz Muhammad Masih-ud-Din Sheikhupuri. Sheikhupuri is near Badayun and the family name is Sheikh Farooqi. The emperor gave him patronage and elevated his status with many titles. He was a sixth-generation descendant of Farid-ul-Makhatib Sheikh Moatassim Khan, a prominent noble in Jahangir and Shahjahan's reigns, who held a post [mansab] that entitled him to an estate with 5000 horses [panch hazari mansabdar; the horses were kept in readiness for the emperor's call, in times of peace or war]. Jahangir had given him an area of 4000 bigha for his residence and cultivation. In that land, he built a fort and named it Sheikhupur after Jahangir, since the emperor had been famous as Mirza Sheikhu during his childhood and youth.

Sheikh Moatassim's father, Nawab Qutb-ud-Din Khan was the maternal grandson of

Hazrat Salim Chisti Fatehpuri, and during Akbar's reign was made Governor of Bihar and in Jahangir's reign was elevated to a *mansab* of 5000, as well as honoured with many other gifts, such as a horse, jewelled saddle, robes and sword. In addition, he was also given the governership of Bengal and Orissa, which implied a status where he would have 50,000 cavalrymen [*sawar*, under his charge and in readiness to serve the emperor].

Hakim Ghulam Najaf Khan came from Sheikhupura with his uncle, Mir Sayyid Ali, who was an officer in British service [*tehsildar*] who helped collect revenue and later, the Nawab Governor Bahadur made him Mir Munshi.

Ghulam Najaf Khan came to Shahjahanabad aged 5, and when he reached an age of decision-making, he chose to reside in Shahjahanabad. His inclination was towards the Unani system of medicine and he studied under Sadiq Ali Khan the son of Hakim Sharif Khan, and practised diagnosis and treatment under Hakim Ehsanullah Khan, to whom he was also related.

He became a famous Hakim of Shahjahanabad and the respected emperor, Shadow of God on earth, gave him the title of 'The Arm of the Empire' Hakim Ghulam Najaf Khan Bahadur. These days the Company Bahadur Sarkar [East India Company] has appointed him for treating sick people. The writer feels that Hakim Ghulam Najaf is blessed with every quality by God, and loves him more than his own brother. His healing powers would require a full book to describe, as I cannot even describe an iota of his miraculous cures. He has healed incurable diseases and even a pinch of dust from his hand has the qualities of an elixir. Even if Socrates and Plato were practising in Hakim's time, they would have taken his diagnosis as their template.

Hakim Sadiq Ali Khan

Hakim Sadiq Ali Khan was the son of Hakim Sharif Khan, and such talented men practising the Unani system of medicine are no longer born. His father was one of the more famous physicians of his time and his fame still remains. Even Aristotle's knowledge would pale in front of his knowledge and skill. In reality, most of the famous physicians of this era are his students. One cannot adequately describe his unique qualities.

Hakim Imam-ud-Din Khan

Quite apart from his expertise in the Unani system of medicine and his qualities as a physician, he was also famous for his knowledge of philosophy, logic and oratory. His memory was such that if all the libraries in the world were to disappear, he could create another library by writing all the books from memory. The emperor rewarded Hakim Imam-ud-Din Khan's children with various distinctions and he himself was appointed a royal physician.

Hakim Ghulam Haider Khan

He was the student of Hakim Sharif Khan and has read and explained the principles of the Unani system of medicine. According to the writer [Sir Sayyid], this could not have been done anywhere else. He also had the honour to serve and benefit from Maulana Abdul Azizi Dehlvi, Maulvi Rafi-ud-Din and Maulvi Abdul Qadir. He had the gift of completely curing the sick. The writer also had the honour of being his student.

Hakim Nasrullah Khan

Hakim Nasrullah Khan was an expert in all the classical fields – logic [ilm-e-mantiq], rhetoric [ilm-e-mani], astronomy [ilm-e-haia't], geometry [ilm-e-hindasa] and philosophy [ilm-e-falsafa]. He learnt all of these from Maulvi Abdul Aziz, Maulvi Rafi-ud-Din and Maulvi Abdul Qadir. He learnt the Unani system of medicine from Hakim Sharif Khan and is an expert in the diagnosis and treatment of diseases. He has written a few books, including *Bahran*, *Daryaft Mizaj*, and *Nuskha-e-Muraqqab*, and this tells us about the depth of his knowledge of medicine. He was employed as a physician with Nawab Faiz Muhammad Khan of Jhajjar, after which he got even better opportunities. He is at present with Nawab Abdur Rahman Khan, the grandson and heir of Nawab Faiz Muhammad, as his physician.

Hakim Fatehullah Khan

Hakim Fatehullah Khan is an expert in his field and is employed as a physician in the state of Pataudi ruled by Nawab Akbar Ali Khan. He is probably the brother of Hakim Nasrullah Khan from whom he learnt the Unani system of medicine.

Hakim Pir Baksh Khan

He is very intelligent and was given the title of 'The Physician of the Era' by [emperor] Muhammad Akbar Shah now resting in paradise. On the paternal side, he is a descendant of Hazrat Omar Farooq, may the mercy of Allah be on him – the Second rightly-guided Caliph after the Prophet – and from his mother's side, his lineage goes up to Ghaus-us-Saqlain Sayyid Abdul Qadir Gilani.

His ancestral village is Thaneshwar, but his birthplace and residence is Shahjahanabad. He studied the Unani system of medicine under Hakim Nasrullah Khan, and he trained in diagnosis and practice of Unani under Hakim Ehsanullah Khan. He was very proficient in his work and was very brotherly towards me. His courtesies and attributes are beyond description. He has been employed as a physician in the state of Nawab Bahadur Jung of Bahadurgarh for quite some time and is very famous for his healing touch in this area. Even the miracle that was the healing power of Jesus's breath [nafs-e-Isa] could not have benefited the people any more than his treatments.

Hakim Hasan Baksh Khan

Chief of the city's dignitaries, he is in fact the best of the best of the learned of the world, an exemplar of the wise men of the era. Hakim Hasan Baksh Khan's ancestral village was Thaneshwar but he was born and lived in Shahjahanabad. He was accomplished in the fundamentals of religion and every knowledge that is cogitated, in logic as well as in reason [*manqul wa maqul*]. He had memorized all the books on the Unani system of medicine in the same way that one learns the Holy Book by heart. No one could hold a candle to his knowledge and if anyone argued with him in any gathering, they were all silenced. He was in the service of Nawab Faiz Muhammad Khan of Jhajjar. After his death, he stayed at home for some time, and was later appointed as a physician to Sahib-e-Alam Mirza Fakhr-ud-Din Bahadur, son and heir of Huzoor Siraj-ud-Din Bahadur Shah [the emperor]. He left this world a few years ago.

Hakim Ghulam Hasan Khan

The brother of Hakim Ghulam Haider Khan, Hakim Ghulam Hasan Khan was very knowledgeable and accomplished in the practice of the Unani system of medicine. He had studied under Hakim Sharif Khan. He left this world a few years ago.

Hakim Muhammad Yusuf Khan

Hakim Muhammad Yusuf Khan is the son of Hakim Ghulam Hasan Khan. After completing his religious studies, he gained knowledge of the Unani system of medicine. Along with these attributes, he is a very courteous, cultured and an altogether incomparable person.

Hakim Abdul Hakim [famous as Abu Khan]

The brother of Hakim Yusuf Khan, Hakim Abdul Hakim, was imparted religious education by Sher Muhammad Khan and an education in the Unani system of medicine by his father. He is considered one of the better physicians of his age, and despite such attributes was very courteous and cultured. Allah has given him the healing touch and even those sick people whom Jesus [the *Masiha*] may despaired of curing could be cured by Hakim Abdul Hakim.

Zikr Ulama-e-Din Raziallahu Anhum Ajmaeen: Description of Religious Scholars, May God Be Pleased with Them

Janab Maulana Maulvi Shah Abdul Aziz,[29] May His Tomb Be Purified and Hallowed

Scholar of scholars, distinguished amongst the eminent, perfect amongst the perfect, sagacious amongst the intelligent, greatest amongst the scholars, pride of dignitaries and contemporaries, pride of ancestors, pride of descendants [though the original words '*rashk*' and 'khalf' have negative connotations, here they are given in positive sense], most learned commentator of Hadith, best of scholars of Islam, preacher and first in greatness Shah Abdul Aziz Dehlvi, may his tomb be purified and hallowed by Allah.

Janab Maulana Maulvi Shah Abdul Aziz [the son of Shah Waliullah] gained knowledge through physical hard work, and spiritually by the Grace of God. He was well versed in logic, astronomy, geometry, philosophy and learnt all these so that he could be a good guide of religious knowledge. He considered these essential to understanding the Quran and the sayings of the Prophet [hadith] peace be upon him.

All his effort and hard work went towards understanding and propagating the sayings of the Prophet and verses of the Quran. He spent his life bringing people in contact with the character of the Prophet, peace be upon him, and in teaching the Prophet's sayings [hadith] and the Quran. He would guide people on moral issues and towards leading better lives. There was no branch of science with which Maulana Maulvi Shah Abdul Aziz was not well acquainted. Knowledge was passed on in his family from generation to generation, just as the Sultanate was passed on in the Timurid Dynasty.

By age 14, he had finished his religious and secular education under the tutelage of his father, Hazrat Shah Waliullah. Upon his father's passing away a few years later, the Maulana Maulvi Shah Abdul Aziz succeeded his father. His brothers Maulana Rafi-ud-Din and Maulana Abdul Qadir were very young at the time and were under his guidance. He was responsible for reviving knowledge in India about the hadith and the commentaries/ explanations of the Quran. All religious scholars born after him benefited greatly from his contribution. He had a wonderful memory and constitution, and had learnt entire books by heart. When he was 80 years old, he wrote a book to counter the teachings of the Ishna Ashriya sect [Shia Muslim believers in the twelve Imams]. He had many arguments with Shia scholars and would quote extensively from their religious texts. He also arranged assemblies twice a week to engage in a discourse with people and to answer their questions. He passed away in AH 1248 [CE 1832–33].

Janab Maulana Maulvi Muhammad Sadr-ud-Din Khan Bahadur, May the Most High God Save and Protect Him

> A thousand times were I to rinse my mouth with essence of roses and musk,
>
> Even then to bring your name to my lips would be extreme disrespect.

[The above is a verse by Urfi].

It is a tradition that when during any conversation one wants to refer to their beloved, then one must describe some incident or anecdote so that the listener's attention is drawn to the beloved without his name being uttered. If more details are needed, then some more qualities are to be praised so that listeners can turn their attention to him. He is on such an elevated status, that it is sacrilege to take his name frivolously.

As far as possible, I too want to take his name with all respect due to his status. However, if there's no alternative but to take his name, then I will use words which will describe him just as Allah refers to His [Own] name in the Quran via a quality attached to Him.

The Beginning of Praise[30]

The most accomplished person in the world, the most learned of the learned in the world, wonderful orator, key to the door of knowledge, magical tablet of knowledge, incomparable mystic, one who arbitrates philosophical discussions, an innately just arbitrator and dispenser of justice, a mirror of fate, garden of virtue, evidence of majesty and beauty, amalgamation of all hidden and evident virtues, one who understands the secrets of the fundamentals of religion and all knowledge that is cogitated, one who knows all the fundamentals of religion, worldly exterior and a spiritual exterior like a *darvesh*, one who knows the secrets of the nation, guide of the world and worldly affairs, Maulana Makhdoomana Mufti Muhammad Sadr-ud-Din Khan Bahadur.

No pen has the strength to be able to write even a single word of praise about him, no tongue can even attempt to speak a word in praise of him. It is impossible to mention even a few, let alone all his virtues and qualities, as they are just so many. When the pen wants to write something about him or the tongue decides to speak out in admiration, it is unable to, feeling as though a lock has been placed on the pen and tongue for the longest time; where does one even begin? Which quality does one describe? Every quality is worthy of being written first.

> The assembly where your praises were being sung is now over, as my life is coming to an end,
>
> But I am still at the beginning of enumerating your innumerable qualities.[31]

There is no other person in the firmament of the world today who is such an excellent scholar. He could solve insoluble problems in the twinkling of an eye and learned people would be awestruck at how he could do it all so easily. He was so intelligent that he could understand everything instinctively; nothing needed repeating, however difficult the subject was. He could understand any subtext or nuance in the conversation or text. Had he not written a treatise on the flower, the nightingale would have remained illiterate.[32]

He was one of those who served religion and the physical world in equal measure and did so very diligently. A worldly exterior hid his spiritual qualities, so he could serve the world too. Had Maulvi Jami been alive he would have said exactly this for him:

> When Pride came in royal garb,
>
> It came because of the arrangement of Allah's devout servants.

He had adopted this manner so that he could be of help to his fellow beings instead of adopting an ascetic life which would take him away from them. He worked as a judge [*mufti*] and dispensed justice with absolute fairness so that even Nausherwan [Nausherwan-e-Adil, the famous Persian king known for his justice, would seem like an unworthy clerk in his court of justice. An accomplished poet and author, he wrote poems [*nazm*] and [*nasr*]. He also wrote a commentary, *La Tashaddur Rihal*, on a *hadith*.

Janab Maulvi Rasheed-ud-Din Khan, May the Mercy of Allah Be on Him

He was accomplished in logic and reason and had mastered the principles and practices of religion and the pillars of religion. He remained incomparable in his era. He was a student of Maulana Shah Rafi-ud-Din who treated him like a son. He even studied under Shah Abdul Aziz and Maulana Abdul Qadir who were brothers of Shah Rafi-ud-Din, but the latter played a greater part in his upbringing.

He was accomplished in every branch of science, but his knowledge of astronomy and geometry was incomparable. He spent his life in the company of imams and wrote many articles on it. Whenever he engaged in discussions or debates, people had no choice but to agree with him as his arguments were so flawless. His devotion and piety were such that no pen possesses the strength to write even a word on it. The rulers of the day wanted to elevate him to the post of religious judge [*qazi*] so that others could benefit from him [his manifold attributes], but he preferred to teach at *Madarsa-e*-Shahjahanabad. At the age of 70, he decided to go for Hajj to Mecca, but was not able to due to a serious ailment and eventually passed from this world.

Janab Maulana Shah Rafi-ud-Din, May God's Mercy Be on Him and May God Forgive His Sins

Great leader, lord of the common man, the practising learned man, the greatest scholar, the model litterateur of Arabs and non-Arabs [used for Persians], best among the best of the companions of mystics, stamp of authority amongst dignitaries, pride of the high and low of the city and neighbourhood, one who breathes life into traditions and laws of Islam, remover of lust and innovations, founder of the foundation of illuminated religion, leader and master Hazrat Shah Rafi-ud-Din, may his tomb be purified and hallowed.

Hazrat was the son of Shah Waliullah, may Allah forgive his sins and grant him a place in paradise and the younger brother of Maulana Makhdoomana Shah Abdul Aziz Dehlvi. His father imparted knowledge to him on most subjects, especially the sayings of the Prophet [*hadith*], peace be upon him, and religious texts. He was also well accomplished in science and in the arts.

[Eventually] when Shah Abdul Aziz could not teach due to old age and ailments, this responsibility fell upon the shoulders of his younger brother [Maulana Shah Rafi-ud-Din]. Even those who had gained every kind of knowledge in the world came to him and when they did, they felt like novices and would learn from him all over again. This is why all the famous scholars of Hindustan are his students. Even if Hasan Basri[33] were alive, he would have felt himself inferior to Maulana Shah Rafi-ud-Din. His generosity was such that he would distribute whatever riches he possessed or received. In conclusion, I would say he was an angel in the form of a man. An entire library could be made if one was to write about even one of his miracles. There are many books of Arabic prose and poetry that have been written by him.

Janab Maulvi Maqsoosullah, May the Most High God Save and Protect Him

A scholar who has acted upon his knowledge is free of envy, best among those who possess knowledge of Islamic jurisprudence in the era, leader of the pious ones in the world, expert, one who has the intellect to understand science, Maulvi Maqsoosullah, son of Maulana Rafi-ud-Din. He was one of the leading scholars and religious leaders of his age. He spent a long time teaching and imparting knowledge to students. For nearly twenty to twenty-five years, he studied under Shah Abdul Aziz, from whom he learnt the art of oratory and was famous for his speeches and discourses. He is now living in seclusion having given up teaching and spends his time in devotion and worship instead.

Maulvi Abdul Qadir, Heaven Is His Abode and May His Tomb Be Purified and Hallowed by Allah

Auspicious presence, source of abundant instruction, seat of forgiveness, accomplished, cream of the learned religious scholars, leader of the pious ones, one who is an authority on all matters of faith, founder of the true shariat, guide of the Shariat, spiritual leader of laws of the Prophet, Maulana Shah Abdul Qadir, may God forgive him his sins.

He was the son of Shah Waliullah and the brother of Shah Abdul Aziz and Shah Rafi-ud-Din. Praising him is akin to lighting a candle to the sun. The tongue doesn't have the power to say a word in his praise and the pen doesn't have the strength to write a word of praise. He was extremely spiritual and gained hidden spiritual knowledge under his father and other elders. It is difficult to meet someone as spiritual and enlightened as him in this era.

I have heard from many trusted people that events occurred as he predicted they would. His reputation was such amongst the people of the city that even nobles who attended his assembly [mehfil] would sit with complete discipline, without his having to say anything. He was responsible for innumerable miracles.

> [Though] the true devotee of Allah is not Allah,
> Yet he is not separate from Him.

He spent his entire life in a room in Akbarabadi Mosque. I could not obtain any of his written work. It is possible that he did not write anything. Hazrat left this world thirty to thirty-five years ago.

Maulana Abdul Hai, May God Forgive His Sins

Distinguished among the eminent, perfect among the perfect, conqueror of the foundation of wrongful innovations and desires, founder of the edifice of piety, and devout, excellent in literary accomplishments, refuge of favours, collection of qualities of glory and beauty, conqueror of the foundation of blasphemy and vice Maulana Abdul Hai,[34] may God forgive him his sins. He was the son-in-law and student of Shah Abdul Aziz. God had blessed him with knowledge. No one could hold their own against him in any discussion and were forced to acknowledge him as the master.

He spent a long period of time engaged in studies and eventually took an oath of allegiance to the late Sayyid Ahmad and stayed with him till the end. He performed Hajj with his master and thereafter, on the orders of his Sheikh [spiritual master], started giving speeches on jihad along with Maulana Ismail. When Sayyid Ahmad Sahib went towards Kohistan, he accompanied him, lived there for a few years and subsequently passed away following an illness.

Maulvi Muhammad Ismail – One Who Breathes Fresh Life into the Traditions Laid Down by the Prophet and Conqueror and Destroyer of Innovations and Wrong Practices in Religion, May the Mercy of Allah Be on Him[35]

The ruler of territories, strengthener of the Shariah, lord of the territories, cherisher of religion of the region, conqueror and destroyer of the foundations of blasphemy, skilled in answering questions with knowledge and certitude, founder of the foundation of apparent and hidden virtues, polite in every state, traveller on the path of guidance and instructions, one who illuminates the mirror of purity and faith, centre of knowledge, eloquent orator, elevated in degree of greatness, leader of high and low, refuge of honour and literary attainments, one who enjoys and can bring to fruition [i.e. write commentary] an understanding of the subtleties of the Quran, one who can discern the subtleties of God's word, a repository of apparent and hidden perfections, one who can examine the subtleties of the word of God and *hadith* of the Prophet, a model for his followers, lord of those with elevated status, one who studies the intricacies of logic and reason, founder of the edifice of excellence among the most excellent, one who lays the foundation of the rules of excellence and perfection, one who is a crusader in the path of true faith, one who establishes faith through irrefutable arguments, leader of the leaders, leader of men, [such is] Maulvi Muhammad Ismail, may his tomb be purified and hallowed.

He was the son of Maulvi Abdul Ghani and grandson of Shah Waliullah and was on brotherly terms with Shah Abdul Qadir, Shah Abdul Aziz and Shah Rafi-ud-Din. After the death of his father, he was brought up by Shah Abdul Qadir as his son who remained deeply involved with the day-to-day details of his upbringing. Later, Hazrat Shah Abdul Qadir's granddaughter was married to Shah Ismail.

Initially, Shah Ismail didn't pay attention to his studies when being taught by Shah Abdul Qadir, but when checked he would recite the previous lesson accurately and would ask probing questions for which even the teacher had to be alert. By the age of 16, he had finished studying logic and reason and the entire city was abuzz with talk of his intellect and grasp over subjects. Scholars would come to him to debate, but go back satisfied by Shah Ismail's answers. He made many notations on books in various libraries and wrote many books, including one on the conflicting views on the *hadith*, titled *Be Qurratul Ainain fi Izbati Raf-e-Yadain*.

He performed Hajj with Mir Ahmad and after that spent his time in the service of the people. During his last days, he went to live in Shahjahanabad on the orders of his master to bring awareness of religious matters to ignorant and heedless people.

He attracted a lot of followers as many were influenced and affected by him. He instilled a love for prayer [*namaz*] in the common people and very soon the crowds in the Jama Masjid for Friday prayers swelled to numbers earlier seen only at Eidgah during Eid prayers. Every Friday and Tuesday, he would preach to an assembly in Jama Masjid. His sermons were so illuminating that they would help clear doubts in the minds of the people. His temperament, sincerity, purity and piety were such that people still continue to follow his teachings. The crowds congregating for Friday prayers even today are being added in his good deeds.

After a few years, his master recalled him to his side and from then on, he travelled with him. Shah Ismail also preached in the mountains on Hindustan's borders along with his Master[*Pir*], Sayyid Ahmad Barelvi. He was martyred along with Sayyid Ahmad Barelvi while engaged in jihad, in AH 1246 [CE 1830–31] in Balakot, Punjab.

Maulana Muhammad Ishaq, Best among Commentators on the Sayings of the Prophet, Peace Be Upon Him, May God Forgive Him His Sins[36]

Lord of lords of men, distinguished amongst the greats, greatest of the time, with the temperament and face of an angel, repository of the secrets of truth and the path of the Prophet – peace be upon him, pride of the religious scholars, pillar of commentators of the sayings of the Prophet [*hadith*], peace be upon him, Maulana Maulvi Muhammad Ishaq.

Maulana Muhammad Ishaq gained knowledge of the sayings of the Prophet [*hadith*], peace be upon him, for twenty years from his maternal grandfather, Shah Abdul Aziz. After his grandfather's demise, his followers turned to Maulana Muhammad Ishaq for guidance. Blessed with a beautiful countenance and temperament, Maulana Muhammad Ishaq put people in mind of the Prophet's (peace be upon him) companions when they saw him. They were convinced that anyone who had been blessed to be in the Prophet's company would have looked like that.

He went for Hajj along with his entire family, and on his return he came back to serve the people and to preach. Thereafter, following a long interval, when he felt that his faith had weakened, he migrated to Mecca along with his family in AH 1256 [CE 1840–41]. The emperor and the people of the city tried to stop him, but he was determined. There he continued to generously help Indians who came for Hajj, and the citizens of Mecca felt that they were blessed to have him in their midst. He lived there for six years [before passing away]. It has been a year since he left this world in AH 1262 [CE 1845–46] in Mecca.

Janab Maulana Maulvi Muhammad Yaqub,
May the Most High God Save and Protect him

Possessor of the example of a disposition set by the Prophet (peace be upon him), authority on the Islamic laws as taught by the Prophet, combination of pre-eminent laudable actions and attributes, one who loves God and is loved by humans [such was], Maulvi Muhammad Yaqub [who was the younger brother of Maulvi Muhammad Ishaq], was well versed in all branches of knowledge and at par with the scholars of his age. He was very content with what he had and could dispense with all worldly things; he even refused gifts from people. He lived within his own means whether comfortably or in difficult conditions. He also migrated to Mecca along with his brother and stayed much in the same manner in the Holy City too.

Janab Maulana Qutb-ud-Din Khan,
May the Most High God Save and Protect Him[37]

He studied under Maulana Ishaq and resembles his Master so much in appearance and style that anyone who has not seen Maulana Ishaq may see him through his [disciple's] visage. His manners and sincerity are outstanding and it is rare to find such positive qualities in a person. His piety cannot be expressed in words. His ancestors hailed from a noble family and were appointed at high posts [mansab] in the royal court. Even now, in his state of spirituality, he has the respect of the emperor and proximity to him. Following in the footsteps of his Master, he preaches to an assembly every fourth day for the benefit of the people. He has translated the Mishkat-ul-Masabeeh, a book on the Prophet's sayings (peace be upon him), [the hadith] into Urdu and proceeded to write a commentary on it as well. The book was sold out as soon as it was written.

Maulvi Abdul Khaliq, May the Most High God Save and Protect Him

His reputation for knowledge and piety is still famous in Shahjahanabad and his temperament, manners and piety are as elevated as his service to religion. There are very few people who combine such temperament, intellect and knowledge, and are so very well-spoken. His teachings and sermons have helped bring many people onto the path of religion. In addition, numerous scholars have benefited from his knowledge.

Janab Maulvi Nazir Hussain, May the Most High God Save and Protect Him

Not merely does he possess the best attributes of the famous personalities of his age, but is also an example of virtue, qualities and accomplishments. He is very knowledgeable, especially in the field of jurisprudence [fiqh] and has surpassed everyone else. Despite having [such noteworthy] attributes, he is a very modest and humble young man, frail of body and with a very mature outlook and knowledge beyond his years.

Janab Maulvi Mehboob Ali, May the Most High God Save and Protect Him[38]

He was from the Sayyid family and had seen more of the world in his travels than the rest of his contemporaries, with regard to knowledge, the sayings of the Prophet (peace be upon him) and jurisprudence. He studied the sciences and religious subjects under the tutelage of the family members of Janab Shah Abdul Aziz. His scholarship and mastery over the intricacies of these subjects was embedded in his memory as permanently as though in *al-lawh-ul-mahfooz*.[39] He had a good relationship with my father and even I benefited from his affection and attention.

Janab Maulvi Nasir-ud-Din Shafi Mazhab, May the Most High God Save and Protect Him

Janab Maulvi Nasir-ud-Din Shafi Mazhab was a student of the late Maulana Muhammad Ishaq who was a very good teacher and so attracted crowds. Maulvi Nasir-ud-Din Shafi Mazhab, may the most high God, save and protect him, has the emperor's patronage as well as access to him but remains very forthright and says what he thinks is right even if it harms his own cause. He never minces his words for fear of consequence and says what he thinks is right. He is content with what he has.

Janab Maulvi Karimullah, May the Most High God Save and Protect Him[40]

He is very accomplished in all the arts and sciences especially religious subjects. He has no comparison in his faith in God and contentment in his lot. Despite having dependants, he is not concerned about material things.

Maulana Fazl Imam – A Learned Man Considered an Authority, an Intellectual Who Knew the Minutest Details, May Allah Keep His Grave Illuminated

The most complete among human beings, one upon whom all kinds of divine favours descended, the fountainhead of faith personified, destroyer of the foundation of deviation from the right path, foundation of the edifice of religion and faith, remover of ignorance, one who destroyed the foundation of evil, giver of new life to the rules of knowledge, founder of the edifice of justice, a support for the religious chroniclers, one who mastered logic and reason [knowledge], the favourite of the greats of the era, refuge of high and low of the age, one who recognized the greatness of greats [and thus displayed his own greatness], a repository of power and beauty, a residence for all virtues from beginning to end, everlasting place for virtues to reside in, one who verified the understanding of every [apparent] particle, one who joins the chain of splendid endeavours in pursuit of knowledge, best among the nobles, pillar of the greats, leader of people, [such was] Maulana Makhdoomana Maulvi Fazl Imam, may Allah grant him the highest station in heaven by his grace and mercy.

I don't have the courage to describe his qualities. Even if I were to write for a thousand years, I would only be able to write about any one of them. Maulana Makhdoomana Maulvi Fazl Imam was accomplished in the arts and sciences. Philosophy, mathematics, literature and the sciences were proud to have a student such as him. In this area it is his family which spread the knowledge of philosophy and reason.

Despite such attributes and virtues, he was very humble and modest. He was always appointed to very high government positions. He was very just and could not tolerate injustice. He tried to help ordinary people in their times of trouble. He was from Khairabad but adopted Shahjahanabad as his home and was counted as one of the nobles here. After an age, he gave up all his positions and returned to his native land and did not return in Shahjahanabad though his family stayed on here. He left this world around nineteen years ago in AH 1244 [CE 1828–29].

The Maulana Whom We Serve, Maulvi Fazle Haq[41]

One in whom all the perfections (hidden and obvious) come together, the foundation of virtues, one who embellishes the garden of perfection, one on whose opinion the opinions of others are based, one whose judgment [advice] is sound, one who occupies the throne of deliberation and good counsel, possessor of good advice, one who possesses the same ethics and disposition as the Prophet, [peace be upon him], one in whom all the virtues from the beginning of time till the end of the world come together, one who has authority to settle disputes, one who issues orders, conqueror of people, one who is the reflection of purity of character, an unprejudiced arbitrator, one who makes the best use of his time, possessor of unique qualities, the Farazdaq and Labid [famous Arabic poets] of his era, one who destroys falsehood and establishes truth [such is] Maulana Muhammad Fazle Haq, son of Maulana Fazle Imam, is 52 years of age now.

He gained his education under his respected father. The pen can only feel proud that it is praising his unique qualities. There is no one he can be compared to in the world. It is as though it is his thought processes that have laid the foundation of logic and philosophy [mantiq o hikmat] in the world. An inspirational orator, he was born in AH 1211 [CE 1796–97]. Allah be praised, what a moment! The planets and stars are envious of the star he was born under.

Janab Maulana Maulvi Muhammad Noor-ul-Hasan, May the Most High God Save and Protect Him

Refuge of excellence, perfection of skills, perfection of virtues radiating from the face like flowing water, one who knows the minutest of details of the Shariat, one who has cognizance of the attributes of Allah, custodian of hidden and tangled secrets from the beginning of time, repository of knowledge and action, one who possesses the nature of Aristotle and Farabi [a tenth-century Arab philosopher], founder of the edifice of perfection of virtues, founder of the edifice of completion of perfection [of virtues], one who gets guidance from heavenly [Bible, Torah, Quran] books, one who treads the shown path of truth [as per heavenly decree], the astrolabe which measures intelligence and knowledge, one who knows the minutest details of all branches of human learning, [such is] Maulvi Muhammad Noor-ul-Hasan, may the most high God save and protect him.

The brilliant student of Maulana Fazle Haq, Janab Maulana Maulvi Muhammad Noor-ul-Hasan, is unique in his knowledge, courtesy and manners. His mind is sharp and his understanding quick. He stands beyond comparison in scholarship. An expert in logic and reason, he can silence anyone with his arguments. In today's era he is a witness to the creation by the Almighty.

One can spend a whole lifetime praising him and only manage one quality and that too would not be described in its entirety. He believes in the Prophet's (peace be upon him) saying that hurting someone is a greater sin than, God-forbid, breaking the Khana-e-Ka'ba.[42] If his knowledge were placed on the highest sky, its burden would be such that it would tear through, all the way down to earth. His piety is such that the saying of a sahabi[43] that 'I would not take all the riches in the world to give up listening to a single call to prayer [azan]', is apt for him too.[44]

Maulvi Karamat Ali, May the Most High God Save and Protect Him

The son of calligrapher [khushnavez] Maulvi Hayat Ali and student of Maulana Fazle Imam, the accomplishments of Maulvi Karamat Ali are beyond description. He left Shahjahanabad a few years ago and went to Hyderabad in search of employment. Travelling is a way to success, and he got a job there at the salary of Rs 1,000 per month.[45] [While still at Shahjahanabad it was evident that] his grasp and knowledge of religious issues was outstanding and [that he] could resolve all queries related to such matters.

Janab Maulvi Mamlook-ul-Ali, May the Most High God Save and Protect Him

He is the student of Maulana Rashid-ud-Din Khan Sahib. His knowledge of logic and reason is outstanding. He knows all the books being used in the current curriculum by heart; even if all these books were to be destroyed his recall alone could help anyone rewrite them. His courteous manners and nature cannot be penned down. Having held the post of a teacher at Shahjahanabad *madarsa* for the past fourteen to fifteen years, he now heads the *madarsa*. He wasn't interested in pursuing a career in writing, had he done so he would have been very famous.[46]

Janab Mufti Sayyid Rahmat Ali Khan alias Mir Lal, May the Most High God Save and Protect Him

Repository of good virtues, one in whom the praiseworthy attributes, best among the last of the learned and intelligent men, patron of the skilful and accomplished, [such is] Sayyid Rahmat Ali Khan alias Mir Lal. He has been given the title of 'lamp of the *ulema*' [religious leaders], and 'light of the mendicants' by the emperor. His hidden and obvious virtues are beyond description. His knowledge, maturity and manners are incomparable. The position of the religious judge who gives the *fatwa*[47] has been in his family for many generations. Now he is at that post. His family and mine have been very close for many generations and because of that, Hazrat is very gracious in paying attention to me. He hasn't written any book because he is engrossed in learning.

Janab Akhun Sher Muhammad, May the Most High God Save and Protect Him

One who treads the path of knowledge and is free from greed and covetousness, one upon whom Allah's favours and bounty descend from beginning from time till end of time, [such was] Akhun Sher Muhammad, may Allah keep his grave illuminated and may paradise be his abode.

He was born in Afghanistan but came to India many years ago for education. When he started living in Shahjahanabad, he studied knowledge and the sayings of the Prophet under Shah Abdul Qadir. He was a classmate of Maulana Ismail. He started residing in the house of Hakim Ghulam Hasan Khan. He stayed away from people and spent his days and nights in acquiring knowledge and in devotion and prayers. He became a spiritual follower of Shah Ghulam Ali Sahib and became his successor though he did not establish his own spiritual retreat [khanqah] where he would take on disciples despite having all the qualities of a Master. Towards the end, with the intention of Hajj and migration, he left for Mecca. On the way to Mecca, on the twenty-ninth [of the Islamic calendar month] of Safar in AH 1257 [22 April 1841], he left this world. Six years have passed since then.

Janab Maulvi Amaan Ali, May the Most High God Save and Protect Him

One who practises complete spiritual incantation, an accomplished person [whose accomplishments will remain even after death], possessor of pure and truthful disposition, best among the perfect ones, model of piety, Maulvi Aman Ali. He is a Sayyid and a student of Maulana Shah Abdul Qadir with whom he also took an oath of allegiance. He has never sought employment and is content with whatever God has bestowed on him even though he is a skilled physician. The writer has had the opportunity of sharing a deep bond with him and he has also showered me with his love. Praising him is beyond my capacity.

Janab Maulvi Muhammad Jaan, May God Forgive Him

He was well versed in the curriculum being taught at the madarsa and had memorized quite a bit of it. He was a respected scholar. He was very influenced by and inclined towards Persian prose and poetry. His courtesy was incomparable and one did not see such maturity in any one else. He held important posts – he headed a regiment [Sar-e-Risaldar] and was also a police officer [Faujdar] – under the British government. A few years ago he left this world. He was closely related to the writer and was therefore very fond of him.

Maulvi Nawazish Ali, May the Most High God Save and Protect Him

He studied under the ulemas of Shahjahanabad.[48] He studied the sayings of the Prophet [hadith] (peace be upon him) from Maulana Ishaq Dehlvi. He was concerned about people and wanted them to return to the straight path and so would hold regular assemblies in his house giving sermons. People would even call him to their homes for assemblies and preaching. His nature was very courteous.

Maulvi Muhammad Rustam Ali Khan,
May the Most High God Save and Protect Him

After finishing with the madarsa curriculum, he studied books on geometry, mathematics and astronomy from my grandfather, Nawab Dabeer-ud-Daulah Amin-ul-Malik Khwaja Farid-ud-Din Ahmad Khan Bahadur Musle Jung. He learnt the sayings of the Prophet (peace be upon him) and jurisprudence from Maulvi Ishaq Sahib. He was accomplished in the Unani system of medicine and sick people would benefit from his treatment. He was reputed to be an excellent scholar.

At the moment he is in the employment of Hazrat Badshah Jam Jaah Siraj-ud-Din Muhammad Bahadur Shah, may Allah keep him and his empire safe. He has a very loving relationship with the writer. The weekly royal newspaper [*Siraj-ul-Akhbar*] is a result of his hard work.

Haji Muhammad, May God Keep Him Safe

He is a resident of Jaunpur and came to Shahjahanabad after the completion of Hajj. He studied books on the sayings of the Prophet (peace be upon him) as well as commentaries on the Quran under Maulana Ishaq and is well versed in all subjects, but an expert in the *hadith*. He is incomparable in piety. I have seen him going into the presence of Maulana Makhdoomana Maulvi Muhammad Sadr-ud-Din Khan Bahadur and that is how I heard of his qualities. Maulana Sadr-ud-Din appointed him as a teacher in *Madarsa* Dar-ul-Baqa.[49]

Mullah Sarfaraz, May the Most High God Save and Protect Him

A reputed scholar, Mullah Sarfaraz is an expert [who has studied and mastered] books on logic, reason, philosophy, mathematics and astronomy and teaches them in great detail. He has studied the sayings of the Prophet (peace be upon him), as well as commentaries on the Quran, from Janab Maulana Maulvi Sadr-ud-Din Khan Bahadur. He has also been appointed as a teacher in *Madarsa* Dar-ul-Baqa by Maulana Sadr-ud-Din.

Zikr-e-Qurra wa Huffaz: Reciters and Preservers of the Quran

By the Grace of Allah there are many reciters and preservers of the Quran in this city and many mosques. During Ramzan, there is no mosque in which two or three people do not finish the Quran in *tarabih* prayers [special prayers offered at night in the Islamic calendar month of Ramzan]. In the Jama Masjid, innumerable recitations of the Quran are finished in *tarabih* prayers during Ramzan. But I will only discuss a few special people.

Qadir Baksh Qari, May the Most High God Save and Protect Him

He recites everything with the correct points of articulation. He has been blessed with the voice of Daood.[50] I am unable to describe the extent of his devotion and piety. He lives his life in a state of happy contentment with what he has. He is now 70 years of age.

Hafiz Ahmad, May the Most High God Save and Protect Him

He is the real brother of Qadir Baksh Qari. Though he is not on the same level as his brother with regard to recitation of the Quran [*qirrat*], but he recites the Quran so accurately that he has no equal. He spends his days and night in devotion and that shows on his face.

Qari Muhammad Baig, May God Forgive Him His Sins

In the knowledge of recitation of the Quran he was far ahead of his contemporaries. His ability to pronunce beautifully using the correct points of articulation was such that the words themselves felt proud to be recited by him. He was a complete scholar and a pious man. Contentment and tolerance were a part of his genes. He never ever looked at wealth in his whole life. He left this world a few years ago.

Qari Ahmad, May the Most High God Save and Protect Him

He is incomparable in his knowledge of recitation of the Quran. I can't describe his virtues, they are innumerable. Qualities such as devotion, piety, contentment, being a stickler for the Shariah, spending in the way of God and staying aloof from all evil, are all in one place in him.

Hafiz Abdur Rahim, May the Most High God Save and Protect Him

Though he is not knowledgeable in the art of recitation of the Quran [qirrat] but by Allah's grace his voice is so beautiful, poignant, expressive and soulful that a flying bird would halt its flight midair upon hearing his voice, and flowing water would become still. Whichever assembly he steps into and indicates that he will recite the Quran, the gathered assembly immediately becomes all ears. Crowds converge wherever he is supposed to recite and when people hear his recitation of the Quran, they forget everything else in the world.

Zikr-e-Bulbul-e-Navayaa'n-e-Sawaad-e-Jannat Abaad Shahjahanabad: Description of the Nightingale-like Sweet Singing People of the City of Shahjahanabad on the Outskirts of Paradise

> Wherever I go I praise my friends,
> One doesn't need to open a shop to display [the excellent qualities of] one's friends.

Janab Mirza Asadullah Khan (Ghalib), May Allah Keep His Shadow over Us for a Long Time

Ghalib is the phoenix that has reached the loftiest heights of glory, His place is in heaven under the lote-tree in paradise [in the seventh heaven], his status is elevated and his degree is of the highest stage, the founder of the edifice of eloquence, the founder of the edifice of expression, nightingale of the garden of poetry, the diffuser of poetry, silver-tongued parrot who brings sweetness into the meaning of every word, he is the height of the sky of superiority, of superior descent, the star of a lofty firmament, he is the sky of authority, the disciple of Rahman [Allah himself probably because he had no formal teacher], the master of Sehban [a poet], he is Ma'l, Luzayi, Farzdaq and Labeed of the age,[51] his name [Asad] is the name of the Prophet's successor [Ali]; [such is] Mirza Asadullah (Ghalib).

People have forgotten about Hafez and other greats so enamoured are they with Ghalib. Sehban-ul-Hind, the famous orator, is awestruck by Ghalib's accomplishments and has cried so much that his eyes are awash with tears. Zulali is like a thirsty soul in front of the spring of Ghalib's talent. Abu Ishaq the generous, who spends his time in feeding others, is also desirous of a morsel from Ghalib's table. Khaqani is as a lowly courtier in front of him. Khusrav stands with bent head ready to serve this emperor of poetry and eloquence [badshah-e-sukhan]. The sweetness of Saadi's poetry is a dependent of Ghalib's table spread. The sweetness of Hafez' tongue is nurtured by the blessing of Ghalib's words.

It is Ghalib's talent and skill that he can paint any paper with his colourful words and make it the house of philosophy. His praise is beyond pen or word. If one were to borrow special aptitude from the intellectual and a flair for writing from fate, even then, one would fall short. It is better not to show one's ignorance by undertaking such a daunting task.

His father's name was Abdullah Beg Khan, he was of Turkish descent and his ancestry went back to Afrasiyab and Pushang. His ancestors were related by blood to the Seljuq Turks. When the Seljuq Empire broke up, his ancestors started living in Samarqand. Due to some misunderstanding with his own father, Hazrat's (Ghalib's) grandfather left Samarqand and came to Delhi.[52] Moin-ul-Mulk befriended him in Lahore. After Moin-ul-Mulk passed away, his grandfather came to Delhi and took up employment with the Mughal Emperor.

Hazrat's father was born in Delhi and he was brought up here. He later shifted to Akbarabad [Agra] where Ghalib was born. When Hazrat was 5 years old his father left this world, leaving the orphaned child in his mother's lap. His paternal uncle, Nasrullah Beg Khan, was the governor [subedar] of Akbarabad, and he took over the task of bringing up the orphaned child. When the British took over the governance of Hindustan, Lord Lake Bahadur appointed Nasrullah Beg Khan as a commander [risaladar] with a cavalry of 400. Nasrullah Beg Khan was very close to Lord Lake Bahadur and accompanied him on many battles.

In return for these services, General Lord Lake gave him an estate [jagir] of two provinces in the area of Akbarabad to be held till his lifetime. In CE 1801, when Nasrullah Beg Khan died, his estate reverted to the state and a pension was fixed in its stead. Hazrat came to Shajahanabad shortly after that, as he was restless there. Once he came here, he tried to live on this pension. In this period he occupied himself by writing verse. He has done a favour to words by penning them down. Every letter and every word is grateful that he uses them.

It is not possible to describe the faith that this sinner has in Hazrat, it will not come on my lips or pour forth from my pen as only the heart feels these. If only my feelings could reach Hazrat; the love I received from him is more than I have received from my own elders. I consider his one word to be better than a book, and one flower from his pen more beautiful than a garden. They are fortunate who have had the good fortune to serve him, learn from him and who have penned down his verses and saved them for posterity. Hazrat is always ready to help others and share his priceless knowledge with whoever seeks his help.

His verses are like priceless precious gems and beyond praise. One compilation [*diwan*] of his poetry [*ghazals*[53] and *qasida*[54]] has been published in more than thirty sections. In the same way he has written prose as well as a concise collection of five prose compositions in a book called *Panj Ahang* which is in fifteen sections. He is at the moment composing a long poem in praise of the battles in which the Prophet, peace be upon him, took part. It is still incomplete and I am sure it will be another priceless work.

Nawab Muhammad Zia-ud-Din Ahmad Khan Bahadur (Nayyar Rakshan), May the Most High God Save and Protect Him

One who illuminates the garden of the state's prestige, founder of the edifice of rank and grandeur, the sun of the sky and firmament, one who controls the axis of fortune, one who has great courage and lofty aspirations to even spin the sky on his fingers, best among the lofty people of the world, [bringer] of a new spring in the garden of ethics and virtue, the gardener of the garden of wealth, dignity and greatness, one who adorns the garden of those of eminent ranks, one in whom God has given wealth [of knowledge and piety], of majestic disposition, the spring of felicity and good fortune, a unique pillar of the world, the incomparable grandee in the city and country, refuge for those who want to attain their desires in the world [such is] Nawab Muhammad Zia-ud-Din Khan Bahadur (Nayyar Rakshan).[55]

In front of his loftiness the sky is lower than the earth and Alexander and Dara are found wanting in front of his rank and status. The dust from his threshold shines from afar because of his status and appears like the stars in the sky. The sky has branded its forehead with the sign marking it his slave. He has earned his pen name 'Nayyar Rakshan' since his words are as bright as the sun in the world. The clouds are overladen with the pearls from his pen and the rivers are enriched by his generosity. Wealth is made wealthy by his wealth.

His generosity is such that calling the ruler generous would be making fun of the latter. His bravery would embarrass Rustam. His munificence could be likened to the river that flows through heaven [Ab-e-Kausar] that satiates thirst forever and his nature is similar to that of Hazrat Khizr.

He has been given such a gift of writing by nature that each word is a gem in itself and cannot be challenged. The maturity of his thought is higher than that of the most senior poet and philosopher. His thought processes are as elevated as angels in the sky. God be praised he is incomparable and even in a thousand years his equal will not be born. His virtues are spread so far that if people were to travel to all the places where his virtues are known, they would not be able to cover those lands even if they travelled their whole lives. It is better not to go down this path of his praise, since it would swallow us whole, yet describe his life only briefly.

He is the son of Nawab Jahaniyan-e-Ma'ab-e-Gardun Janab Mu'alla , who held the title of Fakhr-ud-Daulah, late Nawab Ahmad Baksh Khan Bahadur, the ruler of Firozepur Jhirka. He is not only closely related to Mirza Asadullah Khan Ghalib but is also his disciple. Due to his Master's complete attention on him, his writing is of the same level as that of his teacher, [Ustad] Ghalib. His qualities are such that it could be said that he is following in the footsteps of Muhammad (peace be upon him). He is very fond of and gracious to yours truly and I can neither describe nor write it down and it is mutual. One of his verses is:

> Enter my heart whenever you want, it is your own abode,
> There's no fear of the police chief or guard here.

Nawab Zain-ul-Abideen Khan Bahadur (Arif)

A young sapling of the garden of wealth, the founder of the edifice of dignity, the nightingale of the garden of poetry, the sweet-tongued parrot, cherisher of meanings [of words], the sun in the firmament of the perfect ones, a mirror of the auspicious connoisseurs of poetry, refuge of [poetic] expressions, patron of talent, exalted in resources, pillar of the edifice of grandeur and affluence, a ladder for those desirous of ascending the zenith of grandeur, crème of the incomparable ones in the world, a model for the possessors of wealth in the state and country, one who is fortunate in the world, the chosen one in the world, [such is] Nawab Zain-ul-Abideen Khan Bahadur, 'Arif'.

He is the son of Nawab Ghulam Hussain Khan Bahadur, son of Sharf-ud-Daulah Nawab Faizullah Beg Khan Bahadur Sohrab Jung. He was a student of Mirza Asadullah Khan Ghalib and has learnt Persian [Farsi], from him. He gained a great name in poetry and verse that if the poets of yesteryear, such as Mir, Sauda, Qaim Chandpuri and Kalim were present today, would have been his students. The delicate and real emotions of the lover that came through in every word of his ghazal[56] was enough to give one's life for.

His panegyric [qasida] in praise of kings would bring out the pomp and majesty of the Emperor in a way that none could. Each word of his was dripping with emotions and feelings and one could feel the pain of the lover, the beauty of the beloved, the longing and the heartache. What more can one say than that the teacher [ustad] takes great pride in his student. In this era his talent is well recognized and applauded by all.

Nawab Ghulam Hasan Khan Bahadur (Mahv), May the Most High God Save and Protect Him

One who gives fresh life to the custom of poetry-writing, foundation of nurturing talent, gardener of the garden of expressions, ornament of the creator, adorner of words and embellisher of styles, nightingale of sweet speech, a garden of parrots with perfect voices his voice combines the sweetness of all perfect-voiced parrots found in a garden, best among the possessors of wealth and nobles of state, leader of the grandees, [such was] Nawab Ghulam Hasan Khan Bahadur, pen name Mahv.[57]

He was the son of Nawab Ghulam Hussain Khan Bahadur and grandson of Sharf-ud-Daulah Nawab Faizullah Beg Khan Sohrab Jung. He was also a disciple of Ghalib. His verses were very thought provoking, philosophical and his words had a lot of nuances, metaphors and analogies. His verses were so pure and pristine that the listener could go into a trance. His temperament was such that he could win over everyone. He was very tall. One can't describe the hidden and obvious virtues that he was blessed with. This unique person should be called a collection of contrary virtues as he was young in years but old in accomplishments. My pen does not have the strength to write his praise.

Nawab Zulfiqar Ali (Azar)

Sweet-tongued poet, an orator who illuminates with his speech, one who brings in freshness of expression into ancient speech, manifestation of letters, one who embellishes lofty thoughts, Nawab Zulfiqar Ali, pen name Azar, the son of Hayat Ali Khan, grandson of Moatamad-ud-Daulah Nawab Ahmad Ali Khan, great grandson of Nawab Yaqub Ali Khan who was the brother of Shah Wali Khan, minister of Emperor Ahmad Shah.

The Emperor of Delhi had awarded him the rank of Commandant of the City of Shahjahanabad. He was a very passionate person by nature with a very fiery tongue and his pen name 'Azar' [fire] is very apt. He is one of Ghalib's more famous disciples. One of his verses is:

> It is punishable to utter words of gratitude in front of my beloved,
> How can I dare to put my grievances in front of her?

Janab Maulvi Abdullah Khan (Alavi), May God Forgive Him His Sins

The mirror that reflects [poetic] expressions which were gathering rust, an orator who can ignite the hearer's mind and give new significance to old phrases and words, an abode of beauty [literally, the place where a bride sits], one who embellishes lofty thought, one who polishes the mystical meanings of words, one who embraces the person giving significance to topics and essays, in the embrace of the witty ones, the barmaid [saqi] of the tavern which serves complex mystical thoughts present from time immemorial to date, one who knows the secrets of knowledge and its practice, one who inherently recognizes piety and beautiful character, one who only sits amongst the pious, a reflection of the perfect apparent and hidden virtues [such was] Maulvi Abdullah Khan, pen name Alavi.

By the age of 40, Maulvi Abdullah Khan had the accomplishments of one who is a thousand years old. He hailed from Shamsabad but his childhood and upbringing took place in Shahjahanabad. Because of his inherent qualities and aptitude, he was an expert in every art, especially so in poetry and prose. As he was an expert in Farsi, he spent most of his time studying it (whether prose or poetry), or teaching it. He gained fame in this field. The world cannot produce such a talent again even after a thousand revolutions of the sky. His poetry is more colourful than a flower, and his prose is intoxicating. One can fill registers in his praise.

Some time ago, he went to the east with a heavy heart in search of employment and there a Britisher recognized his virtues and extended his patronage. Unfortunately he had to leave the Britisher's company after a few months. Nevertheless, he had become very famous for his miraculous cures as a physician and so he stayed on at the insistence of the local populace. A nobleman of that area was very impressed by his powers of healing too and decided to extend his patronage to him. He accepted and stayed on and gained a great name in that area. In AH 1272 [sic; CE 1855–56], he left this world.

Janab Maulana Maulvi Imam Baksh (Sehbai)

One who is a mirror of all rusty not-in-use words, one who polishes the mirror of beautiful expressions that are not in use anymore, the gardener of the garden of apparent perfections, one who tears the curtain from the beautiful meanings of things hidden from us, one who can miraculously change the nature of any assembly he attends with his style and choice of expression, one who is worthy of unending praise, the barmaid [saqi] of the tavern of poetry and eloquence, [such is] Maulvi Imam Baksh, pen name Sehbai.

His genealogy goes back all the way to Hazrat Umar Farooq (may the mercy of Allah be on him) from his father's side and from his mother's side till Ghaus-us-Saqlain Sayyid Abdul Qadir Jilani, may the mercy of Allah be on him. His obvious and hidden virtues, his wonderful temperament, made him a very popular man of his era. One rarely sees a man with such a complete personality and so brimming with talents. His knowledge in every subject and his oratory made him unique. He was a master of all the arts, unique in talent in every branch of art. One can't describe his skills, sagacity and accomplishments.

He has written commentaries of many books as well as books on Persian grammar and books on prosody. He has written on many complex matters, which would be difficult for most learned people to comprehend. Worth mentioning are *Risala-e-Gunjeena-e-Rumooz*, *Risala-e-Jawahar-e-Manzoomi* [where each name of Alalh is praised in a separate verse of the quatrain], *Risala-e-Jawahir-e-Manzoom* a treatise written in praise of Emperor Bahadur Shah Zafar; and letters on the lines of Bedil's prose.[58]

His manners and *akhlaq* are beyond description. The words used in his prose and poems are like pearls strung together to make a priceless necklace.

Maulvi Muhammad Husain (Hijr)

Maulvi Muhammad Husain (Hijr),[59] was a disciple of Maulvi Imam and studied the classical Persian texts under him, as well as a composition in rhyme or verse. His prowess in verse reached its peak under his Master. He also learnt the etiquette of poetic assemblies from him. He has expertise in both prosody and verse.

Mir Nisar Ali Nisar

He is the son of Maulvi Abdullah and is from a very noble family. His ancestors were always trustworthy. Maulvi Rahmat-ullah, one of his ancestors was the teacher [*ustad*] of Emperor Muhammad Shah. His great grandfather Maulvi Ashraf Sahib was the teacher of Emperor Alamgir [Aurangzeb]. He himself was the student of Maulvi Imam Baksh, Sehbai, under whose tutelage he learnt Persean classics as well as the art of writing verse. He is very well versed in classical literature and knows how to preserve rare books. His artistry in writing the Nastaliq font is unparalleled.

The way he writes the letter 'alif' makes the tallest cypress bend its head and his 'bay' can make the teeth covered by the most beautiful lips envious. The letter 'hay' is brimming with the water of life. In short his writing is like a painter's palette. I should have written about him in the section on calligraphers, but he is such an excellent poet that I have included him here.

Janab Muhammad Momin Khan (Momin),
May the Most High God Save and Protect Him

One who is a mirror of a rusty not-in-use language and words, one who polishes the mirror of mystical subtleties, giver of new life to rules of perfection in poetry, giver of life to virtues and graces no longer in demand, an abode of beauty [literally, the place where a bride sits] where beautiful topics are imparted fresh grace and beauty, an expanse of uncountable perfections, one who is drunk in the intoxication of poetry, one who inherently recognizes the true, one who dives into the complexities of language, one who is acquainted with the ocean of poetic metre, a pillar adorned by favourable praises, one whose countenance reflects his chosen disposition, one who beautifies the morals and ethics of the Prophet, one in whom is manifested goodness from the beginning to the end, unique in the world, [such is] Muhammad Momin Khan (Momin).[60]

His accomplishments are beyond words and cannot be counted. He is one who can put life into words; just as Jesus could breathe life into dead men, Momin breathes meanings into words. Even if we were to compare him to the sweetness of Hafez's tongue, the attraction of Saadi's verse, the depth of Anwar's thought, the arrangement of words as at the court of Khaqani, the phraseology like the signs of Abul Fazl, meanings such as those of Kamal-ud-Din Isfahani and compare him to every virtue and quality found in every poet we would not find Momin lacking in any way: it is all present in his verse. Sauda is in a frenzy of envy and Mir Taqi Mir's head stands bowed in the face of Momin's verse.

Verse itself has been elevated by him. Nuances of poetry, and depth of thought, drop from his pen as raindrops from clouds. His temperament and conscience are as pure and clear as a mirror. His verses can be taken as examples of how to write poetry. Whether his *ghazals* or his poems in other forms, each word can make a romantic man even more enchanted. If he is talking of the beloved then each word is like the kohl in a beloved's eye. If one were to enumerate his works, a register could be filled.

Janab Muhammad Mustafa Khan Bahadur (Hasrati /Shefta), May the Most High God Save and Protect Him

One who sits on the seat of grandeur and magnificence, the ornament of authority and power, the grand pillar of state, a model for the pillars [nobles] of state, founder of the lofty edifice of poetic possibilities, founder of the lofty edifice [of expression], one who further embellishes the fortune of a lofty garden, one who is a ladder to eminence in the garden of style, one who is like a sherbet from the fountainhead of purity, place from where light of felicity from the beginning of time descends, the place of descent of never-ending light, one who can diagnose the problems of poetic metre and expression with a glance [the metaphor used is of physicians who could diagnose illnesses by just feeling the pulse of the patient], one who is an eloquent orator, one who knows the intricacies of law, one who knows the intricacies of language and [poetic] expression, one who is as generous as Hatim [a sixth century Arabic ruler legendary for his generosity], as sagacious as Utarid [reference to some famous writer], as strong as Rustam the legendary Persian hero [such is] Nawab Muhammad Mustafa Khan Bahadur.

His pen name for Persian verse is 'Hasrati' and for Urdu verse he uses 'Shefta'.[61] If I were to describe his personal bravery and his disposition, I would start shivering with fear at the task I have undertaken. He is at such a lofty position that even the most insignificant words of his make the sky seem lower. A bird flying over the seventh heaven [*Sidra*] could not reach that level even after flying for a thousand years. I am unable to write about his verse because of my severe limitations but want to write about him so that people can know of him.

He is the son of the late Azam-ud-Daulah, Sarfarz-ul-Malik, Nawab Murtaza Khan Bahadur Muzaffar Jung. He is the pride of his family for his obvious and hidden virtues and miracles. The dust of his doorsteps is like a goldmine and the stone of his threshold is a mine of gems. The sun shines only because of the reflection of the radiance of his face. His virtues and good qualities are responsible for spreading perfume in the spring. If a person drawing a portrait of Rustam [legendary Persian hero] takes his name then the painting would start shivering. His sense of justice is so strong that if one were to take the name of Nausherwan [Persian king known for his justice] at the time of praising him, the tongue would be embarrassed. His courage and determination were incomparable. He has been blessed with the highest degree of virtues from birth.

Nawab Muhammad Akbar Khan Bahadur, May the Most High God Save and Protect Him

The gardener of the garden of good fortune, a child of the garden of good fortune, one who is a ladder to the heights of grandeur, one who has power over the inhabitants of the earth and sky, a unique [person] of the age, a step to ascend the heights of glory and magnificence, the unique one of the age, a step to ascend the heights of glory and magnificence, the selected one [such is] Nawab Muhammad Akbar Khan (pen name Akbar), brother of Nawab Muhammad Mustafa Khan Bahadur. He is a disciple of Momin Khan Momin and is very intelligent and accomplished. Though he is very good, he doesn't devote much time to poetry. One of his verses is:

> You burnt the whole world for nothing, not everyone was your enemy,
> Why did the fire from your wails of agony burn the world?

Pandit Narain Das (Zameer)

One who understands the intricacies of poetry, the founder of poetic expression, one who is always engrossed in the intricacies of poetry, one who keeps an eye on poetic expressions, one with an enlightened mind and thoughts, [such was] Pandit Narain Das (Zameer).[62] He was very accomplished in the various arts, including the arts of poetry and oratory. He was well versed in the nuances of writing and was an expert Persian scholar. His poetry was such that each line was capable of arousing envy in others. His prose was also of very high quality. One of his verses:

> Your coquetry, your smile and your flirtatious way,
> And me with my head bent low, to accept whatever you say.

Late Mir Nizam-ud-Din (Mamnoon)

The incomparable one of this age, the unique one of his times, the poet of truth who was the disciple of Rahman [probable reference to Allah, meaning he had no formal teacher], one who removed rust from the mirror of thoughts, gardener of the garden of lofty thoughts, one who illuminated the assembly of eminent topics, one who was a touchstone of illuminated thought [such was] Mir Nizam-ud-Din, pen name Mamnoon. He was the son of Malik-us-Shoara[63] Mir Qamar-ud-Din Minnat. He was a courtier at the emperor's court and was given the title 'Fakhr-us-Shoara'[64]. He was a fresh voice in poetry and gave deep meaning to the words he wrote.

There is a seriousness and finesse in his verse and he used unique metaphors and similes in his writing and speech. No one else has even come close to his dexterity. He transported Urdu poetry into Persian, and Urdu into Dari. No one can come to the level of his panegyrics nor is anyone's verse comparable to his *ghazals*. Every word from his pen is a luminescent pearl. He was an incomparable poet of his era and I don't have words to praise him. He left this world three years ago. Here are two couplets of his:

> Don't be annoyed if I look at you,
> God has made you such that I can't help but look at you!
> The night is short and desires in my heart many,
> Let's make up, we've fought enough.

Shah Naseer, May the Mercy of Allah Be on Him

One whose poetic skills are a measure for the unique and incomparable poets in every age, the incomparable one of this age, one who stood alone in his position of excellence, one who had a pure heart and conscience, Miyan Shah Naseer, may the mercy of Allah be on him, was one of the senior poets of Shahjahanabad.

He would write on very difficult topics, topics no one would dare to think of. In reality, he wrote *ghazals* and panegyrics on issues, which needed mulling over. Despite the fact that he was not very proficient in the techniques of poetry, he would do full justice to the forms he wrote in. No one could find faults in it. He would be heard reciting Urdu poetry loudly to the poetry lovers of Shahjahanabad.

He has written more than two lakh verses but never tried to collect them. There is no exaggeration about the number of his verses, and hundreds would just base the success of their poetry soirées [*mushaira*] on his renditions. Everyone has compiled their poetic compositions [*diwan*] but he never bothered to compile his work. After his death, Maharaj Hari Singh, his disciple, collected whatever he could find and compiled one *diwan*, with at least fifty to sixty sections.

Miyan Shah Naseer went to Lucknow twice and participated in a *mushaira* with Mushafi and Insha Allah Khan. He went to Hyderabad thrice and was well received there. The Rais there rewarded him generously. His greatest patron was Raja Chand Vilal who showered wealth on him. He died in Hyderabad eight years ago on his third visit and is buried there. One of his verses is:

> The desire to catch a glimpse [of Laila] forced him to come,
> Though there were heavy shackles on his [Qais'] feet.[65]

Sheikh Muhammad Ibrahim (Zauq) Khaqani-e-Hind[66]

Distinguished amongst eminent poets, one who guarded the kingdom of [poetic] expression, one who was a guardian of the dominion of [literary] perfection, one who was the foundation of the edifice of virtues and excellence, one who was a repository of solutions for the intricacies [of poetic] art, one who eased difficulty in poetry, one who had complete authority over [poetic] discourse, the best among perfect men, the refuge of connosieurs of poetry, (such was) Sheikh Muhammad Ibrahim (Zauq.)

He held the position of teacher [ustad] to the reigning emperor, Muhammad Siraj-ud-Din Bahadur Shah and had been given the title of 'Khaqani-e-Hind'. His expertise in writing was at a level that no one can match it. His panegyrics, poems and ghazals were all matchless and his ghazals could match those by Sadi and Hafez. His long poems in the form called masnavi, were of the same standard as those by Nizami and his panegyrics at par with Anwari and Khaqani. These famous poets would have been proud to be Zauq's students. His writing was so prolific that only God can count his verses. You can imagine well the level of excellence of the person whose verse was so blessed!

His writing had fluency of language, depth, freshness of style, new meanings, unique simile and allegory, beautiful metaphors and arrangement of words, nuanced allusions and pristine words. His ghazals had firm a rhyming pattern that reflects an exquisite sense of meter. No one else from the past to the present has the felicity of attaining all these qualities in their verse.

Hafiz Abdur Rahman Khan (Ahsan)

A connoisseur of poetry, one who knows the intricacies of poetic language and expression, a unique critic of poetry of the age, the incomparable one of his age, Hafez Abdur Rahman Khan (Ahsan) has a great deal of skill in phraseology and complete mastery over Urdu poetry and has contributed immensely to making the Urdu language even more beautiful.

His sixty to seventy years of practice in writing poetry bear witness to his accomplishments and achievements. He has used various kinds of styles and etymology in his work. Most of the princes in the Red Fort are his students. Despite his old age, he still preserves youthful vigour in his words. One of his verses is:

> The moment you embraced me I forgot all complaints,
> Not that I didn't have many.

Khush Navesaa'n: Calligraphers

Janab Sayyid Muhammad Amir, May the Most High God Save and Protect Him

He belongs to a famous Sayyid family. He is peerless in calligraphy and uses the Nas'taliq form [khat-e-nas'taliq] and can be said to have revived this style. Each letter that he inscribes is a testimony to his skill. During the time that he was practising the art of calligraphy no one even remembered Mir Imad.[67] He was so accomplished and his hand so set that he could write thousands of elegant letters in a moment and not get tired.

Janab Agha Sahib

He is Sayyid Muhammad Amir's student and reached such a degree of perfection that even his teacher was proud of his achievements. Janab Agha Sahib[68] has reached an elevated status with regard to all masters of the art. Apart from this, he is also very skilled in the art of making quills for calligraphy [fan-e-bakiti]. His devotion to his master is exemplary.

Mirza Abdullah Beg

He is also a student of Sayyid Muhammad Amir. Only Agha Sahib can equal his skill. Apart from his skill in calligraphy, his character was exemplary and the pen cannot describe his virtues.

Imam-ud-Din Ahmad Khan

He is the son of Nawab Dabir-ud-Daulah Khwaja Zain-ul-Abidin Khan Bahadur Musleh Jung, and the student of Akhund Abdur Rasul Qandhari and Sayyid Muhammad Amir. He became famous in his time with just a little hard work.

Muhammad Jan Sahib, May Allah Forgive Him

He was the student of Mir Kallan Khush Naves Be-badil. His calligraphy had no match and as long as he was alive, no other calligrapher could flourish. He left this world fifteen years ago.

Akhund Abdur Rasul Qandhari, May the Most High God Save and Protect Him

He is the best among the calligraphers and though a native of Qandhar, has been living in Shahjahanabad for some years. His love for the city has become so much that it feels as if he is a native of Shahjahanabad itself. He is matchless in his use of the Nas'taliq form for calligraphy.

Hafez Kallu Khan Sahib, May Allah Forgive Him

He was uniquely talented in the use of the Naskh form for calligraphy [khat-e-naskh] and was famous for it in his time. He left this world a few years ago.

Mir Imam-ud-Din Sahib, May the Most High God Save and Protect Him

He is the teacher of Sultan-e-Asr Hazrat Zil-ul-laah Siraj-ud-Din Muhammad Bahadur Shah in the use of the Naskh form for calligraphy [khat-e-naskh]. He uses the Naskh form to write about affairs of the judge [of the Shariat law; the qazi] and no one can write it better than him.

Maulvi Hayat Ali Sahib, May Allah Forgive Him

He took the use of the Shikasta form for calligraphy [khat-e-shikasta] to such a level of excellence that the beloved's locks saluted each twist and turn of his letters. He also invented a new style in the use of the Nas'taliq form [khat-e-nas'taliq] and he wrote hundreds of books in it. He died a long time ago.

Pandit Shankar Nath

He was a student of Maulvi Hayat and after him Shahjahanabad has not had a better calligrapher to this day. He left this world some six or seven years ago.

Badr-ud-Din Ali Khan, Engraver of Seals [Muharkun]

He is the student of Sayyid Amir Muhammad Sahib in the nastaliq form of calligraphy and is an expert in the art of engraving seals [muharkani]. He makes the seals for the Nawab Governor General Bahadur and also for government offices.

Musavvira'n: Painters and Artists

Ghulam Ali Khan

He was a matchless artist, in front of whom the picture gallery of the celebrated painter Ma'ani would pale in comparison. Even the paintings of the famous Persian atelier Kamal-ud-Din Behzad seem worthless in front of his brush strokes. No other painter of his calibre has been born to this day. The beauty of his album was such that it appeared as though he had painted nature itself on the eye of a peacock, and all the beauty and grandeur of nature could be seen in it. Even if he painted just a meaningless dot on paper, it seemed as though he had drawn the reality of the world. His paintings brought out the softness of flowers, the hardness of thorns, the antics of animals and the growth of plants.

Faiz Ali Khan

He is Ghulam Ali Khan's brother and is as skilled as him. The luminosity of his paintings is like the candle that lights an assembly, and the fire in his paintings can set fire to the world. Being very religious, he gave up drawing any animate objects and painted only inanimate objects, such as buildings and monuments. God be praised [*Subhan Allah*], he painted these so beautifully that they cannot be described!

Mirza Shahrukh Beg

An incomparable artist of his time, he is very accomplished in the art of painting. It was as though the spirit of one of the houris of heaven has entered his pen and made everything beautiful. The sketches in this book [*Asar-1*] have been made by him, with help from Faiz Ali Khan.

Muhammad Alam

He is a master of art and well versed with all matters pertaining to it. No one else can paint in the style of the ancients as he can.

Arbab-e-Musiqi: Musicians

Himmat Khan

Best among the musicians of his time, most of the musicians and singers were connected to him. His Dhrupad[69] singing was incomparable; so much so that if Tansen were alive, he too would have become Himmat Khan's disciple, and if Baiju Bawra were alive, he would have become his slave for life.

Kings, noblemen and notables from all over the world sent letters and offers in an attempt to employ the maestro, but he was quite content with what he had. He did not consider a single offer, however lucrative, and thus never set a foot out of Delhi. Whoever came to Shahjahanabad to hear him would become oblivious to the world upon hearing just one note, and would make the dust of his feet the kohl in their eyes.

On the second and twenty-fourth of every month, Himmat Khan would hold a musical assembly for the late Hazrat Babarkat Shah Muhamamad Nazir Sahib, the successor of Hazrat Khwaja Mir Dard, may God have mercy on him and forgive his sins. The entire atmosphere would be intoxicated by his voice; it was as if Daood himself were singing. His voice had the pain of the world, the spirituality of a mendicant [*faqir*], the sweetness of piety, and it transported the listener to another world altogether. He left this world for paradise a few years ago.

Ragras Khan

He was unique in his skill at playing the veena[70] and every string of his veena was like a book of guidance for the rest. Just as Himmat Khan had no comparison in singing, Ragras Khan's perfection in artistry and excellence at playing the veena [*been navazi*] had no match. Along with Himmat Khan, he would regale Hazrat Babarkat with his genius on the second and twenty-fourth of every month. He left this world a few years ago.

Mir Nasir Ahmad

Born to a father from a famous Sayyid family, he was married to Himmat Khan's daughter and received his musical learning from his maternal grandfather. He was famous for his singing as well as for playing the veena, and he took both the arts to a zenith. Those who preceded him possessed not even one-tenth of his vocal and instrumental skills. After his grandfather's death, he also sang and played the instrument in assemblies in front of Khwaja Muhammad Nasir, on the second and twenty-fourth of every month. After the demise of Khwaja Muhammad Nasir, he continued his musical soirees for his successor, Maulana Yusuf Ali. His search for employment has now taken him to the district of Awadh.

Bahadur Khan *Sitarzan*

Unmatched in the art of playing the sitar,[71] a phrase used for Hazrat Daood may also be used for Bahadur Khan – that flying birds and running water would go very still hearing him [play]. He left this world five or six years ago.

Rahim Seen *Sitarzan*

This wonderfully talented man hailed from the family of Tansen. The music emanating from the strings of his sitar reminds one of Hazrat Daoud. Six *ragas* and thirty six *raginis* are the servants of his instrument. Nawab Faiz Muhammad Khan of Jhajjhar extended his patronage to him and employed him. After the death of Nawab Faiz Muhammad Khan, his successor Nawab Faiz Ali Khan continued to extend patronage to Rahim Seen much in the same way and thus he remained employed.

Nizam Khan

He had no equal in the art of singing Dhrupad. Even the weakest of his students were better than Tansen and Baiju Bawra. The world lost this talented man a few years ago.

Qaim Khan

He was very skilled in the art of singing the Dhrupad and had mastery over every aspect of this art. Not since the time of Adam has a man been born with such skill, and there is no likelihood that anyone equal to him will ever be born even till Doomsday. He left this world a few years ago.

Gulab Singh *Pakhawaji*

He was a maestro of many musical instruments, especially the pakhawaj.[72] One flick of his wrist would make the pakhawaj resound with a hundred *ragas*. He is responsible for reviving the sitar and was also a very skilled jal tarang player.[73]He passed away a long time ago.

Makhwa *Pakhawaji*

He was unique in his skill with the *pakhawaj* and no one before or after him could hope to match him.

IN CONCLUSION

Praise be to God! [Alhamdulillah], this book is complete; the pen that was frantically writing is now at peace and my mind is at rest. May it please God to make those for whom the book is intended, very happy.

Editor's Notes

1. I have paraphrased this extremely difficult chapter to the best of my ability. I have followed the spirit (and not the letter) of the text, which is beyond my very limited capacity.

2. A complete description is given in *Zameema Maqamaat-e-Mazhari* which was written by Shah Ghulam Ali himself on his Master, Mirza Mazhar Jan-e-Jana.

3. *Zameema Maqamaat-e-Mazhari* mentions his birthplace as Qasba Patiala, Zila Punjab.

4. Commander of the Faithful, a title given to Ali ibn Abu Talib, cousin and son-in-law of the Prophet.

5. *Zameema Maqamaat-e-Mazhari* mentions the date as AH 1180 [CE 1766–67].

6. *Lataif-e-Khamsa* is the actual name of *Maqamaat-e-Mazhari* in which Shah Ghulam Ali wrote about his master. It was published in AH 1309 [CE 1891–92] by Matba Mujtabai Dehli. Azad Bilgrami took the details of his life written by Hazrat Mazhar Jan-e-Jana from the saint himself, and this was included by Lazmi Narayan Shafiq in the chapter on the saint in *Tazkira-e-Chaministan Shohra*.

7. This refers to the traditions and the way in which the Prophet conducted himself as enshrined in the *hadith*. It is considered exemplary conduct to be emulated by every Muslim.

8. Refers to the fact that prayers were initially offered in the direction of the Bait-ul-Muqaddas, a mosque in Jerusalem, however following a revelation brought by Archangel Gabriel to the Prophet, the direction was changed to Ka'ba in Mecca.

9. Khwaja Baha-ud-Din Muhammad Naqshbandi passed away in AH 791 [CE 1388–89]. His mausoleum is in Bukhara.

10. His details were written by his son Shah Abdul Ghani Sahib in *Zamima Maqamat-e-Mazhari*.

11. Imam Rabbani Shaykh Ahmad-al-Faruqi-al-Sirhindi (CE 1564–1624). He has been described as the 'Mujaddid Alf Thani', meaning the 'Reviver of the Second Millennium'.

12. Hazrat Shah *Dargahi* was a Wali by birth and was born in Hazara in AH 1162 [CE 1748–49]. His details are also written by Shah Abdul Ghani in *Zamima Maqamat-e-Mazhari*.

13. Paraphrase of a prayer in Arabic written by Sir Sayyid.

14. Khwaja Yusuf Hamadani was a twelfth-century Sufi saint.

15. Nawab Nizam-ul-Mulk Nizam-e-Hyderabad has written a book on his miracles and his preachings, *Manaqib-e-Fakhriya*.

16. *Risala Tazkirat-ul-Fuqra* by Ahmad Akhtar, grandson of Bahadur Shah II, has complete details. This book gives his date of death as taking place on the eighteenth [of the Islamic calendar month] of Moharram in AH 1223 [16 March 1808]. *Tazkirat-ul-Ansab* gives his year of death as AH 1233 [CE 1817–18].

17. Shah Sulaiman Chisti Fakhri Nizami was the disciple and successor of Maulana Fakr-ud-Din.

18. His real name was Sayyid Qutub-ud-Din Khwaja Mawdood Chisti and he passed away in AH 527 [CE 1132–33]. He was a famous *Wali* and many from his lineage are present in Malkapur, Burhanpur and Hyderabad etc. He has thousands of followers in the Chist and Balkh area. His children are in Herat and Chist, as per the *Tazkirat-ul-Ansab*, p. 132.

19. Sayyid Ahmad in his book, *Tarikh Delhi* (p. 157), writes that the *urs* of both the saints are celebrated on the night of the eighth day of [the Islamic calendar month] of Rabi Awwal. Rs 25 per annum and Rs 2 per month are given from the income of Fatehpuri Masjid for the *urs* and for cleaning to Muhammad Umar Naqib.

20. Maulvi Muhammad Ismail bin Maulvi Abdul Ghani was the grandson of Hazrat Shah Waliullah, and was a famous spiritual leader. He was martyred along with Sayyid Ahmad Barelvi while engaged in fighting infidels in AH 1246 [CE 1830–31] in Balakot, Punjab. There is a book on him in Urdu titled *Sirat Ismail Shahid* [The Character of Martyred Ismail].

21. Maulana Abdul Hai was the disciple and son-in-law of Maulana Shah Abdul Aziz Dehlvi. He was an expert in Hanafi jurisprudence. He wrote *Fatwa Abdul Hai* and brought out the magazine *Nikah Ayyama*. He was also martyred along with Hazrat Sayyid Ahmad Barelvi as per the *Tazkir Ulema Hind*.

22. Each namaz prayer is divided into units of two, three and four, and these units are called *rakat*.

23. A *khutba* is a public sermon, usually preached after congregational prayers on Friday and on Eid.

24. This order started with Hazrat Rasul Shah Saheb Alwari. Mendicants [faqir] of this order apply dust on their faces, keep their eyebrows shaved and place a handkerchief on their heads like a cap. They consider it sacrilegious to sleep at night and those who recite Allah's name are said to often cure exhaustion and physical decline. The history of the oath of allegiance leads back to Sheikh Shahab-ud-Din Suharwardi.

25 He was Sir Sayyid's maternal grandfather Khwaja Farid-ud-Din's brother, and has been mentioned in *Hayat-e-Javed*, Sir Sayyid's biography written by Maulana Hali.

26 'Wajhullah' or 'Face of Allah' is one of the titles of Hazrat Ali. It is based on a *hadith* where the Prophet said that looking at the face of Hazrat Ali is devotion.

27 Of this famous saint of Delhi it was said that his particular blessing was that he could give people a vision of the Prophet, peace be upon him. That is why he was called '*Rasul Numa*' or 'Revealer of the Prophet'.

28 Ghauz-e-Azam and Qutub Shahi are famous Sufi saints.

29 Here, one of the 99 names of Allah, 'Aziz' is invoked, which is a play on the Maulana's own name.

30 The translation of the paeans of praise is paraphrased, as the English language does not contain equivalent words of praise.

31 This is a verse by the famous Persian poet Sheikh Saadi.

32 My pen does not have the capability to translate this exaggerated praise. I am paraphrasing it as praise in Urdu and Persian cannot be translated faithfully as those languages have a different style.

33 Hasan Basri was a very famous eighth century Sufi saint (CE 642–728), who lived in Basra in Iraq.

34 As per the *Tazkir Ulema Hind* (p. 114), Maulana Abdul Hai, disciple and son-in-law of Maulana Shah Abdul Aziz Dehlvi, was an expert in Hanafi jurisprudence. He wrote *Fatwa Abdul Hai* and brought out a magazine, *Nikah Ayyama*. He was also martyred along with Hazrat Sayyid Ahmad Barelvi.

35 For more details, please read *Ittihaf-un-Mubala* (p. 416), *Abjad-ul-Uloom* (p. 916), *Tazkira-e-Ulama-e-Hind* (p. 179), *Al Hayat, Badal Mumaat* (pp. 104 and 115).

36 One gets details about Maulana Maulvi Muhammad Ishaq from *Kitab-ul-Hayat Badal Mamat* (p. 38) and *Hadiaq-ul-Hanafiya* (p. 474).

37 He died in AH 1289 [CE 1872]. *Tzakir-e-Ulama-e-Hind* has more details (p.169).

38 He was born on the first [of the Islamic month] of Moharram in AH 1200 [4 November CE 1785] and died on the tenth [of the Islamic calendar month] of Zilhijj in AH 1280 [17 May CE1864] as per the *Tarikh-e-Dehli* (p. 92).

39 Refers to a sacred tablet in heaven, guarded by angels and on which the decrees of Allah are preserved for eternity.

40 *Tzakira-e-Ulama-e-Hind* has more details (p. 72). Janab Maulvi Karimullah passed away in AH 1291 [CE 1874].

41 In AH 1270 [CE 1853–54], Maulana Fazle Haq was sentenced by the British to transportation for life in the Andamans, because of his involvement in the 1857 uprising.

42 The Khana-e-Ka'ba is a building located in the courtyard of the al-Haram Mosque in Mecca; the Ka'ba is the holiest site in Islam.

43 A word used for a companion of the Prophet, peace be upon him, or a member of his family.

44 Sir Sayyid was his student in his initial years, which fact he mentions in his work *Tohfa-e-Husn*.

45 He wrote a 600-page book *Sirat-ul-Muhammadiya* before 1857. This book is in the Asafiya Library of Hyderabad.

46 One book written by him, *Tarikh-e-Yemeni*, is present in the Bengal Asiatic Society Library.

47 A ruling on a point of Islamic law.

48 Maulvi Nawazish Ali was Sir Sayyid's teacher and he had studied the school curriculum under him.

49 This was a famous *madarsa* near Jama Masjid.

50 The reference is to the psalms of David [Daood] who is said to have been blessed with a beautiful voice.

51 Luzayi, Farzdaq and Labeed were famous poets of the time.

52 Quqan Beg Khan came to Delhi from Samarqand during the reign of Shah Alam and entered the emperor's service as a commander of fifty horses with a personal kettle-drum and standard.

53 The '*ghazal*' is a poetic form with rhyming couplets and a refrain and is often set to music, while a masnavi is a long poem.

54 A panegyric.

55 Nayyar Rakshan means 'bright luminary'.

56 '*Ghazal*' is a poetic form with rhyming couplets and a refrain and is often set to music.

57 *Mahv* means 'absorbed' or 'charmed'.

58 Bedil was a very famous Persian poet.

59 *Hijr* means 'separation from the beloved'.

60 Momin means a believer [in Allah].

61 'Hasrati' and 'shefta' mean 'enamoured'.

62 'Zameer' means 'conscience'.

63 Malik-us-Shoara: The King of Poets.

64 Fakhr-us-Shoara: The Pride of Poets

65 Majnu (meaning insane/madly in love) was the nickname given to the legendary lover. His real name was Qais.

66 Khaqani was a very famous twelfth-century Persian poet and Sheikh Ibrahim Zauq was dubbed the 'Khaqani of Hindustan'.

67 Imad-al-Hasani (CE 1552–1615) was regarded as *the* undisputed master of the use of the Nas'taliq form in calligraphy.

68 Janab Agha Sahib died in AH 1274 [CE 1857–58].

69 'Dhrupad is the oldest surviving form of Indian classical music and . . . though a highly developed classical art with a complex and elaborate grammar and aesthetics, it is also primarly a form of worship in which offerings are made to the divine through sound'. Source: http://www.dhrupad.info/

70 'An Indian stringed instrument with four main and three auxiliary strings; the southern type has a lute-like body; the older northern type has a tubular body and a gourd fitted to each end as a resonator'. Source: https://en.oxforddictionaries.com/definition/veena

71 'A large, long-necked Indian lute with movable frets, played with a wire pick'. Source: https://en.oxforddictionaries.com/definition/sitar

72 'A double-headed drum used especially in the northern part of India. ' Source: https://en.oxforddictionaries.com/definition/sitar

73 'The jaltarang, one of the most rarely heard instruments today, is among the oldest instruments in the world. It consists of china bowls filled with water and struck by two wooden sticks. Earlier, since china clay bowls were not available, artists used to play this instrument with metal bowls. Each bowl can be tuned to the desired frequency by varying the quantity of water in it. ' Source: https://indianraga.wordpress.com/2009/09/16/jaltarang-water-music-of-india/

ASĀR-US-SANADĪD

2

Preface

[This English Preface was published in *Asar-2* and is replicated here verbatim. It is an abridged version of the Preface in Urdu, given later by the author in the book.]

That this work *Asar-oos-Sunnadeed*, was first composed by the Author, and published in the year CE 1846 and CE 1847. The reason for composing the second edition [*Asar-2*] was:

That the first edition [*Asar-1*] of this work was taken by Mr A.A. Roberts to England and presented to the Royal Asiatic Society and met the approbation of its members and Colonel Saxon, a member of the Court of Directors, asked Mr Roberts to translate the work into English. On this gentleman's return to his office in Delhi, he made a translation of the work with the aid of the author. It then appeared necessary to render the work still better with additions and necessary corrections.

That the author begs to offer respectfully, his humble gratitude to Mr Roberts and Colonel Saxon who have patronized him, and he considers that it is through their kindness that he has been able to complete this work, which he thinks will maintain his name for ages to come.

That the author also considers it his duty to offer his gratitude to Mr Edward Thomas through whose aid and kindness he has been able to put the work in type.

That the present edition contains the following additions and ameliorations.

1. The first chapter of this edition is a new addition altogether (which the first edition did not contain), and contains a brief history of the first population of all India and particulars respecting the Capital or Seat of Empire during the old and new reigns.
2. The second chapter of the first edition contained only an account of the fort as well as of all the fortresses erected ever since the City of Delhi was first populated.
3. What the first and third chapter of the first edition contained, is to be found in the third chapter of the second edition, together with additional particulars respecting the old building.
4. In the first edition, there were two faults, viz. that particulars respecting some of the old

buildings were not then satisfactorily ascertained, and secondly, some errors existed in their description. The necessary corrections are however made in the second edition.

5. In the first edition, the description of the buildings was given prominence; but in the new or second edition, the dates of the buildings are regularly given.

6. In the first edition, it was inserted from where the particulars were obtained or gathered. But on the margin of the present edition that historical books are quoted.

7. This new edition contains another thing of great moment, viz. the inscriptions found on the building, are copied and inserted in the new edition in their very original form.

CHAPTER ONE

A Brief Description of Delhi
and Its Old and New Dynasties

[In this brief chapter (which was not a part of the original edition), the author attempted to present a chronology of the prehistory of Delhi (on which there was no 'hard' historical information in the early nineteenth century), but as much of this chronology is not in tune with modern scholarship on the subject, this portion has not been included here. – Editor]

CHAPTER TWO

A List of Forts and Description of the Cities

Table 2.1: Delhi's Forts and Cities through the Ages

No.	Name of Fort or City	Name of Founder	Year	Status and Description
1	Indrapat	Yudhishtir	*c.* 1450 BCE	
2	Delhi	Raja Delu	*c.* 328 BCE	
3	Purana Qila Din Panah Shergarh	Anekpal Tomar	CE 676	Humayun repaired this fort in CE 1533 and called it Din Panah. Later, Sher Shah repaired it and called it Shergarh
4	Qila Rai Pithaura Qasr-e-Safed	Rai Pithaura Qutb-ud-Din Aibak	CE 1143 CE 1205	The entrance of Qasr-e-Safed was Ghazni Gate and it was built inside Qila Rai Pithaura
5	Kushk Lal	Ghiyas-ud-Din Balban	CE 1265	This was made before CE 1265 as it was built a few years prior to his becoming Sultan
6	Qila Marzgan or Ghiyaspur	Ghiyas-ud-Din Balban	CE 1267	Hazrat Nizam-ud-Din's *dargah* is in the precincts of this palace
7	Kilukhari/Kilokhari or Qasr-e-Muizzi	Muiz-ud-Din Kaikobad	CE 1286	Humayun's tomb is on this land
8	Kushk Lal or Naya Shaher or Kushk Sabz	Jalal-ud-Din Firoz Khilji	CE 1289 CE 1289	This was also a palace in Kushk Lal
9	Delhi Alai or Qila Alai or Kushk Siri or Qasr-e-Hazaar Sutoon	Ala-ud-Din Khilji	CE 1303 CE 1303	These were palaces in Kushk Siri
10	Tughlaqabad	Tughlaq Shah	CE 1321	

No.	Name of Fort or City	Name of Founder	Year	Status and Description
11	Adilabad or Muhammadabad or Imarat Hazaar Sutoon Jahanpanah	Muhammad Adil Tughlaq Shah	CE 1327	Delhi Alai was joined to Qila Rai Pithaura
12	Kushk Bijai Mandal or Badih Manzil	Muhammad Adil Tughlaq Shah	CE 1327	This was a tower of the wall of Jahanpanah
13	Kushk Firoz Shah or Kotla Firoz Shah or Firozabad	Firoz Shah	CE 1354	This is the city of the Kotla or Citadel
14	Kushk Jahannuma or Kushk Shikar	Firoz Shah	CE 1354	
15	Khizrabad	Khizr Khan	CE 1418	
16	Mubarakbad	Mubarak Shah	CE 1433	
17	Delhi Sher Shah	Sher Shah	CE 1541	The Kabuli Gate of this city is still extant near the jailhouse
18	Salimgarh or Nurgarh	Islam Shah	CE 1546	A bridge was made in Nur-ud-Din Jahangir's reign and was named Nurgarh
19.	Qila Shahjahan	Shahjahan	CE 1638	The Europeans, especially Italians, were involved in constructing this Fort. The important buildings present in this fort are Delhi Darwaza, Lahore Darwaza including Chhatta, Naqqar Khana or Hathiya Pol, Diwan-e-Aam along with Takht-e-Sangeen (Marble Throne), Khas Mahal, Imtiaz Mahal/ Rang Mahal, marble inlaid screen, with the picture of Orpheus in the style of Raphael, Musammam Burj, Asad Burj, Shah Mahal/Diwan-e-Khas, *Hammam*, Moti Mahal, Bagh-e-Hayat Baksh along with Sawan and Bhado'n, Shah Burj, Mehtab Bagh
20	Shahjahanabad Mahal Bazaar Faiz Canal [*nahr*]	Shahjahan	CE 1648	This is the city attached to the fort and is still inhabited and I pray it stays this way.

DESCRIPTION OF FORTS AND CITIES IN DELHI

See the monuments of the Beloved's city,

The cruel fate has destroyed them all.

Greek philosophers have divided the face of the earth into seven parts and have called these climes. Each region starts from the direction of the equator [*khatt-e-istiwa*] and ends at the outer limits of the north [*qutub-e-shumali*].[i]

1. According to the Greek system, Delhi lies in the third region. The longitude from the Canary Islands [*Jazaier-e-khaldaah*] is 114 degrees [*darjay*] and 38 minutes [*daqiqay*] and the latitude from the equator is 18 degrees and 15 minutes.[1] The longest day here lasts for 13 hours and 50 minutes.

1. English geographers have divided the world into four parts. According to this system, Delhi is in Ashbah [probably refers to Asia] and is specifically located in Hindustan.

[i] *Ain-e-Akbari.*

2. Hindustan has been further divided into three parts, and Delhi lies in the middle of Hindustan. The longitude of Hindustan, as calculated in London by English experts, is 20 degrees less than the Greek system. Apart from this discrepancy, the rest of the calculations are the same.

4. This is a very ancient city and its rulers were under the suzerainty of the kings of Fars [Persia], Kumaon, Kannauj or Deccan. They also ruled independently. Once this city was established, it was never without a king or kingdom.

Only eight periods have passed when there was no kingdom here.

1. When Yudhishtir defeated Duryodhan and ruled in Hastinapur,[ii] [the dynasty] staying there for seven generations. When Nami, also known as Raja Dushtvan,[iii] became king, Hastinapur was drowned in the floods of the Ganga. Dushtvan first went near the Kaushiki River in Deccan and later came to Delhi and made Indrapat his kingdom.

2. When Vikramjit[iv] of Ujjain defeated Raja Bhagwant Kohi and ruled Delhi from Ujjain and appointed a governor for it. It was again made the capital under King Jogvan.

3. When Rai Pithaura made the fort in Ajmer and made it his capital, making his brother Khande Rao the governor.

4. In CE 1191, Sultan Shahb-ud-Din Ghor[v] conquered it and ruled from Ghazni with Qutb-ud-Din Aibak as a governor.

5. When in 1336, Muhammad Tughlaq shifted his capital to Deogarh and called it Daulatabad, all citizens of Delhi were told to shift and forced to leave, and Delhi was desolated. In CE 1341 he reversed the order, and citizens were told they could return, which led to Delhi being inhabited again.

6. When Sultan Sikandar Lodi[vi] made Agra his capital, so that he could conquer Gwalior, there was an old but strong fort in Akbarabad. This fort was later broken and Akbar built a fort there. Sultan Ibrahim also founded a fort there. Babar too ruled from here after defeating Ibrahim Lodi.

7. When Jalal-ud-Din Akbar[vii] made his capital in Agra and kept a governor in Delhi.

8. Now King George III has become the ruler and Delhi is being ruled from London.

To the south of the part of Delhi founded by Shahjahan, there are old monuments, forts

---

[ii] *Mahabharat.*

[iii] *Bhagwat.*

[iv] *Khulasat-ut-Tawarikh* and *Rajavali.*

[v] *Taj-ul-Masir.*

[vi] *Tuzuk-e-Jahangiri.*

[vii] *Akbarnama.*

and palaces stretching for 14 miles. These give evidence of the glory of old kings and the different cities and palaces founded by them. Some are still flourishing and some are in ruins. The aristocracy and rich people also made gardens, inns and tombs for themselves.

Indrapat

Indraprastha was the name of the land between the Khooni Darwaza of Dariba[2] and the Purana Qila [Old Fort]. Indra is the Sky God and *'prastha'* means two hands joined together. According to legend, Indra[viii] had once given a donation of pearls with both hands, and so this place was called Indraprastha. As the name was used regularly, it became known as Indrapat; though as *'pat'* also denotes ownership, it could also be a tribute to Lord Indra who is the king of the skies.[ix]

Hastinapur was the earlier capital of this region. When there was a fight between Yudhishtir and Duryodhan, the former established and populated this area in 3121 BCE. This doesn't seem to be accurate, however, as it is before the Great Flood. The year 1450 BCE seems a more accurate date for Yudhishtir's coronation and inhabitants settling in this city. Though there are no signs of this city any longer, the land to the south of Shahjahanabad, outside Delhi Darwaza [called Delhi Gate today], is called Indrapat. This was the first city of Delhi and other habitations came up near it.

Delhi

Hazrat-e-Dehli is an emblem of justice and charity,
A garden of heaven flourishes and will remain forever.

There are many controversies on how Indrapat came to be known as Delhi. It is said that Raja Dalip[x] established Delhi in his name. However, even this doesn't seem accurate, because though there is mention of Raja Dalip in ancient Hindi texts, there is no mention of Delhi which is mentioned only as Indrapat. It is mentioned that in CE 919 a Tomar king established the city of Delhi near Indrapat.[xi] Because the soil was soft and in Hindi the word 'dehli' is used for soft land, it became famous by that name.[xii] However in CE 919, the Tomars were not ruling Delhi, and this theory seems to be inaccurate as well. What seems most plausible[xiii] is that Raja Delu

---

[viii] *Pothi Indraprastha Mahatma.*

[ix] *Mahabharat* and *Khulasat-ut-Tawarikh.*

[x] *Mirat-e-Aftab-e-Numa.*

[xi] *Tarikh-e-Ferishta.*

[xii] *Nuzhat-ul-Qulub.*

[xiii] *Mirat-e-Aftab-e-Numa.*

of Kannauj, who held suzerainty over the kings of Delhi, established a city near Indrapat in his name, and that the real name was Dehlu.[xiv] Amir Khusrau mentions Dehlu in a verse:

> Give us a horse or any beast of burden from the stables,
>
> Else Command the heavens to carry us to Dehlu.

Raja Delu was a contemporary of Raja Porus of Kumaon and was killed in a battle with him. Porus extended his rule till Kannauj. Alexander conquered his territory later and defeated Porus.[xv] This was in 328 BCE and so this is probably the period of the establishment of the city of Delhi.

Purana Qila

This is the Old Fort, two miles to the south of Shahjahanabad, outside the Delhi Darwaza [Gateway].[3] It is the fort, which was built in the reign of Raja Anekpal Tomar,[xvi] and is mentioned as Qila Indrapat in some historical chronicles of Muslim kings. Anekpal[xvii] had built two stone lions with brass bells around their necks which were rung by petitioners who wanted direct access to the king. The king would then call them and dispense justice.

These lions are known to have been present until CE 1318, but were subsequently destroyed, though there is no record of when they were destroyed. *Ain-e-Akbari* records the building of this fort and mentions Raja Anekpal Tomar as being king in CE 372. This book has led to much confusion, as this year is wrong, since *Ain-e-Akbari* also mentions that there were twenty kings in the Tomar family during 429–847 Samvat [the Hindu calendar era]. Baldev Chauhan became the king and thereafter seven generations of Chauhans ruled for 95 years and 7 months. The last king, Prithviraj Chauhan [or Rai Pithaura], was defeated and killed by Shahab-ud-Din Ghori in CE 1191 and after that, the Muslim kings ruled Delhi.

If we take these details along with the previous Samvat year, then it would mean that Shab-ud-Din Ghori conquered Delhi in CE 886, which is completely incorrect. Shahab-ud-Din Ghori conquered Delhi and established his rule in CE 1191 and that is when Rai Pithaura was killed. These dates are given in all reliable history texts.[xviii] These are the dates also inscribed on the Eastern Gate of the Quwat-ul-Islam Mosque. Even the *Ain-e-Akbari* mentions the same date though it adds a year to it. Thus, Anekpal must have ruled in 733 Bikramjeet/CE 676, which is when he built this fort, and 1176 years have passed since then.

[xiv] *Jawahar-ul-Huruf.*

[xv] *Lubbat-ut-Tawarikh.*

[xvi] *Ain-e-Akbari.*

[xvii] *Nuh Spihir.*

[xviii] *Taj-ul-Masir.*

Din Panah

Emperor Nasir-ud-Din Humayun got this fort repaired and built anew in CE 1533 after the conquest of Kalinjar and Chunargarh.[xix] He built a new city here which he called Din Panah. The clerks [*munshis*] of that period made a chronogram '*Shahr-e-badshah Din Panah*' which records its date.

The walls of this fort were built with lime and local quartzite and were very broad and sturdy, but are now broken in many places. This fort now lies in ruins with the bastions having fallen off in many places, and many of its buildings having broken down as well. The villagers of Indrapat have made mud and stone houses inside it. From among the old buildings only a majestic mosque and Sher Mandal remain.

The fort has three large gates and four windows. One gate to the north-west has been closed for many years and is popularly known as the Talaqi Darwaza [gateway]. It is famously said that an army once left on a campaign from this gate, and it has remained closed ever since. It was said that if the army returned defeated through this gate, the wives would divorce the defeated men. But this seems to be just a rumour. It is not even known during the reign of which emperor, this gate was locked. The river Yamuna used to flow next to the Talaqi Darwaza on the western side, but is now very far from here. It seems that there were moats on all sides of the fort and that water from the river flowed into it. There were bridges in front of the gates to connect it, and one such bridge on the western gate is still standing. Sher Shah also made additions to this fort during his reign and built some monuments inside. In his reign, the fort became famous as Sher Garh.[xx] Nothing remains here from the time of Raja Anekpal.

Qila Rai Pithaura

This fort was built when the kingdom was passed on from the Tomars to the Chauhans and when Rai Pithaura [Prithviraj Chauhan] became the king in CE 1143. The fort now lies in ruins, and only some of its ramparts still stand. It was built on a small hillock with a moat all around it where water from the neighbouring forests was collected for use throughout the year. Even today, there are traces of some dams meant to store water. The western walls and its moats are still standing. The ruins of Ghazni Darwaza [gateway] can also be seen.

I have measured the walls with the help of an astrolabe, and found that the fort is at a height of 65 feet from the moat even today, so it must have been much taller before it broke down. The walls of this fort are very broad. The wall and bastions have been built from the

---

[xix] *Akbarnama.*

[xx] *Tarikh Hidayatullah Khan.*

direction of the moat. Once the wall became equal to the height of the fort, a gap of 17 feet was left and a second 21-foot wide wall was built. Then after leaving a gap of 11 feet towards the fort, another 8-foot wide wall was built. It seems certain that merlons were also built on this wall. This fort was the capital [*dar-ul-khilafat*] of the Muslim kings too, and Sultan Qutb-ud-Din Aibak and Sultan Altamush resided in and ruled from this fort.

In CE 1289, Jalal-ud-Din Firoz Tughlaq established the new city of Kilukhari and this city became famous as Old Delhi. When the nobles of Delhi acknowledged Jalal-ud-Din Khilji as their king, he was brought from the new city of Kilukhari and raised to the throne[xxi] of the old kings in the Qasr-e-Safed or the 'White Palace' [described below] built by Qutub-ud-Din Aibak at Rai Pithaura Fort. The Old Fort [Qila Delhi Kuhna], mentioned in *Tuzuk-e-Taimuri*, refers to this very fort.

Ghazni Darwaza

To the west of this fort was a huge gate. We don't know what this gate was called under Rai Pithaura, but it was named Ghazni Darwaza[xxii] by the Muslims as it was through this gate that the victorious Muslim army entered this fort. There were nine other gates in the fort.

Qasr-e-Safed

Sultan Qutb-ud-Din Aibak (CE 1205–10) built a palace during his reign and called it Qasr-e-Safed or the White Palace. It was in this palace in CE 1241 that Malik Ikhtiyar-ud-Din Aitgin, the Prime Minister of Muiz-ud-Din Bahram Shah was killed while holding court. It was in this palace that Sultan Nasir-ud-Din Mehmood bin Shams-ud-Din Altamush was elevated to the throne. It was in this palace in CE 1259 that Halaku Khan's emissary came to the Delhi Sultanate. A majestic court was held on the occasion such as had never been seen by even the skies. Ghiyas-ud-Din Balban's coronation took place in this palace but now no traces of the structure remain.

Kushk-e-Lal

Sultan Ghiyas-ud-Din Balban built this before he became the king. After he became the king, he built a fort called Marzgan near it. Historical books[xxiii] mention that when the nobles of Delhi agreed to make Jalal-ud-Din Firoz Khilji king and he was brought from Kilukhari to Old Delhi for his coronation, the king came to Kushk-e-Lal and there he disembarked fom his horse and on being asked by his nobles, Jalal-ud-Din said that this palace had been built by his Master,

---

[xxi] *Tarikh-e-Ferishta.*

[xxii] *Tarikh-e-Firoz Shahi.*

[xxiii] *Tarikh-e-Ferishta.*

Ghiyas-ud-Din Balban, who built it before he became the king. It is therefore compulsory for me to show him the same respect today that I showed to him in his lifetime, when he was the king. Thus, we know that this Kushk-e-Lal was made some years before CE 1265.

Balban often lived in this palace even after becoming the Sultan, and when he became fond of hunting, he would leave for a hunt from this palace. Sultan Ala-ud-Din Khilji[xxiv] also lived in this palace before he built the Fort of Siri. Sultan Ghiyas-ud-Din Tughlaq's coronation[xxv] also took place in this palace. There is no description of this palace in any historical book, but the palace known as Lal Mahal near the Sultan's[4] *dargah,* is undoubtedly a part of this palace. This two-storeyed palace was made of bright red sandstone and had beautiful columns. Today, however, it is in a ruined state and is deteriorating daily. There are also a few graves in this palace. There was some doubt earlier about whether this building was Kushk-e-Lal or not, but that doubt has now been laid to rest, and it appears that since the structure was lying uninhabited, people were buried here.

Qila Marzgan

When Sultan Ghiyas-ud-Din Balban sat on the throne in CE 1267, he built a fort near the Kushk-e-Lal and named it Marzgan.[5] It is now famous as Ghiyaspur and Sultan Nizam-ud-Din Auliya's *dargah* is in there. It is written that in the reign of Sultan Ghiyas-ud-Din Balban, it was the custom that if any criminal hid in this palace, he would not be punished, but it is not known why it was named Marzgan, as the words '*marzgan*', which derives from '*magarzan*', means 'hell'. It is possible that this name was not given by the Sultan and may have been named so much later by the people, its real name was Ghiyaspur.

Kilukhari or Qasr-e-Muizzi

Sultan Muiz-ud-Din Kaikobad built this fort in CE 1286 and its name was taken from the village called Kilukhari which existed there. Humayun's Tomb is also found in this locality. Sultan Jalal-ud-Din Firoz Khilji lived in this fort and he completed all the buildings left unfinished by Kaikobad. It is also called Qasr-e-Muizzi,[xxvi] however no traces of this Qasr-e-Muizzi remain now. Hazrat Amir Khusrau has praised it in *Qiran-us-Sa'dain* [Meeting of the Two Auspicious Stars].

> I won't call it a palace; verily it's a spacious heaven,
> On whose doors, the branches of the Tuba tree sweep the dust.

---

xxiv *Tarikh-e-Firoz Shahi.*

xxv *Tarikh-e-Ferishta.*

xxvi Ibid.

Kushk Lal or Naya Shahr

This is another [palace called] Kushk Lal built by Sultan Jalal-ud-Din Firoz Khilji. When he came to the throne in CE 1289, he was not sure of the loyalty of the nobles of the city[6] and preferred to live in Kilukhari, completing its unfinished buildings. He built a garden enclosed with a stone wall on the banks of the river and made one mosque and market, thus populating the new city, and named it Naya Shahr [New City].[xxvii] When Delhi started getting deserted, this new city came to be known as Nayi Delhi [New Delhi]. Kushk Lal [palace] was in this city and Amir Khusrau has praised this palace too with this song:

> Oh Shah! Having encircled the city with walls,
>
> One sees only stones from the merlon to the moon.
>
> [it is difficult to enter your city]

Kushk Sabz

Near the Kushk Lal, Jalal-ud-Din Khilji built another palace which was called Kushk Sabz or the Green Fort. After Jalal-ud-Din was killed by Ala-ud-Din Khilji while getting off his boat from the River Ganga near Katra Manikpur where he had been called under false pretenses, his son Prince Qadar Khan was crowned[xxviii] in this palace as Rukn-ud-Din Ibrahim Shah. No traces of either of these palaces remain as they have completely disintegrated.

Delhi Alai/Qila Alai/Kushk Siri

Sultan Ala-ud-Din Khilji built this fort-palace.[xxix] In CE 1303, he set off to conquer Chittor and sent a huge force towards Telingana's Palace Warrangal. Targhai Nobaan[xxx] the Mughal [Mughal is translated as Mongol in Persian] thought that Delhi was empty and sent a 1,20,000-strong cavalry force to surround the city. Ultimately, after a fierce battle, Ala-ud-Din Khilji prevailed. It was after this that he built this palace. There was a village called Siri on this location and that's why it became famous as Kushk-e-Siri.[xxxi] During Sher Shah's reign, this fort was known as Kushk Siri. It was circular[xxxii] with very strong walls, made of lime, stone and bricks, and had seven gates. This fort had still had not been built when there was a second battle with the Mongols, and 8000 Mongols were captured and killed and their

---

xxvii *Khulasat-ut-Tawarikh.*

xxviii *Tarikh-e-Ferishta.*

xxix Ibid.

xxx *Ain-i-Akbari.*

xxxi *Khulasat-ut-Tawarikh.*

xxxii *Tuzuk-e-Timuri.*

heads buried in its walls in place of stones. This fort is now in ruins but some of its remains can be found while going towards Qutub Sahib [Mehrauli].[xxxiii] In CE 1541,[xxxiv] Sher Shah deserted this city and built and inhabited a new city on the banks of the river near the ancient city of Indraprastha. A village called Shahabad still exists on that location.

Qasr-e-Hazar Sutun

In the same year, in the city of Siri, Sultan Ala-ud-Din [Khilji] built a palace with a thousand columns,[xxxv] which was therefore called Qasr-e-Hazar Sutun. During battle with the Mongols, after many of them were taken prisoner and crushed to death by elephants, their heads were piled up at the entrance of this palace. The palace contained these remnants for many years.

When Raja Bilal Deo, the ruler of Karnataka, was defeated by Khwaja Haji in CE 1311, the treasures from these conquests, which included 312 elephants, 20,000 horses and 96 *maunds* of gold, and pearls, gems and trunks of treasure, were all presented to the Sultan in this palace. When Ghiyas-ud-Din Tughlaq Shah aka Ghazi-ul-Mulk defeated Nasir-ud-Din Khusrau Shah, he too came to this palace and gave condolences to Sultan Qutub-ud-Din and his brothers.

Tughlaqabad

When Ghiyas-ud-Din Tughlaq Shah became the monarch, he started building this fort and city in CE 1321 with many beautiful buildings within. In CE 1323, when Warrangal was conquered and the news reached him that this city was completely ready, Delhi and Tughlaqabad were magnificently lit up in elebration of the news of the victory. Situated on a hill, this fort was built of lime and sandstone and was very strong yet elegant.

Today, however, it is uninhabited and in a bad state. There are portions of the wall which still remain, but the structures inside have crumbled and no signs of them remain, except stones and potholes. In the middle of the fort there used to be a lofty building, which was the sultan's hall of personal audience [*baithak*] and was named 'Jahannuma' [world -reflecting].

This fort and city were made in such a way that it seemed a continuation of each other. It is believed that the size of the fort was unparalleled at the time. It is said that this city and fort had 56 bastions and 52 gates, and it is quite possible that this is true, but since they are now in ruins, I could not verify it. This fort lies 6 *kos* [13.5 miles] to the south of Shahjahanabad under Raja Nahar Singh of Ballamgarh, but now only Gujar herdsmen reside here. They have a wonderful place to live in, in whichever way they please.

[xxxiii] *Tarikh-e-Ferishta, Tarikh-e-Alai.*

[xxxiv] *Mirat-e-Aftab-e-Numa, Tarikh-e-Abdul Haq Sheikh.*

[xxxv] *Tarikh-e-Ferishta.*

Adilabad/Muhammadabad/Imarat Hazar Sutun

When Sultan Muhammad Tughlaq Shah alias Fakhr-ud-Din Juna Ghiyas-ud-Din, son of Ghiys-ud-Din Tughlaq, became the Sultan, he built a new fort near Tughlaqabad in CE 1327 and named it Muhammadabad or Adilabad. He had built a thousand columns in it using local quartzite, which is why it was called Imarat Hazar Sutun [the building with a thousand columns]. Since this Sultan took the title of 'Muhammad Adil Tughlaq Shah', the fort was called Muhammadabad or Adilabad.

The remains of this fort are located on a small hill. It seems as if this building was made only as a leisure palace because to the south of Tughlaqabad there is plain land where there used to be perpetual water, and this palace was built right next to this source of water. A bridge was constructed to this palace from the city of Tughlaqabad with the tomb of Tughlaq Shah being built to the west of the palace. The two were connected via a causeway. Further to the north of the fort walls, Ghiyas-ud-Din Tughlaq built Imarat Hazar Sutun with sandstone columns. The fort is now in ruins, and no remnants of the columns or fort exist. When I saw this palace, I thought it was made just as the twelve-arched pavilions [baradari] are built today. There is no doubt that this building was two-storeyed and could have, in fact, even had three storeys.

Contemporary poet, Badar Saashi, has recorded the date of this palace as AH 725 [CE 1324–25], in a chronogram titled 'Fa-dakhalu-ha' [come in/enter]. Some historians feel that this is the same palace where Ghiyas-ud-Din Tughlaq died because of the structure falling on his head. That, however, is incorrect, as that was another smaller building which was built in three days in CE 1324 near Afghanpur, when Muhammad bin Tughlaq was the heir and not the sultan. This latter building had fallen down on the sultan when he was eating [perhaps] because of a lightning strike, or perhaps because it was not built sturdily enough. This fort was built after Muhammad bin Tughlaq came to the throne.

Jahanpanah

In CE 1327, when Muhammad Tughlaq had completed Adilabad, he joined the walls of Alai Fort and Rai Pithaura Fort, which was famous as Purani Delhi from the times of Jalal-ud-Din Khilji. One end was joined to Siri Fort and the other to Rai Pithaura. He joined Qila-e-Kuhna [Rai Pithaura Fort] and Alai Fort to form a city called Jahanpanah.

These three forts had thirty gates: thirteen gates of Jahanpanah, seven to the south facing east, and six to the north facing west. Siri Fort had seven gates, four of which opened outside and three which opened into Jahanpanah. Rai Pithaura Fort or Delhi Kuhna had ten gates. Some opened outside and some into Jahanpanah. A great city thrived here, but in CE 1541, during the period of Sher Shah Suri, it came to be deserted.

Kushk Bijai Mandal or Badih Manzil

This building is actually only a tower of Jahanpanah Fort, but Muhammad Shah Tughlaq built it with a great sense of aesthetics. On top of the tower was a room with four doors, and stairs leading to the top. Above it there used to be a beautiful twelve-arched pavilion which is now in ruins. It was from the top of this tower that the king would inspect his troops. In the reign of Sikandar Lodi, Sheikh Hasan Tahir lived in this tower and when he passed away in CE 1503, he was buried in the graveyard next to it, where his family members were also buried. Sheikh Zia-ud-Din, who was the successor of Sheikh Shahb-ud-Din Suhrawardy, is buried nearby as well.

Kushk Firoz Shah/Kotla Firoz Shah

When Firoz Shah ascended the throne in CE 1354, he built a new fort in Mauza Kadeen on the banks of the River Yamuna and founded a new city. He built three spacious tunnels in this fort where he could ride along with ladies of his harem. One tunnel led towards the river and measured 5 *jareeb*;[7] one was 2 *kos* [4.5 miles] long and went towards Jahannuma; and one led to Purani Delhi and was 5 *kos* [11.25 miles] long. Purani Delhi here refers to the city and fort of Rai Pithaura [in present-day Mehrauli]. The old residents of Delhi say that this tunnel went towards Badih Manzil and Hauz Khas. Raja Ashoka's pillar, which was brought from the province of Nauhara, in Saalora, in Zila Khizrabad, was installed in this fort near the Jama Masjid mosque.

Shahr Firozabad

In the same year, this sultan [Firoz Shah] built a new city near Old Delhi [Purani Delhi],[8] at a little distance, adjoining Firoz Shah Kotla, and gradually[xxxvi] this city expanded and became densely populated. It was 5 *kos* [11.25 miles] in area, and the area of Turkman Shah Gate and the entire Bulbuli Khana where Sultan Raziya's tomb is, and the Bhojala Pahadi police station [*thana*] of the present day city of Shahjahanabad were part of this city.

Kali Masjid, which is part of the walled city of Shahjahanbad, was also one of the mosques of Firozabad. Thus eighteen villages, including Qasba Andamat, Malik Yar Paran's inn, Sheikh Abu Bakr Tusi's inn, Kadeen administrative division and the land of Kaithwarha administrative division, Ladadat administrative division, Andhawali administrative division, Malka's inn, Sultan Raziya's mausoleum (Bulbulbuli Khana locality), Bhojala Pahadi, the village of Narola and the village of Sultanpur etc., were all part of this city. There was transport on hire to go to each area and locality. This city was so big that when Timur arrived here, he pitched his tents

---

xxxvi *Tarikh-e-Firoz Shahi* by Shams Siraj Afif.

outside the city gates and near Firoz Shah's tomb in Hauz Khas. This indicates that the city extended as far as Hauz Khas.

Raja Man Singh (Tomar) had built a palace at the foot of the Fort of Gwalior and had named it Badalgarh. This palace had a bull cast in bronze which was worshipped by the Hindus. Sultan Ibrahim Lodi conquered this fort and placed that bull on the Baghadadi Gate[xxxvii] of this city. This bull was present in the reign of Akbar.

Kushk Jahannuma/Kushk Shikar

Firoz Shah Tughlaq also built another palace at a distance of 3 *kos* [6.75 miles] from Firozabad and named it Jahannuma.[9] This palace was a hunting lodge. He built a masonry[10] dam near it to collect the water from the hills. The walls of this dam still exist. From Firoz Shah Kotla to this place he built a tunnel which was 2 *kos* [4.5 miles] long, and he would ride into it with the women of his harem.

Gradually, nobles started building houses near this palace and a large population settled here, away from the main city of Firozabad. When Timur came to Delhi initially from the direction of Loni in CE 1398, his army camped near this palace. Raja Ashoka's second pillar was brought from Nawa Meerut and set up in the palace as well. The palace has now completely disintegrated, but one building still stands as a reminder.

Khizrabad

After Timur left Delhi and Khizr Khan became the sultan, he built a new city on the banks of the river in CE 1418, and made many buildings in it. But now, no signs of this fort remain. It is quite possible that the place known today as Khizrabad administrative division may have been this city, but there is no reference to this fact in any history book.

Mubarakbad

When Sultan Mubarak Shah, son of Khizr Khan, ascended the throne, he started building this fort and city in CE 1433, and named it Mubarakbad. The sultan himself supervised the building of this fort. However, before it could be completed, the nobles revolted and killed the sultan in this fort and put Muhammad Shah on the throne. This place, near the tomb of Safdurjang, which includes the sultan's tomb as well as the village next to it, are said to be famous as Mubarakpur Kotla. But in my opinion, after reading history books, I feel that this rumour is untrue, because the sultan had built this city on the banks of the river, and in those days the river could not have possibly flowed next to Mubarakpur Kotla, since some buildings present

---

[xxxvii] *Tarikh-e-Ferishta.*

here are older than the city. In fact, I feel that this city and fort were near the river, on the location where the riverbank of Mubarakpur administrative division still exists.

Delhi Sher Shah

When Sher Shah became the ruler of Delhi, he also wanted to build a new city and he left Delhi Alai and Siri Fort deserted, and built a city in CE 1541 near Indrapat on the banks of the river,[xxxviii] which was well-known as Delhi Sher Shahi. This city was built adjacent to Kotla Firoz Shah.

In fact, it seems that Sher Shah completed the city that Humayun had started building, but could not entirely complete it due to his [Humayun's] downfall and defeat at the hands of Sher Shah. After looking at that area, it is very apparent that there is no other location where Delhi Sher Shahi could have been built.

Kabuli Darwaza, Delhi Sher Shah

Though there are no remains of this city, there is still a beautiful gateway outside Shahjahanabad's Delhi Darwaza [gateway] near the jail. This gate is from Sher Shah's Delhi and the road to Kabul began from here, so it was called Kabuli Darwaza. This gate has been beautifully made of lime mortar and stone and has beautiful small rooms and alcoves. The gateway is made of red sandstone and so is also famous as Lal Darwaza.

Salimgarh/Nurgarh

Islam Shah, son of Sher Shah, built this fort in five years, at the cost of Rs 4 lakh, in CE 1546.[xxxix] However, Islam Shah died before he could complete it, and only the boundary walls were made with the fort being left as it was. In the reign of Jalal-ud-Din Akbar, Murtaza Khan Akbari[xl] built a few buildings here. This fort is still standing to the north east of Shahjahanabad on the banks of the river. Emperor Nur-ud-Din Jahangir built a bridge outside the gateway and it is since then that it has become famous as Nurgarh.

Qila-e-Shah Jahan[ll]

What can one say of a fort where the gardens bloom,
There's perpetual spring, with no sign of gloom.

Emperor Shahab-ud-Din Muhammad Shahjahan ruled from Akbarabad for a long period. In AH 1048 [CE 1638–39], the twelfth year of his reign, he gave orders for a fort to be built in

[xxxviii] *Tarikh Sheikh Abdul Haq* and *Mirat-e-Aftab-e-Numa.*

[xxxix] *Mirat-e-Aftab-e-Numa.*

[xl] *Tuzuk-e-Jahangiri.*

Delhi. In the same year on twelfth [of the Islamic calendar month] of Zil Hijj [16 April 1639] on the banks of the river near Salimgarh Qila, the construction of this fort began.

Ustad Ahmad and Ustad Hamid were uniquely talented architects who were in charge of the building of this fort. However, evidence of a mosaic by an artist from Raphael's Italy, behind the marble throne, depicting a scene from the story of Orpheus, proves that there was involvement of Europeans and particularly an Italian.[12]

In the beginning, Izzat Khan was given the charge of supervision of this fort for five months and two days[13]. The entire foundation of the fort was dug and materials were accrued. In some places the foundation was raised too. In this period, Izzat Khan was appointed to the governership of Thatta and the task was given to Allah Vardi Khan. In two years, one month and eleven days under his supervision, 12-gaz-high walls were built all around the fort. The supervision then passed onto Makarmat Khan and it was completed in the eighth year under him. It took nine years to complete the fort, which was the twentieth year of Shah Jahan's reign. On the twenty-first [of the Islamic month] of Rabi Awwal in AH 1058 [15 April 1648], the emperor held his first court here.

The fort is made of red stone and at regular intervals there are bastions and beautifully made battlements with merlons.[14] It is octagonal in shape, 1000 *gaz* long and 600 *gaz* wide, the entire area covering 6 lakh *gaz*, which is double the size of the Akbarabad Fort. The walls are 25 *gaz* high and its foundations are 11 *gaz* deep. The width is 15 *gaz* at the bottom and tapers to 10 *gaz* on the top. The Yamuna river flows to the east of this fort and on the other three sides a 3600-*gaz*-long, 25-*gaz*-wide and 10-*gaz*-deep moat has been dug and is kept filled with water from the river. In all, Rs 50 lakh was spent on building this fort. In some books it says that Rs 100 lakh was spent:[xli] Rs 50 lakh for building the fort and Rs 50 lakh for the buildings inside it.

Delhi Darwaza and Lahori Darwaza

There are two very big gateways in the fort, the gateway on the south is called Delhi Darwaza and in the west is the Lahori Darwaza. Both these gates have been made with great artistry and have very pretty small dome-shaped pavilions.

The *qiledar* or commander of the palace troops lives on top of Lahori Darwaza. It is well known that there were no barbicans in front of this gate [initially] and one could see very far from here. However, [Emperor] Aurangzeb Alamgir built barbicans in front of both the gates. Both gates also had a wooden plank each, leading to the moat. These planks were converted into masonry bridges in CE 1811, as mentioned in an inscription given on both gates.

[xli] *Mirat-e-Aftab-e-Numa.*

Chhatta Lahori Darwaza

This refers to the vaulted arcade [chhatta] which has been made very well and is very high and extends to a great distance. It has been beautifully ornamented with paintings on the plaster. On both sides are very pleasing and attractive two-storeyed rooms with a square in the middle which has an open roof for light. This vaulted arcade was called 'Bazaar-e-Musaqqaf' or the 'covered market'[xlii] during Shahjahan's reign. Apart from these two gates, there are two smaller gates in the fort, two wicket gates and twenty-one bastions. Out of these, seven bastions are round and fourteen are octagonal.

Naqqar Khana/Hathiya Pol

The gate that leads to the Hall of Public Audience [Diwan-e-Aam] is called the 'Naqqar Khana'. The gate is beautifully made of red stone, there is a room and a five-arched pavilion built on it which is open from all sides. It is in this courtyard that the royal *naubat* drums are played, which is why it is [also] famous as the Naubat Khana. In front of this gate once stood two life-size stone elephants and that's why the gate is also called 'Hathiya Pol'.[15] The elephant sculptures were destroyed during the reign of Emperor Aurangzeb Alamgir.

In front of this gate is a 200-*gaz*-long and 140-*gaz*-wide square with a beautiful tank in the middle. To the south and north of it is a lovely bazaar with a stream flowing in the middle. Only royal princes can go on horseback or elephantback through this gate, everybody else [including the nobles] has to go on foot.

Diwan-e-Aam

The Diwan-e-Aam or Hall of Public Audience is a very famous and very beautiful building, used whenever the emperor held court for the public. There are three divisions inside it.

Nasheman Zille Ilaahi/Sangeen Takht: The Seat of the Shadow of God/The Marble Throne
In the middle of this building, adjacent to the eastern wall, is a marble throne. Its canopy is made of pure marble and is 4 *gaz* square in width, with four columns that support a curved dome. The plinth is higher than a man's height. Behind it is a special recess of marble, which measures 7 x 2.5 *gaz*, with various exquisite types of birds and beasts made in pietra dura, depicting the story of a man singing to the accompaniment of an instrument.[16]

The story of Orpheus as being incomparable in music and singing is famous in Italy. It is said that when he sang, birds and beasts would be engrossed, and when he sat down to sing, they would sit near him. From the same country hailed the famous painter Raphael, who had

---

xlii Ibid.

painted the story of Orpheus and his singing purely from his imagination. He died in CE 1520; this painting became very famous in Italy and England, and its copies are present even today. The painting has been replicated in the recess behind the Mughal throne. Since this painting was famous in Europe, it seems that an Italian was involved in the building of this fort.

At the side of this pavilion is a door with a passage to enter from the inside. The emperor would preside over the Diwan-e-Aam on days that public court was held. In front of this throne is a marble dais. If any noble wanted to address the emperor, he would stand on this dais and speak, and even then, only his neck could reach the emperor's throne.

Dalan Darbar (Main Hall)

Facing the throne is a hall with three aisles, each measuring 67 x 24 *gaz*. Each aisle has nine compartments formed by four columns of red sandstone, which support beautiful engrailed arches, and which have been plastered white to resemble marble, and have stucco and gilded ornamentation on them. The outer hallway (after the middle doorway) has an enclosure with a marble railing in it. It is beautifully decorated with golden finial on its kiosks. Nothing remains of these finials but the marble railing still exists, albeit in a ruinous state.

Gulal Bari

This hall stands in the middle of a plinth that is 104 *gaz* long and 60 *gaz* wide; it is enclosed by a railing of red sandstone which is the size of a man. There were beautiful golden finials on the railings, but these no longer exist. The railing too has been completely destroyed. Mace-bearers and messengers [chaubdars and naqib][17] and state pensioners [ahadis][18] would stand here. The buildings were in a bad state and the Gulal Bari had broken in many places. Emperor Abu Zafar Muhammad Bahadur Shah had the Diwan-e-Aam and the Gulal Bari repaired in CE 1837.

There was a man who had witnessed the reign of three emperors, who described that no emperor had given a public audience in this Diwan-e-Aam since the days of Alamgir II,[19] and it is clear that no one used this after Muhammad Shah. There are doubts whether Muhammad Shah held a court audience there either.

In front of the building is a 204-*gaz*-long and 160-*gaz*-wide courtyard, and around it are palaces with a door from the south leading to them. To the north is the door that leads to the Diwan-e-Khas [the Hall of Special Audience] and the gardens.

Khas Mahal/Chhota Rang Mahal

This palace, with its intricate workmanship, was meant for the chief ladies of the harem. It has a 33 *gaz* long five-arched hall behind which is another hall that is 16 x 8 *gaz* wide. This building is made of marble till the dado level above which there are beautiful decorations in stucco and painting in white plaster. The palace also contains a canal made of marble that is 3-*gaz*-wide, as well as a marble pool. The canal passes through the marble pool and falls like a sheet of water into the octagonal pond situated in the courtyard. There used to be a 67-square-*gaz* garden in the courtyard, with this 25-*gaz*-octagonal pond in the middle of it, and in it there were twenty-five fountains, once upon a time.

Imtiaz Mahal/Bada Rang Mahal

This palace lies behind the Diwan-e-Aam and is the biggest palace in the fort. It used to have a huge courtyard with canals, fountains and gardens, but all of this is now ruined and ugly houses have been built in the charming courtyard.

Earlier, the courtyard had a pond that was 48–50 *gaz* in size and contained five fountains, as well as a stream flowing through which had twenty-five fountains. There was also a garden, 107 x 115 *gaz* in area, with a red sandstone screen around it with 2000 golden finials. Three of its sides had charming mansions and arcades in a width of 70 *gaz*. Towards the west of the buildings, overhanging the river and the Pai'n Bagh [a miniature garden], is the Imtiaz Mahal.

A platform on a plinth is visible from the outside, and below it are two basements. On the terrace is an intricate three-aisled hall with a five-arched façade, which is 57 x 26 *gaz* in size.[20] In front of the middle door towards the courtyard is a huge marble basin with legs that raise it off the ground. The whole is made from a single piece of marble. Into it flows a 3-*gaz*-wide cascade of water from a height of 1.5 *gaz*, down to the sunken lower pond, from where it overflows into canals that in turn flow into the gardens, and its beauty defies description. It has been made entirely of marble.

Engrailed arches were situated in strategic places in the garden with such exquisite embossing and carving that it amazes the mind. On four corners of the roof are four dome-shaped pavilions which magnify the beauty and majesty of the building. During the summers, the corners of the building used to have four marble kiosks, and screens made of vetiver grass would be hung and drenched with water to enable cool air to flow through them and cool the area within.

A Description of the Interior of Imtiaz Mahal

Its façade consists of five arched doors with arched square bays and vaults within. In the middle is a room with a pool, the beauty of which baffles the mind – it is made of marble in such a way that it resembles a flower in full bloom. Inlay work depicting flowers and foliage using various coloured stones within the pool has been executed so exquisitely that it is beyond description.

Although the pool is 7.5-*gaz* square, it is very shallow, just like the palm of a hand. Its beauty is such that when it is full of rippling water, the flowers and foliage inlaid within seem to sway in the morning breeze, giving the impression of a garden in full bloom that reminds one of paradise. Inside this pool is a carved marble cup, which is actually a beautiful flower on whose beauty many thousand flowers could be sacrificed. On every curve and arched cusp, flowers and leaves of coloured stones spring from creeping plants, and the creeping plants in turn emerge from flowers and leaves. Within the cup is a hole and a hidden underground stream that bubbles out of it. The water overflows from the brim, and the swaying of the flowers and plants make the vision seem like a magical moment.

A stream called the Nahr-e-Bahisht flows from Moti Mahal and the Diwan-e-Khas, passes through the middle of this palace and goes out towards the south. There is another stream that flows from the pool from east to west, and cascades into a pond located towards the east of the courtyard in front of the façade. Each channel that these streams flow through is decorated with the same carving, pietra dura and mosaic, that has been used for ornamenting the pool.

Columns supporting the arches in Imtiaz Mahal are made of marble. In fact, this palace, up to the dado,[21] is made of marble and is decorated with inlay work. Almost the entire palace has been gilded with dazzling gold floral designs. They say that this palace had a pure silver ceiling, but in the reign of Farrukhsiyyar it was, for some reason and requirement, replaced with copper. During the reign of Emperor Moin-ud-Din Muhammad Akbar Shah II, this copper ceiling was also removed and was replaced by wood, but even that is now in ruins.

Chhoti Baithak
This building to the south of Imtiaz Mahal is an annexe to the apartments where the emperor sleeps [commonly known as 'Khwabgah', but famous as the 'Badi Baithak', see below]. These apartments are very beautiful and pleasing to the eye. The late Mirza Jahangir Bahadur[22] had made new additions to this area, but it lost its beauty by not remaining the way it was when Shahjahan had built it.

Asad Burj
This is the southern tower of the fort and is built in the same manner as the one to the north, which is famous as Shah Burj. This tower was destroyed in the chaos that followed the bombardment between Octerlony and Harnath Chela, but was restored to its original state in the reign of Emperor Moin-ud-Din Muhammad Akbar Shah II.

Khwabgah/Badi Baithak
This very elegant and beautiful set of apartments is where the emperor retires to sleep. They lie to the north of Imtiaz Mahal and are made entirely of marble. Decorated with beautiful

floral designs and gilded work depicting flowers and foliage, they do not have a parallel on the face of this earth.

In the middle stands a structure that looks like a raised platform, which is the emperor's throne, and to the north and south are two arched marble doorways decorated with glazed-tile ornamentation. The throne structure is 15 x 6 *gaz* in size. An inscription by Sadullah Khan is present on two of its arches, in addition to verses that are inscribed in gold. Beyond the throne area is a hall with five arches; it is very elegant and again made completely of marble. It is exquisitely decorated with pietra dura work and is 20 x 6 *gaz*, with arches and chambers on either side. From the western chambers there is a way that leads to the Diwan-e-Khas, and is called the 'special passageway' [*khasi deorhi*].

In the middle of that hall is a unique marble basin. It does not have a fountain but instead has thousands of beautiful floral decorations in stones of various colours on its layers. The petal of every flower has a hole from which water spouts up like a fountain and into the stream.[23] Beyond this hall lies a large courtyard which has a fascinating floor paved with marble. The paradisical stream, Nahr-e-Bahisht, flows through here and then goes into the Rang Mahal.

Burj Tila/Musamman Burj

To the east of the wall of the apartments where the emperor sleeps, is a tower made of marble from top to bottom and as in other buildings it has gold work, pietra dura and floral decorations. The dome of this tower is also golden in colour, thus giving it the name Sunehri Burj/Burj Tila or Golden Tower. Since it is octagonal in shape, it is also known as Musamman Burj. Three sides of the tower face the apartments where the emperor sleeps, while five jut out towards the river. There are marble screens on these five sides and one has a balcony facing the river. On the western arch, there are inscriptions from the reign of Akbar II.

Shah Mahal/Diwan-e-Khas

To the north of the apartments where the emperor sleeps is a huge square to the east of which is a platform 1½ *gaz* high, 80 *gaz* long and 26 *gaz* wide. In the middle of this stands the Diwan-e-Khas, 34 x 26 *gaz* in size and made of marble from top to bottom. The 4-*gaz*-wide stream, the Nahr-e-Bahisht, flows through the centre of the hall.

In the midst of this edifice is another room of 18x10 *gaz* built by erecting square columns around a platform in the centre. It is on this platform that the Peacock Throne has been placed. When the emperor graces the court with his presence, this is where he sits. The walls, columns and arches are made of marble and inlaid with cornelian, corals and other precious stones up to the dado, in which flowers and foliage have been carved. The beauty of this work forces one to remember God's bounty. From the dado to ceiling, it is decorated with golden work. This famous verse is inscribed on the arches on the inner side of the Diwan-e-Khas in gold:

> If there is Heaven on earth,
> It is here, it is here, it is here.

On its eastern side, this building projects onto the river and has finely carved marble screen doors with perforations that have glass inlay work on them. Towards the west is a 70 x 60 *gaz* courtyard, and around that are mansions and arcades made of red sandstone. Towards the west is the entrance which is connected with the Diwan-e-Aam by a passage. In front of the entrance is a red curtain that screens the door. When the emperor is present and holding court, the nobles present their respects and salutations from near this red curtain. Towards the north is the way to the garden, Bagh-e-Hayat Baksh, and towards the south is the passageway leading to the royal harem.

In front of this entrance towards the courtyard, is a marble enclosure called Chaukhundi Diwan-e-Khas. This building is also a unique wonder as its ceiling was also made completely of silver but was torn off during the Maratha and the Jat rebellions.

Tasbih Khana

On the terrace where this beautiful Hall of Special Audience is built, towards the south, is a hall which is famous as 'Tasbih Khana'. It comprises the rear portion of the apartments where the emperor sleeps. In the middle of this hall is engraved a weighing scale in marble with the phrase, 'Scales of Justice', inscribed on it. It has a lot of golden work. The way to the apartments where the emperor sleeps, called the 'special passageway', is located inside the Tasbih Khana.

Aqab-e-Hammam

To the south of the Hall of Special Audience is an incomparable bathouse, and the buildings are called 'aqab-e-hammam' [behind the royal bathouse].[24]

Hammam

These *hammam* or baths are incomparable and unique. I am convinced there is no parallel to these baths in any country. There are three parts to them and I am describing them separately. The first, called the *jaam-e-kunis,* is like a large room and is made of marble till the dado, with pietra dura decorations. To the east are screens decorated with mirror-work in which flowers, greenery and the river are reflected very clearly.

The second room, called the 'cold room' [*sard khana*], is so unparalleled that even the skies [*chashm-e-falak*] would not have seen anything like it. To the north, there is a throne of marble set in the middle of the room. It is decorated with mosaic and pietra dura. Beyond that is a quadrangle made completely of marble. It has a mosaic of various coloured stones from the floor to the ceiling and has all kinds of floral designs. This mosaic is so beautiful that one spontaneously thinks that a thousand Persian carpets have been laid out. This kind of work convinces one that some Italian master was involved in the building of this fort since that is where [the art of] mosaic [work] was invented.

In the middle of this room is a square pool with pietra dura work. There are four golden fountains, one on each corner and designed in such a way that the jets from all four combine to fall together in the centre of the pool. Adjacent to the wall flows a shallow rivulet that is about a *gaz* wide. No other room is as beautiful as this. The special feature of this room is that as per will or desire and according to the weather, the temperature of the room, and of the water in the stream and of the fountains can be kept cool or warm. Cold or hot water flows from this rivulet as per need.

The third room is called the 'warm room' [*garam khana*]. It is made completely of marble till the dado. Towards the west is a marble pool for hot water and in the centre is a marble platform, which was used for sitting while bathing. Towards the north, as in the second part, is another throne for the emperor's use with a rectangular pool in front that can be filled with hot or cold water. The floor, platform, pools and walls are all beautifully carved and decorated with mosaic and inlay work uptil the dado. The floral inlays are studded with precious and semi-precious stones that create the effect of a garden. Perhaps it was never heated after Shahjahan and Alamgir Aurangzeb. It is famously said that 125 *maunds* of wood were required to heat it.

> The beauty of the building is such.
> That one can't stop gazing at it.

Moti Mahal

This palace is made of red sandstone, then plastered white and generously decorated with floral designs and gilding. The first part is 15 x 8 *gaz* wide and includes two galleries. In the middle is a pool that is 4 x 3 *gaz* wide. Behind each gallery is a section that is 8 x 5 *gaz*. There are lofty rectangular halls with five arches, which overlook the river on the east. Towards the west, they overlook the Hayat Baksh gardens. Each hall is 30 x 7 *gaz* in size.

The inner building is made with marble till the dado, and the rest is made of red sandstone that has been plastered white. There is a pool and a stream from which a 2-*gaz*-wide cascade of water falls into another pool towards the Hayat Baksh Garden via a chute. The pool is unique as one has not seen as faultless a stone as the one from which it has been made. The stone and this wondrous pool are incomparable.

Description of the Pool/Basin

The reality is that this large, flawless stone was mined from the Makrana mines and was incomparable in whiteness and quality. On the orders of the emperor, a basin was made from it, which was 4 *gaz* square and 1.5 *gaz* deep. The entire pool along with its legs was made of one monolithic stone. After it was complete, the basin was brought carefully from Makrana, which is 200 *kos* [450 miles] from the capital city of Shahjahanabad, and was safely installed here. There were mansions to the north and south of the Moti Mahal which still exist, although they now show some signs of damage.

Nahr-e-Bahisht

This stream flows from this palace to the Diwan-e-Khas, and thence to the Rang Mahal and the apartments where the emperor sleeps. From here it is divided into branches which are diverted into every palace and mansion. It is said to resemble the river that flows in paradise called Nahr-e-Bahisht after which it is named.

Bagh-e-Hayat Baksh

> A hundred thousand flowers bloom in this garden,
>
> The greenery is fresh and sweet sound of the water is soothing.

Once upon a time, this garden [*bagh*] was very beautiful and in full bloom, but now lies desolate and in ruins. The present rulers have not paid any attention to its condition. There are a few very beautiful buildings in this garden which are described below. There is one citron-leaved Indian fig tree in this garden which is unique, and its jams/preserves are very beneficial for any ailment of the spleen.

Hauz and Nahr

In the centre of the Bagh-e-Hayat Baksh is a big pool which is 60 x 60 *gaz*. Streams flow around it through channels that are 6 *gaz* wide, made of red sandstone. In the middle of these streams, at some point in time, there were 49 silver fountain jets that worked day and night. At its corners were 112 silver fountain jets which also spouted water day and night. All around this pool were 6-*gaz*-wide water channels made of red sandstone, and every channel had 30 silver fountains. No signs of these fountains remain except for a hole where each of them was installed.

> The lover's heart is always troubled by rivals,
>
> The pain has now become a scar.

The present emperor, Bahadur Shah, has transformed the area once filled by this pool, into Zafar Mahal.

Bhado'n

Towards the south of the garden is an elegant and beautiful building made of marble which is called Bhado'n. An attractive and elegant hall has been built on a platform, with a plinth supported by sixteen columns. These columns divide it into two sections on the east and west creating square bays in between.[25] Below it on the ground is a square marble tank which measures 4 x 15 *tasu* [twenty-fourth part of a *gaz*] and 1 and 1/5 *gaz* deep. A canal flows here from the stream that flows through the palace, and eventually cascades into the tank. From here, another chute flows and falls into the canal.

This building is also very unique and the flowing water and chutes inside it give the impression of rain in the [Hindu calendar] month of Bhado'n[26], thus its name. Small arched niches were made in the pond and the chutes of this building, in which, during the day, flower bouquets were placed, and at night camphor candles would be lit. When water cascaded over these candles and flowers, it created a wondrous impression. There is now no way for water to flow into it. On the four corners of the roof are four golden cupolas.

Sawan

On the northern side of this garden is another exquisite building made entirely of marble. It is identical to the Bhado'n pavilion, with the same arched niches for flowers and lamps, arches, tank, chutes and flow of water. The noise made by the flowing streams is similar to the sound of rain in monsoons and the building was thus named Sawan.[27]

Shah Burj

This three-storeyed tower is also very incredible. It has a diameter of 16 *gaz*. The first storey stands on a plinth of 12 *gaz*. The central hall with a vaulted soffit is round from the inside and level from the outside. It is built of stone with marble upto the dados, and is beautifully decorated with mosaic and inlay work. The rest of it has been plastered white over which floral designs have been painted in gold. This part is octagonal and has a diameter of 8 *gaz*, with four alcoves and two canopied seats that are semi-octagonal and project over the river. The façade is marble and the alcoves on both the northern and eastern sides measure 4 x 4 *gaz*. The ones on the western and southern side are 4 x 3 *gaz*.

In the centre is an extremely attractive tank, 3 *gaz* in diameter. Its ornamentation leaves one breathless and reminds one of divine grace. In the western alcove is a waterfall and small arched niches for flowers in the daytime and lamps at night. In front of the waterfall is a scalloped basin (3.5 x 2.5 *gaz* in area) and from this basin towards the east extends a marble stream 1.5 *gaz* in width. The basin and water channel are beautifully decorated with pietra dura and floral embossing. They are inlaid with cornelian and coral and other priceless precious stones.

Another stream flows from this, falling into the tank on the western alcove and joins the main stream of the tower, subsequently reaching the eastern alcove, via the octagonal tank. Underneath it, towards the river, is a waterfall. From this point onwards, a stream runs through the entire fort, and in fact the water system for the entire fort is controlled from here. Each pipe bears a label of the tank or stream it flows into. The second storey is also octagonal, made very neatly with a diameter of 8 *gaz* and a gallery that is supported on 24 pillars. The third storey is a domed pavilion with 8 pillars. The tower is of marble and its finial is golden. It is a very spectacular building.

Mehtab Bagh

This garden is situated to the west of the Hayat Baksh garden. Once upon a time it must have been a marvellous place but is now in ruins. In the centre of this garden flows a very attractive and large stream. Now Emperor Siraj-ud-Din Muhammad Bahadur Shah has replicated the Jharna[28] of Qutub Sahib[29] to the west of this garden, adding to its beauty.

The City [Shahr] of Shahjahanabad

Everyone will be happy in life,

(If) they settle in Shahjahanabad.

After the fort was built, and the emperor came to live in it in CE 1648, the city also was populated and therefore Mir Yahya Kashi composed the following chronogram: 'Shahjahan built Shahjahanabad' [*Shud Shahjahan abad az Shahjahan abad*].

In the twenty-fourth regnal year corresponding to AH 1060 [CE 1650], on the orders of Shahjahan, a city wall was constructed of mud and stone at the cost of one and a half lakhs, in a period of four months. However, this broke in many places in the monsoons of the next year. Thus Shahjahan ordered it to be built anew of mortar and stone. This was built in seven years in AH 1069 [CE 1658–59] at a cost of four lakh rupees. This is 6664 *gaz* long, 4 *gaz* wide and 9 *gaz* in height. It has 27 bastions, each 10 *gaz* in diameter.

In AH 1218 [CE 1803–04], when the British government took over the reins of Delhi, this wall had broken down in many places. The British government ordered it to be repaired and the moat and wall was renovated.

Outside Ajmeri Darwaza [gateway] was the tomb of Ghazi-ud-Din Khan Firoz Jung, father of Nizamul Mulk Asif Jah, which is famous as the *madarsa*.[30] This was also taken inside the city walls and around CE 1811, an enclosing wall was built around this *madarsa* on the orders of the government. As it was constructed in the reign of Muhammad Akbar Shah Badshah, 'Burj Akbar Shah' was inscribed on its bastion on a marble tablet.

Burj Akbar Shah

The gates of this city are very finely made, and they all mostly look alike. In 1852, on the orders of the British Government, a new double gateway was built, one for entering and one for exiting. It has been named the Calcutta Darwaza, and it contains the inscription 'Calcutta Darwaza, CE 1852'. This city now has fourteen gateways and 14 wicket gates (*khirki*) as listed below.

Gateways

1. Delhi Darwaza
2. Rajghat Darwaza
3. Khizri Darwaza
4. Calcutta Darwaza (closed)
5. Nigambodh Darwaza
6. Kelaghat Darwaza
7. Lal Darwaza
8. Kashmiri Darwaza
9. Badar-roo Darwaza
10. Kabuli Darwaza
11. Paththar Ghati Darwaza
12. Lahori Darwaza (closed)
13. Ajmeri Darwaza
14. Turkman Darwaza

Wicket Gates

1. Zinat-ul-Masajid *ki khirki*
2. Nawab Ahmad Baksh Khan *ki khirki*
3. Nawab Ghazi-ud-Din Khan *ki khirki*
4. Nasirganj *ki khirki*
5. Nai Khirki
6. Shahganj *ki khirki*
7. Ajmeri Darwaze *ki khirki*
8. Sayyad Bholi (Bu Ali) *ki khirki* (closed)
9. Buland Bagh *ki khirki* (closed)
10. Farrash Khane *ki khirki* (closed)
11. Amir Khan *ki khirki*
12. Khalil Khan *ki khirki*
13. Bahadur Ali Khan *ki khirki*
14. Nigambodh *ki khirki*

Urdu Bazaar and Chandni Chowk

In front of the fort's Lahori Gate is a 40-*gaz*-wide and 1520-*gaz*-long bazaar. Old history books refer to it as the Lahori Bazaar.[xliii] Princess Jahan Ara, the daughter of Shahjahan, built this market in CE 1650. There is a 480 *gaz* square after the Lahori Darwaza, with a quadrangle of 80 *gaz*, on which the Kotwali [police station] Chabutra [platform] is set. Beyond this square, at a distance of 80 *gaz*, is another octagonal square measuring 100 x 100 *gaz*, and this is called Chandni Chowk. There are beautiful shops built around it. Towards the north is a garden called Sahibabad or 'Begum ka Bagh'. Beyond this is another bazaar, 460 *gaz* long, with canals flowing inside. At the end of this bazaar is the Fatehpuri Masjid.

Faiz Bazaar

Near Delhi Darwaza of the fort is a 1050-*gaz*-long and 30-*gaz*-wide bazaar. It had stone shops on both sides, and a canal used to flow in the centre. Akbarabadi Mahal, wife of Shahjahan had this bazaar built in CE 1650. The Akbarabadi Mosque is also situated in this bazaar. Some history books, such as the *Mirat-e-Aftab-e-Numa*, also call this the Akbarabadi Bazaar. Both these bazaars [Akbarabadi and Faiz] came into being along with the establishment of the city of Shahjahanabad. The rest of the markets were established gradually over a period of time.

Decoration of the Bazaar and City

At the time of Shahjahan, huge drains were dug out in these bazaars, which kept them clean and prevented sludge. Now this has completely changed. Some of the drains have been closed and some have been destroyed which has resulted in filthy markets. In CE 1852, Mr Arthur Austen Roberts, the Collector and Magistrate of Shahjahanabad decided to undertake cleanliness and ornamentation of the bazaars. He had new drains built in many places and in some places he had the old ones cleaned. Stone drains were laid down under the shops in the big markets, with the waste water draining out of the city. Also, red sandstone platforms were built in front of the shops. Lanterns were used on both sides of the bigger markets at night which added to the beauty and elegance of the city.

Faiz Nahr

The original builder of this canal is Sultan Jalal-ud-Din Firoz Shah Khilji.[xliv] He built this canal in CE 1291 by cutting it out of the river Yamuna in Pargana Khizrabad and took it to a distance of 30 *kos* (about 67.5 miles) to Pargana Safidon where he had a hunting lodge. Subsequent

---

[xliii] *Mirat-e-Aftab-e-Numa.*

[xliv] Ibid.

kings neglected this canal and it became blocked. In CE 1561 during Jalal-ud-Din Akbar's reign, the Governor of Delhi, Shahab-ud-Din Ahmad Khan had this canal cleaned, also brought it into his estates and named it Nahr-e-Shahab. After him, this canal dried up once again. In CE 1638, Shahb-ud-Din Muhammad Shahjahan gave orders for it to be cleaned up to Safidon, and a new canal was to be dug up from there which would reach Shahjahan Fort [Red Fort] and the people of Shahjahanabad. This canal was thus established, and once the fort was ready, its water was released into the fort and city. After a period of time, however, the canal closed down again. Around CE 1820, the British Government again made it operative and it is still functioning today in a well-preserved state.

Editor's Notes

1. As per Ptolemy's *Geography*, latitude was measured from the equator in Africa but expressed in terms of hours rather than in degrees of arc. His Prime Meridian ran through the Fortunate Isles, the westernmost land recorded at around the position of El Hierro in the Canary Islands.

2. So-called because of the bloodshed that happened near it during Nadir Shah's massacre of Delhi; this gateway in Chandni Chowk near Sunehri Masjid, is no longer extant.

3. This refers to the gateway in the city walls and not the one at Red Fort (Qila-e-Mu'alla)

4. It seems possible that this is a reference to Sultan-ul-Mashaik Hazrat Nizam-ud-Din Auliya as there is a building near it called Lal Mahal. But this does not seem possible as Jalal-ud-Din Khilji's coronation took place at Rai Pithaura Fort and he [always] dismounted [as a mark of respect] when he passed by Khushk-e-Lal.

5. There are no traces of any fort of this name in Ghiyaspur which is now called Hazrat Nizam-ud-Din Basti.

6. The older cities, such as Qila Rai Pithaura.

7. A unit of length and is 22 gaz/66 feet, approximately 20.1168 meters.

8. City and fort of Rai Pithaura

9. Known as Pir Ghaib today, it is on the Ridge.

10. Sir Sayyid uses the term *pukhta* which means strong/well-built as well as built of brick or stone or masonry. I have taken it to mean masonry.

11. The name given to what is now known as Red Fort/Lal Qila was Qila-e-Mubarak in Shahjahan's reign. Under the later Mughals it was variously known as Qila-e-Mu'alla and Lal Haveli. Sir Sayyid is referring to it as Qila-e-Shahjahan probably because it was built on the latter's orders.

12. This was probably made by Austin Bordeaux, a Florentine jeweller and imported readymade from Italy according to the note by Sir John Marshall to the Archaeological Survey of India 1902–03.

13. The date given in the first edition is 15 Jamad-ul-Awwal ah 1049/13 September 1639.

14. The solid upright section in a crenellated battlement.

15. The elephant sculptures were placed in front of the Delhi Darwaza under Shahjahan but destroyed in Aurangzeb's reign as he disapproved of statues of animate objects. When fragments of these elephants were discovered in 1903, Lord Curzon had replicas made and installed in front of Delhi Darwaza where they still stand.

16. Sir Sayyid calls it a *do-taara* but it was probably a lyre.

17. They made the announcements and carried the petitions to the emperor.

18. State pensioners could be called on for active service in case of emergency.

19. Alamgir II ruled from 6 June 1699–29 November 1759.

20. In Asar-1, Sir Sayyid mentions this figure as 57 x 36 gaz.

21. The lower part of an interior wall that is decorated differently from the upper part.

22. Mirza Jahangir (ce 1791 to 18 July 1821) was the eldest son of Akbar Shah II.

23. These fountains etc. are no longer present.

24. According to Maulvi Zafar Hasan the *aqab-e-hammam* was the place where garments were removed. Zafar Hasan, *Monuments of Delhi* (Delhi: Aryan Books International, 2008), Vol. 1, p. 22.

25. Sir Sayyid uses the word *bangla* [bungalow] for some reason here which is confusing.

26. The month of the Hindu calendar which corresponds with mid August-mid September and is the rainy season.

27. The second month of the Hindu calendar [which corresponds with the period from 15 July to 15 August] and is the rainy season.

28. A building in Mehrauli with a waterfall or *jharna*.

29. Khwaja Qutub-ud-Din Bakhtiyar Kaki, a Sufi Saint whose *dargah* is in Mehrauli.

30. The madarsa later became the famous Delhi College of the nineteenth and twentieth centuries. Today, the school still functions on the original premises, while Delhi College – now renamed Zakir Hussain College – has shifted to Jawaharlal Nehru Marg, New Delhi.

CHAPTER THREE

Monuments Built by Badshahs and Amirs

Table 3.1: Monuments built by Badshahs and Amirs

No.	Building	Builder	Ruler	Year	Description	Pg no.
1	Lohe *ki lath*	Raja Medhavi aka Dhava	Raja Dhava	Approx. 895 BCE	On this pillar is an inscription of the victory over the Sindhis but tradition proves that these words were inscribed after 5 BCE.	148
2.	Ashoka Pillar/ Minara Zarrin/Firoz Shah *ki lath*	Raja Ashoka	Raja Ashoka	298 BCE	These are pillar-edicts related to Buddhism in old script and Nagari script. On it is inscribed the Fatehnama of Baldev Chauhan, but this was inscribed during the reign of Rai Pithaura.	150
3.	Ashoka Pillar/ *Minaara* Kushk Shikar	Raja Ashoka	Raja Ashoka	298 BCE		154
4.	Anekpur	Anekpal Tanwar	Anekal Tanwar/ Tomar	AH 57/CE 676		155
5.	Anektal	Anekpal Tanwar/Tomar	"	AH 57/CE 676		156
6.	Suraj Kund	Surajpal	"	AH 67/ CE 686		157
7.	Buttkhana situated near Qutub Sahab	Prithviraj aka Rai Pithaura	Prithviraj aka Rai Pithaura	AH 538/CE 1143	AH 587/CE 1191 Qutub-ud-Din Aibak destroyed the temple and built a mosque. On the first part of the pillar is inscribed the Fatehnama. AH 592/CE1195 Sultan Muiz-ud-Din built five arches. AH 627/CE 1239 Sultan Shams-ud-Din Altamash built 3 arches, and added five storeys on the Qutub Minar. AH 710/CE 1310 Sultan Ala-ud-Din sought to enlarge the mosque and make a minaret twice the size of the first, but this was not completed	157–164
	Masjid Quwwat-ul Islam	Qutub-ud-Din Aibak commander	Sultan Muiz-ud-Din			158
	"	Built by Sultan Muiz-ud-Din	"			163
	"	Shams-ud-Din	Sultan Shams-ud-Din			164
	"	Sultan Aladdin	Sultan Aladdin			164

No.	Building	Builder	Ruler	Year	Description	Pg no.
8	Qutub Sahib *ki lath*	Prithviraj aka Rai Pithaura	Rai Pithaura			165
	"	Qutub-ud-Din Aibak/ Fatehnama	Sultan Muiz-ud-Din			166
	"	Sultan Shams-ud-Din	Sultan Shams-ud-Din			167
9	Darwaza Kalan adjoining *lath*/ Qutub Minar	Sultan Ala-ud-Din	Sultan Ala-ud-Din			170
10	Incomplete *lath*/Alai Minar	Sultan Ala-ud-Din	Sultan Ala-ud-Din			172
11	Hauz-e-Shamsi	Sultan Shams-ud-Din Altamash	Sultan Shams-ud-Din Altamash	AH 627/CE 1229	In AH 711/ CE 1311 Sultan Ala-ud-Din got a *burji* made in the centre of this tank.	175
12.	*Maqbara* Sultan Ghazi	Sultan Shams-ud-Din Altamash	Sultana Shams-ud-Din Altamash	AH 629/CE 1231	This is the tomb of Nasir-ud-Din Mahmud, s/o Sultan Altamash	175
13.	*Maqbara* Shams-ud-Din	Raziya Sultan Begum	Raziya Sultan Begum	AH 633/CE 1235		176
14	*Dargah* Shah Turkman		Muiz-ud-Din Bahram Shah	AH 638/CE 1240		179
15	*Maqbara* Rukn-ud-Din Firoz Shah	Muiz-ud-Din Bahram Shah	Muiz-ud-Din Bahram Shah			
16.	*Maqbara* Raziya Sultan Begum	Muiz-ud-Din Bahram Shah	Muiz-ud-Din Bahram Shah	AH 638/CE 1240		179
17	*Maqbara* Muiz-ud-Din Bahram Shah	Ala-ud-Din Masud Shah	Ala-ud-Din Masud Shah	AH 639/CE 1241		180
18	*Maqbara* Sultan Ghiyas-ud-Din Balban	Ghiyas-ud-Din Balban	Ghiyas-ud-Din Balban	AH 683/ CE1284	At the time of the death of Khan Shaheed, his grave and this tomb was made by Sultan Balban himself.	180
19	Hauz Alai/ Hauz Khas	Sultan Ala-ud-Din	Sultan Ala-ud-Din	AH 695/CE 1295	In the reign of Firoz Shah it was named Hauz Khaus.	183
20	*Maqbara* Sultan Ala-ud-Din	Qutub-ud-Din Mubarak Shah	Qutub-ud-Din Mubarak Shah	AH 717/CE 1317		183
21	Baoli *Dargah* Hazrat Nizam-ud-Din	Hazrat Nizam-ud-Din	Ghiyas-ud-Din Tughlaq Shah	AH 721/CE 1321	AH 781/CE 1379 Mohammaed Maaruf made houses on this step well.	148
22	*Maqbara* Ghiyas-ud-Din Tughlaq Shah	Mohammaad Adil Tughlaq Shah	Muhammad Adil Tughlaq Shah	AH 725/CE1324	Muhammad Adil Tughlaq Shah is also buried here.	189
23	*Dargah* Hazrat Nizam-ud-Din		Muhammad Adil Tughlaq Shah	AH 725/CE1324	AH 1063/CE 1652 Khalilullah Khan made a pavilion in the mausoleum.	190
24	Satpula	Muhammad Adil Tughlaq Shah	Muhammad Adil Tughlaq Shah	AH 727/CE 1326		193
25	*Dargah* Sheikh Salah-ud-Din		Firoz Shah Tughlaq	AH 754/CE 1353		194
26	Masjid *Dargah*-e-Nizam-ud-Din	Firoz Shah	Firoz Shah Tughlaq	AH 754/CE 1353		197
27	Jama Masjid Firozi	Firoz Shah	Firoz Shah	AH 755/CE 1354	Prayers were read out with Timur's *khutba* in this mosque	198
28	Kushk Anwar ya Me'nhdiya'n	Firoz Shah	Firoz Shah	AH 755/CE1354		198
29	Bhooli Bhatiyaari ka Mahal	Firoz Shah	Firoz Shah	AH 755/CE 1354		199
30	Kaali Masjid, Kotla Nizam-ud-Din	Khan Jahan	Firoz Shah	AH 772/CE 1370		200
31	*Dargah* Roshan Chiragh Dehli	Firoz Shah	Firoz Shah	AH 775/CE 1373		200
32	Qadam Sharif/ *Maqbara* Fatah Khan	Firoz Shah	Firoz Shah	AH 776/CE 1374		203
33	Masjid Chauraha, Qadam Sharif	Firoz Shah	Firoz Shah	AH 776/CE 1374		204
34	*Dargah* Hazrat Syed Mahmud Bahar		Firoz Shah	AH 778/CE 1376		204
35	Kali Masjid, Shahr	Khan-e-Jahan	Firoz Shah	AH 789/CE 1387		209
36	Masjid Begumpur	Khan-e-Jahan	Firoz Shah	AH 789/CE 1387		209
37	Masjid Kalu Sarai	Khan-e-Jahan	Firoz Shah	AH 789/CE 1387		209

No.	Building	Builder	Ruler	Year	Description	Pg no.
38	Masjid Khirki	Khan-e-Jahan	Firoz Shah	AH 789/CE 1387		210
39	*Maqbara* Firoz Shah	Nasir-ud-Din Muhammad Shah	Nasir-ud-Din Muhammad Shah	AH 792/CE 1389		210
40	Khizr *ki Gumbati*	Abul Fatah Mubarak Shah	Mubarak Shah	AH 824/CE 1421	This is the tomb of Khizr Khan	215
41	Mubarakpur Kotla	Muhammad Shah	Muhammad Shah	AH 837/CE 1433		215
42	*Maqbara* Muhammad Shah	Ala-ud-Din Alam Shah	Ala-ud-Din Alam Shah	AH 849/CE 1445		216
43	*Maqbara* Sultan Bahlol	Sultan Sikandar	Sultan Sikandar	AH 894/CE 1488		216
44	Panch Burja, Zamarudpur	Zamurad Khan	Sultan Sikandar	AH 894/CE 1488		219
45	Basti *Baori*	Basti Khwajasara	Sultan Sikandar	AH 894/CE 1488		219
46	Moth ki Masjid	Shahab-ud-Din	Sultan Sikandar	AH 894/CE 1488		220
47	Maqbara Langar Khan		Sultan Sikandar	AH 900/CE 1494		225
48	Ti-burja	Sultan Sikandar	Sultan Sikandar	AH 900/CE 1494		225
49	Raj'on *ki Bain*	Daulat Khan	Sultan Sikandar	AH 922/CE 1506		225
50	*Maqbara* Sultan Sikandar	Sultan Ibrahim	Sultan Ibrahim	AH 923/CE 1517		226
51	*Dargah* Yusuf Qattal	Sheikh Ala-ud-Din	Babur	AH 933/CE 1526		226
52	*Dargah* Maulana Jamali	Jamali	Babur	AH 935/CE 1528		231
53	Masjid *Dargah* Jamali	Jamali	Babur	AH 935/CE 1528		231
54	Neeli Chhatri	Humayun	Humayun	AH 939/CE 1532		232
55	*Dargah* Imam Zamin	Imam Zamin	Humayun	AH 944/CE 1537		232
56	*Dargah* Hazrat Qutub Sahib	Khalilullah Khan	Sher Shah	AH 948/CE 1541		237
57	Masjid Qila Kuhna	Sher Shah	Sher Shah	AH 948/CE 1541		238
58	Sher Mandal	Sher Shah	Sher Shah	AH 948/CE 1541		241
59	Masjid Maqbara Khairpur	Khair Khan	Sher Shah	AH 950/CE 1543		238 58
60	Khari Baoli	Imadul Mulk Khwaja Abdullah	Islam Shah	AH 952/CE 1545		
61	Maqbara Isa Khan	Islam Shah	Islam Shah	AH 954/CE 1547		247
62	Masjid Isa Khan	Isa Khan	Islam Shah	AH 954/CE 1547		247
63	Masjid *Dargah* Qutub Sahib	Islam Shah	Islam Shah	AH 958/CE 1551	Farrukhsiyar enlarged this mosque	247
64	Arab Sarai	Haji Begum	Akbar	AH 968/CE 1560		248
65	Khair-ul-Manazil	Maham Begum	Akbar	AH 969/CE 1561		248
66	Bhool Bhalaiyya/ *Maqbara* Adham Khan	Akbar	Akbar	AH 969/CE 1561		248
67	*Maqbara* Humayun	Haji Begum	Akbar	AH 973/CE 1565		253
68	Neeli Chhatri/ *Maqbara* Naubat Khan	Nawab Naubat Khan	Akbar	AH 973/CE 1565		254
69	*Maqbara* Atgha Khan	Kokaltash Khan	Akbar	AH 974/CE 1566		255
70	*Dargah* Hazrat Baqi Billah		Akbar	AH 1012/CE 1603		255
71	*Dargah* Amir Khusrau	Imad-ud-Din Hasan	Nur-ud-Din Jahangir	AH 1014/CE 1605		256
72	Jailkhana/ Sarai Farid Khan	Farid Khan	Jahangir	AH 1017/CE 1608		256
73	Barapula	Aga Maan	Jahangir	AH 1021/CE 1612		261
74	Mandi	Agha Maan	Jahangir	AH 1021/CE 1612		261
75	Kos Minara	Jahangir	Jahangir	AH 1028/CE 1618		
76	Pul Salimgarh	Jahangir	Jahangir	AH 1031/CE 1621		262

No.	Building	Builder	Ruler	Year	Description	Pg no.
77	*Maqbara* Sheikh Farid	Sheikh Farid	Jahangir	AH 1033/CE 1623		265
78	Neela Burj/*Maqbara* Faheem	Abdur Rahim Khan-e-Khana	Jahangir	AH 1034/CE 1624		265
79	Chausath Khamba/ *Maqbara* Kokaltash Khan	Mirza Aziz Kokaltash Khan	Jahangir	AH 1034/CE 1624		266
80	*Maqbara* Khan-e-Khana	Abdur Rahim Khan-e-Khana	Jahangir	AH 1036/CE1626		266
81	*Maqbara* Sayyid Abid	Khan Dauran Khan	Shahjahan	AH 1036/CE 1626		271
82	Khas Mahal	Khas Mahal	Shahjahan	AH 1042/CE 1632		271
83	*Maqbara* Sheikh Abdul Haq	Sheikh-ul-Islam	Shahjahan	AH 1052/CE 1642		271
84.	Jama Masjid	Shahjahan	Shahjahan	AH 1060/CE 1650		272
85	Darus Shifa Dar-ul-Baqa	Shahjahan	Shahjahan	AH 1060/CE 1650		282
86	Bagh Begum	Jahan Ara Begum	Shahjahan	AH 1060/CE 1650		283
87	Masjid Fatehpuri	Fatehpuri Begum	Shahjahan	AH 1060/CE 1650		284
88	Masjid Akbarabadi	Akbarabadi Begum	Shahjahan	AH 1060/CE 1650		284
89	Masjid Sirhindi	Sirhindi Begum	Shahjahan	AH 1060/CE 1650		287
90	Bagh Shalimar	Shahjahan	Shahjahan	AH 1064/CE 1654		"
91	Bagh Roshan Ara	Roshan Ara Begum	Shahjahan	AH 1064/CE 1654		288
92	Bagh Sirhindi	Sirhindi Begum	Shahjahan	AH 1064/CE 1654		288
93	Qila Moti Masjid	Almagir	Alamgir	AH 1070/CE 1660		289
94	*Muhajjar* Jahanara Begum	Jahan Ara Begum	Alamgir	AH 1092/CE 1682		289
95	*Maqbara* Sar Nala		Alamgir	AH 1100/CE 1688		290
96	*Dargah* Hazrat Hasan *Rasul* Numa		Alamgir	AH 1103/CE 1691		290
97	*Jharna*	Ghiyaz-ud-Din Khan	Alamgir	AH 1112/CE 1700		293
98	Masjid Aurangabadi	Aurngabadi begum	Alamgir	AH 1114/CE 1703		299
99	*Maqbara* Zebunnisa Begum	Alamgir	Alamgir	AH 1114/CE 1703		299
100	Moti Masjid Qutub Sahib	Bahadur Shah	Bahadur Shah	AH 1121/CE 1709		299
101	Zeenat-ul-Masajid	Zeenat-un-Nissa Begum	Bahadur Shah	AH 1122/CE 1710		300
102	*Maqbara* Ghazi-ud-Din Khan	Ghazi-ud-Din Khan	Bahadur Shah Alam	AH 1122/CE 1710		300
103	*Muhajjar* Shah Alam Bahadur Shah	Jahandar Shah	Jahandar Shah	AH 1124/CE 1712	Shah Alam and Akbar Shah are buried here.	305
104	*Burj Maqbara* Humayun		Rafi-ud-Darajat	AH 1131/CE 1718		306
105	Sunehri Masjid, Kotwali	Roshan-ud-Daulah	Muhammad Shah	AH 1134/CE 1721		
106	Masjid Dariba	Sharf-ud-Daulah	Muhammad Shah	AH 1135/CE 1722		309
107	Jantar Mantar	Raja Sawai Jai Singh	Muhammad Shah	AH 1137/CE 1724	The British also had a part in building this observatory	309
108	Shah-e-Mardan	Nawab Qudsia	Muhammad Shah	AH 1137/CE 1724		321
109	Fakhr-ul-Masajid	Fakhr-un-Nisa Khanum	Muhammad Shah	AH 1141/CE 1728		322
110	Bagh Mahaldar Khan	Nazir Mahaldar Khan	Muhammad Shah	AH 1141/CE 1728		
111	Ghat Nigambodh		Muhammad Shah	AH 1150/CE 1737		325
112	Masjid Roshan-ud-Daulah	Roshan-ud-Daulah	Muhammad Shah	AH 1158/CE 1745		326
113	Bagh-e-Naazir	Naazir Roz Afzun	Muhammad Shah	AH 1161/CE 1748		329
114	Mahjar Muhammad Shah	Muhammad Shah	Muhammad Shah	AH 1161/CE 1748		329
115	Qudsia Bagh	Nawab Qudsia	Ahmad Shah	AH 1162/CE 1749		330

No.	Building	Builder	Ruler	Year	Description	Pg no.
116	Chaubi Masjid	Ahmad Shah	Ahmad Shah	AH 1164/CE 1750		
117	Sunehri Masjid	Javed Khwajasara	Ahmad Shah	AH 1165/CE 1751		335
118	*Maqbara* Mansoor	Shuja-ud-Daulah	Alamgir II	AH 1167/CE 1753		335
119	Kalka Temple		Shah Alam	AH 1178/CE 1764		
120	Lal Bangla	Shah Alam	Shah Alam	AH 1193/CE 1779		
121	*Maqbara* Najaf Khan		Shah Alam	AH 1195/CE 1781		343
122	Jain ka Bada Mandir	Harsukh Rai Mohan Lal	Shah Alam	AH 1215/CE 1800		343
123	Church	Colonel Skinner	King George IV	AH 1242/CE 1826		344
124	Jogmaya	Raja Sethu Mal	"	AH 1243/CE 1827		344
125	Jain ka Chhota Mandir	Panchayati	"	AH 1244/CE 1828		347
126	Kothi Jahannuma	Metcalfe Sahib Bahadur	"	AH 1244/CE 1828		348
127	*Muhajjar* Mirza Jahangir	Mumtaz Mahal	King William IV	AH 1248/CE 1832		
128	Zafar Mahal	Bahadur Shah	Queen Victoria	AH 1258/CE 1842		348
129	Hira Mahal	Bahadur Shah	"	AH 1258/CE 1842		
130	Kothi Dilkusha	Metcalfe Sahib Bahadur	"	AH 1260/CE 1844		351
131	*Baoli* Qutub Sahib	Hafiz Daud	"	AH 1260/CE 1844		351
132	Aahini Pul, Hindan	British Government	"	AH 1263/CE 1847		352
133	Lal Diggi	British Government	"	AH 1263/CE 1847		
134	*Pul* Jadeed (new) Nigambodh	"	"	AH 1268/CE 1852		359

DESCRIPTION OF MONUMENTS
CONSTRUCTED ON THE ORDERS OF THE EMPEROR
AND OF MEMBERS OF THE NOBILITY

Lohe ki Lath

This iron pillar [*lohe ki lath*], made by Dhava, also known as Medhavi, is situated near Qutub Sahib's Minar (Qutub Minar) and is made entirely of iron. While it was being cast, beautiful carvings were made on it. It is 22 feet 6 inches in height, and its width at the base is 5 feet 3 inches. According to a famous story, during the reign of Rai Pithaura, brahmans placed this pillar on Raja Basik's head [mythical ruler of the kingdom of serpents] so that Rai Pithaura's family would rule for posterity. However, this is incorrect as there are three *shlokas* engraved on this pillar in Nagari and Sanskrit which say that the Governor of Sindh gathered an army to fight against Raja Dhava where the latter emerged victorious. He constructed this pillar as a symbol of his victory, but died before it was complete. James Princep[i] writes that nothing further is known about this king except that he was one of the kings of Hastinapur.

This kind of Nagari script was used in CE 3 and CE 4, so it was made much before CE 5 or CE

---

[i] ASI Bengal, Book No. 2, p. 494; Journal No. 7, p. 639.

8.[ii] But I disagree, because the history of kings is available from CE 676 up to the Muslim rule,[iii] and there is no mention of this king. From the lack of engravings of the year, it seems clear this was before the reign of Vikramajit. Moreover, Hastinapur kingdom was on the wane. Therefore I feel that this pillar was made by Raja Medhavi, also known as Raja Dhava, from the line of Yudhishtir. These kings had started living in Indrapat but because they came from Hastinapur they were called Hastinapur kings. From the inscription on the pillar it becomes clear that they were Vaishnavis.

According to the available history,[iv] it is clear that Raja Medhavi acceded to the throne in 1905 BCE. British historians have deduced the date of Yudhishtir's ascension to the throne from which it seems that Raja Medhavi was actually crowned in 895 BCE. It is based on this that I feel that this pillar was made in 9 BCE. Some other king completed it at a later date, maybe in CE 3 or CE 4.

When Rai Pithaura made his fort and temple, this pillar was included in the courtyard of the temple and it still stands in the courtyard of the mosque. The pillar, is unique as it still hasn't rusted. There is just a small dent from a cannon ball that was shot at it. Youngsters encircle this pillar and play a game – whoever manages to grasp it in their arms is supposed to be legitimate [halal] and those who cannot are illegitimate [haram].

Ashoka Pillar/Minara Zarrin/Firoz Shah ki Lath

[This pillar has been variously referred to at various points in time as Ashoka's Pillar/Golden Pillar/or Firoz Shah's Pillar]. It is a stone pillar and people say it is made of sandstone. It has been very neatly made. There were five pillars, one of which is in Radhiya, another in Mattia, a third in Allahabad, the fourth in Navah district of Meerut and the fifth in Nauhra village.

Raja Ashoka made these five pillars, which are also known as Biyasi (Priyadarshini), and they have two of his edicts inscribed on them. The first inscription is in the name of Raja Ashoka and is in Pali and Sanskrit, and the script is the ancient one that preceded Devnagari. The inscription describes teachings of Buddhism, and it commands people to not hurt living beings, prescribing punishment for those who do so, in addition to rules for governance.

But this inscription was not read in earlier times.[v] Firoz Shah gathered Buddhist scholars,[vi] but even they could not decipher it. James Prinsep was the first to read and decipher the

---

[ii] *Royal Asiatic Society Journal*, No. 6, p. 460.

[iii] *Ain-e-Akbari.*

[iv] *Bhagwat, Khulasat-ul-Tawareekh* and *Silsilat-ul-Mulook.*

[v] *Haft-e-Aqleem.*

[vi] *Tarikh-e-Firoz Shahi* by Shams Afif.

inscription.[vii] He says that Raja Ashoka, grandson of Chandragupt and Governor of Ujjain, was crowned in 325 BCE and thereafter built this pillar in 298 BCE, which was the twenty-seventh year of his reign. From Persian histories[viii] it is evident that he was the ruler of Kashmir and ruled over India. During his era there was a discussion on religion which angered the populace, and he had to abdicate. The religious discussions on these pillars make it clear that this is indeed Raja Ashoka whose capital was Kashmir. Using the Persian dating system, we come to know that Raja Ashoka came to the throne in 373 BCE, but I think the previously mentioned date is correct.

When Firoz Shah was building his fortress in Thatta, this pillar was in Nauhra village in Pargana Salora in Khizrabad District[ix] which is 90 *kos* (202.5 miles) away from Delhi, towards the mountains. In that period it was famous that this was the staff used by Bhima [the strongest amongst the five Pandava brothers of yore] whilst grazing cows.

Firoz Shah decided to uproot this pillar and take it to Delhi so that it would be remembered for a long time. He gathered many people from the area surrounding it and got cotton bales stacked around the pillar. The pillar's base was then dug up, and when they reached the base, the cotton cushioned the pillar as it tilted. Then each bale was removed and the pillar lowered to the ground. There was a huge square stone at its root, on which this pillar stood. That stone was also removed, and when the pillar had been completely brought down, it was tied with bamboo and enclosed in raw hide so as to protect it from any damage.

A wagon of forty-two wheels was built to carry it, with strong ropes tied to each wheel. It was lifted with ropes and put on the cart by a large number of people. To make the wagon move forward, 200 men pulled each rope. After such great effort and hard work, this pillar was brought to the edge of the river, which flowed along Nauhra village. From there the pillar was transported to Firozabad in huge ships and finally installed near the mosque, a three-storey building constructed in the Kotla. When one storey was ready, the pillar would be placed on it, and then the second one would be built.

When all three levels were ready, the thick ropes were used to tie one end to the pillar and the other end was tied to a pulley on the ground. Many men were employed to move the pulley. When the pillar was raised to 8 *gaz*, wooden sticks were placed under it, and the gaps padded with cotton to prevent damage to the pillar and building. After many days [of such effort] the pillar was raised to stand straight. The same square stone was put at its base and was strengthened by limestone and rocks. On its head was built a beautiful cupola of white

---

[vii] Archaeological Society of Bengal, *Journal*, No. 6, p. 566; Volume 209, p. 791, *Royal Asiatic Society Journal*, No. 6, p. 469.

[viii] *Ain-e-Akbari* and *Tarikh-e-Kashmir*.

[ix] *Tarikh-e-Firoz Shahi* by Shams Afif.

and black marble with a copper finial gilded with gold installed on top. That is why it was called the Golden Pillar [Minara Zarrin].

Unfortunately the cupola and finial no longer exist. In fact, the top of the pillar has also broken and fallen off. Some say it fell because of lightning and others say it was due to cannonballs. The pillar is 32 *gaz* long, of which 8 *gaz* are underground and 24 *gaz* are visible above ground.

The Second Pillar of Ashoka/Minara Kushk Shikar

This is the second pillar [*lath*] of Ashoka, which was in Mian Doab near Meerut. In the same period[x] when Firoz Shah placed the Golden Pillar [*Minara* Zarrin] in his fort in Firozabad, he put up this second pillar in 'Jahannuma', his hunting lodge. Even though this pillar is smaller than the first one, the same difficulties and problems were faced in bringing it to this location as for the first one. When this pillar was set up, the king celebrated and ordered the entire populace of the city to witness the spectacle, and stations were set up offering sherbet to the people.

After a long time, this pillar broke into five pieces when a magazine blew up near it and the pieces are still lying near the mansion of William Fraser. If these five pieces can be joined together, the pillar comes to 32.75 feet. The width of the thickest piece is 3 feet 2 inches, the thinnest one is 2 feet 6 inches, and all of them together weigh 372 *maunds*. The inscription has been obliterated and is difficult to read.

Anekpur

Three miles from Tughlaqabad Fort, under Raja Ballamgarh, is the village of Anekpur. In CE 676, Raja Anekpal Tomar was the King of Delhi and had a huge dam built in the middle of the hills for his hunting and pleasure activities. On two sides are hills and in the middle a small valley. This valley has been enclosed with a beautiful dam and is still present today inspite of the time lapse. The circumference is 189 feet. There are stairs in the wall of the dam and 17 steps can be still seen above the ground. The older generation describes it from memory and says it was bigger and had more steps visible. The drain is so big that a man can walk in it. However, water doesn't stay in this dam any longer, but seeps out of its bottom all twelve months.

In that era, Raja Anekpal started building a fort on the top of the hill. It is said that only the four walls of the fort were built and even those are no longer extant. There are a few traces of the fragments of the wall in some places. Kunwar Bhopal, the twelfth son of Anekpal, settled here and his descendants still live in this village[xi] as the local landlords.

But the fourth generation after Bhopal brought a Gujar girl whose children took the

---

[x] *Tarikh-e-Firoz Shahi*, by Shams Siraj Afif.

[xi] *Pothi Bhaat.*

lineage further, after which they became a part of the Gujar clan and were no longer Tomars. The landlords of this area are called Gujars. Near this fort is a mine, where great quantities of rare rock crystal are found, but which has been closed down by the Raja.

Anektal

This king, in approximately CE 676, during his reign had a tank built near Mehrauli though that tank is now completely ruined. Near Qutub Minar towards the north, there still exists a deep hole known as Anektal. It seems that till CE 1300 this tank existed because when Sultan Ala-ud-Din started building another minaret and mosque near Qutub Minar, he brought water from this tank till there, and signs of the water channels still remain.

Suraj Kund

This is a concrete, circular, extremely beautiful tank and is very deep, adjoining the Anekpur administrative division and the border of Lakkadpur village. It is said that such a beautiful tank does not exist anywhere else under British rule. The tank contains circular steps, a watering hole for animals on one side, and on the other side steps for the movement of men. There is a path for water to flow in from the mountains, and a structure was built as a palace towards the north on the edge of the tank, connected to the tank via beautifully constructed steps. However, this palace is now in complete ruins though those steps still exist. Kunwar Suraj Pal, the fifth son of Raja Anekpal, built this tank in approximately CE 686.[xii]

In the [Hindu calendar] month of Bhadon Sudhi Chatt, there is a big ritual bathing ceremony held in this tank, and on the edge of the tank on top of the steps is a peepal tree, to which coconuts are offered after prayers. The offerings from here are taken by the Brahmans of Anekpur and Lakkadpur. However, it is not a vey big fair.

But-Khana [Temple] of Rai Pithaura

There was a very famous temple near Rai Pithaura Fort with hallways that were two-aisle, three-aisle and four-aisle deep on all sides with a courtyard in the centre. There were gates on the north, south and eastern sides and on the western side was the idol. There were similar hallways outside the temple too which were used for circumambulation. This temple was also built at the same time as the Rai Pitahura Fort, i.e., in CE 1143.[xiii]

This temple was unique and intricately built by master craftsmen and sculptors and one cannot imagine anything better than the result of their work. Every stone has exquisite

---

[xii] Ibid.

[xiii] *Khulasat-ul-Tawarikh.*

carving with floral designs. Every column, ceiling and wall has beautiful sculptures of idols along with the chain and bell motif. The eastern and northern wings of the temple still survive. The iron pillar of the Vaishnav religion and the sculptures of Gods such as Krishna, Mahadeva, Ganesh and Hanuman convince one that this was a temple of the Viaishnav sect. Even though, the idols have been broken during Muslim rule, one can still identify them. In my opinion, there was a red, sandstone building here too apart from these halls which was destroyed as we can still find remains of sculptured stones of red sandstone.

Masjid Adhina Delhi/Masjid Jami Masjid/ Masjid Quwwat-ul-Islam

Qutub-ud-Din Aibak, the Governor of Muiz-ud-Din Muhammad bin Sam alias Shahab-ud-Din Ghori conquered Delhi in CE 1191.[xiv] He removed the idol from the temple and converted the temple into a mosque. All the idols on the walls, columns and gates were either destroyed or defaced. However, the structure of the temple was kept as it was and the material of twenty-seven temples, which were estimated to be of the value of 54,000,000 *deliwals*, was used to construct this mosque. On the eastern gate, the date of victory (conquest of Delhi) and his own name was inscribed.

Constructions Ordered by Sultan Muiz-ud-Din

When Qutub-ud-Din Aibak returned to Ghazni after the conquest of Ajmer, Ranthambhor, and Naharwala (Gujarat), he was ordered by Sultan Muiz-ud-Din to build something which would represent a mosque in this complex [which still looked like a temple].

On his return from Ghazni in CE 1195, as per the Sultan's orders, Qutub-ud-Din Aibak constructed five arches of red sandstone on the western façade of the mosque, and on the northern door, he got the date of construction inscribed. In CE 1197, this was completed and this date was inscribed on the left jamb of the central arch. Of the five arches, the two on the side are approximately 28 feet tall and the central arch is 48 feet tall and 21 feet wide. There is very intricate and exquisite carving of floral designs on the arches which cannot be described in words. All five arches have verses from the Quran and *hadith* inscribed in calligraphy.

When the mosque was ready, it was crowned by a golden finial.[xv] In these arches, stones from the temples were also used, which can be seen from the gap where a stone from the central arch has fallen down to expose the ones with idols within. These idols can be seen clearly via binoculars.

[xiv] *Taj-ul-Masir.*

[xv] Ibid.

The measurement of the mosque, as per Sultan Muiz-ud-Din and Qutub-ud-Din Aibak, is 72 x 50 *gaz*. Fazl ibn Abul Ma'ali was appointed custodian [*mutawalli*] of this mosque and this was inscribed on one of the columns of the western hall. On a pillar of one of the arches of Qub-ud-Din Aibak's prayer chamber it is written: 'Under the supervision of the slave Fazl bin Abil Ma'ali'.

Construction under Sultan Shams-ud-Din Altamash

Sultan Shams-ud-Din Altamash wanted to expand this mosque later, and in CE 1229, he added three arches each on the northern and southern sides and extended the mosque up to the outside hall of Rai Pithaura's temple. These arches are also of red sandstone which display exquisite workmanship in Naskh and Kufi calligraphy of Quranic verses, along with beautiful carving of floral designs. On the south wing on the left jamb of the central arch, the date of construction is inscribed.

Many of these arches have been damaged, and on the northern side, most of them have fallen down. In CE 1233,[xvi] when Sultan Shams-ud-Din conquered Malwa and Ujjain, the temple of Mahakaal was destroyed, and its idol, along with the statue of Raja Vikramajit, was brought to Delhi and thrown in front of this temple. The three arches on the western wing which were constructed by Sultan Shams-ud-Din, are each 37 *gaz* and 1 foot long, and the central arch is 8 *gaz* wide. There are Quranic verses inscribed in beautiful calligraphy in the Naskh and Kufi script on them. On the southern end is the ancient hallway of the temple, which was made for circumambulation and measures 132 *gaz* in length.

Qutub Sahib ki Lath/Minar/Mazanat

It is impossible to describe the grandeur, beauty and magnificence of this monument, the Qutub Minar. In reality, this monument is such that it has no parallel on the face of the earth. There is a famous saying that when one looks up, those wearing caps and turbans have to hold on to them, or these fall down. From the top of this minaret, persons standing on the ground appear very small as do elephants and horses, and one feels strange seeing them. This minaret is unique and fascinating and it seems as if angels have descended from the skies. Though this minaret is very tall and grand, it has been built so elegantly that one wants to keep looking at it.

The lowest storey has alternate conical and circular projections while the second one has only circular ones, and the third only has conical projections. The two upper storeys are round and built of red sandstone. The fourth storey also has marble with carving and exquisite floral designs. May the curly locks of a thousand beloveds be sacrificed on each of its intertwining

---

[xvi] *Tarikhe-Ferishta.*

tendrils. And may hundreds of rosy cheeked, life-giving lips be sacrificed on each of its tiny flowers and petals.

However, there is some controversy regarding the construction of this minaret. Muslims say that Sultan Shams-ud-Din Altamash constructed it and that's how history books describe it.[xvii] Even the inscription by Sultan Sikandar Bahlol calls it the minaret of Sultan Shams-ud-Din Altamash. In some history books, it is called the 'minaret of the mosque,'[xviii] while some call it Sultan Muiz-ud-Din's minaret.[xix]

However, the entrance of this monument is facing the north, and Hindu temples always face the north as against minarets the doors of which always face east. Therefore, when Sultan Ala-ud-Din started the construction of his minaret, it was east facing. Further, this minaret (unlike Sultan Ala-ud-Din's unfinished one), is not made on a plinth as is the Muslim custom. This minaret follows the Hindu tradition, as they don't have a plinth for their temples. Also, the stones which are above the inscriptions seem to have been fixed in later. As we find the chain and bell motif in the actual temple, we find the same motif on the first storey of the minaret.

The inscription proclaiming the victory of Qutub-ud-Din Aibak, general of Sultan Muiz-ud-Din on the minaret, is very similar to the one on Quwwat-ul-Islam Mosque, and it seems evident that the first storey is from the period when the temple was built. It wouldn't be surprising that wherever there are inscriptions, there were sculptures of idols earlier, and that's why calligraphy and inscriptions giving details of the Muslim sultans and their victories replaced them. There is a famous legend that Rai Pithaura built this minaret along with his fort and temple in CE 1143. This seems true because his daughter worshipped the sun, and Hindus believe that River Yamuna is the daughter of the Sun God, and consequently, worshipping the Yamuna is a very important ritual. Therefore, the first storey was built for his daughter to be able to see the sun and the River Yamuna to offer prayers.

In CE 1191, when the Muslims conquered this temple, they put inscriptions of their victory on it and Fazl Ibn Abul Ma'ali was appointed the custodian and his name was inscribed on the stone near the door. When Sultan Shams-ud-Din Altamash extended the mosque by adding three arches each on either side of the mosque in CE 1229, this minaret was also extended at the same time and had this inscribed on the door of the second storey. Since then, it was named 'Mazanat'. On every storey were installed inscriptions bearing this name and the 'Juma' verse [ayat] from the Quran as well as the names of the architect.

Now, there are five storeys in this minaret. There is no doubt that it had seven storeys

---

[xvii] *Tarikh-e-Firoz Shahi* by Shams Siraj Afif.

[xviii] *Taqweem-ul-Baladan.*

[xix] *Futuhat-e-Firoz Shahi.*

earlier and was also famous as the seven-storeyed minaret [*minara-e-haft manzari*] and where there is a railing today, there used to be merlons like those which are made for a battlement parapet of ramparts. On the fifth storey there was another level, which had doorways all around, and on top of that there was a tall cupola, which made up the seventh storey. Firoz Shah built this in CE 1368 because he writes in the *Futuhat-e-Firoz Shahi* that when he was repairing it, he extended its height from the existing state and he got the description of the repair work on the doors of all the five storeys. After his reign, the minaret again needed repairs and in CE 1503, Fatah Khan repaired it in the reign of Sultan Bahlol Sikandar and got the details inscribed on the top of the first door of the minar.

In approximately CE 1782, it is said that the top storeys had fallen down because of lightning strikes and earthquakes as they were old. Many stones from the base of the first storey had fallen off and were also damaged in many places. In CE 1829, the British Government had it repaired under the supervision of Captain Smith. A strong grill [around the balconies of each storey] replaced the merlons and a beautiful brass screen was installed on the fifth storey. The sixth storey was replaced by an extremely beautiful eight-door stone cupola, and a wooden pavilion replaced the seventh storey on which the flag flew. Unfortunately, both are no longer extant and the stone cupola was removed from the top and put in the grounds. The wooden pavilion has been totally destroyed.

It is very unfortunate that the letters of the calligraphic portions that fell have not been put back in the correct order. If one looks at them closely, one can't make sense of the words as they now only appear to be carvings. There are many glaring mistakes in the calligraphy now. In some places, arbitrary additions of their own compositions [have been inserted by those carving], and these bear no connection with the original inscriptions. The inscriptions of this minaret had never been read and I read them all with the help of binoculars.

The first storey is 32 *gaz* and a few inches high, the second one is 17 *gaz* and a few inches, the third is 13 *gaz* and a few inches, the fourth is 8¼ *gaz* and the fifth is also 8¼ *gaz* high. Thus, the height of the five remaining storeys is approximately 80 *gaz*. The height of the stone cupola that had been built under the British and has now been removed is 6 *gaz*. Along with the wooden pavilion with the flagstaff, the total height of this minaret is 100 *gaz*. It is well known that when all seven storeys of this minaret were standing, then it was 100 *gaz* high. The circumference of the bottom of the minaret is 50 *gaz* and 10 *gaz* on the top. This minaret is hollow from the inside and has a circular staircase built inside it. The first storey has 156 steps, the second storey has 78, on the third storey there are 62 steps, on the fourth and fifth there are 41 steps each. The total steps in this minar are 378 and it seems that these are the same number of steps as were originally built, since there was no way of going upto the sixth and seventh storey.

Construction of Alai Darwaza near Qutub Minar
by Sultan Ala-ud-Din

When Sultan Ala-ud-Din Muhammad Shah Khilji came to the throne he wanted to build new monuments. In CE 1310 he built a huge gateway for this mosque near the minaret. Called the Alai Darwaza, this gateway is built completely of red sandstone[xx] though marble has been used in a few places. It has four entrances on the four sides and has a very high dome. Beautiful carving and floral designs decorate this gateway and there are calligraphic engravings of verses from the *hadith* and Quran. The western, southern and eastern doors have inscriptions of the sultan's name but many stones of this inscription have fallen down and many letters have decayed. After this gateway was completed, the sultan ordered that a fourth section be added to the Quwwat-ul-Islam Mosque.[xxi]

Sultan Muiz-ud-Din had made the central portion and Sultan Shams-ud-Din Altamash had extended it on both sides. The fourth section was constructed on the northern side under the orders of Sultan Ala-ud-Din. This section was 125 *gaz* and a foundation of nine arches was laid. The central arch was 16 *gaz* wide. In CE 1311 this was being constructed but the unfortunate demise of the sultan in CE 1315 left this monument incomplete. Had it been completed then the entire mosque would have measured 241 *gaz* in the east-west direction and 132 *gaz* in the north-south direction. The sultan had started construction of one gateway in this direction but even that was left incomplete. Beautiful carved stones were put in these incomplete monuments as well as inscriptions – the *hadith* has been inscribed. It is not known who took away these stones because one can see the places from where they were removed very clearly. Now only lime, rubble and stones are all that is left. Amir Khusrau has praised this mosque in his book *Qiran-us-Sa'dain*, thus:

> Jama Masjid has been raised by the grace of God,
>
> The sound of the *khutba* echoes up to the moon,

Alai Minar: The Incomplete Minaret

Sultan Ala-ud-Din was very keen to become famous and so when he gave orders for the extension of the mosque in CE 1311, he also ordered that a minaret be built in the courtyard of this mosque, which would be double the size of the existing minaret.[xxii]

Therefore, the construction of a new minaret with a circumference of 100 *gaz* was started, and its foundation was laid as per Islamic rules, with a plinth and a west-facing door.

[xx] *Tarikh-e-Alai.*

[xxi] Ibid.

[xxii] Ibid.

It was decided that it would be 200 *gaz* high. Great care was taken to strengthen this pillar, but the sultan's age let him down, and before even one storey could be completed, he passed away, leaving this unique minaret incomplete to be completed by no other ruler. The stones of this minaret too have fallen off and only rubble remains. Amir Khusrau writes in praise of this minaret, in *Khazain-ul-Futuh*:

> This minaret is like a stone pillar,
> The roof of the sky is lustrous as glass.
> Alas! The roof of heaven has become old and worn out,
> It was for this purpose that the minaret was made.

In history texts this mosque is called Masjid Adina Delhi and Masjid Jami Delhi and nowhere is it called Quwwat-ul-Islam Mosque. It is not clear when this name was given to this mosque. It seems that when this temple was captured and the mosque made here, it was named Quwwat-ul-Islam Mosque. Such mosques are never known by their real names but become famous as Jama Masjid, just as the real name of the Shahjahanabad Jama Masjid is Jahannuma, but it is not known by that name.

Hauz-e-Shamsi

Sultan Shams-ud-Din Altamash built this tank [*hauz*] in the neighbourhood of Qutub Sahib,[xxiii] in CE 1229. It is said that this tank was built of red sandstone, but is now in disrepair. There is only water left with no signs of the sandstone. This tank when it was built was on 276 *bighas*, and had been strengthened by stone. In CE 1311 Sultan Ala-ud-Din got the tank de-silted and cleaned and got a beautiful pavilion built in the middle of the tank, resting on a high platform, which still stands there.[xxiv] Firoz Shah Tughlaq[xxv] also got this tank repaired during his reign and got the water channels to it cleaned. However, today this tank is too clogged up and water doesn't stay in it except for a few months.

Maqbara Sultan Ghazi

This tomb is situated 2 *kos* (4.5 miles) from the *dargah* of Qutub Sahib, towards the west. It is the tomb of Sultan Nasir-ud-Din Mahmood, the eldest son of Sultan Shams-ud-Din Altamash, who was the Governor of Lakhnauti[xxvi] and who died in his father's lifetime in CE 1228. His body was brought to Delhi and he was buried here.

[xxiii] *Tarikh-e-Ferishta.*

[xxiv] *Tarikh-e-Alai.*

[xxv] *Futuhat-e-Firoz Shahi.*

[xxvi] *Tarikh-e-Ferishta.*

In AH 627/CE 1229 Sultan Shams-ud-Din Altamash built this tomb for him. This is a very beautiful tomb and it has buildings all around it. In the west is a small mosque built completely of marble. In the centre is a cave with fifteen steps to descend into it. The grave of the prince lies within. Columns built inside it have covered the cave. On the roof outside is an octagonal platform of 4 feet 7 ½ inches in height. The gateway of this tomb is of marble with Quranic calligraphy in the Kufic script in Naskh form along with inscriptions. The wall around it is made of strong quartzite stone. There are four bastions on the four corners. The entrance of the tomb is made on a plinth and twenty-two steps lead up to it.

Maqbara Sultan Shams-ud-Din Altamash

This famous tomb is near Qutub Sahib's minaret.[xxvii] When Sultan Shams-ud-Din Altamash died in CE 1235 he was buried here. His daughter Raziya Sultan Begum built this tomb in all probability. This tomb is of quartzite stone from the outside and red sandstone from inside. In some places there is marble inside. The walls are covered with Quranic calligraphy and there is exquisite carving on it. It seems that there was a pillared dome on this tomb which has now fallen down. Firoz Shah writes that he repaired this tomband built a sandalwood canopy over it, as well as a stone staircase inside the dome, but there are no traces of any of these.[xxviii]

Dargah Shah Turkman

This *dargah* is in Shahjahanabad near the Turkman Darwaza [gateway]. Shah Turkman is a revered saint[xxix] and his title is Shamsul Arifeen Shah Bayabani. He passed away on the twenty-fourth [of the Islamic calendar month] of Rajab AH 638/CE 1240 in the reign of Muiz-ud-Din Bahram Shah, and this shrine was built at the same time. However, there is no beautiful monument here. There is a marble screen around the grave and limited marble flooring of recent vintage. There is a fair here on every 24 Rajab, and in the [Hindu calendar] month of Bahar, [the festival of] Basant Panchami is celebrated here with great gusto. The Turkman Darwaza near his tomb is named after the saint.

Maqbara Rukn-ud-Din Firoz Shah

This tomb is situated adjacent to the wall of the tomb of Sultan Nasir-ud-Din in Sultangarhi in the village of Malikpur. It is only a domed pavilion with eight columns. This Sultan was

---

[xxvii] *Mirat-e-Aftab-e-Numa.*

[xxviii] *Futuhat-e-Firoz Shahi.*

[xxix] *Mirat-e-Aftab-e-Numa* and *Akhbar-ul-Akhiyar.*

captured and imprisoned after fighting with his sister Raziya Sultan Begum. He died in prison and was buried here. Firoz Shah also got this pavilion repaired.

Maqbara Raziya Sultan Begum

In the city of Shahjahanabad, in Bulbulikhana Mohalla, near Turkman Darwaza, there is a walled enclosure in a state of disrepair, which contains the grave of Raziya Sultan Begum[xxx] that exists in a ruined state. She sat on the throne for a few years and was murdered in CE 1240 in the reign of Muiz-ud-Din Bahram Shah, when this grave was built. Now, there is no remnant of the monarch and only this grave remains.

Maqbara Muiz-ud-Din Bahram Shah

Near the wall of Sultan Ghazi's tomb is Muiz-ud-Din Bahram Shah's tomb.[xxxi] A small domed pavilion with eight columns, it was built when powerful nobles killed him in CE 1241 and proceeded to put Ala-ud-Din on the throne. This pavilion too was repaired in the Firoz Shah's reign.

Maqbara Sultan Ghiyas-ud-Din Balban

This is situated near the ruins of the original house of Qutub Sahib. When Sultan Balban died in CE 1286, he was buried here. This tomb is in ruins now, as all the stones have fallen off and only stones and rubble remain. Next to this tomb is another grave, said to be of his son Khan Shaheed, who was killed in battle in CE 1284 near Lahore. Based on this, one can presume that the Sultan built this tomb in his own lifetime, and when he died he was buried here, too.

Hauz-e-Alai/Hauz-e-Khas

Sultan Ala-ud-Din built this reservoir[xxxii] during his reign in CE 1295. It covered 100 *bighas* of land with a masonry embankment all around it. When Firoz Shah came to the throne, this tank was filled with mud and had become dry.[xxxiii] In CE 1354 approximately, Firoz Shah had it de-silted and repaired and built a *madarsa* on its banks, where he also appointed teachers and enrolled students.[xxxiv] Since then, it became famous as Hauz Khas. The head of this *madarsa* was Sayyid Yusuf bin Jamal Hussaini, who passed away in CE 1388, and is buried in its grounds. Firoz Shah's own tomb is also situated here.

[xxx] *Tarikh -e-Firoz Shahi* by Shams Siraj Afif.

[xxxi] *Futuhat-e-Firoz Shahi.*

[xxxii] Ibid. and *Akhbar-ul-Akhiyar.*

[xxxiii] *Futuhat-e-Firoz Shahi.*

[xxxiv] *Akhbar-ul-Akhiyar.*

Maqbara Sultan Ala-ud-Din Khilji

Near the Qutub Minar, behind Quwwat-ul-Islam mosque[xxxv] is a ruined structure which is the tomb of Sultan Ala-ud-Din Khilji. Though this Sultan died in CE 1315, it still seems that this tomb was built in CE 1317 under the reign of Qutub-ud-Din Mubarak Shah. There was a mosque and *madarsa* near it, but these are also in ruins. Firoz Shah got the tomb, mosque and *madarsa* repaired during his reign[xxxvi] and got a sandalwood canopy put over it. However, now only rubble remains and the grave has crumbled.

Baoli Hazrat Nizam-ud-Din Auliya

It is said that Hazrat Nizam-ud-Din got this step well [*baoli*] built in his own lifetime in CE 1321. The water from this step well is said to be holy and people come here to have a bath with the intention of getting rid of spirits and diseases. This step well is very beautiful and illuminated. There are very well-made steps which lead down to the water.

In CE 1379, Muhammad Maaruf Ibn Wahid-ud-Din built some houses on the southern side of this step well in the reign of Firoz Shah. He also had an inscription with few couplets put up on a stone on the southern side. This inscription is still present there. There have been houses and a graveyard built around the step well and thousands gather here on the day of the annual fair, which is a well-attended affair. Children jump into it from the houses on the sides with the spectators throwing in money and the divers trying to snatch it mid way. The enclosing wall of this *dargah* was in a state of disrepair, but Nawab Ahmad Baksh Khan Bahadur of Firozpur Jhirka had them rebuilt and had the following line written on the wall in gold: 'The Lord has unique ways to honour supplicants'. There is a small building near it, which is referred to as small fortress, but I don't think its worthy of a description or a sketch.

Maqbara Tughlaq Shah

The tomb of Sultan Ghiyas-ud-Din Tughlaq Shah is near the fort of Tughlaqabad. When this Sultan died in CE 1324, his son Sultan Muhammad Tughlaq Shah, who is also known as Muhammad Adil Shah, built this tomb for his father. This tomb is very beautiful with walls made of red sandstone and a dome of marble. There are stripes of marble in the red sandstone with exquisite carving. The tomb has an elevated axis and the stones have been so skillfully joined that there has not been any damage to it till now. Around this tomb there is a triangular wall of lime mortar and local quartzite, with small rooms built on the inside where peasants reside. The entrance of the wall

---

[xxxv] *Mirat-e-Aftab-e-Numa.*
[xxxvi] *Futuhat-e-Firoz Shahi.*

is made of red sandstone and there are thirty-two steps which go inside to the tomb. From here there is a bridge leading to the fort, to provide access to the tomb from the fort, considering there would be water surrounding it. The tomb is very beautiful from the inside.

There are three graves inside this tomb; the one in the centre is that of Sultan Ghiyas-ud-Din Tughlaq Shah himself, the second is of his wife, whose title was 'Maqdooma-e-Jahan' and the third of his son Sultan Muhammad Adil Shah, who died in CE 1351 in Sindh. The headstones of all three graves have vanished and no one knows where they went. Near the entrance is a small dome in the bastion of the enclosing wall with the grave of an unknown person. In the reign of Firoz Shah, this tomb was called Dar-ul-Amaan[xxxvii] and Firoz Shah got a sandalwood canopy built over these graves and installed curtains made from the curtains of the sacred Ka'ba in Mecca. Firoz Shah also received letters of forgiveness from those people and their heirs who had been tortured, maimed, killed or persecuted by Sultan Muhammad Adil Tughlaq Shah. He got these letters sealed inside a box which was kept near the head of the grave.

Dargah Hazrat Nizam-ud-Din Auliya

This famous *dargah* is at a distance of about a mile from the Old Fort. When Hazrat Nizam-ud-Din passed away in CE 1324, there was just a small dome and some stone screens. Firoz Shah installed a sandalwood canopy over the grave. On all the four corners of the grave he hung golden bowls on golden chains. In CE 1562, in the reign of Akbar, Sayyid Faridoon Khan had marble screens placed around the dome, and inside the dome he inscribed a few lines on a tablet that gave details of the date. The next change came in the reign of Emperor Nur-ud-Din Jahangir, when Farid Khan, who had the title of Murtaza Khan in CE 1608, had an exquisite canopy with mother of pearl inlay, built over it. There are a few inscriptions in the carving of the canopy giving the dates. Later, in CE 1652 in the reign of Shahjahan, Khalilullah Khan built a twelve-arched pavilion of red sandstone around the tomb and on the second and fourth arches of this verandah.

In CE 1755, Aziz-ud-Din Alamgir II had an inscription put on the inside of the dome with few Urdu verses on it. In CE 1808, Nawab Ahmad Baksh Khan of Firozpur Jhirka had the columns of red sandstone removed from the verandah which were replaced by attractively made marble columns. In CE 1820, Faizullah Khan Bangash built a copper ceiling on the verandah, with exquisite gold painting and lapis lazuli. After that, in CE 1823, Akbar Shah II built a marble dome with a beautiful golden finial over it. This *dargah* is one of the finest monuments in the city. On the seventeeth [of the Islamic calendar month] of Rabi-us-Sani, the saint's *urs* is celebrated on a grand scale. The festival of Basant is also celebrated here with great style. Firoz Shah built a mosque in this *dargah*.

---

xxxvii *Akhbar-ul-Akhiyar.*

Satpula

This bridge is near the *dargah* of Hazrat Roshan Chiragh Delhi adjoining the Khirki administrative division. Sultan Muhammad Adil Tughlaq Shah built this bridge in CE 1326.[xxxviii] It is actually a dam, and water from distant places has been dammed here. There is a seven-arched sluice gate for the water to flow, which is known as Satpula. There are buildings on top of it with two beautiful gateways. This bridge had broken at one place, where a temporary dam has been made. Near the arches of the bridge there used to be a well which no longer exists, and now only a pit remains inside the drain to gather water. This water is considered holy and used for bathing the sick and infants because of its association with Hazrat Roshan Chiragh Dehli, who had once made his ablutions here. In the [Hindu calendar] month of Kartik, around the time of the Diwali festival, there is an annual fair on Saturday, Sunday and Tuesday, when everyone comes to bathe here to stay safe from evil spirits, magic and the evil eye. During the festival of Diwali, water from this dam is sold in small containers for 6 *takka* each.

Dargah Sheikh Salah-ud-Din

Hazrat Sheikh Salah-ud-Din was a very pious mendicant who lived in the reign of Sultan Muhammad Adil Shah,[xxxix] and was the disciple of Sheikh Sadr-ud-Din. He never minced words with Muhammad Tughlaq Shah and was always harsh with him. When the saint passed away, he was buried close to the Khirki administrative division. This *dargah* was built in CE 1353 in the reign of Sultan Firoz Shah. There is a dome on the mausoleum and screens enclose it. There is a small mosque near to it, adjacent to which is another very large domed mosque. It has crumbled down now and just a few arches remain. Towards the east is a hall called Majlis Khana and a small domed pavilion, which contains more graves. On the twenty-eighth [of the Islamic calendar month] of Safar there used to be an annual *urs* here, but due to shortage of funds it has been stopped.

Masjid Dargah Nizam-ud-Din

This mosque has been referred to as the Jamat Khana [congregation hall][xl] in texts, and is inside the *dargah* of Hazrat Nizam-ud-Din. Sultan Firoz Shah built this mosque in CE 1353 approximately. Firoz Shah writes in his *Futuhat* that he built the Jamat Khana from scratch

---

[xxxviii] Ibid.

[xxxix] *Futuhat-e-Firoz Shahi*; Sheikh Abdul Haq Dehlvi writes in his book *Zikr-e-Sheikh Khwaja* that Shaadi Khan and Khizr Khan, the sons of Sultan Ala-ud-Din Khilji, built this mosque in approximately in CE 1295. Therefore the Jamat Khana of Firoz Shah would be the one that is now known as Majlis Khana and not the mosque.

[xl] *Futuhat-e-Firoz Shahi*.

himself, and that there was nothing there earlier. This proves that the hereditary caretakers of the *dargah*, who feel that this mosque existed before the reign of Firoz Shah, are labouring under a misconception. This mosque is very unique. Its central portion is built of red sandstone and has a dome with a diameter of 14 *gaz*. A golden bowl hangs from the centre of the dome. The Jats fired at it but it didn't fall. There are two sections on both sides of the central portion, which are also covered by two domes each. Therefore, five domes in total cover the entire mosque. The top of the arches of the mosque display calligraphy in Naskh form in the Kufic script. However, no date is given. On the outside wall, towards the courtyard, someone has inscribed the date of the passing away of Hazrat Nizam-ud-Din. It is accompanied by a Persian couplet, but that is of a much later date.

Masjid Jami Firozi

Sultan Firoz Shah built this mosque in his Kotla (citadel) in around CE 1354 and it is still standing, though in ruins, near Ashoka's Pillar. The dome of this mosque was octagonal[xli] and on all eight sides there were inscriptions on stone, which can be gathered from portions of Sultan Firoz Shah's own description of the details of his reign in his book, *Futuhat-e-Firoz-Shahi*. These inscriptions had descriptions of those ordinances issued by the sultan, which were related to religious endowments, public taxation and administrative measures meant for the respite of his citizens. However, there are no traces of this dome and neither do any of the slabs of stones from it exist anywhere. It seems that in the reign of Emperor Jahangir this dome was still intact, but there is no information as to when it fell down after that. In CE 1398, when Timur conquered Delhi, the *khutba* was read out in his name in this mosque.[xlii]

Kushk-e-Anwar/Me'nhdiya'n

This is a very old monument in front of the Kotla Firoz Shah near the jailhouse, but nothing is known about it now. In history texts, it is mentioned as the Kushk-e-Anwar.[xliii] It seems that a king built it, as only royal buildings were known by such names in those days. Since it is so close to Firoz Shah Kotla, it seems that the same ruler built it. It is quite probable that it was built in CE 1354. There is a tradition in India to hold annual ceremonies to honour deceased souls. One is held here, in honour of the Bara Pir or Great Saint [Sayyid Abdul Qadir Jilani- Ghaus-ul-Azam], when small paper and bamboo frames known as *taziya* are made to illuminate the area. These *taziyas* are known as *me'nhdi* and thus the name 'Me'nhdiya'n'.

[xli] *Tarikh-e-Ferishta.*

[xlii] *Tuzuk-e-Taimuri.*

[xliii] *Akhbar-ul-Akhiyar.*

This building looks as if it was built for illumination and has become well known as the Kushk-e-Me'nhdiya'n. The building has been constructed in a new style. It has an arched plinth with five cupolas on top of it – four on the corners and one in the centre. The cupolas are very beautiful, but now this monument is in a very bad shape. Moreover, since it was made of lime and mortar, it has almost fallen down and only a few cupolas remain.

Bhooli Bhatiyari ka Mahal

Outside the city of Shahjahanabad, near Shah Hasan Rasul Numa's *dargah*, there is a dam, built by Firoz Shah in all probability, in CE 1354, at the same time as he built Kushk Shikar. There is a small, haphazardly made building on this dam, once occupied by Bu Ali Khan Bhatti. That name has been corrupted to Bhooli Bhatiyari, by which name it is now famous. The dam is well made and apart from a little damage, is still intact. In the [Hindu calendar] month of Asadh (June–July), on the night of the full moon, the Pavan Pracha fair is held, when Brahmans put their flagstaff in the ground, from which they predict the weather. A huge crowd gathers here on that day.

Kali Masjid, Kotla Nizam-ud-Din

Adjacent to the *dargah* of Hazrat Nizam-ud-Din, this mosque was built by Khan Jahan Firoz Shahi in CE 1370. It is built in the same style as the mosque of Kali Masjid [near Turkman Gate] and the Begumpur Mosque [in Khirki]. It is made of rubble and mortar, and on the entrance there is an inscription giving the date of construction.

Dargah Hazrat Roshan Chiragh Dehli

This is a very famous *dargah* of Hazrat Roshan Chiragh Dehli, who left this world on the eighteenth [of the Islamic calendar month] of Ramzan, AH 757/CE 1356 on a Friday. He was the successor of Sultan-ul-Mashaikh Hazrat Nizam-ud-Din Auliya. Sultan Firoz Shah constructed this *dargah* in CE 1373.

The *dargah* has twelve arches with quartzite pillars. All the arches have stone lattice screens, with the exception of the one on the south, where there is a door for the entrance. The dome of the *dargah* is made of rubble and mortar. It has a golden finial and a golden bowl which hangs inside the dome. A stone eave has been recently constructed by Khwaja Muhammad Khan. Mirza Ghulam Haider, a Mughal prince, had constructed a twelve-arched pavilion around the dome, but it fell down after ten years. In the courtyard of the *dargah* there are two pavilions; the grave of the granddaughter of Hazrat Farid Shakker Ganj is located in the first, and the other has the grave of Maqdoom Zain-ud-Din, who was the former's nephew and successor.

Near this is the grave of Maqdoom Kamal-ud-Din, the spiritual Master of Maulvi Fakhr-ud-Din. On this spot is the grave of Nawab Faiz Talab Khan Bangash. There are two more pavilions belonging to the Afghan period, but the names of the persons buried there are not known. Near the *dargah* is a mosque, dating to the reign of Farrukhsiyyar. The entrance of the *dargah* is domed, and has an inscription in the name of Firoz Shah. In CE 1729, Emperor Muhammad Shah built a boundary wall, with four doors and one wicket gate. It cost Rs 3.75 lakh to build, or perhaps even less.

Qadam Sharif/Maqbara Fatah Khan

This is a very famous *dargah* and is the mausoleum of Prince Fatah Khan, son of Firoz Shah. When Prince Fatah Khan died in CE 1374,[xliv] his body was buried here, and Firoz Shah constructed a mosque, some buildings, and a *madarsa* around the grave. A miracle of the Prophet Muhammad, peace be upon him, resulted in his footprint being imprinted on stone.[xlv] It is said that one of those stones with the footprint of the Prophet came to Firoz Shah, and he placed it in his son's grave in order to sanctify it. Thus, this mausoleum became famous as the Qadam Sharif. There is a tank near this mausoleum, which is enclosed with a marble screen and filled with water, where devotees wash the Qadam Sharif and take the water away as a blessing.

> *O Khizr* the heart finds solace when one drinks it,
> The water of Qadam Sharif is the elixir of life.

On the twelfth [of the Islamic calendar month] of Rabi Awwal, an annual fair is held to celebrate the birthday of the Prophet, peace be upon him. It attracts huge crowds that include thousands of mendicants who gather near the entrance and enjoy themselves to their own music and songs.

Masjid Chaurahiya Qadam Sharif

This mosque was built in the reign of Firoz Shah and is of the same style as the mosques constructed by Khan Jahan. However, it seems that when Firoz Shah built this mausoleum in CE 1374, he built this mosque himself. It is built of rubble and mortar with cupolas and is famous as the Chaurahiya Qadam Sharif Mosque.

Dargah Hazrat Sayyid Mahmood Bahar

This *dargah* is situated on the border of Kilukhari near Barapula at a distance of 4 *kos* [nine miles] from Shahjahanabad. Even though there is no building inside, it is still considered very

---

[xliv] *Tarikh-e-Ferishta.*

[xlv] *Qasida-e-Hamzia.*

sacred. Hazrat Sayyid Muhammad Bahar was a great scholar and saint, and was a descendant of Hazrat Sayyid Nasir-ud-Din Sonepati. He died in CE 1376. According to legend, he once brought a dead man back to life and was thus given the title of Muhayy-ul-Izaam and Raja Haad Goad. An annual *urs* takes place here on the twenty-seventh [of the Islamic calendar month] of Safar.

Kali Masjid/Kalan Masjid

When Firoz Shah was building the city of Firozabad, Khan-e-Jahan the son of Khan-e-Jahan, constructed this mosque on one of the city's localities. When that city was abandoned, Shahjahan built a new one and this mosque came to be included in the city of Shahjahanabad. This mosque is built on a very high plinth with thirty-two steps leading up to its entrance. It has three aisles, and every aisle has five arches, with small domes on the roof.

Masjid Begumpur

Khan Jahan Firoz Shahi built this mosque in the same period as the other mosques, i.e. in CE 1387. This mosque is built solely of rubble and mortar. The style is very inelegant and seems to be of the Pathan period though it is very solid and is still standing. This mosque and the one in Khirki are very similar in style.

Masjid Kalu Sarai

Near the mosque of Begumpur is another mosque built by Khan-e-Jahan Firoz Shahi. This is also made using rubble and mortar with small cupolas. Khan-e-Jahan built all these mosques approximately at the same time, so the date can be set at CE 1387. The northern and southern portions of this mosque have been completely destroyed and occupied by peasants.

Masjid Khirki

Khan-e-Jahan built this mosque in the village of Khirki near Satpula, in CE 1387, in the reign of Firoz Shah. Peasants now occupy this mosque and they have closed all the arches and made their homes inside them. This mosque is square on the exterior and is divided into four equal quadrangles inside. In between the four quadrangles, lies an open court, like a crown. It has doors on three sides except the side that faces west [the direction of Mecca]. The whole mosque has numerous columns that form the aisles. There are nine domes in each square and under every dome there are four columns. Apart from these, there are other pillars as well. There are also four open squares in the courtyard inside the mosque. This is a unique mosque built in the style of the mosques of Rum (Turkey), and it doesn't have a parallel in this area.

Maqbara Firoz Shah

This mausoleum is situated on the banks of the Hauz Khas reservoir. When Firoz Shah died in CE 1388, he was buried here. In my opinion, this mausoleum was built in the reign of Nasir-ud-Din Muhammad Shah in CE 1389. It is built of stone and lime mortar. On its entrance, there is an inscription in cut-plaster, but many of the letters have not survived. There are small cupolas in this compound, and the graves of Nasir-ud-Din Muhammad Shah [Firoz Shah's son] and Ala-ud-Din Sikandar Shah [Firoz Shah's grandson] are also situated here. There is a small pavilion [which contains the graves] of Shahab-ud-Din Taj Khan and Sultan Abu Saeed with an inscription on it.

Khizr ki Gumbati

The mausoleum of Khizr Khan is on the bank of the river in the Okhla administrative division, at a distance of 6 *kos* [13.5 miles] from Shahjahanabad. Khizr Khan's son Abul Fatah Mubarak Shah had it built in CE 1421. It is not very well constructed. It had only one dome that no longer exists, and only one cupola remains in the surrounding wall. However, it is still a beautiful spot from where one can see the river flowing past, dotted with boats.

Mubarakpur Kotla

This mausoleum is situated in the village of Mubarakpur, 4 *kos* [9 miles] to the south of the city of Shahjahanabad. It was built when Muiz-ud-Din Abul Fatah Mubarak Shah died in CE 1433. This mausoleum is very beautifully made of local quartzite, and is worth seeing. Some say that the king had wanted to construct the city of Mubarakbad at this spot, but this is not accurate, as he had wanted to build Mubarakbad city where the village of Mubarakbur Reti stands.

Maqbara Muhammad Shah

This mausoleum is situated opposite the tomb of Mansur [Safdarjung] in the village of Khairpur. It is the mausoleum of Sultan Muhammad Shah, son of Farid Khan, son of Khizr Khan, who succeeded Sultan Muiz-ud-Din Abul Fatah Mubarak Shah. When he died in CE 1445, he was buried here and his son Ala-ud-Din Alam Shah built this tomb. This tomb is made of stone and mortar but its construction is of a very high order. The interior, the surrounding aisles, and the cupolas on the top have been very beautifully constructed.

Maqbara Sultan Bahlol Lodi

When Sultan Bahlol Lodi died in the village of Bhadaoli, near Saket, in CE 1488, he was buried near the *dargah* of Hazrat Roshan Chiragh Delhi. His son Sultan Sikandar Lodi built this mausoleum. It has been built in a very unique style with twelve arches and five cupolas on top and it looks very beautiful. A graveyard has come up here, with many graves inside the red-stone screen enclosure. From here the walls of the *dargah* of Roshan Chiragh Dehli and one of its entrances can be clearly seen.

Panch Burja Zamarudpur

The village of Zamarudpur is 6 miles south of Shahjahanabad. It was earlier known as Kanchan Sarai and it seems that in the reign of Sultan Sikandar Bahlol, it was included in the landholding of Zamarud Khan and was thus renamed Zamarudpur. Zamarud Khan's graveyard is in this village and there are small pavilions supported on columns built on the graves. There are five domed pavilions in this location made of lime and stone and they contain many graves. It seems quite obvious from the style that it is from the reign of Sultan Sikandar and was built in CE 1488 i.e. in the fifteenth century. There is no inscription on the graves.

Basti Baori

This tomb is near the *dargah* of Hazrat Nizam-ud-Din. In the reign of Sultan Sikandar Bahlol there was a eunuch named Basti, who built this tomb for himself in CE 1488. There is a very beautiful step well near this tomb. It has very attractive hallways made on different levels. To the west of the step well is a mosque with Quranic verses engraved in cut-plaster. This step well seems to be the tank (for ablutions) of the mosque. But it is now dry. The inscriptions on the mosque can't be read as they have become faint due to age and disrepair.

To the left of the mosque is a domed gateway which was used as a common passage. The dome of a tomb can be seen opposite the gateway's dome. It was built on a high plinth with many buildings on it. There are stairs to reach the top and on top there is a domed pavilion on the grave with beautiful red stone columns. The screens, which were there earlier, have been taken away and only the pavilion and columns remain. The plinth itself has been beautifully made with four cupolas on its four corners, out of which three still remain, while one has broken down.

Moth ki Masjid

Just a little ahead of Mubarakpur Kotla is this beautiful mosque and a well. It is a very famous mosque, built of stone and lime mortar. The gateway, which was once more beautiful than the mosque itself, with Quranic verses engraved on marble, is now in ruins.

There is a famous legend that someone picked up a grain of lentil [*moth*] from the ground and sowed it. He kept repeating this process till he had a full harvest in a few years. He built this mosque from the proceeds of selling that harvest and that is why it is called Moth ki Masjid [the *moth* mosque]. Inside the well there is an inscription on red stone. However, its letters have crumbled, but it seems clear from the remaining letters that this mosque was built in the reign of Sultan Sikandar Bahlol in approximately CE 1488.

Maqbara Langar Khan

This mausoleum is on the border of the village of Raipur, which is near Zamarudpur. This is the tomb of Langar Khan who was a noble in the reign of Sultan Bahlol Lodi and so its date of its construction has been placed at CE 1454. It is a very ugly monument built of lime mortar and stone. Its unique feature is that the grave inside has been built on such a high plinth that if a man stands near it and raises his arms, his fingers will not reach the top of the grave. Near this mausoleum is another square domed pavilion with a grave that probably belongs to someone from the same family.

Ti-burja

There are three [teen or ti] domed pavilions [burja] near the Moth ki Masjid but no one knows whose tombs these are, though it seems evident that they were built in the reign of Sultan Sikandar in approximately CE 1494. These three tombs are made of lime mortar and stone. The first one, built of red stone, is better constructed than the rest.

Rajo'n ki Bain

This step well is in the vicinity of the dargah of Qutub Shah, near Dilkusha Mansion. Daulat Khan built it in CE 1506, during the reign of Sultan Sikandar Lodi. It has a very beautiful design, and is made completely of lime mortar, which is completely intact even today. There is a mosque near it, and a small pavilion with a dome supported by stone pillars. Once upon a time, masons (raj) used to live in this step well; since then it has been known as Rajo'n ki Bain [step well].

Maqbara Sultan Sikandar Bahlol

Sultan Sikandar Lodi's mausoleum is near the village of Khairpur. His son, Sultan Ibrahim Lodi, built it in CE 1517. This tomb is made of lime mortar and stone but its interior and the surrounding verandah and the cupolas and dome on top are beautifully constructed.

Dargah Sheikh Yusuf Qattal

This dargah is near the Khirki Mosque. It is the tomb of Sheikh Yusuf Qattal who was the disciple of Qazi Jala-ud-Din Lahori. He left the world in CE 1526, and Sheikh Ala-ud-Din, the grandson of Sheikh Farid Shakarganj, built this monument, as mentioned in an inscription. The burj and screens of this dargah are made of red stone, while the dome is plastered with lime mortar and has glazed tile decoration on its edges. There is a lime mortar mosque near it which is now in ruins.

Dargah Maulana Jamali

This is a very famous *dargah* in the environs of the *dargah* of Qutub Sahib. Sheikh Fazlullah Maroof Jalal Khan built this room in CE 1528,[xlvi] and used to live a secluded life in it. When he passed away in CE 1535, he was buried in the same room. He was a very famous poet of the reign of Babar, Humayun and Sultan Sikandar, writing under the pen name of 'Jamali'. That is why this *dargah* is famous as Maulana Jamali's *dargah*. This room is exquisitely made with glazed tiles and ornamentation. Verses written by him are incised in plaster around the four walls immediately under the ceiling.

Masjid Dargah Maulana Jamali

This mosque is near the *dargah* of Maulana Jamali. It is a very grand stone and lime mortar mosque and was also built by Maulana Jamali in his lifetime in CE 1528.[xlvii] The mosque is situated on the same location where Qutub Sahib used to live earlier and there are still ruins of the old structures near it. In fact when Rai Pithaura built his fort, this area was inhabited.

Neeli Chhatri

There is a small twelve-arched pavilion near Salimgarh on the banks of the river at Nigambodh Ghat. It is a pavilion with a curved roof [*chhatri*], which has blue [*neeli*] glazed tile work on it, and that's why it is called Neeli Chhatri. Emperor Humayun built it in CE 1532,[xlviii] to enjoy the view of the river. However, Hindus say that this pavilion was built in the time of the Pandavas. Even if this is not true, the fact remains that the tiles on this building have come from some other Hindu monument as they have carved sculptures which have been defaced. As per Hindu traditions,[xlix] Raja Yudhishtir performed a sacrificial rite on this *ghat* [series of steps leading down to a sacred river/waterbody] and it is entirely possible that later, under the Hindu rule, building this pavilion commemorated this event, and it was renovated under Humayun. In CE 1618, when Jahangir passed through Delhi on his way to Kashmir, he had an inscription placed on the building, and when he returned in CE 1620, he had another inscription put there.

[xlvi] *Akhbar-ul-Akhiyar.*

[xlvii] Ibid.

[xlviii] *Tuzuk-e-Jahangiri.*

[xlix] *Pothi Indraprashta Mahatma.*

Dargah Imam Zamin/Maqbara Sayyid Hussain Paa-e-Minar

This mausoleum of Imam Muhammad Ali Mashhadi, who is also known as Sayyid Hussain Paa-e-Minar,[1] [near the minaret], is near the Alai Darwaza next to the Qutub Minar. This saint came to Delhi in the reign of Sultan Sikandar from Mashshad Tus, Iran, started living in this spot and built this tomb himself. When he passed away in CE 1537, he was buried in this tomb as per his will. This tomb is vey well made and consists of a beautiful dome and a marble floor. There is an inscription on the door.

Dargah Hazrat Qutub Sahib Rahmatullah Alaihe

This *dargah* is of Hazrat Qutub-ul-Aqtab Khwaja Qutub-ud-Din Bakhtiyar Kaki (May Allah's mercy be on him). He left this world on the night of Monday on the fourteenth of [the Islamic calendar month] of Rabiawwal AH 634/15 November 1236, and was laid to rest here. However, there was no building here at that time. In CE 1541, during the reign of Sher Shah, Khalilullah Khan got an enclosure built. This enclosure no longer exists. In the reign of Islam Shah, Yusuf Khan got a gateway built in this *dargah*. The chronogram Khwaja Aqtab gives its date as AH 958/CE 1551. Later in CE 1707, Shakir Khan got a gateway built on the southern side, during the reign of Shah Alam Bahadur Shah. This gateway still exists. In CE 1717, Farrukhsiyyar had a fine marble screen put around the shrine, along with beautiful marble doors that also contain inscriptions.

Masjid Qila-e-Kuhna

When Sher Shah became the emperor, he built this mosque on the northern wall of the Old Fort [Purana Qila] in CE 1541. This is a very beautiful mosque from that era. The façade and interiors are made of red sandstone with marble placed in a beautiful pattern. There is beautiful calligraphy in the Naskh and Kufic script in the mosque.

Every *mehrab*, niche and corner is decorated with calligraphy and inlay work. It is extremely pleasing to the eye. The superstructure has been very well and skillfully made with carved red stone. The courtyard contains a beautiful sixteen-sided tank which is in very bad shape due to neglect. The abutments of the mosque are very wide and have staircases to climb to the roof. Attractive rooms and corridors have been built inside it.

One dome is still standing on the mosque while the other two domes on either side have broken down. This mosque is referred to as the Jami Masjid in the *Akbarnama*. Perhaps it was the Jami Masjid made in the reign of Humayun.

---

[1] *Mirat-e-Aftab-e-Numa.*

Sher Mandal

Sher Shah built a tall three-storeyed building near the Kuhna Mosque in the Old Fort, which he named the Sher Mandal in CE 1541. It is still famous by this name. It is made entirely of red sandstone. Between the first and second floors there is a room with a verandah encircling it with a staircase going up to the top. On the third level there is a pavilion which is meant solely for pleasure.

When Humayun came to the throne for the second time, he made this building into a library.[li] In CE 1555, Humayun came to this building in the evening to see Venus which was about to rise. As he was going down, he lost his footing on the narrow steps and fell. He suffered grievous injury to his temple and died a few days later. Mirza Hidayatullah Khan, in his book on the history of Delhi, opines that Humayun himself built this building, but that is not true.

Masjid Maqbara Khairpur

This mausoleum and mosque are undoubtedly from the Pathan era and were probably built in CE 1543 in the reign of Sher Shah. Though the name of the builder is not known but there is no doubt that this tomb is of a Pathan noble from whose name the village also gets its name. The mosque is also made at the same time.

It is made of lime-mortar and stone but is very pleasing to the eye. There is beautiful stucco decoration on the mosque. Quranic verses are inscribed on the facade. It is rare to see such a refined structure during the Lodi period.

Khari Baoli

There used to be a well here, built by Imad-ul-Mulk, who was also known as Khwaja Abdullah. It was built in the reign of Islam Shah in CE 1545. Six years later, a step well was added in front of the well, and it was included into the city of Shahjahanabad after it was built. There are many buildings here, and the area has become a proper locality.

Tomb of Isa Khan

Near Arab Sarai [inn] there is an enclosure called Isa Khan ka Kotla [Isa Khan's Citadel] within which lies this tomb. Isa Khan was an important noble in the reign of Islam Shah and is one of the beautiful monuments from the Pathan period. There is a dome in the middle, with a beautiful verandah made of local quartzite running around the tomb. The cupolas on top have red sandstone columns. There are many graves inside the tomb. Villagers live in this tomb and they are ruining it. There is an inscription inside the tomb on its western side with verses

---

[li] *Akbarnama.*

from the Quran on it as well as details of the builder and the year. From that, it becomes apparent that Isa Khan himself built this tomb in his lifetime in CE 1547.

Masjid Isa Khan

This mosque is inside the Isa Khan ka Kotla and near the tomb of Isa Khan and was built by him at the same time in CE 1547. This mosque is made of local quartzite, lime mortar with some red stone in the *mehrab*.

Masjid Dargah Hazrat Qutub Sahib

This mosque is near the screens of the *dargah* of Qutub Sahib. It has three sections divided by aisles. The first one with two arches is made of mud and was built by Qutub Sahib himself. In front of this section made of mud, another section was added in CE 1551 in the reign of Islam Shah. Later, in CE 1717, Farrukhsiyar got a third section built in front of it with the date inscribed on its façade. It contains the chronogram: 'The House of the Benevolent God'.

Arab Sarai

This inn [*sarai*] was built near the tomb of Humayun by Nawab Haji Begum, wife of Humayun, in CE 1560 in the sixth year of Akbar's reign. Three hundred Arabs resided here and that's why it got this name. This inn is now very different though the original gateway built here still retains its beauty.

Khair-ul-Manazil

This is a *madarsa* and mosque built in CE 1561 by Maham Begum, the wet nurse of Emperor Akbar, in front of the Old Fort. This monument is built of lime mortar and stone and is now is in ruins.

Bhool Bhulaiyya'n: Adham Khan's Tomb

In the vicinity of the *dargah* of Qutub Sahib is this tomb of Adham Khan, foster brother of Emperor Akbar and son of Maham Anga. Adham Khan murdered Shams-ud-Din Mohamamad Khan Atgha in CE 1561. As punishment, the emperor threw him from the ramparts of Agra Fort and killed him. Maham Anga also died soon after that. Both the bodies were brought from Akbarabad and buried here, and a tomb was built on the orders of Akbar.[lii]

This tomb is made of mortar and stone. It has a staircase in one of the walls with a skillfully made labyrinth which misleads one into thinking that this will lead back to the staircase. It is easy to get lost in it, and so it has become famous as Bhool Bhulaiyya'n or *Maqam-e-Gum Gushtagi* (the place where one gets lost).

[lii] *Masar-ul-Umara.*

Humayun's Tomb

Anybody who wants a glimpse of Heaven on earth,

Should be invited to see this tomb and garden of Humayun.

There is a mausoleum, 2.5 *kos* [5 miles] to the south of Shahjahanabad, in the city of Kilukhari [built by Muiz-ud-Din Kaikobad] that contains the tomb of Humayun Badshah. It is a matchless monument and has been built using marble and red stone. The marble is of such purity that it could put a pearl to shame. The red stone is so exquisite that it resembles the leaves of a red rose. The dome is made entirely of marble and looks as if it is a pearl from the bounty of God. The design is so beautiful that the sky seems like a water bubble in comparison. It is so well-proportioned that it appears delicate in spite of its size.

The layout, with its gardens, courtyard and water bodies, are very beautifully designed. The courtyard and its buildings are extremely attractive and pleasing to the eye. The red stones with white stripes mesmerize one's senses. The flowers and vines of different colours that have been inlaid in stone are also an amazing spectacle. Earlier there used to be a splendid garden, with water channels on all four sides, tanks at frequent intervals, flowing fountains, blooming flowers and chirping birds, but unfortunately, it is desolate today. There are no signs of the flowers and birds now, the streams have broken down, the tanks are choked, the fountains are silent, the wells are blind and there are no remnants of the waterfalls either. Only a few signs of these can be found in some places. In CE 1565, Nawab Haji Begum, the wife of Emperor Humayun, started the construction of this tomb[liii] in the fourteenth year of Akbar's reign. It took sixteen years to complete and it cost Rs 15 lakh. This is also a graveyard of the Timur family.

Neeli Chhatri: Naubat Khan's Tomb

This lies near the Purana Qila and it is the tomb of Nawab Naubat Khan Akbari. He built it in CE 1565, during his own lifetime. The dome was made with blue glazed tiles, and thus it became famous as Neeli Chhatri. Now, the dome no longer exists and the entire structure is in a poor state.

Maqbara Taka (Ataka/Atagha) Khan

This is the tomb of Shams-ud-Din Muhammad Khan Ghaznavi whose title was Azam Khan [and was also variously known as Taka Khan, Ataka Khan and Atagha Khan]. He was the husband of Emperor Akbar's wet nurse (Jiji Anga) and was killed by Adham Khan in CE 1561.[liv] The emperor killed Adham Khan in retaliation by throwing him twice from the ramparts of Agra Fort. After

---

[liii] *Mirat-e-Aftab-e-Numa.*

[liv] *Masar-ul-Umara.*

Ataka Khan was murdered, his body was brought to Delhi and was buried near the *dargah* of Hazrat Nizam-ud-Din. In CE1566, his son, Kokaltash Khan, built this tomb. This is a very beautiful structure of red stone and white marble, decorated with Quranic verses and floral designs. The date of construction is inscribed on top of the door.

Dargah Hazrat Khwaja Baqi Billah, May Allah Have Mercy upon Him

This *dargah* is at a distance form the city of Shahjahanabad outside the wicket gate of Farrashkhana. It is the *dargah* of Hazrat Khwaja Baqi Billah Naqshbandi who passed away in CE 1603. This mausoleum was built at the same time. Later, a mosque was also built and many graves came up in the vicinity. Near the tomb there is a wall which has niches to put lamps in.

Dargah Hazrat Amir Khusrau

Hazrat Amir Khusrau's or Abul Hasan tomb is near the *dargah* of Hazrat Nizam-ud-Din. He passed away in CE 1324 and was buried here on the spot known as Yaarani Chabutra [or the terrace for the assembly of friends]. There is a chronogram inscribed on his tomb which has the date of his death. The first line reads the 'incomparable one' [*adeemul misl*], and the second reads 'sugar-tongued parrot' [*tuti-e-shakkar-e-miqal*]. In CE 1588, Saiyyed Mehdi made only an enclosure around the grave. Imad-ud-Din Hasan built the present marble structure in CE 1605. Inside the dome there are a few verses by Hazrat Amir Khusrau and the date of construction is inscribed. In this *dargah*, on the seventeenth [of the Islamc calendar month] of Shawwal, a fair is held and the festival of Basant celebrated.

Jailkhana/Sarai Farid Khan

This is in fact an inn [*sarai*] built by Nawab Farid Khan Jahangiri who had the title Murtaza Khan. It was probably built in CE 1608. When Old Delhi was deserted, this inn was deserted too. The British Government thought it was suitable for a jailhouse [*jailkhana*] and had it repaired and converted into one. This inn has a grand gateway with apartments on its upper storey. The superintendent of the jailhouse can easily live there. Nearby, a lot of buildings, including a lunatic asylum and a cattle house have sprung up.

Barapula

This bridge is situated 4 miles to the south of Shahjahanabad. There is no other bridge in the area that is as refined as this one. Meherban Agha or Aghayaan who held the title of Agha-e-Aghayaan, built it in the reign of Emperor Jahangir in CE 1612. He was a very well-known *khwajasara* [a eunuch] in the reigns of Akbar and Jahangir.[iv] The bridge is made of lime mortar and stone. There is an inscription with a few verses on it which give the date of construction, the name of Meherban Agha as builder and praise Emperor Jahangir.

Mandi

Meherban Agha Khwajasara built this grain market [*mandi*] at the same time as he had Barapula Bridge constructed in CE 1612. The entrance gates of the grain market are very beautiful, and the name of the person who built them has been carved on them. There was an extremely well-made mosque inside the market, which is now broken. However, a step well that contains water still exists and is famous. There are many such step wells in the region of Malwa, but the step well here is unique.

Kos Minara

During his reign, Emperor Jahangir had a road constructed from Bengal via Agra to the River Attock with trees on both sides. In CE 1618, he gave orders that there should be a *minar* built at every *kos* from Agra to Lahore,[lvi] and a well to be built at every 3 *kos* [6.75 miles]. These strong structures of lime mortar and stone, which could be seen from afar, still exist. There seems to have been a gap left to install a milestone with numbering on it, but these were not installed.

Pul Salimgarh

It seems that when Salim Shah built the fort of Salimgarh, the river flowed by its side and there was no water on its southern side which was used for entry. There was a gateway towards the north, on the bank of the river. It is probable that over time, the river washed the southern side away and thus, the fort was surrounded by water on all sides, leaving no access to it. Then Emperor Nur-ud-Din Jahangir had this bridge built in CE 1621 in front of the southern entrance gate. The bridge, which is still standing, is made of lime-mortar and stone and is very well built. There are two inscriptions on the bridge. When Shah Jahan built the fort, this bridge was so well integrated that it seemed as if it was built particularly for this fort.

Maqbara Sheikh Farid

This tomb is near the Begumpur Mosque of Sheikh Farid ibn Sheikh Ahmad Bukhari who was given the title of Murtaz Khan in the reign of Jahangir. The building is now in ruins and only the

iv *Tuzuk-e-Jahangiri.*

lvi Ibid.

gallery remains. In CE 1663, he died and the date is inscribed on his grave. This tomb was made at approximately the same time.

Neela Burj or Maqbara Fahim

This tomb lies near Humayun's tomb. According to some people, it is the tomb of the barber and according to others, it is that of Fahim. The first claim is definitely wrong, and if the second is true, then Abdur Rahim Khan-e-Khana has built this tomb. In CE 1623, when Mahabat Khan imprisoned Abdur Rahim Khan-e-Khana by fraudulent means, he sent a message to Fahim Khan who was a close disciple of Abdur Rahim Khan-e-Khana. Fahim refused to betray his master[lvii] and died fighting, along with his son and forty followers. It is obvious that when Khan-e-Khana was released in CE 1624, he built this tomb. This tomb is of made of bright and beautiful glazed tiles and is so well ornamented that it is a delight to the eyes. The tiles on its dome [burj] are blue [neela], which is why it's known as the Neela Burj.

Chausath Khamba

Near the *dargah* of Hazrat Nizam-ud-Din, this tomb belongs to Mirza Aziz Kokaltash Khan, son of Khan-e-Azam Ataka Khan. When Mirza Aziz Kokaltash died in Ahmadabad in CE 1624 in the reign of Jahangir, his body was brought and buried here and this tomb was built on his grave. The tomb is built in a new style that is without parallel. It is built entirely of marble with 64 marble columns from which it derives its name. The arches and their arrangement are very beautiful.

Maqbara Khan-e-Khana

This mausoleum is near Barapula Bridge and the tomb of Humayun. It is the tomb of Abdur Rahim Khan-e-Khana, son of Bairam Khan. He died at the age of 72 in CE 1626, and was buried here.[lviii] The chronogram: 'The Khan who was the commander of the army' [*Khan-e-Sipahsalar*], is the chronogram for the date of his death. The tomb used to be very beautiful and elegant with a marble dome, and the rest of it in red stone with stripes of marble interspersed in between. There was beautiful marble mosaic work on it. During the time of Asaf-ud-Daulah, the stone of this tomb was removed, taken to Lucknow and sold, thus destroying its beauty. This tomb is now a bare skeleton of lime mortar and brick. Khan-e-Khana was an important noble from the reign of Akbar and Jahangir. He was a Sanskrit scholar who penned some wonderful verses.

[lvii] *Masar-ul-Umara* and *Tuzuk-e-Jahangiri*.
[lviii] *Masar-ul-Umara*.

Maqbara Saiyyed Abid

Saiyyed Abid Khan was a friend and associate of Nawab Khan Dauran-e-Khan who was killed in battle. This tomb was built probably in CE 1626 near the building called Lal Bangla [red bungalow]. It is built of lime mortar and bricks and in places there are glazed tiles for decoration. It is a well-built monument. There used to be a tank in the courtyard with water channels all around, which are now choked. The gate is also well made with a three-arched pavilion over it.

Khas Mahal

There was a palace near Purana Qila from the period of Shahjahan, which was built in CE 1632 by the daughter of Zain Khan, whose title was Khas Mahal. It is now in ruins with only the gate remaining.

Tomb of Sheikh Abdul Haq Muhaddis

The tomb of Sheikh Abdul Haq Muhaddis, a very famous scholar during the reign of Akbar and Jahangir, lies near Hauz Shamsi. The tomb was built at the time of his death in CE 1642. Inside the tomb, on the wall at the head of the grave, are given details about the Sheikh. The tomb is simply built, of lime-mortar and stone. Its main attraction is its location on the edge of the Hauz Shamsi.

Jama Masjid/Masjid Jahannuma

This mosque is situated on a small hillock to the west of Shahjahanabad (1000 *gaz* distance from it) and completely hides the hill.[lix] Emperor Shahab-ud-Din Muhammad Shahjahan built this mosque. It's impossible to describe its exquisite design, delicate work and beauty. There is no other mosque of similar beauty on the face of earth. It is built of the same colour of red stone from top to bottom with marble used up to the dados. The red stone is interspersed at intervals with stripes of marble and black stone inlays. The domes are completely of marble with black stripes of black stone. The architect has made this mosque with such artistry that not a single wall, arch, *mehrab* is free of design.

The foundation of this mosque was ceremoniously laid in the tenth [of the Islamic calendar month] of Shawal AH 1060 (6 October 1650) in the twenty-fourth year of Shah Jahan's reign under the supervision of Prime Minister [Diwan-e-Aala] Sadullah Khan and Fazil Khan, the Officer in charge [Khan-e-Saman] of the Office of Household Expenses [Khan Samani]. A labour force of 5000 masons, stonecutters and labourers worked on it. This mosque was completed in six years at the cost of Rs 10 lakh.

[lix] *Shahjahan Nama* and *Mirat-e-Aftab-e-Numa*.

The mosque has three beautiful domes, which measure 90 x 20 *gaz*. There are seven *mehrab* on the interior and eleven arches in the façade, with a lofty central arch and five arches on each side of it. There are very beautiful lofty minarets on either side of the arches with a staircase to reach to the top. There is a very attractive twelve-arched pavilion on the minarets built of marble. The view of the city from the top is magnificent. The whole city is spread out in front of the spectator. The northern minaret had fallen down due to a lightning strike and had damaged the courtyard in places. The British Government had both the minaret and courtyard repaired during the reign of Muin-ud-Din Muhammad Akbar Shah, in CE 1817.

Innumerable devotees flock here to offer prayers by the grace of Allah, and as it is not possible for the Imam's voice reciting the *Takbir* [*Allah ho Akbar*] to reach all of them, Prince Mirza Salim, son of Muin-ud-Din Muhammad Akbar Shah, had built a platform of a light salmon-coloured stone built in front of the central arch. Now the *mukabbir* stands on this and repeats '*Allah Ho Akbar*' and '*Rabbana lakal Hamd*' [a prayer] after the Imam so that all can hear it.

The floor of the mosque is of marble with demarcated prayer 'mats' made in black stone. The pulpit is of marble and beautifully made. Towards the north hallway, there are some relics of the Prophet, peace be upon him, and this place is known as the *Dargah* Asar Sharif. The courtyard is very attractive, measuring 136 *gaz* square, in the middle of which stands a tank made of marble. It is very attractive and pleasing, measuring 15 x 12 *gaz*, containing a fountain in its centre, which flows on Fridays and on the festivals of Eid and Alvida Juma during Ramzan. On the west of this tank, there is a small stone enclosure built because of a dream seen by Muhammad Tahsin Khan Khwajasara in CE 1766, who saw the Prophet, peace be upon him, sitting there.

All around the mosque are beautiful aisles, hallways and rooms. On all four corners of the mosque are four pavilions with a twelve-arched pavilion that adds to their attraction. In front of the south-east gallery, there is a sundial to indicate the time of prayers. There are three very majestic gateways on three sides of the mosque.

Masjid Jami: Southern Gateway

The southern gateway is located near the Chitli Qabr market area and is very attractive. There are rooms within it for living comfortably. Thirty-three steps lead up to it and are generally crowded in the afternoon with peddlers puting up their shops and selling their wares. The smell of the sherbet, kabab and *falooda* sold here, attract people. Various types of pedigreed birds and animals, including gaming cocks, are also sold here on the steps. Friends roam around arm-in-arm, enjoying themselves.

Masjid Jami: Northern Gateway

The northern gateway is near Pai Wa'alon ka Bazaar. This is also very well made with comfortable rooms for living within. It has thirty-nine steps leading up to it and peddlers use these to sell their wares. Kabab sellers and others are found here too, but the main attractions are the jugglers [*madari*] and storytellers [*dastango*]. In the afternoon, storytellers sit on stools and narrate evergreen tales such as the *Dastan-e-Amir Hamza, Qissa-e-Hatim Tai,* and *Dastan-e-Bostan-e-Khyal.* Huge crowds gather to hear them even as the jugglers show their sleight of hand and magical tricks.

Masjid Jami: Eastern Gateway

The eastern gateway is towards the Khas Bazaar. It is a very lofty gateway with many buildings on it, and has thirty-five steps in front of it. A cloth market sets up here everyday and is one of the attractions of Shahjahanabad. There are thousands of different types of clothes displayed so attractively here that it seems like a garden in bloom. Young men, with a variety of animals in cages, come here and show off their possessions. There are men selling pigeons on one side and horses on the other which can be bought for cash by those interested.

Dar-ul-Shifa and Dar-ul-Baqa

Around this mosque was a wide bazaar with two large tanks on the eastern side. These tanks are now closed and buildings have been constructed over it. On the north-western side stood a *dar-ul-shifa* [hospital] with physicians appointed by the emperor, where the sick would get treatment. Now it no longer exists and the descendants of the emperor have constructed residential buildings here. There is a *madarsa* or *dar-ul-baqa* on the southern side. This *madarsa* had also become desolate with buildings in a state of disrepair. Maulvi Muhammad Sadr-ud-Din Khan Bahadur, the chief judge [Sadr-us-Sudur] of Shahjahanabad, has taken it from the emperor by a grant and has renovated it and restarted the school. He has brought worthy students and teachers to reside here and once again teaching has been resumed. Both these buildings are from the reign of Shahjahan and its construction was started at the same time in approximately CE 1650.

Begum ka Bagh/Sahibabad

This garden is near Chandni Chowk in the city of Shahjahanabad. Malika Jahan Ara Begum, the daughter of Emperor Shahjahan, built it in CE 1650.[ix] Once upon a time this garden was

---

[ix] *Mirat-e-Aftab-e-Numa.*

very beautiful, with grand houses inside it and canals flowing in it. But now it is in a very bad state. It measured 970 x 240 *gaz*.

Masjid Fatehpuri

This mosque is in the city of Shahjahanabad beyond the Urdu Bazaar and Chandni Chowk. Nawab Fatehpuri Mahal Begum, wife of Shahjahan, constructed it in CE 1650.[lxi] The mosque measures 45 x 22 *gaz* and is built completely of red sandstone. There are three arches, and three aisles, on each side of the dome. The flooring is of marble and there are minarets on either side of it. These are 35 *gaz* in height but their cupolas have now broken. There is a red sandstone platform in front of it, which is 45 x 35 *gaz*, in front of which there is a red sandstone tank, which is 16 x 14 *gaz*. The courtyard of this mosque is beyond that and measures 100 x 100 *gaz* and around the courtyard there are 69 rooms for students to reside in.

Masjid Akbarabadi

This mosque is situated in Shahjahanabad's Faiz Bazaar. It was constructed by Nawab Aizazun Nisa, also called Akbarabadi Begum, wife of Emperor Shahjahan, in CE 1650.[lxii] It has three domes and seven arches, is built completely of red sandstone, and measures 63 x 17 *gaz*. The marble *mehrab* is beautifully ornamented. Beyond it lies an enclosed red stone platform, 63 by 57 *gaz* and set at a height of 3½ feet with a red stone tank in front of it. The courtyard of the mosque is 154 x 104 *gaz*, with rooms around it for students to reside in. At the gateway of the mosque is an inlaid inscription in black stone which gives the date of construction.

Masjid Sirhindi

This mosque still exists outside the Lahori Darwaza. Even though the wall around the courtyard has fallen into the moat, the galleries of the mosque are still intact. Sirhindi Begum, wife of Shahjahan, built this mosque in CE 1650. This is built completely of red sandstone but it is now falling down in many places because of age.

Bagh Shalimar

This garden was laid out by Emperor Shahjahan and is situated at a distance of six miles from Shahjahanabad.[lxiii] He started building this garden in approximately CE 1653 after completing

---

[lxi] Ibid.

[lxii] Ibid.

[lxiii] *Mirat-e-Aftab-e-Numa.*

the construction of Shahjahanabad. The garden has beautifully built buildings, tanks and canals. There were many different varieties of trees in the garden, of which a few mango trees remain which are not available anywhere else. Shahjahan himself named this pleasure garden, as in Hindi the word 'shala' means window and 'mar' means pleasure and luxury.[lxiv]

Bagh Roshan Ara

This garden was among those laid out in the reign of Shahjahan. It is located in the wholesale vegetable market. Roshan Ara Begum, the daughter of Shahjahan, laid it out. Later, when she died in the thirteenth year of Aurangzeb's reign,[lxv] she was buried here. This garden was probably made in CE 1653 when Shahjahan had given orders to the royal ladies of his household and noblemen to build mansions and gardens. This is a very beautiful garden with a tomb in the middle and canals flowing on all sides. This garden is still green and flourishing.

Bagh Sirhindi

This garden is near the Sabzi Mandi and Sirhindi Begum, wife of Emperor Shahjahan in CE 1653, laid it out. This must have been a very attractive garden at one time but now it is in ruins. Sirhindi Begum has been buried in this garden.

Moti Masjid

Emperor Aurangzeb built this mosque in the second year of his reign[lxvi] in CE 1659 near the Hayat Baksh Garden. It is built completely of marble. Its flooring, walls, engrailed arches, mehrab, parapets and ceiling are all of marble with beautiful ornamentation done on it. The floral designs on it are exquisite. In reality, no other building in the entire fort can match the beauty of workmanship and ornamentation of this mosque.

This mosque has three attractive arches, two small minarets and three golden domes because of which many refer to it as theSunehri Masjid. There is a small water tank in the courtyard of this mosque which is supplied water by the Bhado'n Pavilion and keeps overflowing. There is a small room to the northern side of the mosque for the purposes of prayers and study. This room also contains a small, shallow but very beautiful tank. It is decorated by glass mosaic. This mosque was completed at a cost of Rs 1,60,000.[lxvii]

[lxiv] *Tuzuk-e-Jahangiri.*

[lxv] *Mirat-e-Aftab-e-Numa.*

[lxvi] *Masar-ul-Alamgiri.*

[lxvii] *Mirat-e-Aftab-e-Numa.*

Muhajjar Jahan Ara Begum

This stone enclosure is situated in the courtyard of the *dargah* of Hazrat Nizam-ud-Din Auliya. It is made completely of marble with marble screens on all sides. There are four graves in it, three of adults and one of a child. Jahan Ara Begum, daughter of Emperor Shahjahan, built this enclosure in CE 1681 in her own lifetime. She died in the same year and was buried here. She had great faith in the Chisti order and it is said that she had willed all her property worth Rs 3 crore to the *dargah*'s hereditary caretakers. But after her death, Alamgir [Aurangzeb] gave only property worth Rs 1 crore and said that only one-third of one's property can be willed away by a person, as per law.

Maqbara Sar Nala

Near the *dargah* of Hazrat Roshan Chiragh Delhi, at the end of the lower water channel, is a tomb. Its flooring and pillars are of red sandstone. It is not known who is buried here or when it was built, in spite of vigorous investigation. From the style of construction, it seems as if it was built approximately before CE 1688.

Dargah Sayyid Hasrat Hasan Rasul Numa

Hazrat Sayyid Hasan Rasul Numa was a descendant of Sayyid Usman of Narnaul. His tomb lies in the place famous as Gulabi Bagh. He used to live here and when he passed away in CE 1691, he was buried here. The date of his death is inscribed on the outer verandah in a chronogram: 'Rasul Numa remained firm with the Prophet' AH 1103 [CE 1691/1692]. In CE 1748, Haji Muhamamad Tahir built a mosque near this *Dargah* which had an existing *hauz* built by Muhammad Saeed. In AH 1818, Mir Muhammad Shafi, who is one of his descendants, took financial help from Nawab Amir Khan of Tonk, and built a stone enclosing wall around it. This has two attractive gateways.

Jharna

There is a building near Hauz-e-Shamsi in the vicinity of the *dargah* of Qutub Sahib which has a very old wall belonging to a dam, which may have been built at the same time as Hauz-e-Shamsi to stop its water from overflowing. This wall had an outlet from which excess water would flow via the Naulakha water-channel towards Tughlaqabad and Adilabad. In around CE 1700, Nawab Ghazi-ud-Din Firoz Jung built a pavilion in front of the wall and beyond that a 25-feet-square tank. A waterfall would flow here from the water of Hauz-e-Shamsi. There would be fountains flowing from its roof too. The water would then flow into the square tank. Now all these fountains and waterfalls are still though there is a way for water to come into the tank.

Akbar Shah II had got a few stone buildings constructed on its northern and southern side.

Now Bahadur Shah has built a twelve-arched stone pavilion in the middle of it. In the [Hindu calendar] months of Sawan and Bhado'n every year a grand fair is held here with people gathering for eight days. From Wednesday to Friday there is a large crowd here. The main day of the fair is a Thursday. There are no less than a lakh or lakh and a half people gathering here for this fair. The cost of this fair is around Rs 2.5 lakh to Rs 3 lakh. Flower sellers, artisans and craftsmen who make floral fans come here and take their works for offering at the *dargah* of Hazrat Qutub Sahib. That's why this fair is called Phool Walo'n ka Mela. There is a grand spectacle on this location on the days of the fair with thousands bathing in this tank and diving into it from the roof of the pavilions, top of the walls, trees etc. and they slide from a slippery stone which measures 18 feet in length and 7.5 feet in width. They put up swings on the mango trees which are flowering. Unfortunately, this fair is not included in the list of holidays in the courts of Delhi.

Masjid Aurangabadi

This mosque is in the Punjabi Katra of Shahjahanabad. Nawab Aurangabadi Begum, wife of Aurangzeb in approximately CE 1703, built this mosque. This mosque is built completely of red sandstone with a tank in the courtyard that is fed by water from a canal. The courtyard of this mosque was very large, but now people have encroached upon it for water supply to their own homes. Punjabi traders live in this area and so it is now known as Punjabi Katra.

Maqbara Zeb-un-nisa Begum

This mausoleum is outside Kabuli Darwaza in Shahjahanabad. Nawab Zeb-un-nisa Begum, the eldest daughter of Emperor Alamgir, died in CE 1702 and this mosque and mausoleum were built in the reign of Emperor Alamgir. There is a headstone on the grave.

Moti Masjid

This mosque is near the *dargah* of Qutub Sahib with only a wall in between. It is built completely of marble with even the flooring being of marble with black stone *mehrabs* which denote prayer mats on the floor. This mosque has three arches and three domes with two marble minarets on the two corners of the mosque's courtyard. Shah Alam Bahadur Shah built this mosque in CE 1709. In the reign of Shah Alam, the middle dome fell down because of an earthquake and was immediately repaired.

Zeenat-ul-Masajid

This mosque is on the banks of the river, in the city of Shahjahanabad. Zeenat-un-Nisa Begum, the daughter of Emperor Alamgir, built this mosque and an enclosure for her tomb in around CE

1710. This is made completely of red sandstone and has three marble domes with black stone stripes in it. It has two lofty minarets and can be seen from afar. This mosque has seven arches with one large one in the centre and the rest of smaller size. There is a tank in the courtyard which used to be fed by a well which is no longer functional. To the north is a marble enclosure and another enclosure of fawn-coloured stone. The one on the inside contains the grave of Zeenat-un-Nisa Begum with a marble headstone bearing a Quranic verse and the epitaph.

Maqbara Ghazi-ud-Din Khan

Outside the Ajmeri Darwaza is the mausoleum of Mir Shahab-ud-Din bearing the title of Ghazi-ud-Din Khan Bahadur Firozjung who was the father of Nizam-ul-Mulk Asif Jah. He was one of the notable nobles from the reign of Alamgir. He built the tomb himself during his lifetime.[lxviii] When he died in CE 1710, the fourth year of the reign of Shah Alam Bahadur Shah, in Ahmedabad, his body was brought to Delhi and buried in this tomb. It is built completely of red sandstone with a beautiful gateway. There is a large courtyard in the tomb. There are rooms and galleries on the northern and southern side.

Towards the east there is a Tripoliya [three-arched] Gateway, and towards the west there is a grand red sandstone mosque. On both sides of the mosque, leaving aside some space for a courtyard, are halls. The southern hall boasts an enclosure of salmon-coloured stone, and this has another marble enclosure inside with very delicately made screens surrounding it. The graves of Nawab Ghazi-ud-Din Khan and his descendants are inside this enclosure. For a long time, the British Government ran a *madarsa* here and so this place became famous as the *Madarsa*. Itmad-ud-Daulah Nawab Fazl-e-Ali Khan of Lucknow donated Rs 1,70,000 for the maintenance of this *madarsa*, and this fact has been inscribed on the wall.

Muhajjar Shah Alam Bahadur Shah

This enclosure is adjacent to the Moti Masjid near Qutub Sahib's *dargah*. When Emperor Shah Alam Bahadur Shah died in CE 1712, he was buried in this enclosure. Later, when Emperor Sultan-e-Aali Gauhar Shah Alam died in CE 1806 he was also buried in this enclosure. Later, when Emperor Muhammad Akbar II died in CE 1837, he was also laid to rest here. Though the date of his death is not inscribed on the headstone but Raqim Asim writes it in a chronogram which may be translated as:

> He is God. He is great and powerful,
> Shah Akbar, the giver of light to the world,
> Was eclipsed, like the full moon, by death.

[lxviii] *Masar-ul-Umara.*

Of the date [of his death] Victory said:

The empyrean of Heaven is the resting place of the exalted in dignity,

AH 1253 [CE 1837–38]

Pavilion inside Humayun's Tomb

There is a small pavilion of red sandstone with traces of marble in it. There are two marble graves. These are unidentified graves but they seem to have been made much later, in fact quite recently, and I place this at approximately CE 1718.

Sunehri Masjid Kotwali

This mosque is near the Kotwali Chabutra in the city of Shahjahanabad. Nawab Roshan-ud-Daulah Zafar Khan built it in CE 1721, in the reign of Muhammad Shah. Even though it is made of lime-mortar and bricks, it is very attractive. The dome and finials are golden (gilded), which is why it is known as the Sunehri Masjid. The dome had been damaged and was replaced by the dome from Roshan-ud-Daulah's other mosque. There are a few verses inscribed on the central arch of the mosque [which record the construction of the mosque by Nawab Roshan-ud-Daulah Zafar Khan for Shah Bhik, his spiritual master].

Mosque and Madarsa Built by Sharf-ud-Daulah

This mosque is in Dariba Bazaar of the city of Shahjahanabad with a *madarsa* near it. Nawab Sharf-ud-Daulah Bahadur built it in the reign of Emperor Muhammad Shah in CE 1722. This mosque is built of lime-mortar and bricks but it has three marble domes. However, this marble is so yellow that it appears to be of brass. There is an inscription on its façade.

Jantar Mantar

'*Jantar*' means an instrument, and here it refers to instruments used for observing stars. The word '*mantar*' is meaningless and has just been added to give it a colloquial feel, such as the phrase '*khana-wana*'.[2] Raja Sawai Jai Singh of Jaipur built this observatory in the seventh year of Emperor Muhammad Shah's reign in CE 1724.[lxix] Similar observatories were built in Jaipur, Mathura, Banaras and Ujjain. For accuracy, the instruments were made of lime mortar and stone. This observatory is now in a state of disrepair, all the instruments have broken down, and the measurement units on them have faded. None of them are fit to be used to measure anything now. There are three instruments made of lime mortar and stone, which still exist, albeit in a ruinous state.

[lxix] *Zich-i-Muhammad Shahi.*

Jai Prakash

This is an instrument to measure shadows. A pillar has been put as a measuring tool on an upper level, with a horizontal circumference of 53 feet and 8 inches. Four levels have been built around it like a well with one level sunk in the ground and three above the ground. This has been further divided into 60 sections in which niches have been created which are left alternatively open or filled up. Circles have been drawn on the inside wall, which have been divided into measurement units for the measurement of degrees and above, the circle of the circumference and horizon, have all been divided.

Ram Jantar

This instrument is a raised platform, which is positioned towards the north and has four arcs. There are stairs on both sides of the arc so that the effect of the shadows can be studied. Two more arcs have been taken out from below the platform. Each arc had measurement units to record the time and zodiac. However, the signs on this raised platform have all been erased, and the arcs are also broken in many places.

Som Samrat Jantar

This building is essentially a measuring instrument itself. A ramp of lime-mortar and stone has been built in the middle of an equatorial sundial with a radius of 18 *gaz*. All the measuring units are given on it. This ramp has stairs to climb to the top. Similarly, there are stairs on both sides of the sundial arcs to facilitate the observation of shadows. The units on this instrument have also been ruined. Even though the Raja of Jaipur gave the task of maintenance and repair of the ramp to the Archaeological Society of Delhi in CE 1852, it was left incomplete. Sawai Jai Singh invented these three instruments and that's why they have been given Hindi names.

Karah-i-Maqar[3]

Below this observatory, two concave hemispheres are placed in such a way that the axis of the zodiac is incomplete without either. The sphere or *karah* is completed only when one half is placed on the other. There are twelve arcs in these spheres. The signs of the zodiac have been divided in such a way that six are filled in and six are empty. There were signs of measurements everywhere and perhaps it had an axis, but all these have broken and the units have been erased. In every empty arc there are stairs that allow one to climb to the top to study the shadows. The diameter of these spheres is 26 feet each, and they are very solidly built of lime-mortar and bricks.

This observatory was the first of its kind to acknowledge and use principles of modern English astronomy. Prior to this, the principles of Greek astronomy were in use, which is why this observatory is very unique and well known amongst those built around the same time. In the fourteenth year of Muhammad Shah's reign in CE 1731, Raja Sawai Jai Singh sent many mathmeticians along with Father Manuel to 'Firingistan' [perhaps referring to England and other foreign countries], from where he got telescopes and other astronomical instruments. These men visited observatories there from where there they brought back an instrument for star gazing which was called Lear. Comparing it to this observatory (Jantar Mantar), they found that that there was a difference of half a minute in the lunar calendar and during the period of the lunar eclipse and solar eclipse, there was a difference of 15 seconds.

These facts confirm that the English were also involved, and in fact this explains why the observatory, which was built according to Greek principles, followed the English system. There was much argument and dispute by those who followed the Greek system and they demanded that these new facts should be verified and rationally proved. However, the new calculations made from both these new and old instruments corresponded with each other, therefore either attention was not paid or they could not establish these new rules/findings. Now, at this spot, there is a brief list of those principles, which were contrary to Greek astronomy but were accepted here.

1. The outer circumference of the centre of the sun was accepted.
2. The movements of the moon around its circumference were to be recorded.
3. It was accepted that Venus and Mercury were illuminated by the sun (like the moon), and that they also waxed and waned.
4. It was accepted that Saturn was pear-shaped, and not spherical.
5. Four celestial bodies were found around Jupiter which have been called Jupiter's moons.
6. Numerous objects around the sun were identified and after observing their behaviour, it was determined that it took a year for them to complete an orbit.
7. It was also proved that many fixed stars were actually planets and not stars.

In this observatory, there was no need to measure the appearance of the new moon, the visible and invisible stars (constellation) and the stages in the rising and setting of the moon, since they could be easily seen during the day with the help of a telescope. With the help of these English and Greek instruments in use at this observatory, a set of astronomical tables named the *Zich-i-Muhammad Shahi* was prepared. There is no doubt that this table is absolutely accurate when compared with other existing tables.

In this same observatory, a new *tarikh* [calendar] was taken out, called the 'Tarikh-e-Muhammad Shahi'. It started on Saturday, the first day [of the Islamic calendar month] of Rabi us Sani AH 1131/ 21 February 1719, and this date has been taken as the first year of Muhammad Shah's reign, though in reality his reign did not start on this date. When Jala-ud-Din Farukhsiyar died on the eighth of that month, [28 February 1719], Rafi-ud-Darajat and after him Rafi-ud-Daulah ascended the throne. Muhammad Shah became the emperor only after that. Since the two only ruled for a few months before Muhammad Shah, their period of rule was considered non-existent, the eight days of the lunar month which had passed already were also invalidated, and the first day of Rabi-us-Sani was taken as the first day of Muhammad Shah's reign.

This date is as per the lunar calendar and the days and years also follow the lunar cycle, similar to the Hijri calendar. The only difference between the two calendars is that while the Hijri starts with the month of Moharram, the Muhammad Shahi starts with the month of Rabi-us-Sani. Here, it should be noted that in the Muhammad Shahi calendar, 1 July 1852 was 14 Ramzan 1308 according to calculations and 12 Ramzan 1308 according to lunar sighting.

Shah-e-Mardan[4]

This is a *dargah* in front of Mansur Ali Khan Safdar Jung's tomb. Udham Bai, the wife of Emperor Muhammad Shah, who was given the title of Nawab Bai and then Nawab Qudsia Sahib-us-Zamani belonged to the Shia faith. In CE 1724, she received a stone with the imprint of a footprint, which was said to be the footprint of Hazrat Ali. Nawab Qudsia got it placed in a marble tank at this location. And under it, she got marble flooring laid and made an enclosure around it. Since then this *dargah* flourished.

In the reign of Ahmad Shah, Nawab Qudsia got a compound wall, an assembly hall, and a mosque with a tank constructed under the supervision of Jawed Khan Khwajasara in CE 1748. In CE 1808, Ishrat Ali Khan got the assembly hall reconstructed. In CE 1821, Sadiq Ali Khan got a drum house made. This is a very well-maintained and beautiful *dargah*. On the twentieth of every month [according to the lunar calendar] there is a gathering, and on the twentieth of the month of Ramzan[5], there are huge crowds here. During Moharram, *taziyas*[6] are brought and there are huge crowds. The place where the *taziyas* are laid to rest is called Karbala. Mirza Ashraf Beg built a boundary wall for this.

Fakhr-ul-Masajid

This mosque is located inside the city of Shajahanabad, near the Kashmiri Darwaza. It was built by Fakhr-un-Nisa Khanum, wife of Nawab Shujaat Khan in CE 1728. This is not a very big mosque but it is very exquisitely designed with beautiful domes and its appearance is very elegant. Its façade is of marble with stripes of red sandstone at intervals. Inside the mosque till the dado there is very tastefully placed marble. The domes are of marble with lines of black stone. The finial is golden in colour. Inside the mosque the flooring is marble and outside it is of red sandstone. On the northern side is a hall which opens on two sides with a very beautifully made tank in front of it but the tank and its fountain are now broken.

Bagh Mahaldar Khan

This garden is a little away from the wholesale vegetable market. It was built by Nazir Mahaldar Khan in the reign of Muhammad Shah in CE 1728. This is a very beautiful and famous garden. There is a very attractive twelve-arched pavilion and a big masonry tank in it. This tank is always full with water from the canal. He built a bazaar in front of the gateway. The gateway itself is a three-arched one which is famous as Tripolia Darwaza. The date is inscribed on the gateway:

> By the Grace of God and the Prophet of the age (Muhammad) Mahaldar Khan Nazir built such a road, bazaar and tripolia that the events may be marked in the revolutions of the world. There came a voice from the invisible crier 'May this house be everlasting!' AH 1141/CE 1728.

Ghat Nigambodh

This ghat lies on the banks of the river to the north east of the city of Shahjahanabad. The word '*nigam*' means '*Ved*' in the 'shastras' [Hindu religious text] and '*bodh*' means knowledge or enlightenment. According to Hindu faith[lxx] at the beginning of the Dwapar Yug (as per their calculations 4953 years have passed since), Brahmaji had forgotten all the Vedas when he came here, Parmeshwar again rekindled his memory and gave him knowledge of the Vedas. That is why this ghat was named Nigambodh.

It is also said that Raja Yudhishtir performed an important sacrificial rite here and to commemorate that, a pavilion was built on the spot. It wouldn't be strange to say that it was this pavilion that was broken by Emperor Humayun and another one built by him under Salimgarh Fort. Hindus also believe that a corpse burnt here requires less wood to burn and he/she gains high status in the afterlife. Around CE 1737 the Hindus got a red sandstone ghat made here. There is a unique crowd of men and women who come to bathe and the beauty of the scene even affects the sun which comes out orange.

Masjid Roshan-ud-Daulah

This mosque is situated in Qazi Wada near the wholesale flower market and Faiz Bazaar. Nawab Roshan-ud-Daulah Zafar Khan built this mosque in the reign of Emperor Muhammad Shah in CE 1745. All the domes of this mosque were golden [copper gilt]. Some time ago, the copper gilt plates were taken out from here and put on the Sunehri Mosque near the Kotwali Chabutra. This mosque was very finely made but now is in a ruinous state. It seemed ready to collapse but Qazi Faizullah Khan got it repaired from the goodness of his heart.

[lxx] *Mirat-e-Aftab-e-Numa.*

Bagh-e-Nazir

This garden is in the Navah of Qutub Sahib at a short distance from the Jharna. Nazir Roz Afzun Khwajasara built in the reign of Muhammad Shah in CE 1747. It has small stone buildings scattered in all four corners. In the centre is a very fine red sandstone building with a tank in front of it. During the reign of Muhammad Shah this garden must have been very well maintained, but now just a few trees remain.

Muhajjar Badshah Muhammad Shah

This stone enclosure [muhajjar] is in the courtyard of Hazrat Nizam-ud-Din's dargah. Emperor Muhammad Shah died in CE 1748 and was buried here. It is said that Muhammad Shah himself made this enclosure. It is very tastefully built and is very attractive and elegant. The marble used here is so pure and white with a beautiful sheen that a pearl would pale in comparison. It is beautifuly decorated with inlay and stone carvings. This enclosure has a beautifully decorated marble door, with each side of it being carved from a single piece of marble. Its beauty is enough to stun the viewers. Apart from the grave of the Emperor, it also contains the graves of his wife, Nawab Sahiba Mahal, Mirza Jigar [his grandson] and Mirza Ashoori and three other graves of princes of the royal family.

Qudsia Bagh

Qudsiya Bagh has been built on the banks of the river, outside Kashmiri Gate. Udham Bai, the wife of Emperor Muhammad Shah and the mother of Emperor Ahmad Shah, built it. Her son first gave her the title of first Nawab Bai and later Nawab Qudsia Sahib-uz-Zamani. Thereupon she made this garden in approximately CE 1748. The dome in this Bagh is very beautiful. There is an attractive twelve-arched stone pavilion and a very beautiful mosque built inside it.

Chobi Masjid

Emperor Ahmad Shah built this mosque and as its pillars and arches were wooden, it was called Chobi Masjid. It was built in CE 1750. It is in a very bad state and was repaired by the government in CE 1850.

Sunehri Masjid

This mosque is built in the city of Shahjahanabad, outside the fort and at a lower level than it. It is made completely of fawn-coloured stone and has two beautiful minarets. All the pinnacles and the three domes were golden. But the domes were broken and in CE 1852 Emperor Bahadur Shah II got them taken down and replaced with domes of fawn-coloured stone. Khwajasara Javed Khan, who was a trusted confidante of Nawab Qudsia Begum, mother of Emperor Ahmad Shah, had this mosque built in CE 1751. He had been given the title of Nawab Bahadur. This mosque had a tank for ablution but that is dry now.

Maqbara Mansoor Safdarjung[7]

This is the tomb of Abul Mansur Khan Bahadur Safdarjung, who was Prime Minister of Emperor Ahmad Shah. When he died in CE 1753, he was buried here. His son, Nawab Shuja-ud-Daulah, built it under the supervision of Shaidi Bilal Muhammad Khan. The cost incurred was Rs 3 lakh.

The tomb is very beautiful, made of red sandstone interspersed with stripes of marble. It has a marble dome and marble has been used till the dados inside the tomb. The headstone is also of marble. The actual grave is in the basement/underground room below. The monument is so delicate and and finely made that there is nothing comparable to it. The planning of the structure and garden has been very well done. The enclosing wall has been made of lime and stone and it has a beautifully made garden inside it. There are canals and tanks on all sides.

There are attractive buildings on three sides of the garden. The one on the south is called Moti Mahal while the one on the west is Junglee Mahal. The building on the north is known as 'The Emperor's Favourite' [Badshah Pasand]. In the east is a gateway that is very lofty with numerous rooms and apartments built in it. There is a beautiful mosque near the gateway towards the north, which is built of red sandstone. There are cupolas on the four corners of the wall and with very fine-latticed screens of red stone, which give it a very attractive look.

Kalka

This temple is built on the border of Bharpur village, 6 *kos* [13.5 miles] south of Shahjahanabad. As per Hindu mythology, millions of years ago, there were two demons, Simba and Nasba, who gave a lot of trouble to the gods living there. The gods complained to Lord Brahma who refused to interfere but recommended that they pray to Goddess Parvati. They conducted a religious ceremonial rite and the goddess Kaushiki Devi was born from the mouth of Goddess Parvati.

Kaushiki Devi killed the leader of the demons, Raktbhanch. But from the drops of his blood, which fell to earth, thousands of demons were born. Then Goddess Kali was born from the eyebrows of Kaushiki Devi. Goddess Kali, 'whose lower lip rested on the hills below and the upper lip touched the sky above' drank the blood of the demons before it could fall on the ground, as Kaushiki Devi slaughtered them. Thus Kaushiki Devi was victorious over the demons. In the end of the [Hindu] Dwapar Age, which was 4953 years ago, Kali Devi took up residence on this hill. The present temple was built in CE 1764.

Originally, there was a vaulted twelve-arched pavilion here and the deity (which is an unfinished stone slab) was enshrined in a marble enclosure. On her left side is an inscription with her name and date: Sri Durga Singh is mounted on a lion – 1821 Fasli.

In CE 1816, Raja Kedarnath, who was the Accountant in the Commissariat [nazarat] in the reign of Emperor Akbar Shah, had a tall pinnacle built over the vaulted structure. He built a thrity-six-arched circumbulatory verandah around it. Now many buildings have sprung up, built by the moneylenders to accommodate the people who come to the temples during the half-yearly fairs held here on the eighth of the [Hindu calendar] month of Chait. In front of the door of this temple stand two red sandstone lions and a trident. As per Hindu faith, the lions pull the goddess' chariot and that's why they are stationed at the doorway.

The temple priest does prayers twice a day, in the morning and evening, and at 11 a.m. he makes offerings of food etc. to the deity. The stone diety is covered by heavily decorated red cloth and there's a small, very well-decorated bed kept inside the Goddess' enclosure where she is said to rest at night. A clarified butter lamp is kept lit throughout the day and placed on the enclosure. It is considered inauspicious for the lamp to die out. When the wishes of the devotees and pilgrims come true they also offer small canopies and coverings for the diety.

Every people/every sect has its own way of worship which it considers the right path; this is a very famous saying by Hazrat Nizam-ud-Din Auliya.

Lal Bangla

This tomb of Lal Kunwar, the mother of Emperor Shah Alam II, is near the Old Fort [Purana Qila]. This mausoleum was built by Emperor Shah Alam II in CE 1779. Lal Kunwar's grave is in the building with the small dome, and the building with the bigger dome holds the graves of Begum Jaan, the daughter of Shah Alam II.

These buildings including the dome and halls are made completely of red sandstone and coupled with the name of Shah Alam's mother, Lal Kunwar, have led the two to be called Lal Bangla. Now, in this area there are many graces of the scions of the family of Timur. In its courtyard recently Bahadur Shah II had an enclosure built with the grave of Nawab Fatehbadi Begum and another one of Mirza Bulaqi.

Najaf Khan's Tomb

The tomb of Nawab Zulfiqar-ud-Daulah Mirza Najaf Khan Bahadur is near Shah-e-Mardan *dargah*. He was the brother-in-law of Mirza Hasan, Safdarjung's brother. He was buried here in CE 1780 after his death. Though this tomb is not remarkable in any way as it is constructed from lime and stone, it is the tomb of a very important chief of the era.

Large Jain Temple

Lala Harsukh Rai and Lala Mohan Lal built this temple in Dharampura, in the city of Shahjahanabad. Its construction was started in CE 1800 and it took eight years to complete.

The first prayer here was held on the fifth of [the Jain calendar month] Vaisakh Sudi in CE 1807. The temple is built of brick and lime-mortar with generous use of marble inside. The pinnacles are golden. It cost Rs 5 lakh to build and it is said that one pedestal was built for Rs 1.25 lakh.

Church

This church is in the city of Shahjahanabad near Kashmiri Darwaza. Colonel James Skinner Sahib Bahadur built this *masihi masjid* [Christian mosque]. Its construction started in CE 1826 and was completed in ten years at a cost of Rs 90,000. The cost of the marble flooring is not included in this figure. It is difficult to describe the beauty and majesty of this church. In reality, there must be very few churches which are as beautiful as this. The grave of William Fraser Sahib is in the courtyard of this church inside a beautiful enclosure.

Jogmaya Temple

This is a very famous temple near Qutub Minar. According to Hindu belief, when the atrocities of the demon, Kans, crossed their limits, Lord Brahma took the avatar of Krishna and was born in the end of the [Hindu] Dwapar Age, which was 4,953 years ago, in the family of Vasudev to his wife, Devki. Due to fear of Kans harming the child, baby Krishna was left in the safe custody of Yashoda in Gokul and was replaced in the jail by Yashoda's infant daughter. When Kans came to know of the girl child, he picked her up and wanted to smash her to the floor in a rage, but she flew away from him like lightning. This temple is devoted to her.

Raja Sidhmal, a courtier during Emperor Akbar Shah II's reign, built the temple as recently as CE 1827. The temple is 41 feet high with mirrors on the golden pinnacle which reflects from quite a distance. It has no idol; a stone, enclosed by a marble screen, is worshipped as the Goddess. The temple has a weekly fair which is very popular with traders as it does not involve animal sacrifice [animal sacrifice goes against the beliefs held by the trader class].

Small Jain Temple

This temple is in Seth Gali (Kucha Seth, Dariba Kalan) in the city of Shahjahanabad. It has been constructed by the Jains of the city and is famous as the Panchayati Mandir. Its construction was started in CE 1828 and it took seven years to build. The deity was established in CE 1834. This temple is made of lime mortar and brick with marble used in many places inside. It has a golden pinnacle. Many lakhs of rupees were spent on constructing it.

Kothi Jahannuma

Jahannuma mansion is situated outside Kashmiri Darwaza and was built by Hakim-e-Rais Parwar Muazam-ud-Daulah Amin-ul-Mulk, Ikhtisas Yaar Khan Farzand-e-Arjumand ba Jaan-e-Paivand-e-Sultani[8] Sir Thomas Theophilus Metcalfe Baronet Bahadur Firoz Jung Sahib Senior, Commisioner of Dar-ul-Khilafat Shahjahanabad. The construction was started in CE 1828. This is an extremely beautiful mansion. It is very worthy of this verse:

> What a beautiful monument, that the spectator
>
> Cannot tear his gaze away from it.

Muhajjar Mirza Jahangir

Mirza Jahangir was the son of Akbar Shah II. He died in Allahabad and his body was brought and buried in the compound of the *dargah* of Hazrat Nizam-ud-Din Auliya. His mother Mumtaz Mahal built this marble enclosure in CE 1832. It has very fine and attractive work, particularly the screens. The doors are made of a single-piece marble and are very attractive.

Zafar Mahal/Jal Mahal

Hazrat Abu Zafar Siraj-ud-Din Muhammad Bahadur Shah Badshah Ghazi got this palace built about four or five years ago, in the tank situated in Bagh-e-Hayat Baksh. It is made completely of red sandstone. There is an empty and open space in the middle, and around it are built alcoves and enclosures for sitting. On one side is a bridge, which serves the purpose of entrance and exit.

Hira Mahal

To the north of the bathhouse is Moti Mahal, and between it and the bathhouse is a small courtyard through which flows a 4-*gaz* canal made of marble, taking a winding course, which is a continuation of the stream that flows through the Hall of Special Audience [Diwan-e-Khas] and Rang Mahal till here. In the middle of the courtyard, to the side of the canal, is a twelve-arched pavilion made of marble, and on its roof on all four corners are four small cupolas which have golden domes. This marble pavilion is very delicately and aesthetically made.

This is not an old building but was built four to five years ago under the orders of Hazrat Abu Zafar Siraj-ud-Din Muhammad Bahadur Shah Badshah Ghazi, May God preserve his reign. It has been very finely made and its attractions can't be penned down. The course taken by the canal in this courtyard also defies description. In yesteryears, there used to be golden and silver fountain jets installed in this canal but now this canal is in ruins, and there is no trace of those fountains.

Kothi Dilkusha

This is a pleasure house and is called *Kothi* [mansion] Dilkusha. It is owned by Sahib-e-Waala, Manaqib-e-Aala, Munasib Farzand-e-Arjumand, ba Jaan-e-Paivand-e-Sultani Muazmuddaulah, Ain-ul-Mulk Ikhtisaas Yaar Khan[9] Sir Thomas Theophilus Metcalfe Sahib Baronet Bahadur Firoz Jung Sahib Senior, of Shahjahanabad. Sahab Bahhadur bought this mansion[10] in CE 1844 and began further construction. This verse is very apt for it:

> If there is a Paradise on earth,
> It is here, it is here, it is here.

Baoli Dargah Hazrat Qutub Sahib

Nadeem-ud-Daulah Khalifat-ul-Malik Hafiz Muhammad Daud Khan Bahadur Mustaqim Jung built this step well in CE 1844 near the *dargah* of Qutub Sahib, in front of the mosque. It was completed in CE 1846. It's a beautiful step well made of lime and hardstone. Around Rs 14,000 were spent on it, and that is not including the cost of the stone.

Iron Bridge on River Hindon

Near Ghaziabad there is a river named Hindon. The British Government got an iron bridge constructed over it in CE 1846. This is a unique bridge as beams were hung on iron springs. A path has been made on the beams. If a heavy object crosses the bridge, it starts shaking and the springs absorb the shock. There is no other bridge in this area quite like it.

Lal Diggi

This tank was built on the orders of Lord Ellenburough Bahadur in CE 1846 under the fort in Shahjahanabad, just in front of the Khas Bazaar. This tank is built completely of red sandstone. It has four beautiful cupolas on all four corners of it. There are steps made on both sides on the width. The tank is always full from the waters of the canal. It is 500 feet long and 150 feet wide. After construction of this tank, many wells have had their brackish water turn sweet and this is a source of relief for many people.

New Nigambodh Bridge

The British government built a bridge on the river in CE 1852 at the Nigambodh Ghat in front of Calcutta Darwaza near Salimgarh. This bridge is constructed of lime-mortar and bricks but it has been very sturdily and beautifully built. It has well-proportioned arches which amaze the viewer. It has added to the beauty of the river and the *ghat*. During the monsoons, hundreds of people go walking on it to see the spectacle and there's a daily atmosphere of a fair there.

Editor's Notes

1. In all probability it refers to only the copper-plating of the domes, as it would be difficult to shift entire domes.
2. 'Food etc', just a rhyming pattern of meaningless words.
3. Called 'Jai Prakash'.
4. 'King of men' was a title given to Hazrat Ali, cousin and son-in-law of the Prophet.
5. Hazrat Ali was the cousin and son-in-law of Prophet Muhammad and the fourth Khalifa. As per Shia belief, he was the rightful successor and is designated as the first Imam. A poison-coated sword wounded him on the nineteenth day of the month of Ramzan and he passed away two days later, on the twenty-first. Even today there are assemblies held on 19, 20 and 21 Ramzan in Shah-e-Mardan.
6. Moharram is a month of mourning for Shias when they mourn the martyrdom of Hazrat Ali's son, Imam Hussain. *Taziyas* are replicas of the mausoleum of Imam Hussain.
7. Since his given name was Abul Mansoor Khan, and Safdarjung his title, this mausoleum was known as Mansoor ka *Maqbara* till quite recently. There are still some old signages with 'Mansoor *ka Maqbara*'.
8. Honorifics that state he was: 'a ruler who looked after his nobles. The most honourable person of the government, custodian of the country, the exalted son and most beloved of the emperor'.
9. The most honourable one, one with virtues of the highest degree, the exalted son and most beloved of the emperor, the most honourable person of the government, custodian of the country, the most distinguished light of the state.
10. Sir Sayyid calls it a mansion [*kothi*] and not a mausoleum [*maqbara*] which it actually was.

Urdu Bayaan ke Bayaan Mei'n:
An Explanation in Explanation of Urdu

Under the Hindu rule, the spoken and written language was Hindi. In AH 587/CE 1191/1248 Bikramjit [Hindu calendar era], when the Muslims established their reign here then the court language became Persian; the common people, however, continued speaking in Hindi. By AH 894/CE 1488 even though Persian was well-established in the court, the masses were not conversant with it. In the reign of Sultan Sikandar Lodi, the kayasths[i] who were always involved in admininistration, were the first to learn to read and write Persian. Gradually others also started to learn Persian and it became popular amongst the Hindus.

There had been no change or evolution in Hindi till the reign of Babar or Jahangir: the Muslims spoke in Persian and the Hindus conversed in bhasha.[ii] Amir Khusrau started including words of bhasha in Persian under the Khilji Sultans in the thirteenth century. He wrote some riddles, mukarni[iii] and verses in a language that combined bhasha with Persian.

Though Persian words had started being combined in the bhasha, since then there was no language that could be called distinct or separate. When Shahjahan built and populated Shahjahanabad in AH 1058/CE 1648, and people from all over the world gathered here, there was a mixing of Persian with Hindi dialects. Frequent usage led to a change and evolution of certain Persian and Hindi words. Thus a new language was born in the Royal Army [Lashkar-e-Badshahi] and the 'Exalted Camp' [Urdu-e-Mu'alla][iv] – that is why the language was called Urdu. Frequent use of this language cemented the name Urdu, and it developed a culture and life of its own.

In AH 1100/CE 1688, in the reign of Aurangzeb Alamgir, poets started writing in this language. It is well known that the first poet to use Urdu for poetry was Wali [Deccani]. From

---

[i] A sub-caste in Hinduism who were traditionally scribes.

[ii] Local dialects.

[iii] The actual term is 'keh mukarni': keh (say), mukarni (deny) and is a type of riddle.

[iv] It means 'exalted camp' and referred to the city of Shahjahanabad.

Wali's verses, however, it seems that others had also written poetry in this language, as he made satirical comments on other poets using Urdu. Urdu verse in those days was not very refined. Poets improved it day by day, and Mir Taqi Mir and Sauda took Urdu poery to its zenith.

Mir's language was so pristine and pure with beautiful and spontaneous metaphors and idioms that even till today they are parsed. Sauda's language is also excellent and his choice of subjects is superior to Mir's, but he could not match the purity and excellence of Mir's language.

Among Urdu prose writers, Mir Amman, the author of *Bagh o Bahar*, is the best. He has the same command over prose that Mir had over the art of writing *nazm* [a form of Urdu poetry].

Maulvi Abdul Qadir Sahib and Maulvi Rafi-ud-Din Sahib were the first to translate Arabic into Urdu. Maulvi Abdul Qadir's Urdu translation of the *Kalam-ullah* [The Holy Quran] is a huge contribution to the Urdu dictionary. Maulvi Rafi-ud-Din's translation is an excellent benchmark for arrangement of Urdu syntax.

Urdu poetry has followed the Persian style of poetry in such a way as if a young man is writing a verse in praise of a beautiful lad.

In Hindi *bhasha*, ardent verses were written in a feminine voice for men. This is sometimes used in Urdu too and called *rekhti*.[v] Approximately in AH 1220/CE 1805, Insha Allah Khan popularized the genre of *rekhti*.

The metre and rhyme pattern of Persian poetry were absorbed in Urdu poetry too. Only *mukarni* and riddles were written in a different metre and with a mix of *bhasha* words.

In this many references and words are used, which seemingly have no connection to each other and the person addressed is asked to find a word, which is a common thread in all. The word may turn out to be totally different in meaning.

In the riddle the attributes and qualities of something are described and the person addressed is asked to solve it and give the word for it. The riddle has to be solved in such a way that the name of the person or thing is found and yet it is totally different.

The *mukarni* is in the feminine voice, with use of double entendre where one reference is to the beloved and the other to something totally different. One negates the other.

The following is an example of *keh mukarni* by Amir Khusrau:
The riddle: It shakes itself, and shakes me too, the shaking really pleases me; It has become
                so frail by continuously shaking.
The answer: Is it the beloved? No dear, a fan![vi]

---

[v] Verses written in the feminine voice, expressing the desires and longings peculiar to women.

[vi] Explanation taken from http://www.angelfire.com/sd/urdumedia/kemukar.html

Nisbat: Amusing Questions and Answers

Q. Why wasn't the meat eaten?

A. *G'la na tha!* [It wasn't tender (*g'la*); Didn't have a neck/throat (*g'la*)].

Q. Why wasn't the pomegranate eaten? Why wasn't the minister appointed?

A. *Daana na tha.* [It had no seeds (daana); he had no intelligence (daana)]

Q. Why wasn't the samosa eaten? Why wasn't the shoe worn?

A. *T'la na tha* [It wasn't fried (t'la). It had no sole (t'la)].

Rekhti: Urdu Verse

> *Achha jo khafa ham se ho tum, ai sanam achcha*
> *Lo ham bhi na bolenge, Khuda ki qasam achcha*
> [If you are angry with me, O Beloved, then so be it
> Even I won't speak to you, I vow in God's name, so be it]
> – Insha Allah Khan Insha

Sher-e-Urdu: Couplets in Urdu

> *Ishq karte hain us pari ruh se*
> *Mir sahib bhi kya diwaane hain*
> [He adores the one with a fairy-like face
> Mir sahib is also crazy]

> *Mir in neem-baaz aankhon mein*
> *Saari masti sharaab ki si hai*
> [Mir, in the half-closed eyes of my beloved
> Lies all the intoxication of wine]
> *Hum huye, tum huye, ke Mir huye*
> *Uski zulfo'n ke aseer huye*
> [Whether it's you, Mir, or me
> We are all prisoners of her tresses for eternity.]

APPENDICES

An Update on the Status of the Monuments

RANA SAFVI

Purana Qila

This mention may be a bit confusing for Delhiites today, as it would seem to refer to Purana Qila near Pragati Maidan. However, Sir Sayyid is actually describing a fort now known as Lal Kot, which is situated in Sanjay Van. Only some portions of the walls of this fort still remain.

Din Panah

The walls of the Purana Qila (as we call it today) still stand strong, as do its gates. In 1924, the Archaeological Survey of India (ASI) evacuated entire villages from its premises.

Rai Pithaura Fort

Neither the fort nor any of its gates exist today. The walls of Rai Pithaura Fort still stand in a few places but all else has been destroyed. The area of Lal Kot has been turned into a medicinal forest called Sanjay Van. The walls around the *mazaar* of Haji Rozbih are still intact. A hereditary caretaker looks after it, and people come to offer flowers and burn incense. The name of Prithviraj Chauhan's daughter is now famous as Bela.

Kushk-e-Lal

According to Carr Stephen, Sultan Balban built himself a Kushk-e-Lal and Qila-e-Marzgan *inside* Rai Pithaura Fort. Kushk-e-Lal was built before Balban became the emperor, and Qila-e-Marzgan after he ascended the throne. Sultan Jalal-ud-Din Khilji is said to have visited it after his coronation at Qasr-e-Safed [the White Palace], which was in Rai Pithaura Fort. The other incident connected with Kushk-e-Lal is the burial of Sultan Balban. His corpse was taken out of Kushk-e-Lal and carried to its resting place inside Rai Pithaura Fort. These words allude to a very short journey, though in those days, if indeed Kushk-e-Lal was situated within the present-day Hazrat Nizam-ud-Din Basti, it was a long distance to travel. Thus, Kushk-e-Lal and Lal Mahal seem to be two different monuments.

Delhi Alai

Some walls, and a few tombs and mosques from this city are now located in the area of Shahpur Jat village.

Qasr-e-Hazar Sutun

There still exist a few stones with holes in them inside the Bijai Mandal grounds, meant to denote where the columns may have been placed, and these are probably the remains of this palace.

Tughlaqabad

Though the inside is in ruins, the magnificent walls and bastions, and other parts of this fort still exist.

Adilabad/ Muhammadabad/Imarat Hazar Sutun

The ruins of this city exist near Ghiyas-ud-Din Tughlaq's tomb, and the magnificent doorway testifies to its erstwhile grandeur.

Jahanpanah

Some of the walls and ruins of the city still exist.

Kushk Bijai Mandal or Badih Manzil

'Badih Manzil' here means extraordinary or unique, not big or large. Badih Manzil still stands but is sadly neglected. It appears to be a favourite meeting place for youngsters as one finds shards of beer bottles on the roof. The grass is overgrown and unkempt in the grounds around, so one needs to be careful when walking here.

Kushk-e-Firoz Shah/Kotla Firoz Shah

This is one of my favourite places in Delhi, and its ruins are well looked after. It is said that it was stripped during the building of the city of Shahjahanabad, leaving it in ruins. On Thursdays, huge crowds gather here to offer incense and respect to the djinns that are said to reside in the underground cells and chambers. From what I could gather, the djinns are a recent phenomena; they came up after 1977 when Ladoo Shah started coming here. According to Anand Vivek Taneja's *Jinnealogy: Time, Islam and Ecological Thought on the Medieval Ruins* of *Delhi* (Stanford University Press, 2017), Ladoo Shah was a musician and a healer. He gained powers to heal from the djinns by coming to the Kotla frequently. It was his gift of healing, given to him by the djinns, that started bringing people here. Ladoo Shah had a huge following as he was said to be able to talk to the djinns and forward the requests of his followers to them. Gradually the ruins with their underground cells, being conducive to spirits, became famous. The Ashoka Pillar here is now famous as 'Lath-wale Baba' or 'Pillar Baba', and the chief djinn is said to reside in it. On Thursdays one finds mendicants, etc., offering to mediate on behalf of the innumerable supplicants who come here to pray. The pillar itself is inside an iron cage, and it shows signs of great wear and tear because of the pollution and exposure.

Kushk-e-Jahannuma/Kushk-e-Shikar

A single monument, mysterious and attractive, known as 'Pir Ghaib' still stands. Pir Ghaib is a name that is used by local people, who say a saint disappeared from here. A room on the first floor is dedicated to the saint, and some locals come and burn lamps and incense sticks there and offer large green sheets of cloth called *chadors*. The monument was used by British officers during the uprising of 1857 and was damaged in that war. A heavy battery was stationed near it. The British called it an observatory. There is a pair of ramp-like steps very similar to that in one of the instruments in Jantar Mantar, but there is no evidence that the two were connected. A cylindrical structure with a round hole in the middle on the roof could have been used as a sundial or for some kind of measurement. Sir George Everest used it as a survey tower when he was making the baseline measurement for the Great Trignometrical Survey. At that point some changes were also made to the monument. There is a step well nearby which must have been part of the hunting lodge, and the tunnels that Sir Sayyid mentions were probably in this step well.

Khizrabad

Nothing remains of this city.

Mubarakbad

Mubarakpur Kotla is now an overcrowded area of the city of Delhi, with buildings mushrooming haphazardly all around. There are just a few remains of the lintels of the gateway, but as they are sandwiched between constructions, only those who actively seek them can discover these.

Dehli Sher Shah: Kabuli Darwaza

It is now famously known as Khooni Darwaza because of the bloodshed and killing of the Mughal princes by Major Hudson in the aftermath of the 1857 uprising. There was an incident of rape here involving a female student from Maulana Azad Medical College, and since then the gateway is kept locked.

Salimgarh/Nurgarh

Nurgarh saw much action during 1857, and there are only the ruins of a mosque and battery here. Temporary structures, put up as jails for officers of the Indian National Army (INA) in 1945, have now become museums. Railway lines run right down the middle of Nurgarh, and one has to cross over a railway bridge to reach it. The portion towards the fort is used as residential quarters by the Central Industrial Security Force (CISF) who are stationed there.

Qila-e-Shahjahan

Delhi Darwaza and Lahori Darwaza

Delhi Darwaza still stands, as imposing as ever. Lord Curzon replaced the stone elephants destroyed by Aurangzeb in 1903 with two elephants minus mahouts, as in the original scuplture. The area in front of Lahori Darwaza is the venue for the Prime Minister's speech every 15 August.

Chhatta Lahori Darwaza

This gateway with a vaulted arcade houses a tourist bazaar now, where one can buy souvenirs, etc. The ceilings have been painted white.

Naqqar Khana/Hathiya Pol

In the first edition of his book (*Asar-1*), Sir Sayyid has described the elephants as being in front of the Delhi Darwaza, which opinion he changed in *Asar-2*, thus creating some confusion. The elephants in fact stood in front of the Delhi Darwaza. According to Carr Stephen, the reason for the drum house being called Hathiya Pol is that it was here that everyone, except for princes of royal blood, had to dismount from their elephants/horses before proceeding to the court.

The tank in front of the drum house in front of Chatta Bazaar saw the massacre of British women and children on 16 May 1857, as a result of which the British destroyed it after they came to power on 20 September 1857. The drum house witnessed a lot of changes after 1857. Maulvi Zafar Hasan writes that it served as the main entrance to the Diwan-e-Aam. Between this and the east end of the vaulted arcade (Chhatta Chowk), there earlier existed a court of some 200 feet in length and 140 feet in breadth, surrounded by arcaded apartments that served as quarters for the nobles on duty in the Emperor's Guard. At the south-west corner of this square stood certain public buildings wherein the emperor's steward transacted business, while its central feature was a tank fed by the stream that ran north–south down the centre of the arcaded streets and the quarters of the lesser nobles and officials, and leading respectively to the Royal Gardens and Delhi Darwaza. A stone railing is said to have fronted the drum house, but all traces of it, together with the square and its surrounding arcades, have disappeared. Today, it is the only building which has been re-plastered white, and it houses the offices of the Archaeological Survey of India as well as a War Museum.

Diwan-e-Aam: The Hall of Public Audience

Nasheman Zille Ilahi/Sangin Takht

Gordon Sanderson[1] has written that

> this tablet was removed after the capture of the palace in 1857 and placed in South Kensington Museum in London, while eleven of the other inlaid panels were also removed. They were restored to their original position some years ago, at the instance of Lord Curzon. It was fortunate that old drawings of the mosaic existed, from which it was possible to restore the decoration to its original form, and for his purpose an Italian 'mosaicista' was especially brought to India, and the work completed in 1909.

Sir John Marshall reported in the *ASI Annual Report 1902–03* that it was hoped the plaque would be restored in time for the Delhi Durbar (of 1903), but it arrived too late for that. He added, the panels 'have now been replaced behind the throne, and many other panels have also been cleaned of the lac with which they were covered, and their mutilated surfaces repolished. There still remain some of the gaps where panels are partly or wholly missing'. These were supposed to be filled up as per the original design after procuring the precise stones from Europe, and the work was either to be done in Europe or by artists brought from Italy. The work was completed in 1909. The panel still exists behind the marble throne but it is in small sections, and since the throne is sealed off by a glass covering, one has to strain to see it.

Main Hall

Maulvi Zafar Hasan noted in 1916 that 'the hall now robbed of its former gilding and stucco, is built throughout of red sandstone', and thus it remains today as well.

Gulal Bari

To the north of the Diwan-e-Aam was a gateway leading to the twin courtyard in front of the Diwan-e-Khas, which was destroyed in 1857 by the British. In the middle of the western wall of the first courtyard was a gate, the entrance to the Diwan-e-Khas. According to Sanderson, a red cloth awning was stretched in front of it, and so it was called Lal Pardah. Gulal Bari was an ante-court built outside the Diwan-e-Aam that was reserved for minor officials, while the general crowd attending court stood outside this last enclosure. This structure is no longer present.

Maulvi Zafar Hasan has noted: 'the lawns in front of the Diwan-e-Aam are intended to represent the original courtyard, and the shrubberies at the sides and ends, the former columnades.'

Khas Mahal/Chhota Rang Mahal

Gordon Risley Hearn[2] called this the Mumtaz Mahal and so it is known as even today. This building is now an ASI museum and was probably named so post 1857, since Sir Sayyid makes no mention of this name. It was the residence of the princesses, and in all probability Princess Jahan Ara lived here, which is probably why it came to be named after her mother. After 1857, according to Sanderson, it was used as the Sergeants' Mess and its appearance was completely changed. Originally there must have been a range of arcades forming the southern boundary of the garden of the Rang Mahal running all the way through to the front of the east wall of the fort. The east wall would also have had screens to prevent people getting a glimpse into the harem from the riverside. One can see some of the original design in a very faded condition on the inner portions of the engrailed arches inside it. The rest of the building has been plastered white both inside and outside.

Imtiaz Mahal/Bada Rang Mahal

This was its nomenclature in the time of Shahjahan, but later the coloured stones used for its decoration gave it the name Rang Mahal. It is in a bad state today due to misuse over the years. The ceiling has gaping holes that are badly in need of repair, and callous visitors have defaced the walls. The base of the flower fountain is in good shape but the flower-like cup, in which the fountain was embedded, has disappeared. There are no working fountains, and the jewels or inlay work and floral designs have long since disappeared. It is a testimony to the cruelty of time.

Chhoti Baithak

This structure is no longer extant. According to Hearn, a small pavilion known as the Chhoti Baithak and a structure known as Darya Mahal or Floating Palace (which finds no mention by Sir Sayyid) were situated between the Rang Mahal and Mumtaz Mahal.

Asad Burj

This is still intact, in a part of the fort where visitors are not allowed. It can be viewed from the road. There are many colonial structures in this area which were built by the British.

Khwabgah/Badi Baithak

No such marble basin exists there today.

Burj Tila/Musamman Burj

The tower's original dome, as mentioned above, was golden in colour and made in different sections and covered by gilded copper. After the uprising of 1857, however, it disappeared, and the present one covered with lime plaster is the result of repairs. The tower is in otherwise good condition, and all the verses written on it are intact and can be read by those who know Persian.

Shah Mahal/Diwan-e-Khas

Fanshawe, in his book *Delhi: Past and Present*, written in 1902, wrote:

> In front of it (Diwan-e-Khas) was a marble pavement and at the sides low marble screens separated it from the other buildings, as in the case of the Khas Mahal in the Agra Fort. Why these and the fountain in front of the Diwan-i-Khas, which fell over niches containing lighted lamps and the arcades of the court, should have been removed after 1857, is inconceivable, as they could not possibly have been objectionable on sanitary grounds, and the area they covered was not needed for any military purpose.

He added that two pavilions on either side of the Diwan-e-Khas, with roofs of curved Bengal pattern similar to those flanking Khas Mahal, were also removed, apparently before 1857, as they do not appear in the photographs of that year which depict the riverside of the palace. It was this building that was a mute spectator to the changing fortunes of the Mughal Empire. It was in this hall that Muhammad Shah surrendered to Nadir Shah. It was also in this hall that the sepoys who came into the Red Fort in May 1857 proclaimed Bahadur Shah II as the Emperor of Hindustan under whose banner they would fight the British. It was here that Bahadur Shah II was tried for sedition. A lone, yellowed marble throne stands in the exact place where the splendid peacock throne once stood. It is a forlorn token of the once glorious Mughal Empire. One has to strain to see the famous couplet, '*gar firdaus bar ru-e-zameen ast*' [if there were heaven on earth…], as it is discoloured due to grime and age.

Today, one feels like weeping looking at the yellowing marble and decaying paintwork on the ceilings. The precious stones were gouged out of the pietra dura; the wooden ceiling has been damaged in many places and repairs are underway.

Tasbih Khana

The marble screens in the Tasbih Khana too are broken and contain gaping holes. The marble, as everywhere else, is yellowed. The inscription is surprisingly intact.

Aqab-e-Hammam (Behind the Royal Baths)

All buildings between the Diwan-e-Khas and the bathouse have been demolished.

Hammam

The bath-house is kept locked now. The inlaid precious stones have been removed and it is a shell of what it was in its heyday. However, compared to the rest of the fort, it is well preserved.

Moti Mahal

It is no longer extant. According to Hearn, Moti Mahal was demolished after the 1857 uprising because it prevented free passage of air to the barracks. In fact, he expresses surprise as to why the rather unimportant Hira Mahal was left standing. The mansions and arcades on the north and south side of the gardens were destroyed, as was the Khas Khana. The British presumably removed the monolith tank, which defies any description after 1857, and it stood in the Queen's gardens till 1911 when it was brought back to the Fort. It now stands in the centre of a large tank in front of the Rang Mahal and Diwan-e-Khas.

I read about the monolithic marble basin the night before I visited the Red Fort. It has been kept in the middle of a tank in front of Rang Mahal and normally remains out of bounds. For purposes of my work, I took permission to see it, and went with a great deal of excitement to witness its beauty first hand. I cannot describe my disappointment when all I saw was what looked like a bathtub with a broken fountain stub in its centre.

Nahr-e-Bahisht

Only the marble and sandstone channels remain as a mute reminder of this stream that once ran through the fort and its palaces.

Bagh-e-Hayat Baksh

A part of it was used to build the military barracks and the remaining part of this 'iram' (paradise) like garden has grass and a few shrubs that were planted by the British.

Hauz aur Nahr (Bagh-e-Hayat Baksh)

The fountains have disappeared and only a tired looking building now rests in a dry pond.

Bhado'n

A yellowing Bhado'n pavilion now stands as a mute witness to the desolation of the Red Fort.

Sawan

It exists in a state similar to the Bhado'n. As the stream and its fountains have been destroyed, it is difficult to appreciate or understand the beauty and purpose of these two buildings.

Shah Burj

This bastion suffered damage prior to 1857 as the Rohillas under Ghulam Qadir 'stripped many of the rooms of their marble ornaments and pavements and have even picked out the stones from the borders of many of the floorings'. They also spent three days digging up the floors for treasure which they believed Emperor Shah Alam had hidden in this palace. Sanderson wrote:

> For many years after the Mutiny the building served as an officer's residence, but in 1902, conservation work was taken up and the marble cascade reconstructed and modern additions removed. The earthquake of 1901 so damaged the structure that it was necessary to take it almost entirely down and rebuild it.

The dome of the bastion was also destroyed post 1857, and it no longer exists. Today it is out of bounds for the public. It is not in a good state of preservation, and though the niche and fountain bed are still intact, it is heartbreaking to compare them to paintings by Mazhar Ali Khan in the 'Imperial Delhie' album.

Mehtab Bagh/Moonlight Garden

This garden was planted with white flowers and flowering trees and was used in the evening and at night. The British uprooted it post 1857 and barracks were built here. The ASI, in 2016–17 conducted excavations here to rediscover the old parterres and water causeways, to see if they can be restored. There are no remains of a *dargah*.

Shahjahanabad City: Jama Masjid

Jama Masjid: The Area around the Southern Gateway

This is today's Gate 1. It is the most crowded as it is the gate closest to the Chawri Bazaar metro station as well as the Matia Mahal area.

Urdu Bazaar and Chandni Chowk

The first part of this market is the present-day location of the Jain temple that was originally named Urdu Mandir because of its location in the Urdu Bazaar or Camp Bazaar, so called because of the soldiers camped there. Today, the road in front of Jama Masjid Gate No. 1 is called Urdu Bazaar, not for its military connotations, but because of the presence of shops selling Urdu books here. The fourth section of the road up to Fatehpuri Masjid was known as the Chandni Chowk, and today it is an extremely overcrowded and busy bazaar. I often feel that the present state of her beautiful market would make Princess Jahan Ara turn in her grave.

Faiz Bazaar

Both the bazaar and Akbarabadi Mosque are no longer extant. The British destroyed the mosque after 1857. Sir Sayyid was heartbroken. According to the proceedings of the meeting of the Madrasatul Ulum committee, published in the Institute Gazette in June 1886, these inscriptions were presented to Sir Sayyid by Shahzada Sulaiman Jah Bahadur, to be used in the middle *mihrab* of the Muhammadan Anglo American College, Aligarh's Jama Masjid. Recently, some remains of the mosque were found as a result of the digging underway for metro construction in the area. Much of this area is now covered by roads packed with heavy traffic.

Imam ki Gali

This entire area is now called Matia Mahal after the erstwhile palace and is famous for its eateries, especially Karim restaurant. Shops selling sweets and other food items have replaced Ghazi Bharbhunja ki Dukan. The Imams of Jama Masjid now live in an area near Dariba and Chah Rahat, and their residence is part of the Jama Masjid compound near Gate 3.

Matia Mahal

Matia Mahal is now a generic term for the entire area; the building itself disappeared in the nineteenth century. The area around this erstwhile palace was given to Azizabad Begum, wife of a Mughal prince and became famous as Azizabad ki Haveli [mansion]. Nothing remains of it but memories.

Janab Maulvi Muhammad Sadr-ud-Din Khan Bahadur Sadr us Sudoor's Haveli

This has been broken down to give way to many houses and shops. Only the gateway remains. The entire area is a warren of houses, shops and small workshops with electric wires hanging in glorious confusion above. It is difficult to locate and identify the rest of the *havelis* mentioned by Sir Sayyid, but I found the *haveli* of Sayyid Muhammad Amir Khushnavez.

Sayyid Muhammad Amir Khushnavez's Haveli

This has been encroached upon on all sides and a part of it is occupied by small workshops. The calligraphic inscriptions have been painted over and so cannot be read. The upper part of this huge mansion was occupied by a school run by the Municipal Corporation of Delhi.

Sayyid Rafa Sahib ki Masjid

This has had a makeover and the bright new shining mosque is very popular with shopkeepers of the area. Chitli Qabr is the name of the entire area. Most are unaware of the small shrine which is mostly kept locked and which is looked after by a neighbouring shopkeeper.

Azam Khan ki Haveli

This mansion is now just a name for the area. Thousands of people live in the small residences that have sprung up inside its compound. Post 1947, the shape of Shahjahanabad was considerably and irretrievably altered. The *havelis*/mansions gave way to residences for the refugees who came in the wake of Partition, and in most cases only the gates remain.

Bangash ka Kamra and Amir Khan ka Bangla

These have long since disappeared and been replaced by a readymade-clothes market. However, Tiraha Bairam Khan still survives and the Phool ki Mandi [wholesale flower market] still thrives under a huge tree on the Tiraha itself.

Dai ki Masjid and Auliya Masjid

Both are functioning mosques and have been rebuilt. The *haveli* where Sir Sayyid was born is opposite Auliya Masjid. As is the case with most such *havelis*, only the original gateway remains. Inside there are many houses and some of the area has been sold to real estate developers.

Jama Masjid: The Area around the Eastern Gateway

For some reason, Sir Sayyid does not mention the most famous landmark of the area, the Shaheed Sarmad shrine. It is painted bright red and adjoining it is the Hare Bhare Shah ki Mazar which is painted bright green. Khas Bazar is now an extremely crowded market, and Sadullah Khan ki Chowk has been swallowed up by rampant construction.

Jama Masjid: The Area around the Northern Gateway

R'hat ka kuan or the well with the Persian wheel is on a narrow alley behind Jama Masjid, and the area is known as Chaah Rahat. The old wooden doors are locked and decaying, and an inscription proudly proclaiming the well which supplied water to the Jama Masjid looks out of place. The Persian wheel itself is in a small compound next to it. It has been taken over by some factory workers and their families. We went inside and had a look and felt dejected at the state of neglect of such an important part of our heritage. We tried to enter from the back but it was pitch dark and full of debris, and we were warned that there could be rats and snakes, so we desisted.

Pai'nwalo'n ka Bazaar and Dariba

These are still names of the shopping areas, only the items being sold have changed.

Khooni Darwaza

This gateway no longer exists; the name has been given to Kabuli Darwaza near Firoz Shah Kotla.

Samru Begum ki Kothi

The area where this *kothi* once stood is today a warren of shops selling electrical items, called Bhagirath Palace. The main building houses the Central Bank of India, and its famous steps are filled with debris and rubbish.

Punjabi Katra

The area retains its name and the mosque, renovated, still stands and is functioning.

Behind the Jama Masjid
Chawri Bazar

This is now a busy area full of shops selling bathroom fittings and stationery items.

Shah Bola ka Barh

A tree stands here with vendors selling food under it, but it is hard to say if it is the same tree.

Qazi ka Hauz

The tank has long since disappeared but the name remains. The Chawri Bazar metro station is located here.

Lal Kuan

This area, with the same name, today houses small residential and commercial properties.

Khari Baoli

This is today Asia's largest spice market.

A Description of Monuments Built by Emperors and Noblemen

Lohe ki Lath/Iron Pillar

This pillar has now been fenced in, as people trying to clasp it were damaging it. The translation of the inscription is given on a plaque near the north gate of the Quwwat-ul-Islam Mosque.

Ashoka Pillar/Minara Zarrin/Firoz Shah ki Lath

Today, this pillar is known as 'Lath-wale Baba' or 'Pillar Baba'. According to popular belief, the chief djinn of the city of Firozabad (which is said to be populated by djinns) lives here. Every Thursday, believers throng here to offer flowers and to pray for their needs. The pillar has now been enclosed by a high iron grill to prevent further deterioration due to human touch.

The Second Pillar of Ashoka/Minara Kushk Shikar
This pillar came into the possession of Hindu Rao whose house was nearby. He gave pieces of it to the Asiatic Society. The Executive Engineer of Delhi then sawed off the inscribed portions and sent them to the Asiatic Society in Calcutta. In 1866, experts at the Asiatic Society put the pieces together and re-erected it at the original location.

Anekpur
The dam is called Anangpur Dam now, and it is in a village of the same name in Faridabad district.

Anektal
Today, the tank is overgrown by vegetation and only a hollow depression is seen in Sanjay Van (forest) from which it is difficult to imagine that the tank was once the lifeblood of Lal Kot.

Suraj Kund
A fair of the same name continues to be held every year and is very popular. The lake [kund] itself is very impressive and is in a well-preserved state.

Rai Pithaura's Temple
Many idols can be seen carved on the pillars of the Quwwat-ul-Islam Mosque.

Masjid Adhina Delhi/Masjid Jami Masjid/Masjid Quwwat-ul-Islam
Very popular with tourists and in a good state of preservation.

Qutub Sahib ki Lath/Minar/Mazina
Very well-maintained though one is not allowed to go inside.

Construction by Sultan Ala-ud-Din, the large gate near the Qutub Minar/Alai Darwaza
In an excellent state of maintenance.

The Incomplete Lath/Alai Minar
The Quwwat-ul-Islam Mosque, the Qutub Minar, Alai Darwaza, Alai Minar, tomb of Altamush, and tomb and madarsa of Ala-ud-Din Khilji, all today fall under the Qutub Complex, which has been declared a World Heritage Building by UNESCO.

Hauz-e-Shamsi/Qutub Sahib ka Talab

This tank is now restricted to a very small area and is used by locals for bathing. The pavilion is on the south-west and can be accessed from there. The locals use it for dumping rubbish.

Maqbara Sultan Ghazi

The villagers of Mahipalpur and Rangpur revere this *maqbara* and look after it. They light lamps and incense sticks and pray to the prince who is buried here, referring to him as Pir. They hold his *urs* too. It is in very good condition considering its age.

Maqbara Sultan Shams-ud-Din Altamash

This is one of my favourite places in Delhi and the cenotaph of Sultan Altamash is very well preserved. There are some signs of deterioration but not much, and the calligraphy in the *mehrabs* and walls except for a few places is well preserved. The domeless tomb seems a befitting resting place for the Sufi king.

Dargah Shah Turkman

The actual *dargah* of Shah Turkman Bayabani, as described and sketched by Sir Sayyid, lies in the *mohalla qabristan* behind Turkman Darwaza. However, a recent unknown grave has been renovated and named Dargah Shah Turkman, which many people confuse with the original. Sir Sayyid's sketch has no resemblance to the grave near Turkman Darwaza.

Maqbara Rukn-ud-Din Firoz Shah

There is only one pavilion near Sultan Ghari but there is no grave in it now. It is not known if it is Rukn-ud-Din Firoz Shah's or his brother Muiz-ud-Din Bahram Shah's, who is also said to be buried in the vicinity.

Maqbara Raziya Sultan Begum

Located in the narrow lanes of Bulbulikhana, the tomb is difficult to find. The locals have set up a mosque on its western wall and look after the grave. The Imam lives in a portacabin next to it.

Maqbara Muiz-ud-Din Bahram Shah

Only one pavilion remains and there is no grave to indicate which brother is buried here.

Maqbara Sultan Ghiyas-ud-Din Balban

It is in a state of deterioration, though in recent years some repairs have been carried out. The grave of Khan-e-Shaheed is revered locally with offerings of lamps and incense sticks.

The ruins of the rooms at the back hold the remains of a tomb very similar to that of Khan-e-Shaheed, and in all probability it is the cenotaph that was built over Balban's grave.

Hauz-e-Alai/Hauz-e-Khas

Hauz Khas is now a fashionable area of Delhi with speciality restaurants and eateries. On one side of the tank is a deer park with three tombs which is popular with morning walkers. The tank is of course restricted to a much smaller area.

Maqbara Sultan Ala-ud-Din Khilji

It is in the same ruined state and only the crumbling walls remain.

Baoli of Hazrat Nizam-ud-Din Auliya

The step well has been boxed in from all sides and buildings next to it have been encroached upon. The water is not very clean despite periodic efforts at cleaning it.

Maqbara Tughlaq Shah

No Gujar herdsmen live here any more and the tomb is very well maintained.

Dargah Hazrat Nizam-ud-Din Auliya

One of India's most popular Sufi shrines, the *dargah* has a regular stream of visitors from all over the world.

Satpula

The seven-arched bridge still stands, though the reservoir is dry and is used as a playground.

Dargah Sheikh Salah-ud-Din

Located in West Savitri Nagar, Sheikh Sarai, it is in a good state, though the approach to it is crowded with car-repair shops.

Masjid Dargah Nizam-ud-Din

The mosque still stands tall despite signs of age. It is under conservation by the Aga Khan Trust for Culture.

Masjid Jami Firozi

This mosque is still functional, with prayers conducted five times a day. Though it is still an impressive structure, there is no sign of a roof and the walls have also broken down in places.

Kushk-e-Anwar/Me'nhdiya'n

The graveyard, popularly known as Me'nhdiya'n, still exists, although it has been thoroughly encroached upon. The Sufi saint Shah Waliullah is buried here, as is the poet Momin Khan Momin. The main building has disappeared. Maulana Azad Medical College now stands at this location.

Bhooli Bhatiyari ka Mahal

The entrance gateway is very impressive and it leads on to an inner gateway, which in turn opens out on to an open space. There are ruins of rooms on two sides and some more on an elevated space. The walls surrounding it are in good condition. There is a lake near it but no dam. It is said to be haunted because of the wilderness around.

Kali Masjid, Kotla Nizam-ud-Din

This is a functioning mosque under the Delhi Waqf Board. It has been whitewashed and is in a good state of preservation, but visitors are not encouraged.

Dargah Hazrat Roshan Chiragh Dehli

There is another legend about how the saint got his title. It is said that during the construction of the step well in Hazrat Nizam-ud-Din's *dargah*, since Sultan Ghiyas-ud-Din Tughlaq had banned the sale of oil to the *dargah*, the saint lit lamps with water instead as his workers were secretly working there at night. The *dargah* has been severely encroached upon, but is still very popular. Additions have been made inside the structure in order to better accommodate devotees.

Qadam Sharif/Maqbara Fatah Khan

This monument is now a heartbreaking sight. The gateways are in ruins, and one has to navigate through narrow alleys to reach the *dargah*. What was once Qila Qadam Sharif is now a travesty of its former self. It is badly maintained and encroached upon from almost every direction. The Qadam Sharif itself is kept by the custodian [*mutawalli*], who only takes it out on request. The few graves which still remain in the graveyard are in a state of disrepair. On the walls of the tank which contains the footprint of the Prophet, the following lines are inscribed:

> This piece of land, which bears the print of the sole of thy foot, will continue for years to be worshipped by sagacious persons. When Yusuf, at the footprint of Muhammad, built this enclosure by the help of God, For the date of the completion of its erection I heard the invisible crier say, Well done! (AH 1067/CE 1656–57).

Masjid Chaurahiya Qadam Sharif

No mosque from that era survives in the area. It is entirely possible that it was converted into a residence after Partition.

Dargah Hazrat Sayyid Mahmood Bahar

The *dargah* and adjoining mosque have been renovated and are well maintained. Only the domed gateway survives in its original form. It is located within a residential colony in Kilukhari.

Kali Masjid/Kalan Masjid

It is a functioning mosque and is very well maintained. It has been painted a bright green.

Masjid Begumpur

It is in a state of disrepair and most of the domes have fallen. However, the gateway and courtyard are still impressive.

Masjid Kalu Sarai

In a state of extreme deterioration with half of it having fallen, it is now occupied as a residence.

Masjid Khirki

The mosque's name has intrigued me for a while as naming a mosque after its rather ordinary windows did not make sense to me. Sir Sayyid's description makes it clear that it was named after the village where it was located. It is now boxed in by buildings, but remains in a fair state of preservation despite having been used by the villagers in the past.

Maqbara Firoz Shah

The mausoleum is well preserved and very popular with visitors to the Hauz Khas area.

Khizr ki Gumbati

I have been unable to locate this Gumbati; probably, it has been destroyed.

Mubarakpur Kotla

It is in a state of grave deterioration with buildings boxing it in from all sides. Moreover, it was not very clean when I visited. I was informed that the locals consider Mubarak Shah to be a *pir* (saint). They make offerings of flowers and sweets at his grave every Thursday, and clean the grave too.

Maqbara Muhammad Shah

It is located in the Lodi Gardens and is well preserved.

Maqbara Sultan Bahlol Lodi

It has been considerably encroached upon and is in a state of disrepair.

Panch Burja Zamarudpur

It is located behind Blue Bells International School at walking distance from Kailash Colony Metro Station. The tombs have been encroached from all sides, and the locals are suspicious and unfriendly. As one enters, the first tomb can be seen boxed in from all sides by houses. The residents wouldn't let us check inside. I had a tough time locating all the tombs. One of the tombs has been boxed in from all sides by high-rise buildings and I could locate it only after a local lady mentioned, 'There is some kind of a building here.' We had to climb six flights of stairs to the top of a tenement to find that the walls of modern buildings form a kind of well at the bottom of which a small dome can be seen.

The largest of these buildings is a cattle shed, and a part of it has been rented out to ragpickers. Another building is a twelve-arched pavilion (*baradari*) and is used by locals as a place to dry clothes. This area is outside municipal limits and so buildings have sprung on every side with rooms being offered for rent.

Basti Baori

This is the Jama Masjid of Defence Colony and a *madarsa* functions here. The gateway, which is used as a storeroom, was shut when we went there. The original building has been added to and the mosque is well maintained. The grave on top, however, is neglected. The step well or *baoli* was abandoned a long time ago. There is a modern tank for ablutions.

Moth ki Masjid

This is in the middle of a bustling locality of the same name. It is in a fair state of preservation, but has been hemmed in by buildings on all sides.

Maqbara Langar Khan

I have not been able to locate this tomb.

Ti-burja

Two of the tombs, known simply as 'Bade Khan' and 'Chhote Khan', are located inside a park in South Extension Part 1, and are well looked after. The third tomb, located near these two, is now known as 'Bhure Khan'. There is an ongoing dispute between a trading company and the ASI regarding the land between Bade Khan, Chote Khan and Bhure Khan, which is why Bhure Khan has been fenced in with barbed wire. What is known as Kale Khan's Gumbad is at a short distance in the same area, and exists in good condition as a stand-alone structure inside a park.

Rajo'n ki Bain
It is one of my favourite places in Delhi, located inside the Mehrauli Archaeological Park, and is very well maintained.

Maqbara Sultan Sikandar Bahlol
The tomb is situated inside the Lodi Gardens and is very well maintained.

Dargah Sheikh Yusuf Qattal
It is in Khirki and is well maintained. The locals revere it and light lamps and incense sticks.

Dargah Maulana Jamali
This *dargah* is like a jewel box with its colourful ceiling and decorations. It is inside the Mehrauli Archaeological Park and is kept locked to prevent vandalism.

Masjid Dargah Maulana Jamali
A very impressive and well-maintained mosque, it is located inside the Mehrauli Archaeological Park.

Neeli Chhatri
It is located opposite the Zafar Gate of Salimgarh Fort near the Nigambodh Ghat. The building is new, but it houses an ancient Shiva *lingam*. The temple is very revered, and while I was there, I saw many devotees. A priest keeps a fire burning at the spot where the original *yagya* conducted by Yudhishtir (the eldest Pandava in the *Mahabharata*) is said to have taken place.

Dargah Imam Zamin/Maqbara Sayyid Hussain Pa-e-Minar
Located inside the Qutub Complex, it is very well maintained.

Dargah Hazrat Qutub-ul-Aqtab
This is a very popular *dargah*. There have been many additions, including a dome in the main shrine of Qutub Sahib. There have been many encroachments on its periphery, and one of the

gateways to the Naubat Khana houses a gurudwara. However, once inside, the *dargah* itself is well maintained.

Masjid Qila Kuhna
It is not a functioning mosque but is well maintained.

Sher Mandal
It is closed to the public but is well maintained.

Masjid and Maqbara Khairpur
Known as the Bada Gumbad and Mosque, these are well-maintained structures, located inside Lodi Gardens.

Khari Baoli
There is now a street called Khari Baoli near the Fatehpuri Mosque, which is famous as Asia's largest wholesale spice market. Nothing remains of the step well (*baoli*).

Isa Khan's Tomb and Masjid
These are now inside the Humayun's Tomb complex and are well maintained. The Aga Khan Trust for Culture has done conservation work on the tomb.

Masjid Dargah Hazrat Qutub Sahib
The mosque is still in use and has undergone many renovations.

Arab Sarai
The Arab Sarai gateway has been restored recently by the Aga Khan Trust for Culture and is quite impressive. Some of its broken walls have also been rebuilt.

Khair-ul-Manazil
The mosque is still functioning and is looked after by 90-year-old Janab Bashir Ahmad Sahib, who lives in the premises. Living on donations and being a caretaker is difficult, as the place has no electricity and it is expensive to buy oil for the lamps needed to light the mosque at night. Besides, the rooms of the *madarsa* have mostly broken down and only a few remain. But there is a strange sense of peace in the place. The water from its well provides relief to many a thirsty tourist, and is also used for ablutions by the faithful.

Khas Mahal still existed in 1919, when Maulvi Zafar Hasan wrote *Monuments of Delhi*, though he describes it as being in a ruined state. It was an inn, and only the gateway and series of arched cells remained. Today, however, there is no trace of this structure.

Bhool Bhulaiyya'n/Tomb of Adham Khan

It was used as a rest house by the British who removed the two cenotaphs from inside. At some point of time, one of them was brought back. It is in a bad state despite continuous repairs. All the colour outside has been stripped off. The ceiling was repaired but looks desolate. The labyrinth has been closed off.

Humayun's Tomb

The Humayun's Tomb complex was declared a UNESCO World Heritage Site in 1993. It has been restored by the Aga Khan Trust for Culture in partnership with the Archaeological Survey of India (ASI), and is one of the most popular monuments in Delhi.

Neeli Chhatri or Tomb of Naubat Khan

This monument used to be within the premises of Delhi Public School, Mathura Road. Friends who studied there in the 1960s and 1970s remember it. It has since been demolished.

Maqbara Taka (Ataka/Atgha) Khan

Though the tomb itself is well preserved, it has been severely encroached upon. It has to be approached through the cluster of houses of people who live in this crowded area.

Dargah Hazrat Khwaja Baqi Billah

The *dargah* is very well maintained. Surrounding the mosque and shrine is a crowded cemetery.

Dargah Hazrat Amir Khusrau

The shrine itself is well maintained and very popular, but it is hemmed in on all sides by various additions that have been made to the *dargah*. In the outer enclosure to the south is buried Shams-ud-Din Mahru, the son of Amir Khusrau's sister.

Jail Khana/Sarai Farid Khan

The inn (*sarai*) no longer exists.

Barapula

A new flyover has been constructed here, which is also known as the Barapula. The old Barapula still exists, but it is in a state of disrepair and is used by vendors to sell vegetables and other things. It has been encroached upon on both sides and as I was counting, of the twelve *pulas*, I found that two were being used as a cycle-stand by the houses behind. It is quite filthy too.

Mandi
The wholesale market (*mandi*) no longer exists; the residents of Arab Sarai were resettled in Jangpura.

Kos Minara
There is a well-preserved Jahangiri Kos Minar inside Delhi Zoo and another one behind Apollo Hospital.

Pul Salimgarh
There is a well-maintained bridge connecting the two forts.

Maqbara Sheikh Farid
This tomb is located in a small compound, but as there are hutments all around, it is not very easy to access.

Neela Burj/Maqbara Fahim
Neela Burj is now a stand-alone monument that is located behind Humayun's Tomb, with a railway line running next to it. It has been treated badly by time, with the beautiful tilework having succumbed to the ravages of time. The Aga Khan Trust for Culture has undertaken restoration work on it, but even after restoration only two panels have survived – that too in a ruined state.

Chausath Khamba
This is a beautiful building. Unfortunately, however, it too has been encroached upon. The Aga Khan Trust for Culture has recently restored it.

Maqbara Khan-e-Khana
The Aga Khan Trust for Culture is currently restoring it. Somehow, to me, the shape of the building gives the impression of a plucked hen.

Maqbara Sayyid Abid
It is located inside the Delhi Golf Course complex with the swimming pool in front of it.

However, I go by the description and sketch by Sir Sayyid which shows the tomb and gate in front of the swimming pool. The ASI has marked a nearby tomb as Sayyid Abid's, but I disagree with that labelling.

Khas Mahal

Zain Khan Koka, son of Khwaja Masud of Herat, was Akbar's foster brother. His mother, Picha Jaan, was Akbar's wet nurse. This structure no longer exists.

Tomb of Sheikh Abdul Haq Muhaddis

It is in a good state of preservation and has a functioning mosque inside the complex.

Jama Masjid/Masjid Jahannuma

It still stands tall and is fairly well maintained. However, the steps that once were the heart of Delhi's cultural ethos are now home to beggars. There are no storytellers or sellers of unique animals. The surrounding area is now overcrowded, dirty and full of shops.

Dar-ul-Shifa and Dar-ul-Baqa

Both are no longer extant. Dar-ul-Shifa had collapsed by CE 1744 and houses were built over it.

Begum ka Bagh/Sahibabad

Begum Bagh was renamed Queen's Gardens by the British. Today, a statue of Mahatma Gandhi stands in the centre of the garden. It is situated north of the Town Hall. Its area has also been severely restricted.

Masjid Fatehpuri

Post-1857, the British auctioned this mosque to Rai Lala Chunnamal for Rs 19,000. In 1877, it was acquired by the government in exchange for four villages, and was restored to the Muslims. It is in a fair state of preservation and is a functioning mosque. Traffic snarls in front of it and the shops of Khari Baoli next to it hamper easy access.

Masjid Akbarabadi

The British destroyed this mosque after the Revolt of 1857. Sir Sayyid used the calligraphic inscriptions on it and set these up in another mosque made in its image, in Aligarh Muslim University. In 2012, the remains of a Mughal building were found in Subhash Park by the DMRC while they were digging for metro work. However, there is no conclusive proof that these are the remains of the Akbarabadi mosque.

Masjid Sirhindi

It is outside Lahori Gate and has fared badly at the hands of time and poor maintenance.

Bagh Shalimar

Its original name was Azizabad Bagh, most probably after Shahjahan's wife, Akbarabadi Begum, whose given name was Aziz-un-Nisa Begum. It was here that Aurangzeb crowned himself Emperor on 31 July 1658. The *khutba* was read out at his second coronation. Today, the garden is in North Delhi, and is very popular with locals for walking and relaxing. The Shish Mahal still remains as do two pavilions, and these are fenced off from the rest of the gardens. They are in ruins, and permission to enter is given on request. The British Residents Octerlony and Charles Metcalfe used the garden as a summer retreat.

Bagh Roshan Ara

It is situated in Shakti Nagar near the Kamla Nagar Clock Tower. Only two buildings remain in the garden: a gate and a central pavilion, which became Princess Roshan Ara's tomb. The British converted the four-lawn (*charbagh*) arrangement into a European-style park in the nineteenth century. In 1922, the British established the elite Roshan Ara Club here. A road runs between the Cricket Club and Roshan Ara's tomb pavilion, dividing them into two separate parks.

Bagh Sirhindi

I have been unable to locate this garden.

Muhajjar Jahan Ara Begum

Relatives of mentally disturbed women bring them to the stone enclosure [*muhajjar*] built around Princess Jahan Ara's tomb and tie them here for miraculous cure. It is quite a heartrending sight.

Maqbara Sar Nala

I could find no contemporary reference to this *dargah*. It probably no longer exists.

Dargah Sayyid Hazrat Hasan Rasul Numa

During the eighteenth century, this *dargah* was the scene of many cultural activities, along with the *dargahs* of Qadam Sharif, Hazrat Nizam-ud-Din Auliya and Roshan Chiragh Dehli. Situated on Panchkuian Road of today, it is surrounded by slums. The tomb area itself has received a makeover, but people living all around block its approach.

Jharna

It has been encroached by houses on all sides and is used as a playground for children. It is no longer used during the *Phool Walo'n ki Sair*. There exists one broken-down rock which could have been the *phisalna pathhar* [stone to slide down upon], but it is outside the present boundary and there is wild vegetation all around. It was recently restored by the Indian National Trust for Art and Cultural Heritage (INTACH), but it remains a pale shadow of its former glory.

Masjid Aurangabadi

It no longer exists and was probably demolished after the 1857 Revolt.

Maqbara Zeb-un-Nisa Begum

The inscription on the headstone of Zeb-un-Nisa's tomb reads: 'A fountain of learning, virtue, beauty and elegance. She was hidden as Joseph was, in the well. I asked Reason the year of her death. The invisible voice exclaimed "The moon became concealed."'

Moti Masjid

It is boxed inside Zafar Mahal and Qutub Sahab's *dargah*. The marble is yellowing and there are signs of deterioration. There were two attractive pavilions on the minarets, but Emperor Bahadur Shah Zafar got them taken down in the year 1846 as they had been damaged and there was a fear of them falling down. It is unfortunate indeed that the structure has not been repaired.

Zeenat-ul-Masajid

This mosque was badly damaged during the Revolt of 1857, and it was used as artillery barracks in its aftermath. The marble pulpit was removed. It was also used as a bakery for the troops. The tomb was destroyed immediately after the events of 1857, the marble monument was removed and the grave levelled to the ground. The tomb has now been rebuilt on the southern end of the mosque in a corner, as a memorial to the princess who built the mosque, with the rest of the space being taken up by an office of the Jamaat-e-Ulema-e-Hind.

Maqbara Ghazi-ud-Din Khan

This *madarsa* housed the famous Delhi College which was later renamed Zakir Hussain College. The college has now shifted to new premises but the Anglo-Arabic School continues to be run in the old *madarsa*. The mausoleum with its exquisite carved screens is still beautiful. It is closed to visitors.

Muhajjar Shah Alam Bahadur Shah

Like the rest of Zafar Mahal, this stone enclosure (*muhajjar*) too is in a state of total disrepair. The marble screen has broken in many places and the finials are missing. This enclosure is now famous as the *sardgah* (the place where he wanted to be buried) of Bahadur Shah Zafar, who had wanted to be buried here with his father. An empty grassy space denotes the area. The headstones and verses inscribed on the doorway have all disappeared.

The Burj inside Humayun's Tomb

Today this tomb is famous as the Barber's Tomb for unknown reasons.

Sunehri Masjid Kotwali

The mosque is of considerable historical importance as it was from here that Nadir Shah ordered and witnessed the massacre of the citizens of Delhi. Shops have encroached into its premises, limiting it to an upper storey only. There are residences on the first floor, built very close to the main mosque.

Mosque and Madarsa of Sharf-ud-Daulah

I have not been able to locate this mosque. Perhaps it no longer exists.

Jantar Mantar

Though severely damaged during the 1857 Revolt, it was subsequently restored and now exists as a popular tourist spot.

Shah-e-Mardan

This now lies within B.K. Dutt Colony and is the centre of Shia religious activities. Considerable additions and alterations have been made to it and it is well maintained. Gatherings are now held throughout the year and particularly during the month of Muharram. There is an ongoing dispute between the *dargah* authority and the owners of Rajdhani Nursery, which is situated on leased land in the Karbala. Anjuman-e-Haideri, which looks after the *dargah*, claims that the lease has expired, while the nursery owners claim that the court recognizes them as lease-holders. There have been several clashes and protests, and as a result there is always a heavy police presence in the Karbala.

Fakhr-ul-Masajid

The left wall of the mosque and the colonnade on the same side were damaged during the siege of Delhi by the British in 1857. A cannon ball also dismantled the pavilion of the minaret in the north-eastern corner. Like all other monuments it is encroached upon and is showing signs of deterioration. The mosque is on the first floor and there are shops underneath it. A *madarsa* functions here with the students living on its premises.

Bagh Mahaldar Khan

The Tripolia Gate still stands but the garden has disappeared. Repairs undertaken to preserve the gate resulted in a lowering of the level of the road under it. The gateway to the garden still stands forlorn. There are car-repair shops where once the garden existed.

Ghat Nigambodh

This ghat on the Yamuna river, behind Red Fort, still functions as a cremation ground for Hindus. It has an electric crematorium built in the 1950s as well as a CNG-run crematorium added in 2006. The Municipal Corporation of Delhi (MCD) manages it.

Masjid Roshan-ud-Daula

This mosque was also known as Qazi-Zadiyo'n ki Masjid. I have been unable to locate it.

Bagh-e-Nazir

From what I could gather from the monks in Ashoka Mission, the family of Roz Afsun fared badly in the riots that followed the Partition of India in 1947. The lone survivor, a young boy, migrated to Pakistan. In 1948, Prime Minister Jawaharlal Nehru gifted the land to the Cambodian monk, Dharmavara Mahathera, on behalf of the Indian state for establishing a Buddhist institution. It was he who founded the Ashoka Mission there. It is now the official Buddhist Mission in Delhi.

Muhajjar Badshah Muhammad Shah

Although this stone enclosure is not in the best of conditions, one can imagine what its former beauty must have been.

Qudsia Bagh

In 1857, a battery was located in this garden and it was badly damaged. Most of the buildings have disappeared and all that remains now are a gateway in a dilapidated condition and a colonial-style guest house. The mosque is a functioning one and although one can see the battlemarks of 1857 on it, it is well maintained. A large part of the garden was used to construct the Inter-State Bus Terminus (ISBT) and the adjacent tourist campsite. It is a popular park for locals.

Chobi Masjid/ Wooden Mosque

This mosque must have been destroyed post 1857, when the British built their barracks in Mehtab Bagh, as no trace of it exists now. According to Maulvi Zafar Hasan, the mosque probably came up at the site of a structure built by Emperor Farukhsiyar, where he imprisoned the saint Shah Muhammad Ali Waez who had come to seek the emperor's protection from the atrocities of the Governor of Gujarat, Chanpat Singh. Chanpat Singh instigated the emperor to imprison the saint. Later Farukhsiyar had a dream asking him to set the saint free, which he promptly did. The saint spent his time preaching and living in the Jama Masjid of Shahjahanabad.

Sunehri Masjid

The mosque is a functioning one even today, its structure is well maintained and the upkeep, good.

Mansoor's Tomb (Safdarjung's Tomb)

It is in very good condition and it is a popular tourist spot. The mosque is used for Friday congregational prayers and kept locked on all other days.

Kalka Temple

The temple is extremely popular in Delhi and I had to stand in a long line to enter the premises. One is allowed very little time to see the main idol and there are many priests inside. There are also many buildings built all around the main temple.

Lal Bangla

These monuments are in the parking lot of Delhi Golf Club and are under the ASI. They are in a fairly good state of preservation. There are no stone enclosures and the courtyard has been curtailed, with the kitchens situated very close to it. Only the smaller domed building has two tombs which, judging from the *takhti*, have female occupants. The bigger building has no centotaph or tomb.

Tomb of Najaf Khan

In good condition, the tomb is popular with the locals because of its sprawling and well-maintained gardens.

Larger Jain Temple

It is beautifully maintained and many additions have been made.

Church

Many changes, additions and extensions have been made. This beautiful church, known as St James Church, holds regular service on Sundays. It saw hectic fighting during the 1857 Revolt and suffered some damage. The copper ball and cross on the top, which are said to be replica of a church in Venice, were damaged in 1857 and were later replaced. The Church Committee approached INTACH (Indian National Trust for Art and Cultural Heritage) in 1996 for repairs, and along with a grant from the Delhi government and the support of Queen Elizabeth II of Britian, the Indian Army Regiment of Skinners Horse, INTACH UK Trust, British Council, and personalities, such as Mrs Sumitra Charatram, Mrs Roula Shriram, Lt. Col. C.R.D. Gray and Sir Bernard Feilden, it was successfully restored.

Jogmaya Temple

This is a very popular temple. Under Akbar Shah II, the *Phool Walo'n ki Sair* started from here with a floral offering being made to the deity. The tradition continues till today, though the offering is made on the second day. Many additions have been made to the medieval temple.

Small Jain Temple

Interestingly, this is now known as the Shree Digambar Jain Bada Mandir.

Kothi Jahannuma

It was damaged during the 1857 Revolt, but was later repaired by Thomas Metcalfe's son, Sir Theophilus Metcalfe, who inherited it. It was more popular by the name Matka Kothi – a corruption of the name, Metcalfe – given to it by the labourers working there . After passing through the hands of various owners, it was finally acquired by the Government of India. Between 1920 and 1926, it was the seat of the Council of State of the Central Legislative Assembly. It is now the office of the Defence Scientific Information and Documentation Centre, Defence Terrain Research Laboratory and many other divisions of the Defence Research and Development Organization (DRDO), and is out of bounds to the general public.

Muhajjar Mirza Jahangir

This enclosure is now in a sorry state of disrepair. It is used as a shortcut to enter the Dargah of Hazrat Nizam-ud-Din Auliya. The prince remains forgotten.

Zafar Mahal

British officers used the tank as a swimming pool post-1857. It is now empty, and a forlorn Zafar Mahal pavilion stands in the centre.

Hira Mahal

A solitary pavilion stands all by itself looking quite out of place without its fountains and canals. It is out of bounds for tourists.

Kothi Dilkusha

The maximum praise in the first edition of Sir Sayyid's book is reserved for Metcalfe, to whom the book is dedicated. Kothi Dikusha (built on a former tomb) now lies within Mehrauli Archaeological Park. The adjoining buildings made by Metcalfe are in a ruinous state, but the tomb itself has been restored. The rooms that were added on the plinth of the tomb have disappeared.

Baoli Dargah Hazrat Qutub Sahib

This step well is kept closed and out of bounds. I was fortunate to be allowed to visit it by the hereditary caretaker (*khadim*). The structure is still strong but dirty from being closed off. The water in the step well, despite repairs, is filthy.

Iron Bridge on River Hindon

It is now a concrete bridge.

Lal Diggi

It was destroyed in 1857.

New Bridge of Nigambodh

All bridges now are of concrete.

Notes

[1] Gordon Sanderson, *Delhi Fort: A Guide to the Buildings and Gardens*, Delhi: Asian Educational Services, 2000; reprint of the facsimile edition of 1914.

[2] Gordon Risley Hearn, *The Seven Cities of Delhi*, Delhi: W. Thacker & Company, 1906.

[3] *Asiatic Review*, Vol. 4, London.

Inscriptions

I am including here, for the benefit of the reader, inscriptions that have been referred to but are not a part of the first edition (*Asar-1*). The first two inscriptions below are from Gordon Sanderson, *Delhi Fort: A Guide to the Buildings and Gardens* (Delhi: Asian Editorial Services India, 2000; reprint of the facsimile edition of 1914). The other inscriptions are taken from Maulvi Zafar Hasan, *Monuments of Delhi* (Delhi: Aryan Books International, 2008).

Inscriptions on Burj Tila or Musamman Burj

The inscriptions on the western arch of Musamman Burj, inscribed in the reign of Akbar II, read as follows.

The first inscription:

> Praise and thankfulness are worthy of the Lord of the World.
>
> Who made such an Emperor the King of the Age;
>
> Who is descended from a royal father and a grandfather down from Timur;
>
> (And is the) protector of the world having his court (as high as the) sky, and soldiers (as numerous) as the stars,
>
> Muin-ud-Din Abu-n-Nasr Akbar, Ghazi,
>
> King of the World, conqueror of the age, and shadow of God,
>
> On the face of Musamman Burj, built anew such a seat that the sun and the moon sewed (fixed) their eyes on it.
>
> Sayyid-us-Shu'ara was odered to record its date, so that the black letters may endure on the white (ground)
>
> The Sayyid wrote the chronogram of this building:
>
> 'May the seat of Akbar Shah be of exalted foundation. The year AH 1223'.

The second inscription:

> O! Thou who hast fetters on the legs, and a padlock on thy heart, beware! And thou who hast thine eyelids sewn up and feet in the mire, beware!

Bound towards the west and having thy face to the east, O Traveller who hast
turned thy back on thy destination, Beware!

Inscription on the arches of the balcony:

Praise and commendation are due to the Lord of the World (God) who made the King of
the age, like the Emperor who is descended from a royal father and grandfather up to
Timur, and is the protection of the world, having sky-like mansions and soldiers as (as
numerous) stars Muin-ud-Din Abu Nasr Akbar, the champion of the faith, the king of the
world, the world conqueror of the age, and the shadow of God.

On the face of octoganal tower built anew, such a seat that the sun and the moon fixed
their eyes on it.

The Sayyid-us-Shu'ara (poet-laureate) was ordered to find its date, in order that black
letters may remain written on the white (ground).

The chief poet wrote down as the chronogram of this building: 'The seat of exalted
foundation is Akbar Shah.' The year AH 1223.

Tasbih Khana

Translation of the inscription on the wall:[1]

May the Emperor of the World, Shahjahan, by his good fortune, the second Lord of felicity,
In the royal palace, with great magnificence, ever be like the sun in the sky.
As long as foundation is indispensable with his building,
May the palace of his good fortune touch the highest heaven.
Wonderfully charming is this adorned palace,
A paradise embellished with a hundred beauties
Dignity is a sign to represent its greatness;
Felicity is in the embraces of its hall
[incomplete]
[incomplete]
Whoever rubbed his head sincerely against its foot,
His honour increased, like (the swelling) of the (river) Jun (Yamuna)
When time erected its wall,
It set a mirror before the face of the sun.
The face of its wall is so decorated, that it demands from the painters of
China a fee for showing its face,
Time extended such an (affectionate) hand over its head,
That the sky borrowed height from it.
In its playing fountains, and river like tank,

The sky washed its face with the water of the earth.

As it is the seat of a just king

So it is the King of all buildings.

Iron Pillar – Quwwat-ul Islam Mosque

The inscription on the pillar:

He on whose arm fame was inscribed by the sword, when in battle in the Vanga countries, he kneaded (and turned) back with (his) breast the enemies who uniting together, came against (him):-he, by whom, having crossed in warfare the seven months of the river (Sindhu), the Vahlikas were conquered: he, by the breezes of whose prowess the southern ocean is even still perfumed;-

[Line 3] He, the remnant of the great zeal of whose energy, which utterly destroyed (his) enemies like (the remnant of the great glowing heat) of a burned out fire in a great forest even now leaves not the earth; though he, the king, as if wearied, has quitted this earth, and has gone to the other world, moving in (bodily) form to the land (of paradise) won by (the merit of his) actions, (but) remaining on (this) earth (by the memory) of his fame;-

[Line 5] By him, the king,- who attained sole supreme sovereignty in the world, acquired by his own arm and (enjoyed) for a very long time; (and) who, having the name Chandra, carried a beauty of countenance like (the beauty of) the full moon, having in faith fixed his mind upon (the God) Vishnu, this lofty standard of the divine Vishnu was set up on the hill (called) Vishnupada.

The Edicts on the Ashoka Pillar in Firoz Shah Kotla

Edict I

The Principles of Government

Thus saith His Sacred and Gracious Majesty the King: When I had been consecrated twenty-six years, I caused this pious edict to be written. Both this world and the next are difficult to secure save by intense love of the Law of Piety, intense self-examination, intense obedience, intense dread, intense effort. However, owing to my instructions, this yearning for the Law of Piety, this love of the Law from day to day have grown and will grow.

My Agents, too, whether of high or low or middle rank, themselves conform to my teaching and lead others in the right way – fickle people must be led into the right way – and the Wardens of the Marches act in like manner. For this is the rule – protection by the law of Piety, regulation by that Law, felicity by that Law and protection by that Law.

Edict II

The Royal Example

Thus saith His Sacred and gracious Majesty the King: 'The Law of Piety is excellent'. But wherein consists the Law of Piety? In these things, to wit, little impiety, many good deeds, compassion, liberality, truthfulness and purity.

The gift of spiritual insight I have given in manifold ways; whilst on two-footed and four-footed beings, on birds and the denizens of the waters, I have conferred various favours – even unto the boon of life and many other good deeds I have done.

For this my purpose have I caused this pious edict to be written, that men may walk after its teaching and that it may long endure; and he who will follow its teaching will do well.

Edict III

Self-examination

Thus saith His Sacred and gracious Majesty the King: Man sees his every good deed and says, 'This good deed I have done'. In no wise does he see his evil deed and say, 'This evil deed I have done, this act called impiety'.

Difficult however, is self-examination of this kind. Nevertheless, a man should see to this, that brutality, cruelty, anger, pride and jealousy are the things that lead to impiety and should say, 'By reason of these may I not fall'.

This is chiefly to be seen to – 'the one course avails me for the present world, the other course avails me also for the world to come'.

Edict IV

The Powers and Duties of Commissioners

Thus saith His Sacred and gracious Majesty the King: When I had been consecrated twenty-six years I caused this pious edict to be written. My commissioners had been set over many hundred thousands of the people, and to them I have granted independence in the award of honours and penalties in order that the Commissioners confidently and fearlessly may perform their duties, bestow welfare and happiness to the people of the country and confer favours upon them.

They will ascertain the causes of happiness or unhappiness and through the subordinate officials of the Law of Piety will exhort the people of the country so that they may gain both this world and the next.

My Commissioners, too, are eager to serve me, while my agents will obey my will and orders and they too, on occasion, will give exhortations, whereby the Commissioners will be zealous to win my favour.

For, just as a man, having made over his child to a skilful nurse, feels confident and says to himself, 'the skilful nurse is zealous to take care of my child's happiness' even so my Commissioners have been created for the welfare and happiness of the country, with intent that fearlessly, confidently and quietly perform their duties. For that reason my Commissioners have been granted independence in the award of honours and penalties. For as much as it is desirable that there should be uniformity in judicial procedure and uniformity in penalties, from this time forward my rule is this: 'To condemned men lying in prison under sentence of death a respite of three days is granted by me.'

During this interval the relatives of some of the condemned men will invite them to deep meditation, hoping to save their lives, or, in order to lead to meditation him about to die, will themselves give alms with a view to the other world or undergo fasting. For my desire is that, even in the time of their confinement, the condemned men may gain the enxt world and that among the people, pious practices of various kinds may grow, including self control and distribution of alms.

Edict V

Regulations Restricting Slaughter and Mutilation of Animals

Thus saith His Sacred and gracious Majesty the King: When I had been consecrated twenty-six years the following species were declared exempt from slaughter, namely: parrots, starlings. Adjutants, Barhamany ducks, geese, nandimukhas, gelatas, bats, queen-ants, female tortoises, bones fish, vedaveyakas. Gangapuputakas, skate, (river) tortoises, porcupines, tree squirrels, barasingha stags, Brahmany bulls, monkeys, rhinoceros, grey doves, village pigeons and all four footed animals which are not utilized or eaten. She-goats, ewes and sow, that is to say, those either with young or in milk are exempt from slaughter as well as their offspring upto six months of age.

The caponing of cocks must not be done.

Chaff must not be burnt along with living things in it.

Forests must not be burned, either for mischief or so as to destroy living creatures.

The living must not be fed to the living. At each of the three seasonal full moons, and at the full moon of the month of Tishya (December–January), for three days in each case, namely the fourteenth and fifteenth days of the first fortnight and the last day of the second fortnight, as well as on the fast days throughout the year, fish is exempt from killing and may not be sold.

On the same days in elephant preserves or fish ponds no other classes of animals may be destroyed./On the eighth, fourteenth and fifteenth days of each fortnight as well as on the Tishya and Punarvasu days, on the seasonal full moon days and during the fortnights of the seasonal full-moons the branding of horses and oxen must not be done.

During the time up to the twenty-sixth anniversary of my consecration twenty-five jail deliveries have been affected.

Edict VI

The Necessity of a Definite Creed

Thus saith His Sacred and gracious Majesty the King: When I had been consecrated twelve years I caused pious edicts to be written for the welfare and happiness of mankind, with the intent that they, giving up their old courses, might obtain growth in piety, one way or another.

Thus, aiming at the welfare and happiness of mankind, I devote my attention like my relatives, to persons near and to persons afar off, if haply I might guide some of them to happiness, and to that end I make my arrangements.

In like manner I devote my attention to all communities, for all denominations are revered by me with various forms of reverence. Nevertheless, personal adherence to one's own creed is the chief thing in my opinion. When I had been consecrated for twenty-six years I caused this pious edict to be written.

Edict VII

Review of the King's Measures for the Propagation of the Law of Piety

I. Thus saith His Sacred and gracious Majesty the King: The kings who lived in tmes past desired that men might grow with the growth of the Law of Piety. Men, however, did not grow with the growth of the Law of Piety.

II. Therefore, thus saith His Sacred and gracious Majesty the King: This thought occurred to me: In times past kings desired that men might grow with the growth of the Law of Piety in due proportion; men, however, did not in due proportion grow with the growth of that Law.

III. By what means, then, can men be induced to conform? By what means can men grow with the growth of the Law of Piety in due proportion? By what means can I lift up some at least of them through the growth of that Law?

Therefore, Thus saith His Sacred and gracious Majesty the King: This thought occurred to me : I will cause the precepts of Law of Piety to be preached and with instruction in that Law will I instruct, so that men hearkening thereto may conform, lift themselves up and mightily grow with the growth of the Law of Piety.

For this my purpose the precepts of the Law of Piety have been preached, manifold instructions in that law have been disseminated, so that my Agents, too, set over the multitude will expound and expand my teaching.

The Commissioners, also, set over many hundred thousands of souls, have received instructions – 'In such and such a manner expound on my teaching to the body of subordinate officials of the Law.'

IV. Thus saith His Sacred and gracious Majesty the King: Considering further the same purpose, I have set up Pillars of the Law, appointed Censors of the Law, and composed a precept of the Law.

V. Thus saith His Sacred and gracious Majesty the King: On the roads, too, I have had banyan trees planted to give shade to man and beast; groves of mango trees I have had planted; at every half kos I have caused wells to be dug; rest-houses have been erected; and numerous watering-places have been provided by me here and there for The enjoyment of man and beast.

A small matter, however, is that so-called enjoyment.

With various blessings has mankind been blessed by former kings, as by me also; by me; however, with the intent that men may conform to the Law of Piety, has it been done even as I thought.

VI. Thus saith His Sacred and gracious Majesty the King: My Censors of the Law of Piety are employed on manifold objects of the royal favour affecting both ascetics and householders and are likewise employed amongst all denominations. Moreover, I have arranged for their employment in the business of the Church and in the same way I have employed among the Brahmans and the Ajivikas and among other Jains also are they employed and in fact, among all the different denominations.The ordinary high officers shall severally superintend their respective charges, whereas the officers who are Censors of the Law are employed in the superintendence of all other denominations in addition to such charges.

VII. Thus saith His Sacred and gracious Majesty the King: These and many other high officers are employed in the distribution of the royal alms, both my own and those of the Queens; and in all the royal households, both here (capital) and in the provinces, those officers indicate in diverse ways the manifold opportunities for charity.

VIII. I have also arranged that the same officers should be employed in the distribution of the alms of my sons and the Princes, the Queens' sons, in order to promote pious acts and conformity to the Law of Piety. For the pious acts and conformity referred to to are those who whereby compassion, liberality, truth, purity, gentleness and saintliness will thus grow among mankind.

IX. Thus saith His Sacred and gracious Majesty the King: Whatsoever, meritorious deeds I have done, those deeds mankind have conformed to and will imitate, whence follows that they have grown and will grow in the virtues of hearkening to father and mother, hearkening to teachers, reverence to the aged, and seemly treatment of Brahmans and ascetics, of the poor and wretched, yea even of slaves and servants.

Thus saith His Sacred and Gracious Majesty the King: Among men however, when the aforesaid growth of piety has grown, it has been affected by twofold means, namely by pious regulations and meditation. Of those two means pious regulations are of small account, whereas meditation is superior.

Nevertheless, pious regulations have been issued by me to the effect that such and such species are exempt from slaughter, and there are many other pious regulations which I have issued. But the superior effect of meditation is seen in the growth of piety among men and the more complete abstention from killing animate beings and from the sacrificial slaughter of living creatures.

For this purpose has this edict been composed that so long as sun and moon endure, my sons and descedants may conform thereto, and by such conformity the gain of both this world and the next is assured.

When I have been consecrated twenty-seven years I caused this pious edict to be written.

X. Concerning this his Sacred Majesty saith: Wheresoever stone pillars or tables or stone exist, there must this pious edict be inscribed, so that it may long endure.

The second inscription on this pillar is in the name of Bisaldev Chauhan, the King of Sambhar, from where the Chauhans originated. He attacked the Tomars of Delhi and attained victory over them. Rai Pithaura got a proclamation of his victory inscribed on it in CE 1163. The inscription is in Nagari and Sanskrit. These *shlokas* can be easily read. This inscription praises Bisaldev and enumerates his virtues and describes that he conquered India and established peace. The inscription is:

In the year AH 1220 or (CE 1163) on the 15th day of the bright half of the month of Vaisakh, this moon of the fortunate Visala Deva, son of the fortunate Vella Deva, king of Sakambhari. As far as the Vindhyas, as far as the Himadri, having achieved conquest in the course of travelling to holy places; resentful to haughty kings, and indulgent to those whose necks are humbled, making Aryavarta once more what its name signifies, by causing the barbarians to be exterminated; Visala Deva, supreme ruler of Sakambhari and Sovereign of the earth is victorious in the world. This conqueror, the fortunate Vigraha Raja, King of Sakambhari, most eminent of the tribe which sprang from the arms (of Brahma) now addresses his own descendants: By us the region of the earth between Himavat and Vindhya has been made tributary; let not your minds be void of exertion to subdue the remainder. Tears are evident in the eyes of the enemy's consort; blades of grass are perceived by their adversaries' teeth; thy fame is predominant throughout

space; the minds of thy foes are void (of hope); their route is the desert where men
are hindered from passing; O Vigraha Raja Deva! In the jubilee occasioned by their
march, may thy abode, O Vigraha, sovereign of the earth be fixed, as in reason
it ought, in the bosoms (akin to the mansion of dalliance) of the women with beautiful
eyebrows who were married to thy enemies! There is no doubt of thy being the highest
of embodied souls. Did thou not sleep in the lap of Sri whom thou didst seize from the
ocean, of the bright half of the month Vaisakh. This was written in the presence
of and by Sri-pati, the son of Mahava Akhyastha, of a family in Ganda at this time
the fortunate Lakshana Pala, a Rajputra, is Prime Minister. Siva the Terrible and the
universal Monarch.

Qutub Sahib ki Lath/Qutub Minar

Inscription in the basement

On the doorway of the minar is inscribed:

> ... of this Minarah was Fazl Abul Ma'ali

Inscription on the first band

> The Amir. The commander of the army, the glorious, the great.[2]

Inscription on the second band

> ... necks of the people, master of the kings of Arabia and Persia, the most just of the
> Sultans in the world, Muiz-ud-dunya-wa-din... the shadow of God in East and West, the
> shepherd of the servants of God, the defender of the counties of God... the firm... sky,
> victorious against the enemies... the glory of the magnificent nation, the sky of merits.
> .. the sultan of land and sea, the guard of the kingdom of the world, the proclaimer of
> the word of god which is the highest, and the second Alexander (named) Abul Muzaffar
> Muhammad ibn Sam, may God perpetuate his kingdom and rule. And Allah is high, besides
> whom there is no God; and knows what is revealed and he is Most Compassionate and
> Merciful.

Inscription on the third band

This band cites the first six verses of Sura 48 of the Holy Quran.

Inscription on the fourth band

> The greatest Sultan, the most exalted emperor, the lord of the necks of people, the
> master of the kings of Arabia and Persia, the sultan of the sultans of the world, Ghiyas-
> ud-Dunya-wa-Din, who rendered Islam and the Muslims powerful, the reviver of justice
> in the worlds, the grandeur of the victorious government... the magnificent, the bright
> blaze of the khilafat, the propagator of kindness and mercy amongst created beings, the
> shadow of God in East and West, the defender of the countries of God, the shepherd of

the servants of God, the guards of the kingdoms of the world, and the proclaimer of the word of God, which is the highest, Abu... Bin Sam, an ally of Amir-ul-Momineen, may God illumine his arguments.

Inscription on the fifth band

This band cites Surah 59, verses 22 and 23 from the Quran.

Inscription on the sixth band

This band cites Sura 2, verses 255–260.

Inscription on the entrance doorway

The Prophet, on whom be God's blessing and peace, said, 'He who builds a mosque for God, God will build for him a similar house in paradise.' The fabric of the minar of his holiness and majesty, the king of kings Shams-ud-Dunya-wa-Din, who has received God's pardon and forgiveness (the deceased), may his grave be purified, and may paradise be his resting place was injured. The said minar during the reign of the great, the illustrious and exalted king, Sikandar Shah, the son of Bahlol Shah Sultan, may God perpetuate his kingdom and exalt his power and prestige and reign under the superintendence of Khanzada Fath Khan and son of Masnad-e-Ali Khwas Khan was restored, and its upper storeys were repaired together with setting in order the quadrangle and filling in joints. On the first day of Rabia II in the year AH 909 (23 September CE 1503).

Inscriptions on the second storey

Lower band inscription:

The most exalted Sultan, the great emperor, the lord of the necks of the people, the pride of the kings of Arabia and Persia, the shadow of God in the world, Shams-ud-Dunya-wa-Din, the help of Islam and the Muslims, the victorious governments, the majesty of the shining religion, helped from the heavens, victorious over his enemies, the bright meteor of the sky of the khilafat, the propagator of justice and kindness, the guard of the kingdoms of the world and the proclaimer of the word of the high God (named) Abul Muzaffar Altamush-as-Sultani, the helper of the prince of the faithful, may God perpetuate his kingdom and rule and increase his power and rank.

Inscription on the upper band:

This band cites Sura 14, verses 29–30 and Sura 62, verses 9–10 of the Holy Quran.

On the doorway (to the balcony) is inscribed:

The completion of this building was commanded by the king, who is helped from the heavens (named) Shams-ul-Haq-wa-Din Altamush-al-Qutbi, the helper of the prince of the faithful.

Inscriptions on the third storey

The great sultan, the most exalted emperor, the lord of the necks of the people, the master of the kings of Arabia and Persia, the king of kings in the world, the protector of the lands of God, the helper... khalifa of God... of Islam and Muslims, the help of the kings and sultans, the defender of the lands of God, the shepherd of the servants of God, the right hand of the khilafat, and the promulgator of justice and kindness (named) Abul Muzaffar Altamush-as-Sultani, the helper of prince of the faithful, may God perpetuate his kingdom and rule, and increase his power and rank.

On the doorway:

The great Sultan, the most exalted emperor, the lord of the necks of the people who vies with the kings of Arabia and Persia, helped from the heavens, victorious over his enemies, the sultan of the earth of God, the protector of the lands of God, the proclaimer of the word of the high God, the splendour of the victorious rule, the administration of the refulgent religion (named) Shams-ud-Din-Duniya-wa-Din, the help of Islam and the Muslims, the shadow of God in the world, the crown of the sovereignty and the people, the source of justice and mercy, the king of kings of the empire and religion, the right hand of the Khalifa of God, the helper of the prince of the faithful.

On the side of the door:

This building was completed under the superintendence of the slave, the sinner, Muhammad Amir Koh.

Inscription on the fourth storey

The erection of this building was ordered during the reign of the most exalted Sultan, the great emperor, the lord of the necks of the people, Shams-ud-Dunya-wa-Din who renders Islam and the Muslims powerful, who affords security and protection, the heir of the kingdom of Solomon (named) Abul Muzaffar Altamush-as-Sultan, the helper of the prince of the faithful.

Inscription on the fifth storey

On the doorway:

This minaret was injured by lightening (in the months of) the year AH 770. By the divine grace Firoz Sultan, who is exalted by the favour of the most Holy, built this portion of the edifice with care. May the inscrutable Creator preserve from all calamities.

There are two Nagari inscriptions in this storey. The first is dated Samvat 1425 (CE 1368) and contains the name of Firoz Shah, and the second, on the outer door *jamb*, is dated a year later than the first one, but contains the same name. The latter also gives the name of Nana Salha, son of Chahada Deva Tala, as the architect responsible for the repair work.

Alai Darwaza: Qutub Complex

On the marble architrave around the eastern archway:[3]

The erection of this noble edifice and foundation of this lofty building were undertaken in

the reign and during the kingship of the lord of the kings of the world, the king of Darius
like splendour, the sultan of perfect justice and abundant benevolence, the emperor
whose orders are universally obeyed, the exalter of the pulpits of Islam, the reviver of the
impressions of the commandments (of God), the founder of the pulpits of Islam, the exalter
of the foundation of the places of worship, the founder of the guiding cities, the destroyer
of erring countries... the crown of kingdom... the throne of royalty, the expounder of the
laws of holy war, the elucidator of the arguments of ijtihad [legal or theological decision],
the master of the counties... the exalter of the foundation of the mehrabs and mimbars
of Islam, the destroyer of the foundation places of idol worship, the maker of the rules of
charity, the destroyer of drinking houses, the king, the conqueror of countries, the shadow
of the mercy of God, helped with the help of God (named) Abul Muzaffar Muhammad Shah
the king, the right arm of the khilafat, the ally of Amir-ul-Momineen may God perpetuate
his kingdom in reward of his building of mosques, and continue his rule forever for his
illuminating of places of worship and preserve him in his kingdom and rule as long as the
world exists and this Sura is read: 'Praise be unto Him who transported His servants by
night from the sacred mosque (of Mecca) to the Masjid al Aqsa.'[4] [Constructed] on 15th
Shawal, the year AH 716 (7 March 1311).

On the arch face upper band (marble):

By the order of the chosen of the merciful God, the master of the countries of the
world, the Solomon-like king, great in the world and in faith, the consoler of Islam and
the Muslims, the bestower of honour on kings and princes, the founder of a charitable
building.... Athiests, the exalter of the foundation of mehraba and mimbar (named) Abul
Muzaffar Muhammad Shah, the king, the right arm of the khilafat, the ally of the Amir-ul-
Momineen, may God perpetuate his kingdom until the day of judgement, this mosque of
delightful pillars and firm foundations was erected.

On the arch face lower band (red sandstone):

This famous congregational mosque... The chosen of the merciful God, the Alexander of
his age, great in the world and in the faith, king of kings of the world, compeer of the moon
... Abul Muzaffar Muhammad Shah, the king, the right arm of the khilafat, the ally of the
Amir-ul-Momineen

On the marble architrave around the western archway:

When the Almighty God whose glory is great and whose names are exalted, chose the
Lord of the kings of the world to revive the observances of the faith and raise the banners
of religion so that the foundation of the religion of Muhammad become increasingly
firm every moment, and the foundation of the law of the religion of Ahmad may be
increasingly strengthened every instant, and for the perpetuation of the kingdom and

the administration of the government, and the erection of the mosques for worship, in compliance with the order of Him except Whom there is no God; ' He shall build the mosque who believeth in God[5]... Abul Muzaffar Muhammad Shah, the king, the right arm of the khilafat, the ally of the Amir-ul-Momineen, may God continue his kingdom until the day of resurrection, exalt him for the erection of mosques of Islam and preserve him long enough to perform benevolent action, on the 15th of Sjawal, the year AH 710 (7 March 1311).

On the face arch, upper band (marble):

His majesty the great, the lord of the kings, of dignity like Mustafa, humbly submitting to the command of God, the chosen by the favour of the most Merciful, great in the world and in faith, the consoler of Islam and the Muslims, the bestower of honour on kings and princes, firm with the help of the Merciful (named) Abul Muzaffar Muhammad Shah, the king, the second Alexander, the great arm of the khilafat, the ally of the Amir-ul-Momineen, may God perpetuate his kingdom, erected this place for the Sunnat-o-Jamaat.

On the face arch, lower band (red stone):

This mosque which is as famed among the people of the world as is the Kaba, with pure faith and intention firm as destiny, the exalted, the lord of the kings of the age, great in the world and in faith, the king of land and the sea, helped with the help of the Merciful (God) (named) Abul Muzaffar Muhammad Shah, the king, the right arm of the khilafat, the ally of the Amir-ul-Momineen... until the day of judgement.

On the marble architrave around the southern archway:

By the grace of the peerless God and with the help ... 'Verily the foundation of a mosque is laid on piety' Whose command and glory are high and Whose justice and peace are great ... commanded 'Turn thy face towards the holy temple (of Mecca) as Muhammad the prophet of God, may peace be upon him, said, 'He who builds a mosque for God, God builds a house for him in Paradise;' the exalted, the lord of the kings of the age, the emperor of Moses-like splendour and Solomon-like dignity, the custodian of the commands of the law of Muhammad, the helper in the observances of the religion of Ahmad, the strengthener of the pulpits of the places of learning and of mosques, the supporter of the rules of the schools and places of worship, the strengthener of the foundation of the observances of Islam, the builder of the foundation of the faith of Noman (Abu Hanifa), the uprooter of the dead (old) principles of evil doers, the destroyer of the fundamental doctrines of the infidels, the demolisher of the foundation of the places of idol worship, the exalter of the foundation of congregations of Islam (mosques), the medium of manifestation of (Divine) signs, the suppressor of infidelity. .. the uprooter of evil-doing from the face of earth, the conqueror of forts... the master of places of strong foundations... beneficent (God) Abul Muzaffar Muhammad Shah, the king, the right arm of the khilafat, the ally of the Amir-ul-Momineen: may God extend the shadow of his dignity over the heads of mankind until the day of resurrection! Built this mosque, which is the mosque of paradise for saints and... men of piety, a place of assembly of the eminent angels, and an edifice inhabited by the souls of the chief prophets, on the 5th of Shawal, the year AH 710 (7 March 1311).

On the arch face upper band (marble):

This mosque, which in extent and height is like unto Bait-ul-Muqaddas, nay, is the second Bait-ul-Mamur (Kaba) was built with pure faith and good intention by his exalted majesty, the lord, the diffuser of grace and beneficence, helped with the help of the benevolent King (God), great in the world and in the faith, victorious (named) Abul Muzaffar Muhammad Shah, the king, the right arm of the khilafat, the ally of the Amir-ul-Momineen.

On the arch face lower band (red stone):

During the auspicious reign of the exalted majesty... world and faith, exalted by the armies of victory (named) Abul Muzaffar Muhammad Shah, the king, the right arm of the khilafat, the ally of the Amir-ul-Momineen, may God extend the shadow of his kingdom over the heads of mankind until the day of resurrection, (built) this mosque to which is accorded the attribute 'He who enters it acquires salvation'

Maqbara Firoz Shah

The inscription on the south doorway of the tomb incised in plaster:

... Sultan, Sikandar, son of the king of kings Sultan Bahlol Shah, may God perpetuate his reign and kingdom and exalt his order and glory, on the 20th of the august month of Ramzan, the year 913... King Sultan Firoz Shah, may his dust be sanctified and paradise be his resting place....[6]

Rajo'n ki Bain

On the face of the pavilion there is an inscription:

During the auspicious reign of the great Sultan, who has trust in the merciful (named) Sikandar Shah, son of Bahlol Shah Sultan, may God perpetuate his kingdom and sovereignty, this pavilion was built by the slave, the expectant of mercy of the omnipotent (named) Daulat Khan... Khwaja Muhammad, on the first of Rajab the year AH 912.

Dargah Imam Zamin: Qutub Complex

The inscription on it is as follows:

In the name of God who is merciful and compassionate.

May continual praise (of God) and prayer be offered by the residents of the sacred enclosure and the dwellers in this favourite tomb as a sacrifice to God, whose friends have sacrificed this world and the next in His path and made of the immense treasures of life and heart a sacrifice to His court.

May manifold praises reach the sweetly scented and illumined grave of the intercessor on the day of judgement (the Prophet) and his pure descendants and friends and his holiness the charitable and announcer of good news to the world, who made the divine grace a friend of his holiness, the guide of men and chosen of Muhammad (named) Muhammad Ali of the Chistia sect, descendant of Hussain, a support of the great Saiyyeds, the best of the revered devotees of God, a Jesus of the world of recluse and asceticism, a Moses of the mountain of retirement and seclusion, helped from God who is rich, the polestar of religion and faith, and a Saiyyed descended from Hasan and Hussian, in that he erected this holy and elegant building and left his parting advice that when his life... should come to an end and favoured with the call, 'Enter therein (Paradise) in peace and security' it should fly to the sacred enclosure and favourite garden, this celebrated building should become the bright tomb of his holiness.

This building was completed in the year AH 944.

Dargah Qutub Sahib

On the marble balustrade surrounding the mud grave of Qutub Sahib:

Offered by the slave of the slaves and the devoted servant (named Muhaiy-ud-Din Bahadur Shams-ul-Umara Amir Kabir Khurshid Jah, on the 20th of the month of Safar, the victorious, the year AH 1300 (CE 1882–23).

On a marble slab containing niches and used as a lamp post north of the grave:

1. 786 (numerical value of the word 'Bismillah')

Crown

There is no God but Allah and Muhammad is his prophet. Khwaja Qutb-ud-Din Bakhtiyar Aushi Kaki Chisti, may God have mercy upon him, the successor of the Sultan of Hind, the cherisher of the poor (named) Khwaja Muin-ud-Din.

2. Bismillah ir Rahman ar Raheem

O god forgive those who drink a cup of the wine of love, stake their life if they meet a gamester. The lamp-post of the sacred grave of his Holiness Qutbul Aqtab Sahib, may God have mercy on him. [On the] 14th Rabi Awwal, the year AH 635. Offered by the humble Sardar Mirza, holder of rent-free land in Delhi. [On the] 27th Rabi Awwal the year AH 1332, Fida Husain, stonecutter Akbarabad (Agra).

Dargah Hazrat Amir Khusrau

Inscription engraved in one line on the walls inside, over the latticed marble screens:

1. *O thou! Who hast the sweet drink of joy in thy cup, and receives messages constantly from one friend*

   The house of Farid is ordered by thee, hence is it that thou art entitled Nizam

   Immortal is the slave Khusrau, for he with his thousand lives is thine own slave.

2. *My name is 'Nek' (righteous) and 'Great Khwaja' (it contains) two sheens, two laams, two gafs and two jeems[7]*

   If you can evolve my name from these letters I shall know that you are a wise man

   (The scribe of the above is the grandson of Sheikh Farid Shakkarganj)

3. *O! Khusrau, peerless in the world, I am a supplicant at thy tomb.*

   It has been built by Tahir; eternal blessing is always found here

   Wisdom thus spake the date of its foundation, 'Say to the tomb that it is a place of secrets.'

   (The composer of these lines and founder of this building is Tahir Muhammad Imad-ud-Din Hasan, son of Sultan Ali of Sabzwar, in the year AH 1014 (CE 1605–56). May God forgive his sins and conceal his faults. The scribe is Abdun Nabi, son of Ayub).

Inscription on a stone tablet in a niche on the northern wall immediately below the roof:

In the reign of the emperor, the asylum of the world, the father of victory, the just king (named) Nur-ud-Din Muhammad Jahangir, the champion of faith, may God perpetuate his kingdom and reign, and extend his beneficence and benevolence.

Inscriptions on the doors of the tomb:[8]

Verses of a chronogram

Amir Khusrau of Delhi is such that his door is as the door of Paradise.

Why should not the supplicant at his tomb be favoured, he who is the minister of the court of Nizam-ud-Din.

The poor and humble servant Miyan Jan, who is a faithful servant and servant of the poor, erected these bright doors in the year AH 1280 (AH 1663–64).

And

What honour and dignity if you accept them (the doors) O! Amir Khusrau, dear of God!

Miyan Jan offers the pair of doors; may he achieve the heart's wishes, and may his heart be illuminated.

Inscription written in Nastaliq characters on the south-east panel of the marble balustrade around the grave of Amir Khusrau:[9]

Offered by the slave of the slave, the humble Muhaiy-ud-Din Khan Shams-ul-Umara

Amir Kabir Khurshid Jah, on the 20th of August Ramzan, in the year AH 1303 (22 June 1886).

Pul Salimgarh

The two inscriptions are:

1. *God is Great!*

   (This bridge) was built by the command of Shah Nur-ud-Din Jahangir, the Great

   The year and the building (are to be found- in the words): The auspicious, straight and firm road. Year AH 1031.

2. *(God is Great)[10] By the command of the King of the Seven Worlds (The Lord of Majesty and Bounty)*

   Emperor, just, equitable and politic (The Most Holy)

   (The Helper) Jahangir son of the Emperor Akbar (The Revealer)

   (The beneficent) His sword has subdued the world (The Living)

   (The year 17)[11] When the bridge was built in Delhi (regnal year)

   The praise of this bridge should not be written (of Jahangir)

   (Under the superintendence) Thought gave the date of its completion (of Husain Halbi)

   The Bridge of the Emperor of Delhi Jahangir (a glorious inscription)

Tomb of Najaf Khan

The inscription on the tomb is:

He (alone) is living, who will never die.

The sky with its uncertain revolution, with its back like a bow and full of arrows,

(is certain) that its arrows of affliction (will) never miss its mark.

It shot (an arrow) at a mark, which was one of the respected Saiyyeds:

The blood (of the Sayyids) and the Sayyids of the Safvi (dynasty) were honoured by him.

He was a precious fruit of the tree of the garden of the Twelve (imam);

He was a pure light of the two pearls (Hasan and Hussain) and a pearl of the nine shells (the sky);

Bakshi-ul-Mulk, Amir Najaf Khan, the Lion-Hearted;

Conquerors of the territories of Hind, with the help of (the command) 'be not afraid'.

He is a hero (of such power) that if he held the (sword of Ali) Zulfiqar in his hand,

The King Lafatha (Ali) himself would exclaim: A worthy son.

Notes

1 The inscription has been obliterated now and is no longer visible. Translation taken from Gordon Sanderson, *Delhi Fort: A Guide to the Buildings and Gardens*, Delhi: Asian Educational Services, 2000; reprint of the facsimile edition of 1914.

2 These titles apparently refer to Qutb-ud-Din Aibak, but his actual name does not appear to be visible anywhere.

3 The inscriptions have been mostly obliterated and drawings of the inscription in Asar-us-Sanadid remains one of the sources for them and their translations.

4 Quran, Sura XVII, verse 1.

5 Quran, Sura 9, verse 18.

6 It was probably inscribed in the reign of Sikandar Shah as it refers to the repairs done by him as the date is given as AH 913/1507–08 CE.

7 These refer to the Perso-Arabic alphabet and its numerical values:
   2 sheens = 2 x 300 = khe
   2 laams = 2 x30 = 60 = seen
   2 gaafs = 2 x100 = 200 = re
   2 jeems = 2 x 3 = 6 = wao
   = Khusrau

8 Miyan Jan gave a pair of copper doors.

9 The pierced marble balustrade which surrounds the grave.

10 The words in brackets are medallions placed in between the inscription containing praise of Allah and some of His 99 names.

11 Given in three medallions.

An Extract from
Maulana Altaf Husain Hali's[1]
Biography of Sir Sayyid,
Hayāt-i-Javed

When Sir Sayyid was posted in Delhi as a judge (*munsif*), he thought of researching its old and new monuments and cities. He wanted to publicize his brother's newspaper *Sayyid-ul-Akhbār*, compile articles on the monuments of Delhi, and to publish a book on them. He would often travel outside Delhi to investigate monuments, and his friend the late Maulana Imambaksh Sehbai would accompany him. It was difficult to investigate the monuments outside Delhi since most were in ruins and broken down, their inscriptions could not be read, nor could anyone provide the complete details because no one was familiar with these inscriptions.

Moreover, since the monuments lay broken, it was difficult [for Sir Sayyid] to figure out who had built them and why. It was necessary to refer to historical records to find out about these buildings. Many had become so dilapidated that it was difficult to find out anything about them. It was a difficult task to identify and read the inscriptions. It was an extremely difficult task to measure the monuments, to get artists' drawings of all the monuments and their ruins and the details of 125 monuments, to remove the dirt of the ages from the inscriptions and read them in their correct historical context.

Some of the inscriptions on Qutub Sahib ki Lath [the Qutub Minar] were so high that they could not be read, so Sir Sayyid got a basket (*jheenka*) strung between two poles, which would be pulled up so that he could get close enough to read the inscriptions. He [Sir Sayyid] says that whenever he sat in this makeshift pulley to go up, his friend Maulana Sehbai would be so apprehensive that he would turn pale with fright.

This was the first step of the future successes of Sir Sayyid, and his condition is encapsulated in this Arabic verse by Abu Tamam:

He is climbing up with such enthusiasm,

That people think he has some work in the sky

In spite of all these difficulties, the first edition of *Asār-us-Sanadīd* was published within a year and a half.[2] The composition of this second edition, free of colourful phrases, exaggerations and the ceremonious style of the earlier edition, was a little dull by comparison.

The first edition had a few shortcomings as regards historical accuracy, but was very well composed. Its first three chapters painted a beautiful picture of Delhi's old glory and majesty. The last chapter described a city full of accomplished people of art, culture and knowledge. The first edition was published in 1847. Mr Roberts, Collector and Magistrate of Shajahanabad, took one print of *Asār-us-Sanadīd* to London and presented it to the Royal Asiatic Society, and the members appreciated it greatly. They requested Mr Roberts to get it translated into English. When Roberts returned, he tried to translate it with Sir Sayyid's help, but Sir Sayyid thought it better to rewrite it thus correcting the mistakes he had spotted in it. Though he wrote it anew, with corrections and additions, the second edition was written very simply and was free of exaggerations and ceremonious language that had characterized the first edition. Sir Sayyid had also prepared maps, but before it could be published, the mutiny of 1857 took place and those maps were destroyed. Some maps were found later and are in the library of Aligarh Muslim University.

The fourth chapter of the first edition, which had a description of Delhi's famous personalities, is not included in this edition. These changes can be attributed to Mr Edward Thomas, the Sessions Judge of Delhi at the time, who was very fond of investigating antiquities. It was on his request that Sir Sayyid decided to put the matter he included in the second edition in this order.

The second edition was printed in 1854, but most of the prints were destroyed in the mutiny. Mr Roberts, the Collector and Magistrate of Delhi, tried to translate it into English taking Sir Sayyid's help, but before he could make much headway, he was transferred. There is no information on whether it was ever completed, or whether it was ever translated into English. It was translated into French in 1861 by famous French orientalist Garcin de Taussey, who gave one copy to Sir Sayyid as well. In 1864, on the basis of this book, he [Sir Sayyid] was granted honorary membership of the Royal Asiatic Society.

Notes

[1] 1837–1914

[2] In 1847 Sir Sayyid had published the first edition of this book. The present edition was recomposed, as Sir Sayyid felt it imperative that the book be rewritten with additions and improvements.

Glossary

Ab-e-hayat: A river that flows through heaven

Alhamdulillah: Praise be to Allah

Aramgah muqaddas: The emperor's retiring rooms

Arbab-e-mausiqi: Musicians

Auliya: Saint

Ayat or *ayat-e-Qurani*: Verses of the Quran

Badshahi naqqar khana: Royal drum-house

Baoli (also *bain, baori*): Step well

Baradari: Twelve-arched pavilion

Batini: Matters hidden from the world

Biddat: That which is forbidden in Islam as innovation with regard to true/pure Islam

Bikramjiti: A Hindu calendar era

Bhog: Food offerings made to an idol

Bhool bhulaiyya'n: A maze

Bulbul-e-navayaa'n: Poets

Burji: Tower/cupola/dome/pavilion; Sir Sayyid uses this word variously in his book

Chabutra: Platform

Chadar-e-nur: Sheet of light

Chajja: Eaves

Chashm-e-falak: Inhabitants of the skies

Chashm-e-khizr: Fountain of life and immortality

Chhatri: Canopy

Chowk: An open space in a town or city

Dalan: Hall

Dar-ul-khilafat: Capital city; metropolis

Diwan: Compilation of poems

Diya: Small lamp

Fad-kuluha: Come in, enter

Fan-e-bakiti: Skilled in the art of making quills for calligraphy

Fan-o-ilm: Science

Faqir: Mendicant

Fiqh: Jurisprudence

Furuh-e-din: Principles and practices of religion

Gaz: A measurement

Ghafrallahu: May God forgive him his sins (used for the dead)

Ghazal: A poetic form with rhyming couplets and a refrain; often set to music.

Gumbad: Domed

Hajjam: Barber

Hakim (also '*tabib*'): Physicians

Hammam: [Royal] Baths

Haveli: Mansion

Hazrat: An honorific for a person worthy of great respect, as in Hazrat Daoud (Prophet David)

Hisar-e-falak: The boundary of the sky

Hujra: Small room

Ilm-e-arooz: Prosody

Ilm-e-haia't: Astronomy

Ilm-e-hikmat/ilm-e-falsafa: Philosophy

Ilm-e-hindasa: Geometry

Ilm-e-maani: Rhetoric

Ilm-e-mantiq: Logic

Jagir: Fief, landholding

Jahannuma: World-reflecting; also the name given to the hall where Sultan Ghiyas-ud-Din Tughlaq used to give personal audience

Jahil: Ignorant, illiterate, wretched

Jali: Lattice-work

Jam-e-kun: Changing rooms

Jam-e-ziddain: A collection of contrary virtues

Jazb: Totally oblivious to the world

Jazb illallah: A state of total absorption in Allah

Jyot: Flame

Ka'ba: The most sacred place in Mecca

Kahkashan: Heavenly constellations

Kalsis: Pinnacles

Kamilat: Miracles; miracles wrought by prophets are however called *mojeza*

Karamat: Miracles

Kar-kashani: Tile work on monuments

Khadim: Hereditary caretaker (usually of a *dargah*)

Khalifa: Successor

Khan Samani: Office of Household Expenses

Khan-e-Saman: Officer-in-charge of Household Expenses

Khanqah: A place for gathering of the Sufi brotherhood/a retreat

Khat-e-naskh: Calligraphy (using the Naskh form)

Khat-e-nas'taliq: Calligraphy (using the Nas'taliq form)

Khuld aramgaah: One who now rests in paradise

Khurshid Talat: One whose countenance is like the sun

Khush navez: Calligrapher

Khwabgah: Also known as Rang Mahal, the emperor's private/sleeping quarters

Kos: A measure of distance equivalent to 2.25 miles

Kot: Bastion

Kotla: Citadel

Mahajan: Moneylender

Mahpara: A piece of the moon (refers to beauty)

Mahv: Absorbed in, or charmed by

Majazib: Men who experience divine ecstasy

Majlis khana: Meeting hall

Majlis-e-wa'az: Preaching to an assembly on religious topics

Makan-e-nur: House of light

Makharij al-ḥuruf: Using the correct points of articulation while reciting the Quran

Manqul wa maqul: Logic and reason

Mansab qiladari (of Shahjahanabad): Rank of commandant of the city of Shahjahanabad

Mantiq o hikmat: Logic and philosophy

Manzil-e-mah: Destination of the moon

Manzum: A composition in rhyme or verse

Maqbara: Mausoleum

Marpech: River/stream taking a winding course

Masha'ikh: Sufi masters

Masnavi: A long poem

Mauza: An administrative division

Mazaar: Mausoleum

Me'nhdiya'n: Lanterns

Mizan-e-Adl-e-Ilahi: The Divine Scales of Justice

Muhajjar: An enclosure made of stone; usually a marble enclosure around a grave.

Muharkun: Engraver of Seals

Munshi: Clerk, scribe

Munsif: Official belonging to the lower ranks of the judiciary

Mureed: Disciple/follower

Musawwiran: Artists

Nala: Water channel

Naqqar khana: Drum-house

Naqqar-shahi: Art of playing the drums

Nasheman: Alcoves

Naskh: A calligraphic form

Nasr: Prose

Nas'taliq: A calligraphic form

Naubat: Kettledrums

Navah: Area

Nazm: Composition

Nigar khana: Picture galleries

Nur: Light

Panchakki: Water mill

Peshkar: Accountant

Pichikari: Inlay work

Pir: Master

Piri: Mastership

Purana: Old

Qasida: A panegyric

Qazi: Islamic judge of the Shariat law

Qila: Fort

Qirrat: Recitation of the Quran

Quddisa sirru-hu: May his tomb be purified or hallowed (used in speaking of a deceased king or a great man)

Qurra and *hafiz*: Those who recite and memorize the Quran

Rahmatu'l-lah 'alai-hi: May God have mercy on their souls (an honorific used for those are dead)

Rekhta-goi: Urdu poetry

Sairgah: Recreation spot

Sallamahu'l-laho ta'ala: May the most high God save and protect him (an honorific used for those who are alive)

Sandal: Sandalwood

Sang-e-khara: Local quartzite

Sang-e-rukham: Alabaster

Sarai: Inn

Sard khana: Cold room (at the bathhouse)

Sehan: Courtyard

Sema: (In a) divine trance

Sheikh: Title bestowed on one well versed in religion and henceforth the surname of his family

Shikargah: Hunting lodge

Shikhar: Pinnacle

Sher o shayri: Poetry and verse

Sidra: The seventh heaven

Silsila: Order, as in the order to which a saint belonged

Subedar: Governor

Subhan Allah: Glory be to Allah

Tabarruk: A token of blessing

Tabib, also *hakim*: Physician

Tafseer: Commentary on the Quran

Takiya: Place where members of a spiritual sect dwell

Takkas: Currency

Taqriz: Praise/Review

Tasbih khana: Prayer hall

Taziya: Small paper and bamboo frames

Trishul: Trident

Uloom-e-deen: Religious knowledge; pillars of religion

Uloom funoon: Accomplished in science and the arts

Waliullah: Friends of Allah

Wakil Mutlaq: Imperial regent

Yak-fanni: Master of all arts

Zahiri: Matters obvious to the world

Illustrations